AF321595

OUT OF CHAOS

BEN URI: 100 YEARS IN LONDON

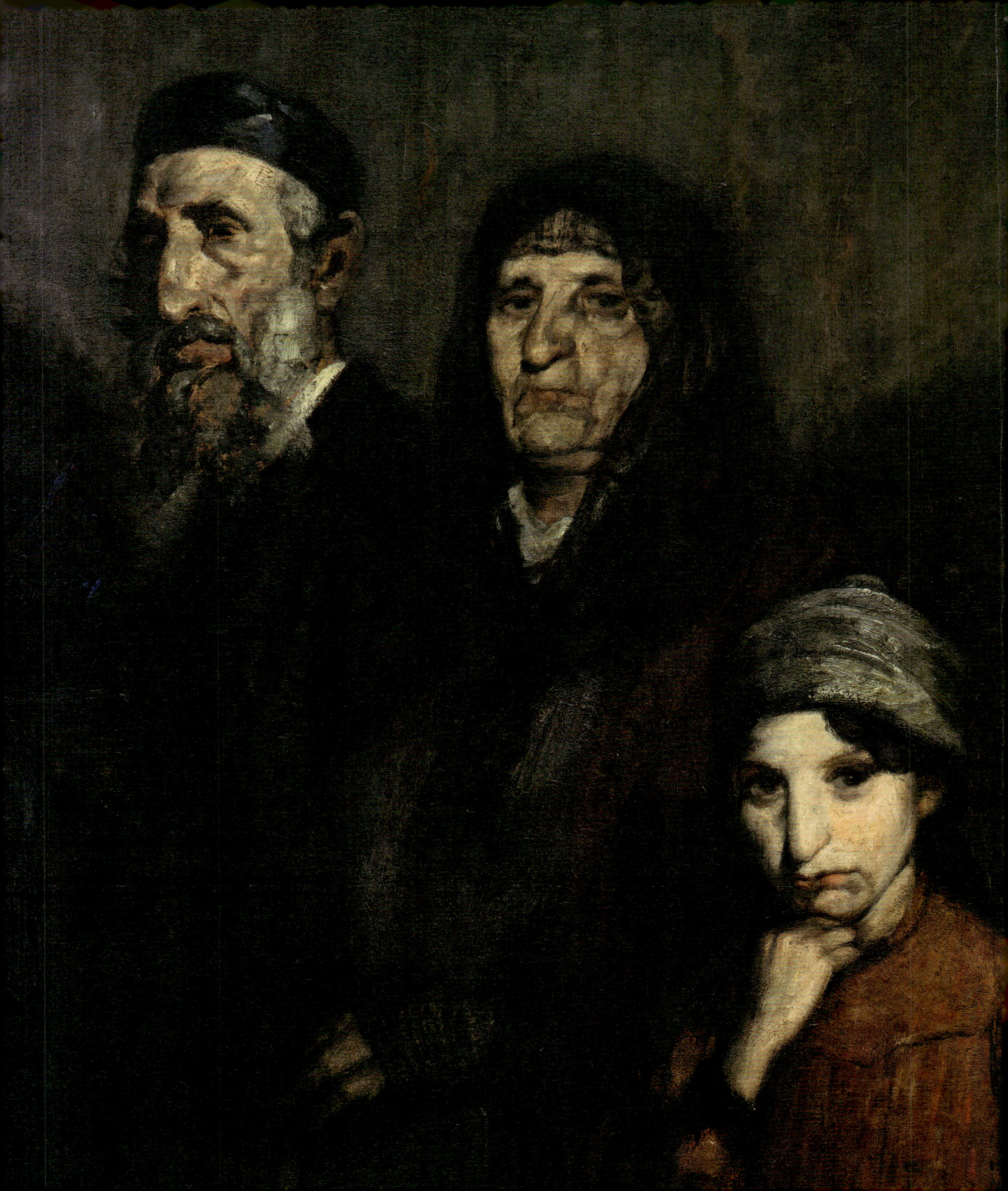

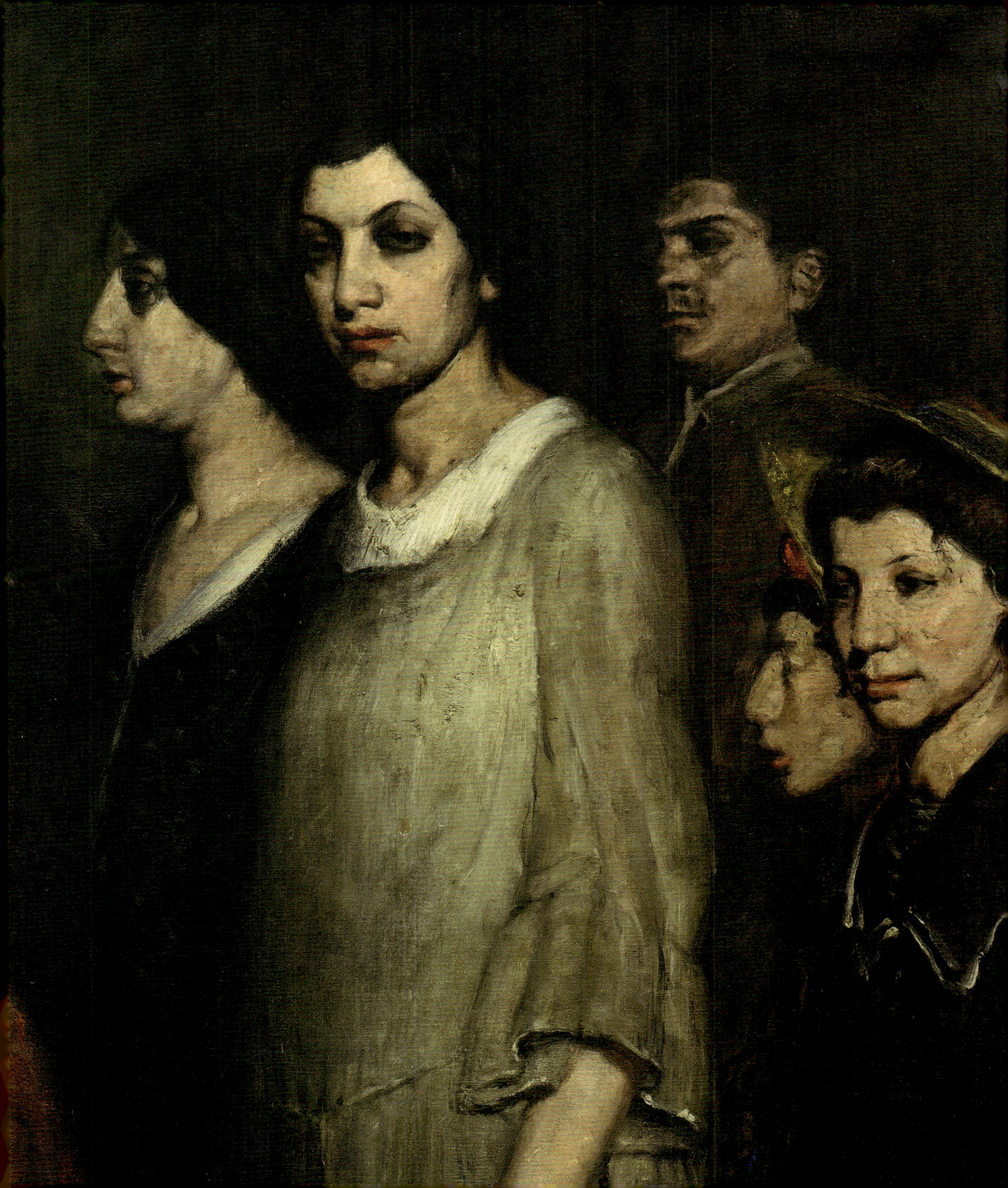

OUT OF CHAOS

BEN URI: 100 YEARS IN LONDON

AUERBACH · BOMBERG · CHAGALL · EPSTEIN · GERTLER · GROSZ · KOSSOFF · LIEBERMANN · SOUTINE

CONTRIBUTORS

Richard Cork

Sarah MacDougall

Rachel Dickson

David Herman

James Hyman

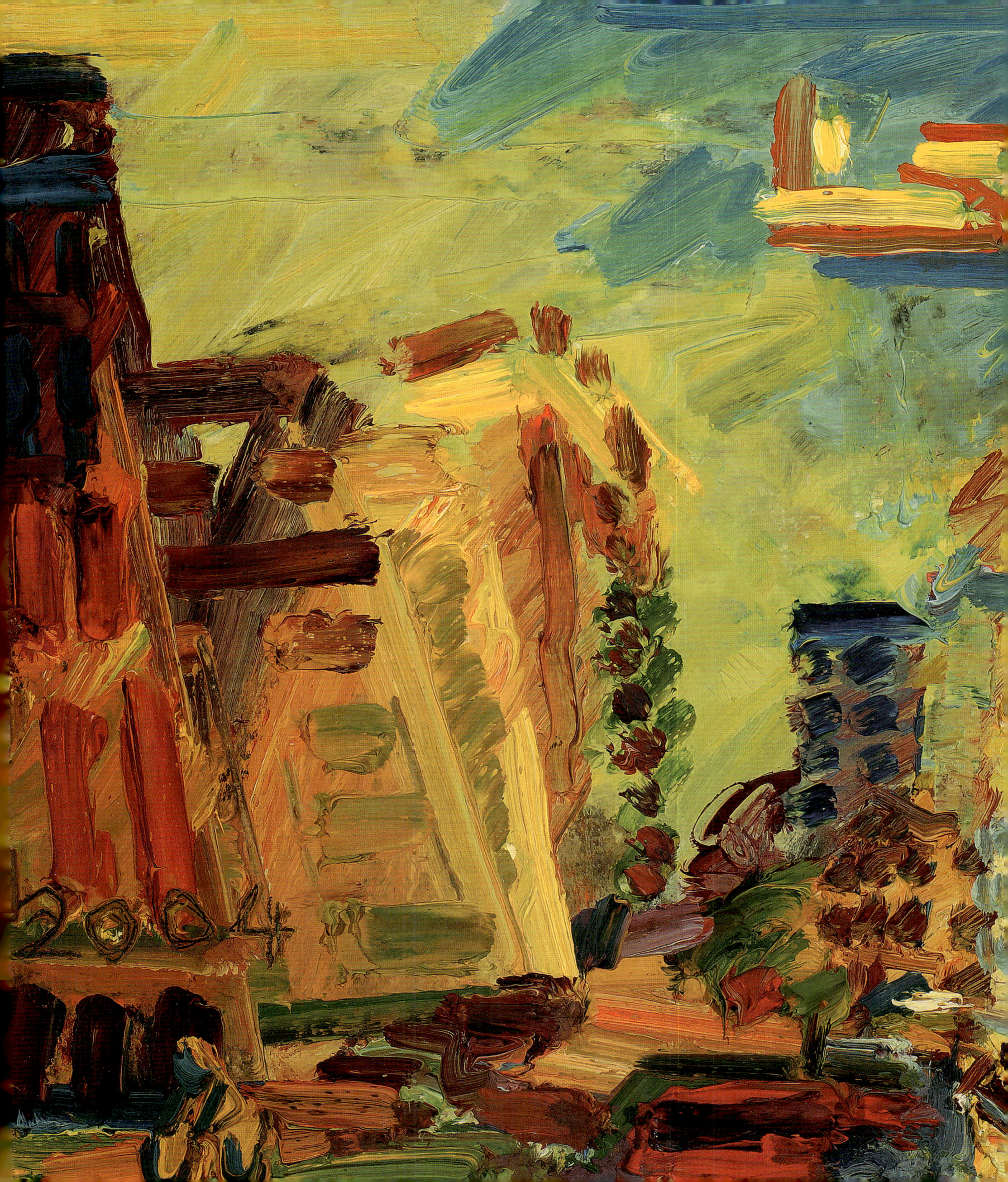

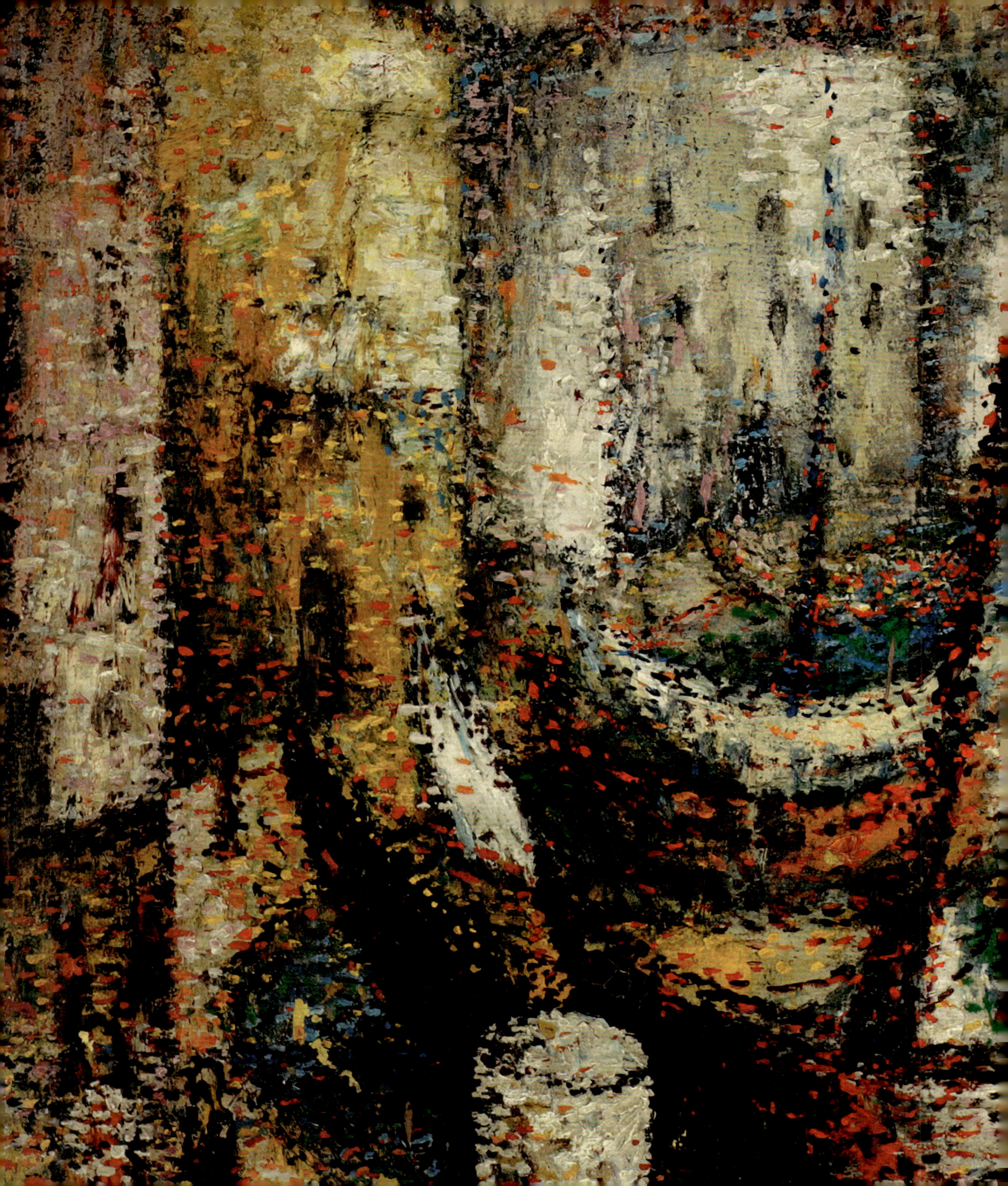

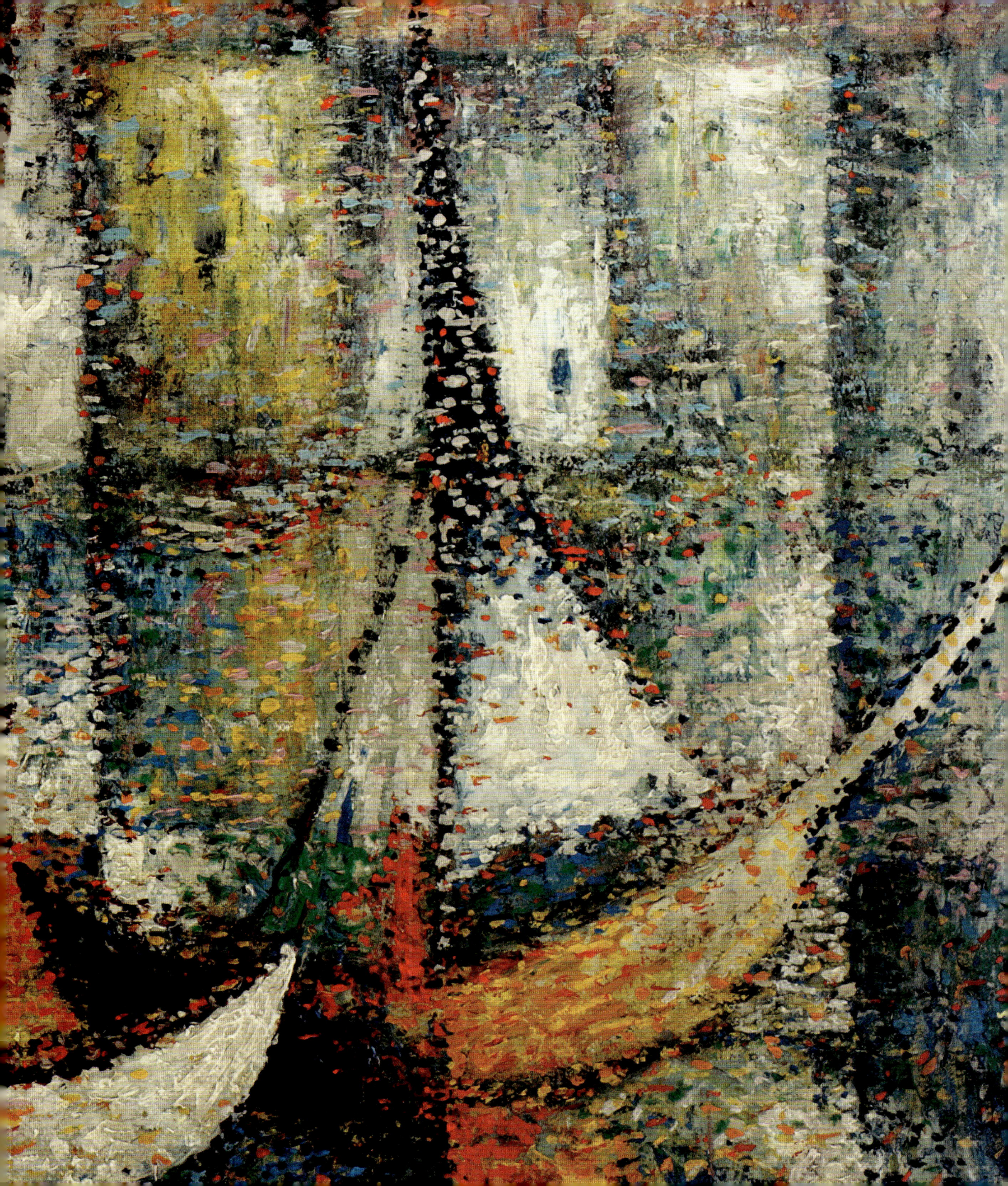

This book has been dedicated by Jonathan Symons
in honour of his late parents Cyril and Hazel Symons.

First published in 2015 by
Ben Uri
108a Boundary Road,
London NW8 0RH

www.benuri.org.uk

Copyright © 2015

British Library Cataloguing-in-
Publication Data
A catalogue record for this book is
available from the British Library

ISBN 978-0-900157-53-0

Edited by Rachel Dickson and
Sarah MacDougall

Picture research by Hadeel Eltayeb
and Nicola Baird

Catalogue designed and produced by
Isambard Thomas, London

Printed by OGM, Padova

DETAIL ILLUSTRATIONS

pp. 2–3: Victor Hageman,
The Emigrants (detail), *c.*1910

p. 5: Frank Auerbach, *Mornington
Crescent, Summer Morning II* (detail),
2004

pp. 6–7: Arthur Segal, *Halen,
La Ciotat* (detail), 1929

pp. 10–11: Chana Kowalska, *Shtetl*
(detail), 1934

pp. 16–17: Mark Gertler, *Merry-Go-
Round* (detail), 1916

pp. 20–21: Jacob Kramer, *The Day of
Atonement* (detail), 1919

pp. 23: Mark Gertler, *Rabbi and
Rabbitzin* (detail), 1914

ACKNOWLEDGEMENTS

The editors would like to extend
particular thanks to the following for
their help in realizing this exhibition
and related publications:
Irum Ali, Nicola Baird, Dr Helen Beer,
Sima Beeri, Jenna Birley, Amy Bowker,
Alice Calloway, Lizzie Cowden, Laura
Dellapine, Edward Dickenson, Hadeel
Eltayeb, Philomena Epps, Jordanna
Greaves, Simona Horelicanova, David
Herman, Sophie Hill, Elaine Homer,
Simona Horelicanova, Claire Jackson,
Laura Joens, Agata Korbus, David
Mazower, Huw Molseed, Alice Odin,
Ioanna Papagkika, Kathrin Pieren,
Harriet Powney, Aimée Taylor,
Isambard Thomas, Lena Watson and
Katie Wilson. We also thank Alison
Duthie, Leanne Hammacott and
Sophie Cornell at the Inigo Rooms,
Somerset House East Wing, in
association with the Cultural Institute
at King's College London.

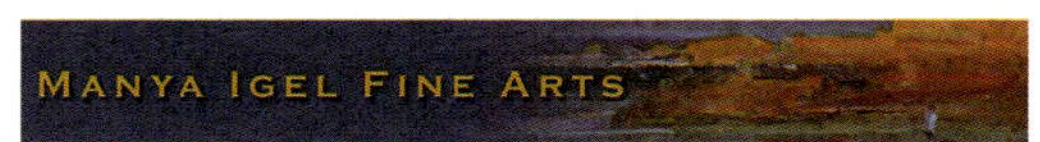
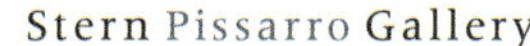
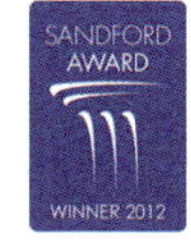
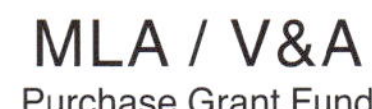
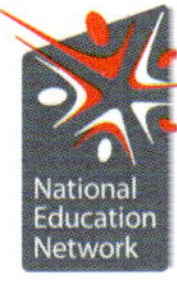
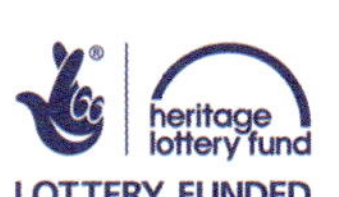
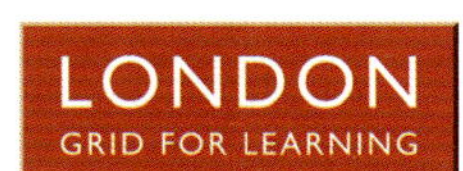
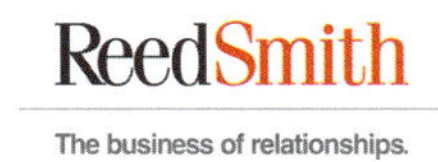
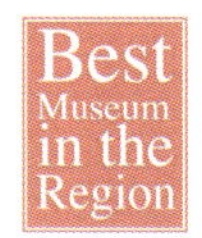
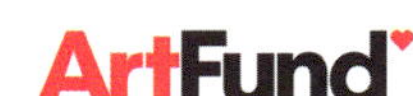
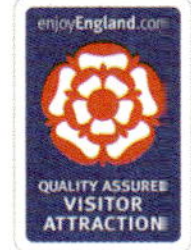

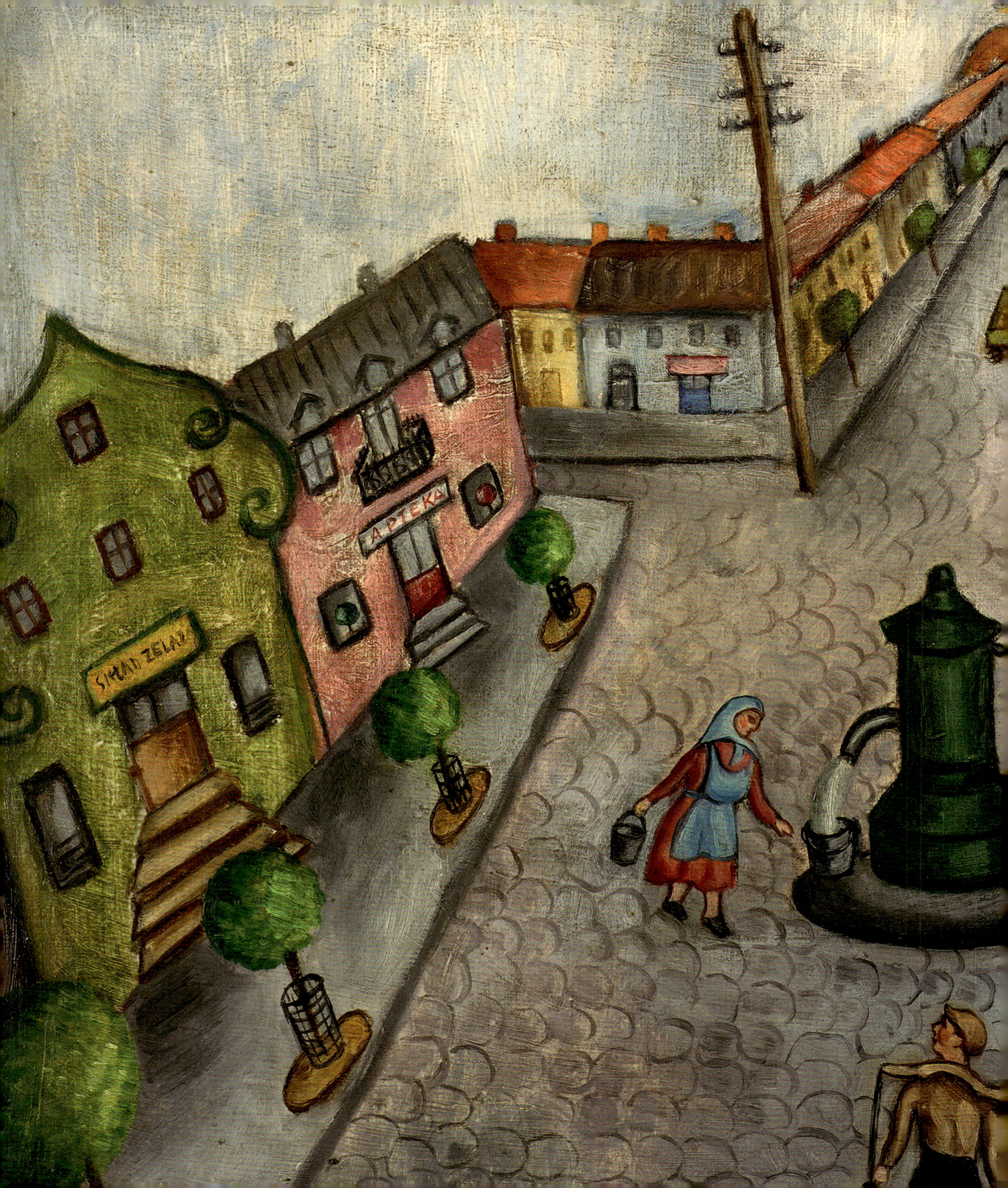

APTEKA
SKŁAD ŻELAZ

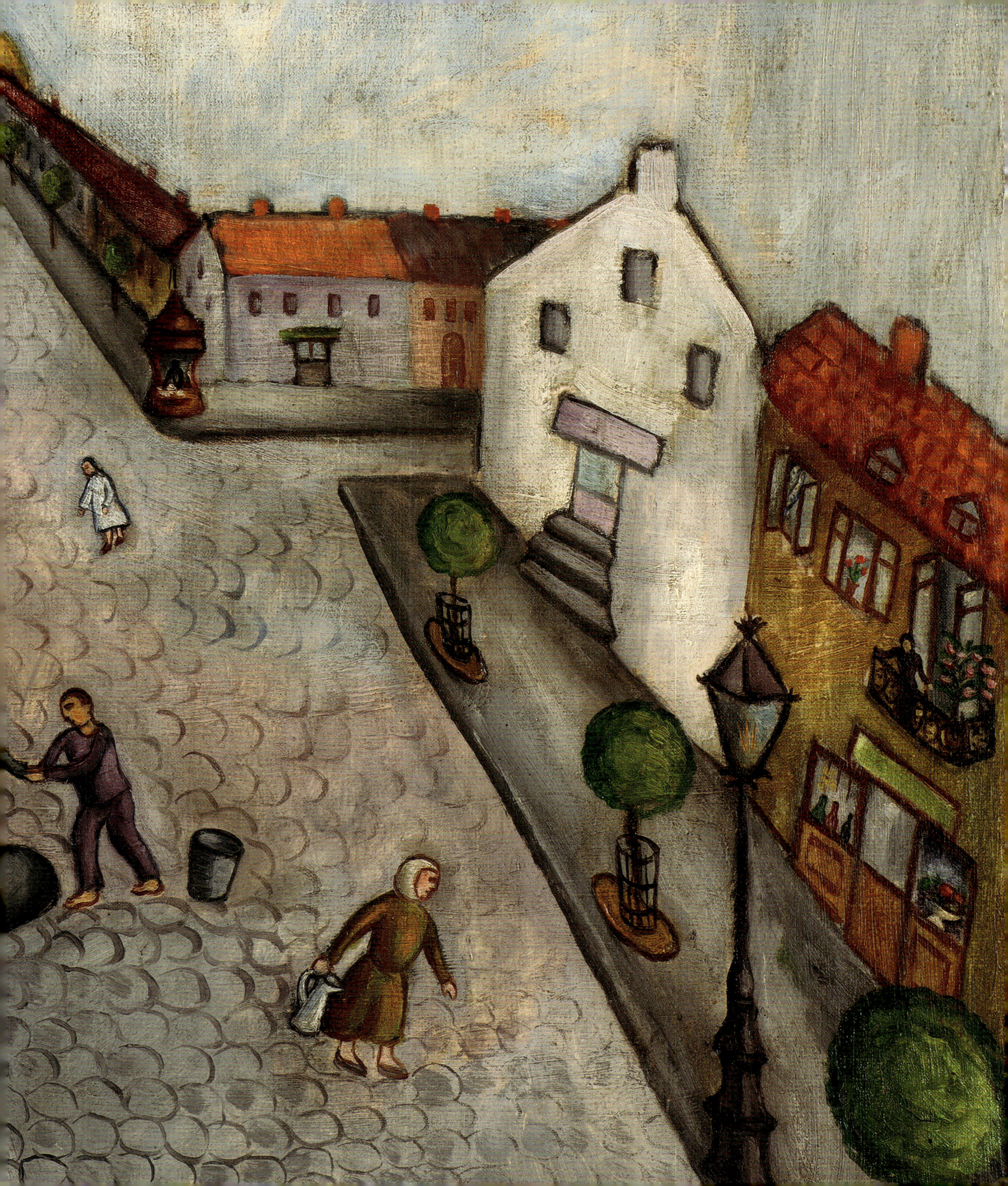

Out of Chaos:
Shaping the future from the past

'Out of Chaos' is often an understatement of the trauma involved in journeys of migration – each narrative is defined by the precise context of 'from what to what' and 'from where to where'. Right at this moment there will be a banker, or a lawyer, and his or her family, crossing the Atlantic first-class, transferring from Wall Street to the City of London. When they reach their new home, the temporary chaos of moving will end sweetly. Equally, right now, there are refugees being trafficked or cast adrift in unseaworthy, decrepit boats at extortionate financial and personal cost as they flee tyranny and uncertainty to find a new life in Europe, gambling on beating the odds of the high risk of drowning in the Mediterranean and surviving the journey. For them, it is not when, but *if*, they reach land, as they exchange one chaos for another. This is the way it has always has been for those fleeing for their lives. This too is our context and reflects the history of Ben Uri, The Art Museum for Everyone, and the art and scholarship we share.

Out of Chaos, Ben Uri: 100 Years in London explains our history via visual stories, both traditional and modernist vocabularies frame the artists' 'forced journeys' from Russian pogroms at the turn of the 20th century, and from Nazi persecution and genocide in Europe during the years 1933–45. The London narrative begins in a congested, tightly-knit immigrant society in Whitechapel, where two languages (Yiddish and English) were spoken.

The institution, Ben Uri, was founded in July 1915 by Russian-Jewish émigré Lazar Berson, a decorative artist who had recently left Paris, where he had shared an apartment with the famous sculptor Jacques Lipchitz. Ben Uri was originally intended as an 'Arts Society' to provide support for Yiddish-speaking, Jewish immigrant artists and craftsmen who were working outside the cultural mainstream. It was named after Bezalel Ben Uri, the biblical creator of the tabernacle in the Temple in Jerusalem, and to indicate kinship with the Bezalel School of Arts and Crafts in Jerusalem, established nine years earlier in 1906. Its vision was to become a National Museum of Jewish Art and Crafts in the mould of the Bezalel School, and Berson and the founding fathers aspired to build a permanent collection of work by Jewish artists, the majority of whom were immigrants.

Stop for a second and imagine the scene: a Russian émigré arrives in London from Paris in 1914. His language is Yiddish and he inspires a mix of mostly left-wing intellectuals and thinkers, small business-men, artisans and, of course, artists, to create a Jewish art society with the ambition of becoming a National Museum. The charisma, foresight and tenacity of Berson and his fellow founders must have been extraordinary in an area as poor and cramped as Whitechapel at the best of times, but this occurred in the first two years of the First World War, when concerns were elsewhere as many residents were fighting and dying for King and country. Berson was both politically aware and engaged, which conflicted with the founding members' view that the institution should be non-political and non-religious, solely focussed on art and creativity (a policy also adopted by the new Board in October 2000, some 85 years later). Following a dispute about Berson's political activism, he left London suddenly in late 1916. Soon after, the creative parameters of the Society were extended to embrace the 'plastic arts' and to facilitate the formation of a collection of outstanding importance, not just for Ben Uri but for the nation at large.

A century later, the collection, principally in store, comprises in excess of 1300 works by some 380 artists (67% of émigré, 27% women, 33% contemporary) from 35 countries, with significant bodies of work by many important British artists, including Frank Auerbach (11 works), David Bomberg (14), Jacob Epstein (6), Mark Gertler (11), Josef Herman (10), Jacob Kramer (12), Simeon Solomon (13), alongside celebrated examples by European masters including Marc Chagall, George Grosz, Max Liebermann, Reuven Rubin and Chaïm Soutine. 42 of the 67 works featured in this survey have been acquired in the past thirteen years.

Our curators Sarah MacDougall and Rachel Dickson write about the collection as a whole, and the Jewish School of Paris and the 'forced journeys' of émigré artists later in this book. Further texts by Richard Cork, David Herman and James Hyman, address the historical, artistic and social contexts from which Ben Uri emerged, and the impact its artists had, in turn, on 20th century and contemporary art in Britain and abroad. I thank them all for their partnership and scholarship.

During its formative years, Ben Uri moved frequently within the East End, and to and from the West End, eventually acquiring its first permanent premises – a Georgian townhouse at 14 Portman Street, behind Marble Arch – in late 1943, where it remained until 1961. In 1964, it moved to the fourth floor of a synagogue building in Dean Street, in 'swinging' Soho, where it was eventually awarded museum status, but was served notice in 1995 and forced to close in 1997, when the site was redeveloped as The Soho Theatre. Ben Uri subsequently became homeless and moved from one office to another, successfully kept alive by a determined and committed leadership. In October 2000 a new Board, inspired by the richness and diversity of the collection, took over responsibility for the museum. Fired by a radical vision and strategic plan to reposition an intensely heritage-proud Ben Uri as a fully-engaged mainstream art museum, it implemented far reaching changes and established art, identity and migration in

London as the principal focus. Successfully re-launched as 'The London Jewish Museum of Art: The Art Museum for Everyone' in January 2001, Ben Uri quickly found a temporary new gallery / home in Boundary Road, St John's Wood, in June 2002, where it still uncomfortably exists, having long outgrown both the physical space and the north London location.

A centenary is a rare achievement and provides an opportunity to reflect and explain what makes the museum distinctive. More people visit museums every weekend across the country than sporting fixtures, but without the same sense of passion and ownership. London has some ten 'national' art galleries, attracting some 25 million visitors each year, and they are the dominant players, presenting to the public unparalleled, world-leading exhibitions and engagement. We visit regularly but how many of us or London's minority communities feel ownership – feel they're ours?

We had to think afresh when we set about the challenge of forging a new direction for Ben Uri in order to secure its future for the final 15 years of its first millennium, and the whole of its next. We had to address one fundamental question if we were to find a route to be distinctive, meaningful and successfully compete for London's time and attention: What is the real opportunity for museums to make a continuous difference to people's lives and the society we live in as it has to be bigger than simply sharing great collections? Work that out and we could analyse how the smaller museum (Ben Uri) can add incremental value to its society; how we could generate a communal sense of ownership; how we can engage six figure visitor numbers and share experiences; how in a world of increasing options and reduced funding we could be distinctive and sustainable. Our conclusion was that museums have an unique opportunity to exploit their assets –

collections, scholarship, communication skills and inventive programming – as an effective and valuable vehicle for 'social integration' which is, and will continue to be, one of contemporary society's greatest challenges. That remains our over-arching objective and our programming is the vehicle.

Art is an extraordinary leveller. People of diverse ethnicity, social status and age stand together in front of it, or draw and paint side by side, and the differences melt away. Art is a universal, unspoken language between them. Museum programing has to constantly exceed expectations but, for smaller institutions like Ben Uri, to survive and prosper we have to generate measurable incremental value, to actively shape our programming as a whole to widen audience appeal, much in the vein that the immigrant artists, who were the backbone and beneficiaries of Ben Uri a century ago, found ways to integrate without subsuming their personal or artistic identities. London today has over 3.5 million immigrants, richly contributing to the success and diversity of our incredible city, and this number will continue to grow exponentially for as long as London is a world-leading economy and a safe haven from corruption and autocracy. Exhibitions of African, Korean and Caribbean artists in recent years demonstrate our unswerving commitment to this philosophy.

Having clarified our purpose, we could design the vehicle. We give our exhibitions – both historical and contemporary – a complementary agenda addressing issues of migration and identity. We tour our exhibitions nationally and internationally in partnership with other museums. We publish scholarly but accessible books distributed world-wide. We maintain a spotlight on Nazi looted art and the moral stance that has to dictate actions. We continually develop new pupil and teacher resources, available to over 16,000 schools through the London Grid for Learning and the National Education Network. We pioneer wellbeing and art therapy programmes. We offer IPad-drawing, as well as life-drawing classes. All this has resulted in significant increased visitor numbers which, by our analysis, are now some 80% secular and increasingly multi-cultural, compared to less than 5% a decade ago.

The future for Ben Uri in our second century will continue to focus on social integration as its principal purpose, through our twin strategic initiatives: the first, an astutely located new 'Museum of Art, Identity and Migration' which will uniquely share its space with fellow minority communities so that they, alongside us, can tell stories of their recent émigré journeys to London and together we will exhibit contemporary art emerging from within our communities. The second is a large, carefully located central London home for Ben Uri, where the current formula of sharing our world-class collection, combined with innovative, critically-acclaimed exhibitions, embracing two centuries of creativity, can be expanded appropriately to attract and engage significant visitor numbers. We continue to search for the right location to present individually, or combine both visitor engagements, as our planned acquisition of some 60,000 sq. ft. on the South Bank would have delivered, but just slipped through our hands to an in-funds commercial bidder – the perennial challenge of the not-for-profit sector.

The visitor potential for a museum focussing on identity and stories of migration through high art and emerging artists, much presented by individual communities themselves, is based on the reality that minorities in any context feel strength and confidence in numbers and, in this context, the greatest pride in seeing their heritage being explained and shared with large, wide-ranging audiences by them, not others. We believe this is the key to creating a real sense of diverse community ownership and ever increasing visitor number engagement. The opportunity is to stimulate and engage with new generations of visitors many of whose communities don't see the traditional 'we present to you' museums relevant or of interest. Museums can play an important role in enabling social integration. Generating pride in differences (through art) is a much preferable alternative to suspicion and scapegoating easy targets, particularly the immigrant population, for society's problems, as this museum's Jewish founders and so many of its artists collected over the first 50 years, would testify.

Life and choices today are, of course, very different but to give you a measure of the potential of community pride and sense of ownership, in 1906 at the Whitechapel Gallery over 150,000 people visited the exhibition *Jewish Art and Antiquities* in the six weeks to 16th December. The opening hours were between 12 noon and 10 pm daily to facilitate the majority who worked extended hours every day to survive. 100,000 Jews lived in Whitechapel at the time. Was it community pride or wide general interest across London generating 150,000 visitors – 25,000 visitors each week? The principles demonstrated a century ago are as valid today.

This book, the centenary exhibition and the wide range of achievement over the past 14 years could not have been delivered without the passion, commitment and expertise of key colleagues, too numerous to mention all but, given the auspicious occasion of our centenary, I must recognise some: Board colleague Mike Posen, who has served the museum with distinction for well over twenty years, David Stern, Irving Grose and the late Peter Gross who were all

key partners in the transformation of the museum; Curators Rachel Dickson and Sarah MacDougall who together have cemented our reputation for scholarship and exhibitions over the past thirteen years; Educators Alix Smith and Aimée Taylor who have transformed the visions of a National Learning programme and a Wellbeing programme for the elderly and those living with dementia, into meaningful reality; Longstanding supporters Daniel and Pauline Auerbach, Richard and Miriam Borchard, Sir Harry and Lady Djanogly, David and Patsy Franks, Sir Michael and Lady Heller, Manya Igel, Edward and Agnes Lee, Marks Barfield Architects, Anthony and the late Marilyn Rosenfelder, Jonathan Symons and George and Judit Weisz; Beate Planskoy, who instituted the Eva Frankfurther Curatorial and Research Fellowship for the Study of Émigré Artists which has facilitated so much of our expertise; institutions, particularly the Heritage Lottery Fund, who are the principal sponsors of the six month long centenary exhibition at the Inigo Rooms, King's College London at Somerset House as well as supporting important acquisitions to trigger expansive, innovative public learning and engagement; and other institutional supporters of our major acquisitions, The Art Fund and the V&A Purchase Grant Fund, who provide us, and the museum sector at large, the opportunity and privilege to acquire key works for our collections and the public at large.

And finally, it is to you, our public, that I direct our largest thanks for understanding our purpose and engaging with our programing to make Ben Uri a jewel in London's rich cultural crown, albeit still desperately in need of a permanent home in the centre of our great city. Together we can deliver the vision and secure the museum's exciting future

David J Glasser, *Executive Chairman*

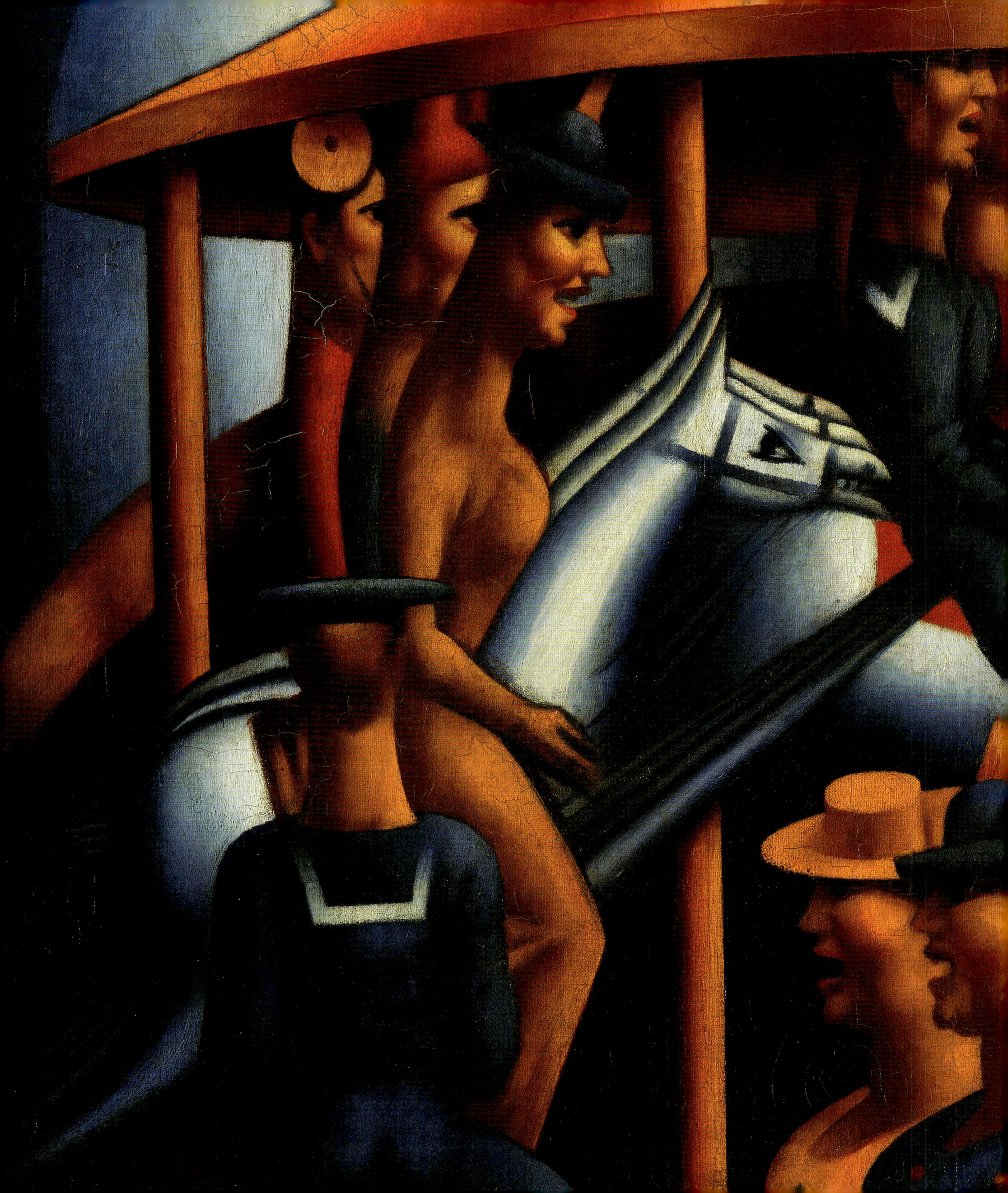

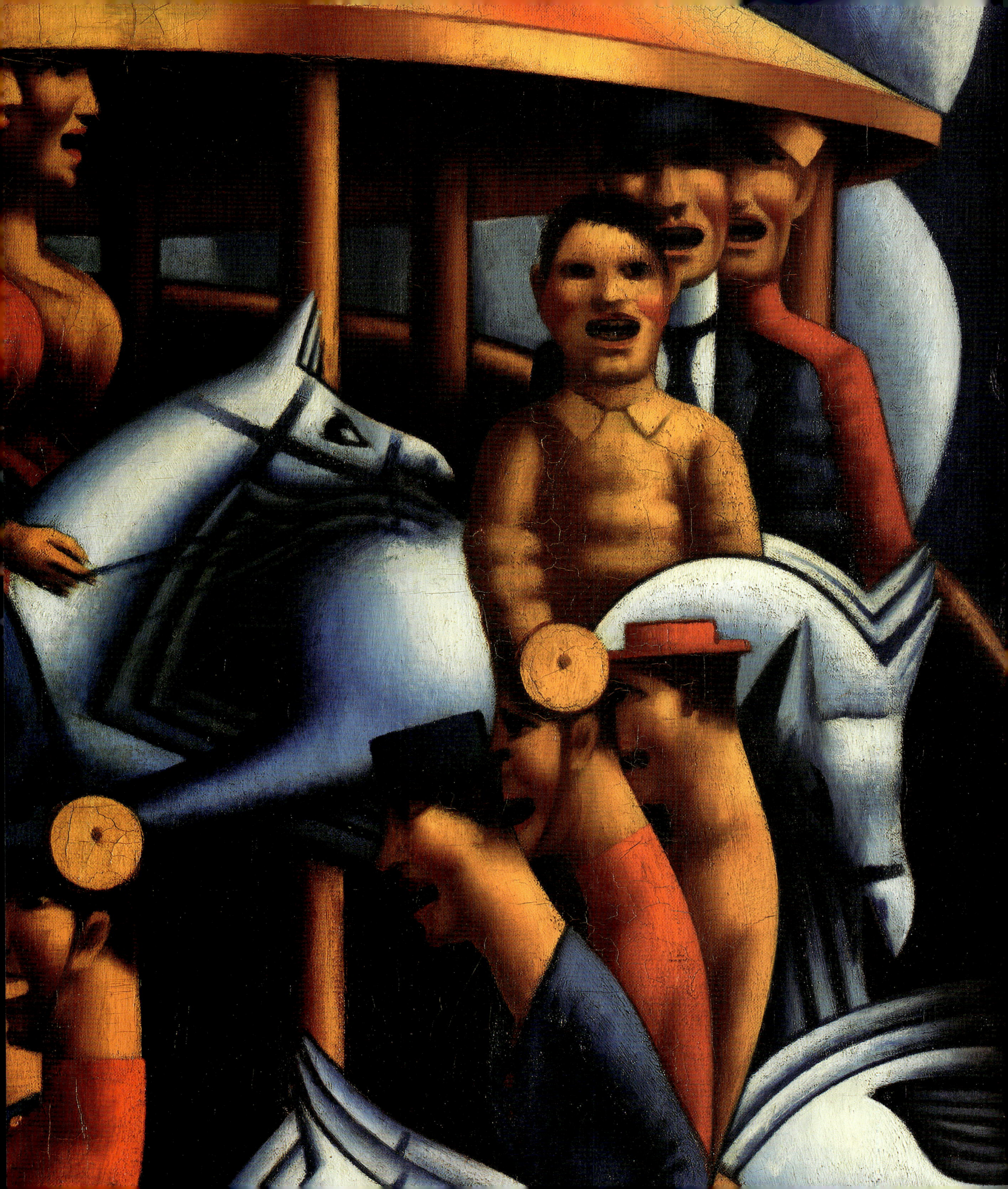

The Ben Uri Collection:
A century of engagement with British and European Art

From 1919, the Ben Uri started to positively acquire important works including a tranche of late nineteenth century works by disgraced Pre-Raphaelite, Simeon Solomon (cats. 2 and 4), and the following year, David Bomberg's East End masterpiece, *Ghetto Theatre* (1920, cat. 16), was acquired directly from the artist, fresh from its display at the progressive London Group exhibition. For many years, it was Ben Uri's single most requested loan work. In 1923, significant funds (£142 and 10/-) were raised to acquire Samuel Hirszenberg's monumental *The Sabbath Rest* (1894, cat. 3), one of the finest nineteenth-century pieces in and outside the collection, painted in Poland, depicting a world obliterated by events of the twentieth century. In 1928, Bomberg's fluently-handled *Jerusalem landscape Mt Zion with the Church of the Dormition: Moonlight* (1923) was acquired; and in 1937 Jankel Adler's intriguing *Still Life* was added to the collection, paid for in instalments.

From just 80 works in 1930, the collection has now grown to more than 1,300 across a wide variety of media, including painting, sculpture, drawing, printmaking, film, video, photography, textiles, ceramics, collage and installation. It is a unique body of work representing a distinct academic and visual survey of artistic and social life, primarily of artists born into the Jewish faith, and it forms a significant part of both British art / history and the cultural heritage of British Jewry.

The analysis of the collection is both fascinating and revealing and is unique within a British and European museum context. The collection also features a growing amount of related work by non-Jewish artists, including old master prints by Rembrandt van Rijn and Albrecht Dürer, alongside works by Frank Brangwyn, Royal Academician Anthony Whishaw, German/American George Grosz and photographer Sophie Robertson.

Works are comprehensive in style and technique across a wide-range of subject-matter. A minority depict aspects of Jewish life ranging from religious observance in Emmanuel Levy's joyous *Two Rabbis with Scrolls of the Law* (c.1943) and two recently acquired early masterpieces of Wolmark's oeuvre, *In the Synagogue* (1902) and *Sabbath Rest* (1909–1910) to traditional scenes including *Shtetl* (1934, cat. 27) by Chana Kowalska (who perished as a result of the Holocaust), and celebrations of Yiddish culture and shtetl life in Anatoly Kaplan's portfolio, *Tevye the Milkman* (1959).

Landscapes are prolific, including Lucien Pissarro's Impressionist *The Pagoda, Kew* (1919), Irma Stern's Expressionist *Mediterranean Scene* (1950, cat. 42) and contemporary colourist Philip Sutton's *Parliament Square* (1988), as well as powerful representations of city and village life, including Josef Herman's *Street Scene, Ystradgynlais* (1945, fig. 31) and Lesser Ury's *Berlin Street Scene* (1921, cat. 20). A number of striking nudes also feature, the most celebrated being Mark Gertler's *Sleeping Nude* (1938) and Frank Auerbach's two early life room drawings from 1954 (cat. 43).

The collection is particularly strong in portraiture ranging from the tender Art-Nouveau-inspired *Girl with a Rose* (1910) by Eugen Spiro to Isaac Rosenberg's beautifully observed *Portrait of Sonia* (1915, fig. 8) and Clara Klinghoffer's remarkable *Portrait of Orovida Pissarro* (1962, cat. 46), as well as a number of notable self-portraits, including those by Max Liebermann (cat. 23) and Reuven Rubin (cat. 32).

Overall, the collection is particularly rich in works by first and second generation émigrés, notably the

East End-based 'Whitechapel Boys', including David Bomberg, Mark Gertler, Isaac Rosenberg, Jacob Kramer, Bernard Meninsky, 'Whitechapel Girl' Clare Winsten (cat. 15), and the more senior painter, Alfred Wolmark - many of whom were involved with Ben Uri from its earliest years.

It also has a strong representation of works by those who made 'forced journeys' during the years of the Nazi regime from 1933-45, including Jankel Adler (cat. 22), Martin Bloch (cat. 28), Hans Feibusch (fig. 26), Fred Feigl, Naum Gabo, Josef Herman (cat. 36), Erich Kahn (fig. 25), Alfred Lomnitz (known as 'Lom', cat. 35), Else Meidner (fig. 33) and Ludwig Meidner (cat. 21).

In recent years, Ben Uri has also begun to build its collection in relation either directly or indirectly to the First and Second World Wars, including recent acquisitions of very different works by Isaac Rosenberg (*Self-portrait in Steel Helmet*, 1916 cat. 13), Barnett Freedman (*D-Day Preparations,* 1943, cat. 38) Emmanuel Levy (*Crucifixion*, 1942, cat 37), George Grosz's *The Lecture* (also known as *Anti-Semite,* 1934, cat. 29) and *Interrogation* (*c.*1936–38, cat. 33) and Marc Chagall's gouache *Apocalypse en Lilas, Capriccio* (1945–7, cat. 40), which depicts a naked, hermaphrodite Christ.

A number of works by important Israeli painters also feature in the collection, among them four fine early rare oils by Moshe Elazar Castel, the celebrated *Self-Portrait* (1937) by Reuven Rubin, as well as works by Emmanuel Mané-Katz, Nahum Gutman and Issachar Ber Ryback.

Ben Uri is exceptionally proud of its most recent major acquisition, *La Soubrette* (*c.*1933, cat. 26) by Chaïm Soutine. This significant work forms the centrepiece of the museum's growing collection of work by European masters, particularly *Les Peintres Juifs de L'Ecole de Paris.*

Almost 200 new works have entered the collection in the last 15 years, many with the generous and greatly appreciated support of the Art Fund, The V&A / MLA Purchase Grant Fund, The Heritage Lottery Fund (HLF), the Government 'In Lieu' scheme, artists and donors.

There are still many gaps and progressively fewer opportunities to acquire significant examples to fill them. Ben Uri currently has no works by Lucian Freud, Anthony Caro or Anish Kapoor. We very much need a great oil by Leon Kossoff, an early portrait by Frank Auerbach and a Toledo or Ronda landscape by their tutor David Bomberg. We are missing work by Modigliani and Kisling from the École de Paris; the American émigré artists including Bloom, Levine, Soyer brothers, Gropper, Shahn and Weber; the Abstract Expressionists including Newman, Gottlieb and Rothko; the Russian school of Vitebsk, El Lissitzky and the contemporary post-perestroika artists; the Israeli artists post-establishment of the State in 1948; and the list goes on.

We are nonetheless very honoured to be the custodians of such a wide-ranging and significant collection and hope that it will continue to inspire and delight viewers for at least the next century.

Sarah MacDougall, *Head of Collections,* and
Rachel Dickson, *Head of Curatorial Services*

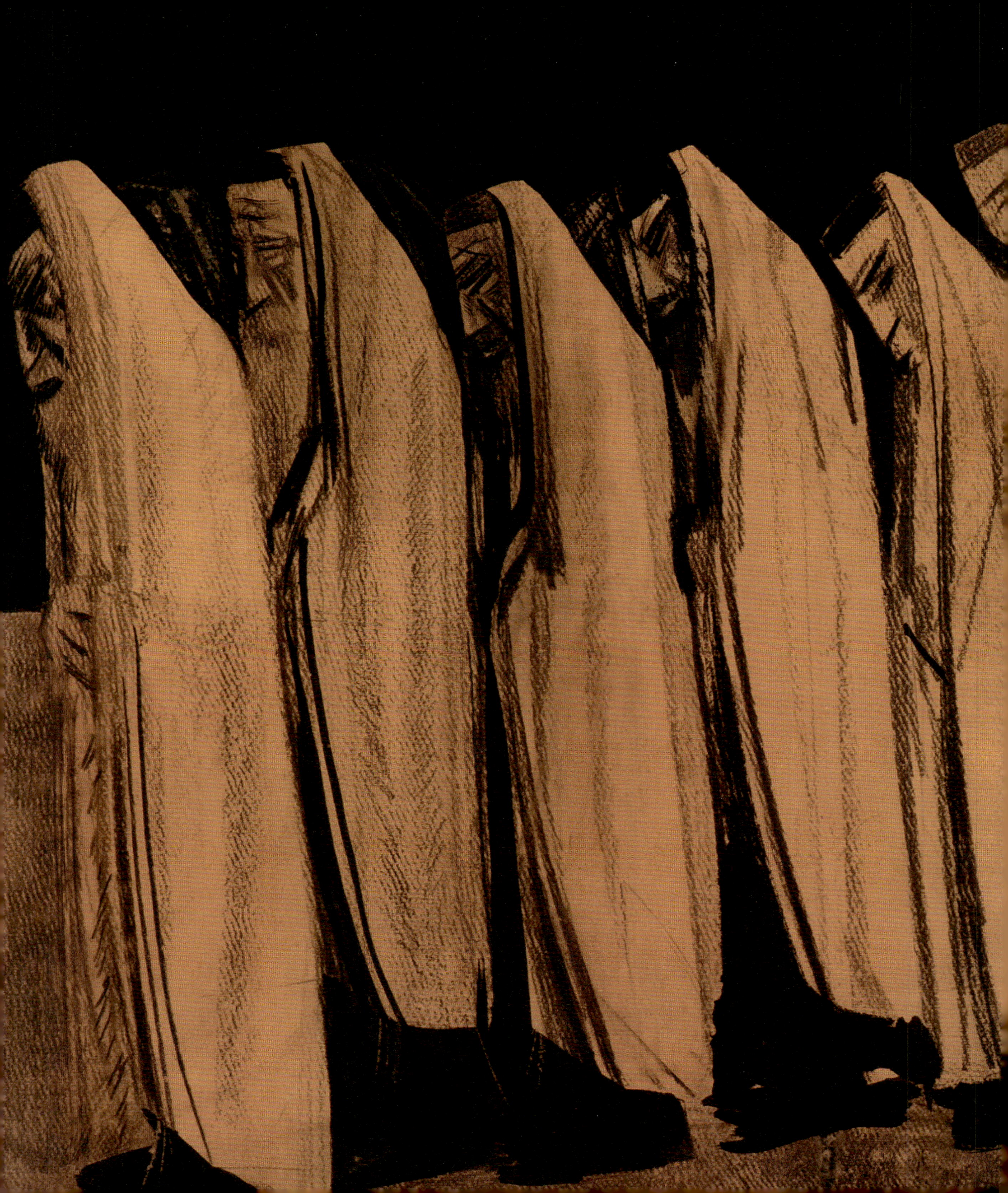

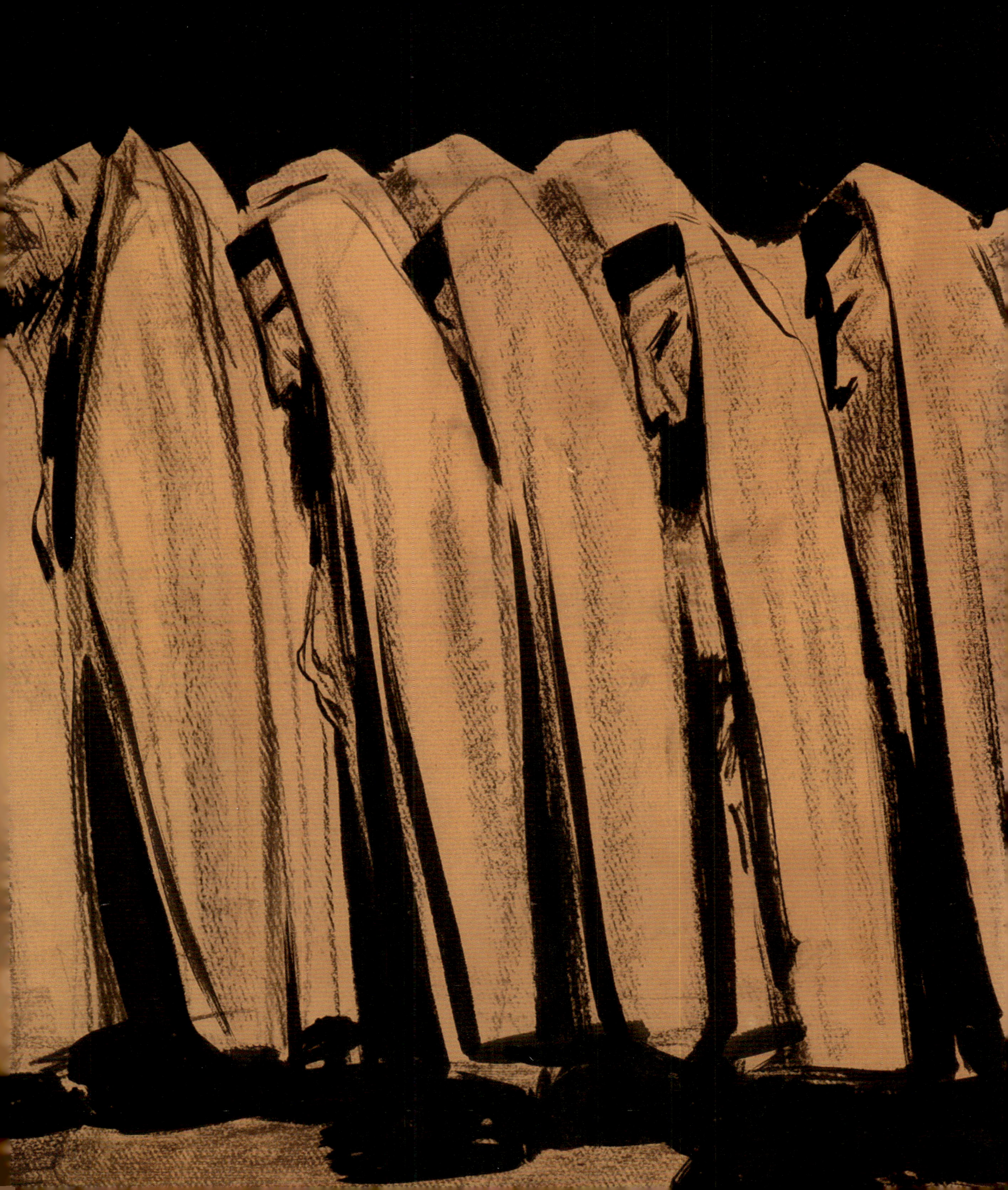

Catalogue

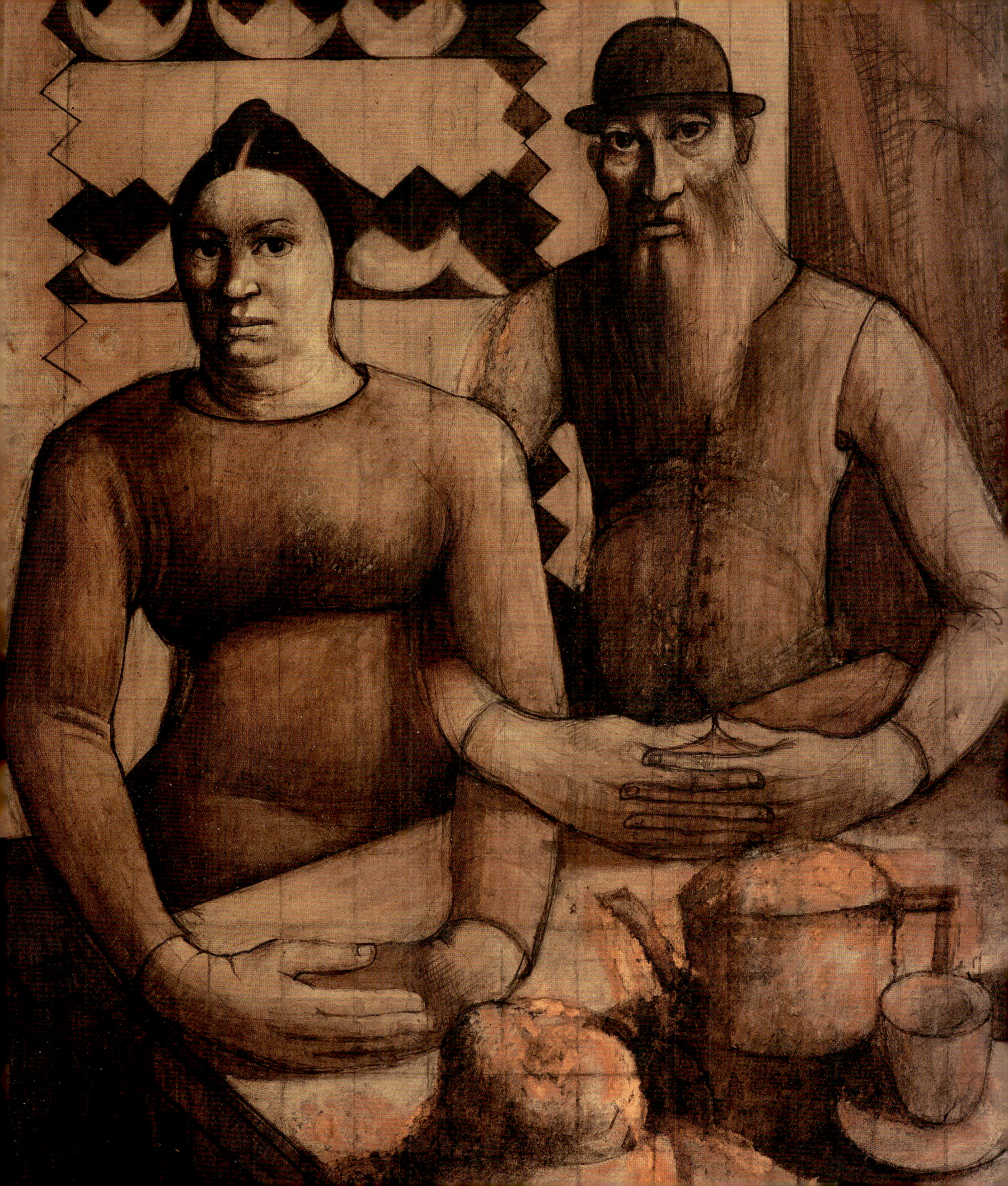

I

Portrait of Queen Victoria, 1842

SOLOMON ALEXANDER HART, RA

(1806 Plymouth, England – 1881 London, England)

FOOTNOTES

1   Joseph Leftwich, 15 June 1951, *Festival of Britain Anglo-Jewish Exhibition 1851–1951, Art Section*, Ben Uri Art Gallery, 14 Portman Street, W1, 9th July – 3rd August 1951, Ben Uri Archive.

2   The London School of Jewish Studies was founded as Jew's College, a rabbinical seminary, in 1855. The rabbinical training programme was later suspended, and much of the historical holdings of the library were sold off. Re-focussed and renamed in 1999, it now has an emphasis on providing a broader range of adult educational courses and training for the wider Jewish community. Since 2012, LSJS once again offers rabbinical training, in partnership with the programme set up by the London Sephardi community.

Born in Plymouth in 1806, Solomon Alexander Hart has been called 'the first important Anglo-Jewish artist';[1] his father, Samuel, and older brother, Mordecai, were well-known engravers. Barred from the local Grammar School because of his Jewish origins, Hart was taught by a Unitarian minister, and, unable to afford an apprenticeship premium, learned to draw by copying ancient sculptures at the British Museum. In 1823 Hart entered the Royal Academy to study painting, supporting himself by making copies and colouring theatrical prints. His earliest painting, a portrait miniature of his father, was shown at Somerset House in 1826, the year he also began exhibiting at the Royal Academy; he exhibited his first oil painting, *Instruction* in 1828. In 1830 Hart showed his first Jewish subjects, *The Elevation of the Law* (Suffolk Street Gallery) and *Polish Synagogue* at the Society of British Artists – the latter was well-received and brought him many commissions. Elected an Associate Royal Academician in 1835, Hart became the first Jewish Royal Academician in 1840, Professor of Painting (1854–63), and finally, librarian in 1864.

An influential figure, Hart was also curator of the Painted Hall, Greenwich, and an adviser to the British and South Kensington museums. Among his friends were J. W. M. Turner and Sir William Collins, who introduced him to his children saying: 'This is Mr Hart, whom we have just elected Academician [...] Mr Hart is a Jew, and the Jews crucified our saviour, but he is a very good man for all that, and we shall see something more of him now'. Hart's *Conference between Manasseh ben Israel and Oliver Cromwell*, bought by F. D. Mocatta, was presented to Jews' College (now the London School of Jewish Studies).[2] He died in London in 1881.

Celebrated as a painter of historical scenes, Hart visited Italy, *c.*1841–42, making an elaborate series of drawings later used for works on Italian themes. His *Portrait of Queen Victoria* wearing the badge of her office (the Order of the Garter) emphasises both her youth and her imperial authority and is unlikely to have been a commission. Painted five years into Victoria's reign and two years into Hart's Academicianship, it conveys his social and artistic integration with Britain, identifying him with the ultimate symbol of the establishment. It can also be seen as a self-portrait – the outsider as insider – signifying Hart's achievements as a painter and perhaps satisfying his aspirations of belonging to the British establishment and the artistic elite.

This is one of two works by Hart in the Ben Uri Collection.

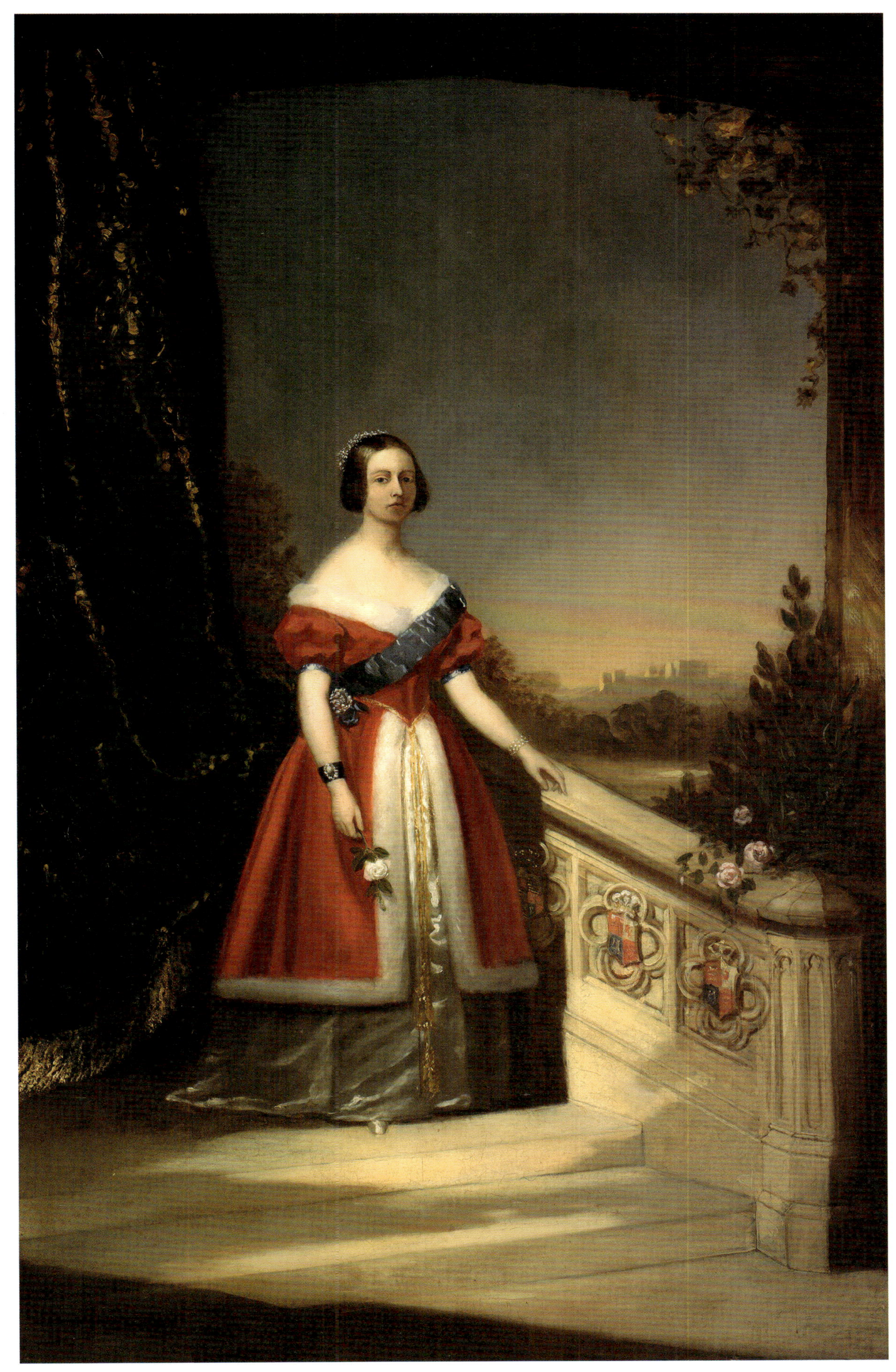

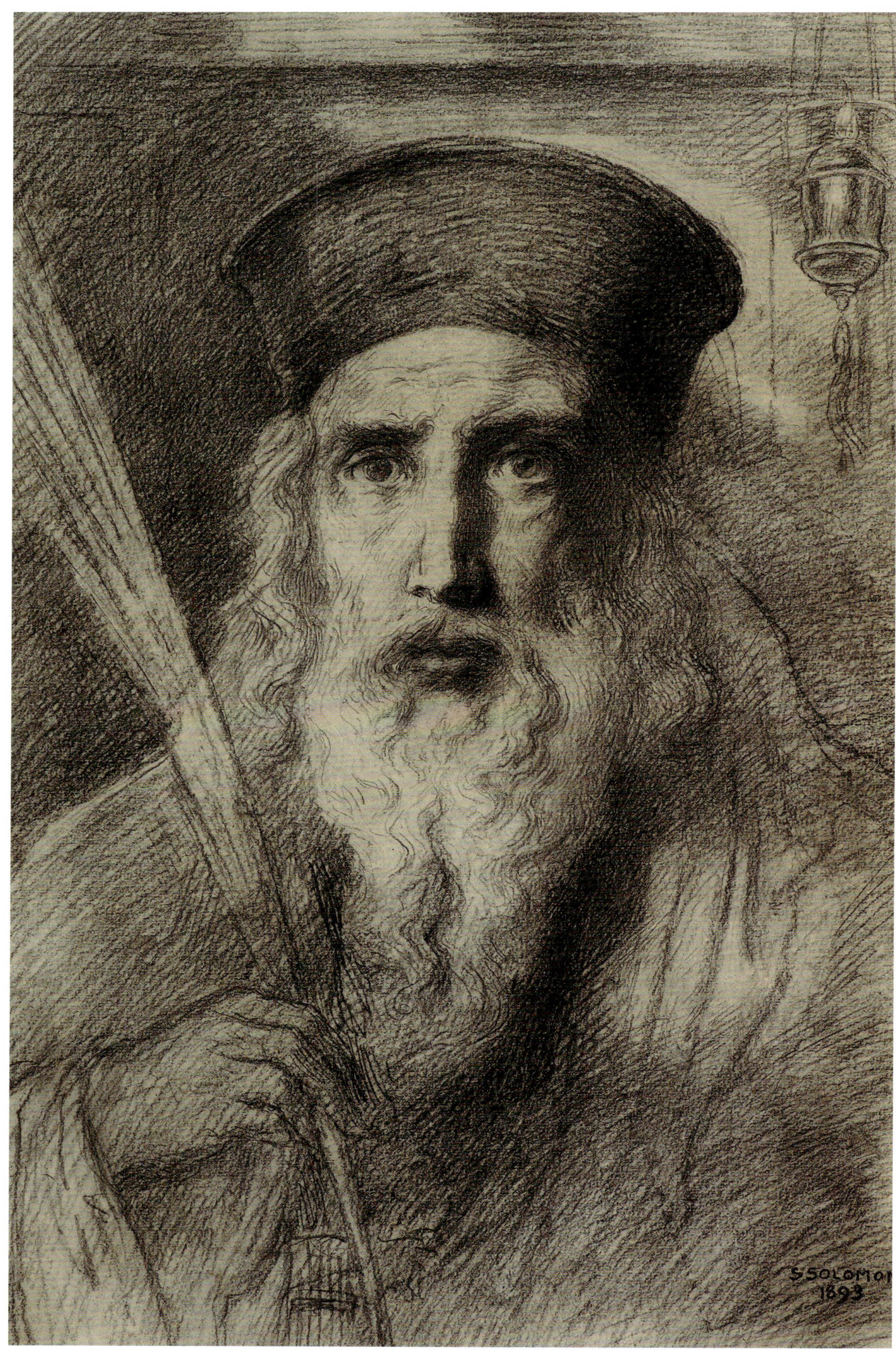
S.SOLOMON
1893

2

The Rabbi, 1893

SIMEON SOLOMON

(1840 London, England – 1905 London, England)

Charcoal on paper
51.2 × 34.2 cm
Signed and dated (lower right)
'S Solomon 1893'

Ben Uri Collection
Purchased with the assistance of
Moshe Oved 1919

SELECTED EXHIBITION HISTORY
*Ben Uri Gallery and Club, opening
exhibition*, London, 1925; *Burne Jones
and His Followers*, Isetan Museum of
Art, Tokyo; Ishibashi Museum of Art,
Kurume; Tochigi Prefectural Museum
of Fine Arts, Utsunomiya, Yamanashi
Prefectoral Museum of Art, Kofu,
1987; *Love Revealed: Simeon Solomon
and the Pre-Raphaelites,* Birmingham
Museum & Art Gallery; Ben Uri,
London; Museum Villa Stuck, Munich
2005–2006; *Homeless and Hidden I,*
Ben Uri, London, 29 Jan–24 Feb 2008

FOOTNOTES
1   Abraham Solomon, who achieved
fame for his paintings of the railway,
was also elected an Associate Royal
Academician, receiving news of this
honour upon his deathbed.

2   According to Joseph Leftwich,
Foreword to Ben Uri catalogue, 1951,
p. 4., M. H. Spielmann ranked her
second only to Simeon himself. She
also died of alcoholism.

3   Succot is a harvest festival, and
takes place at the time when the last
crops were gathered in the Holy Land
during biblical times. The four plants
(or species) used in the ceremony are
date palm (lulav), myrtle (hadas),
willow (aravah) and a citrus
fruit (etrog).

4   Cyril Roth, Jewish Art (London:
W. H. Allen/ Israel: Masadah – P. E.
C. Press Ltd, Tel Aviv, 1961), p. 567.

5   See David Mazower
in this volume.

Simeon Solomon was born in London in 1840 into a middle-class Jewish family, the youngest of the eight children of Meyer Solomon and Katherine (née Levy), an amateur miniature painter. Raised in Bishopsgate, he trained at F. S. Cary's Academy (1852–56), and in the studio of his elder brother Abraham (1824–1862),[1] who he followed to the Royal Academy Schools (1856–60). Their sister, Rebecca (1832–1886) was also a gifted artist and a regular RA exhibitor, employed as a copyist and drapery painter by John Everett Millais.[2] Simeon made his exhibition debut at the Royal Academy with a drawing at the age of 17, where he showed regularly until 1872. Two years later he exhibited a controversial oil painting, *Moses* (Private Collection, New York) but was supported by the novelist William Makepeace Thackeray. His earliest works, mostly on Old Testament subjects, were inspired by Jewish culture and tradition. Solomon was introduced to and became a member of the Pre-Raphaelite circle around 1857. In the following decade he regularly exhibited works at the progressive Dudley Gallery, London and was elected a member of the Savile Club.

In 1873 Solomon was arrested in a public lavatory, convicted of gross indecency and sentenced to 18 months imprisonment (subsequently suspended). Without support, he drifted into alcoholism, living on charity and a meagre living as a pavement artist. Following a brief stay in a lunatic asylum, he spent years in the St Giles Workhouse, Holborn, where he died of a heart attack in 1905.

Solomon's fascination with faith and the the aesthetic qualities of religious ritual often produced work featuring young men in idealised roles as rabbis, priest or acolytes rapt in mystical contemplation. His young Rabbi is shown in synagogue with the *ner tamid* (everlasting light) behind him, holding a *lulav* (palm leaf), one of the four species (*arbah minim*) usually bound together, indicating that this is the festival of Succot.[3] Although the three other plants used in the Succot ritual are missing from the picture, Solomon had probably not witnessed the celebrations since childhood. Nevertheless, his Jewish subject paintings have been called 'among the best of what is commonly called Jewish art, notwithstanding the fact that the artist, early in life, had become converted from nominal Jewish orthodoxy to a fervent Catholicism'.[4]

In 1920 both *The Rabbi* and *Thou Shalt Not Tempt* (1894), another charcoal drawing in the Ben Uri Collection, were reproduced in *Renesans* ('Renaissance'), the short-lived Yiddish journal, which ran for six issues under the editorship of Leo Kenig drawing on a cohort of writers and artists closely associated with Ben Uri.[5] There are 13 works by Solomon in the Ben Uri Collection·

3
Sabbath Rest, 1894

SAMUEL HIRSZENBERG

(1865 Lodz, Poland – 1908 Jerusalem)

Oil on canvas
149.5 × 206.5
Signed and dated (lower right)
'S. Hirszenberg, 1894'

Ben Uri Collection
Acquired by subscription with the
assistance of Moshe Oved, 1923

SELECTED EXHIBITION HISTORY:
Opening exhibition, Ben Uri, London,
1925; *Homeless and Hidden*, Ben Uri,
London, 2008

FOOTNOTES
1   See Richard Cohen and Mirjam
Rajner, "Invoking Samuel
Hirszenberg's Artistic Legacy"
International Conference "Memory
and Journey. Dimensions of Israeli and
Jewish Art," Dusseldorf, Germany,
July 1–3, 2013 for a wider discussion of
this work.

2   Shimon Milner, cited ibid.

Born in Lodz, Poland in 1865, Samuel Hirszenberg was a traditional history painter in the realist tradition, influenced by the Polish masters Jan Matejko (1838–1893) and Maurycy Gotlieb (1856–1879). He entered the Academy of Fine Arts in Krakow at the age of 15 and studied there for two years, afterwards completing his training at the Royal Academy of Arts in Munich (1885–1889). Hirszenberg returned to Poland in 1891 and re-settled in Lodz two years later. He went on to become well-known for his monumental paintings depicting the condition of impoverished Jews in Poland, where frequent anti-Semitic pogroms caused many to flee to the West. He exhibited regularly in Paris before moving to Jerusalem in 1907, where he taught at the newly-established Bezalel School of Arts and Crafts until his death in 1908.

Hirszenberg was preoccupied with themes of exile and wandering. His painting, *Exile* (1904, now lost),[1] was reproduced in the Yiddish magazine "Ost und West" to great acclaim the following year. However, *Sabbath Rest*, a later version of an 1890 work of the same title and similar composition in the Museum of Modern Art, Lodz, shows how his interest in this subject pre-dates this composition. In this version, several details have been altered to emphasise the narrative of migration. Three generations are gathered in one room around the bedridden matriarch to keep the Sabbath. Their piety is indicated by the candlesticks on the table and the hanging star-shaped *Judenstern* lamp, which burns for 24 hours. A young boy leans on his grandfather, his parents seated at

the table; the muted palette conveys their poverty, but two older grandchildren by the window are symbolically closer to a brighter future. Their traditional way of life is contrasted with the encroaching industrialization of the Lodz workers' quarter just glimpsed through the window behind them. The elder grandson reads aloud from a 'Letter from Argentina', an alternative title for the painting according to 'Ruth' (Hirszenberg's convert wife) in "Ost und West". The theme of migration is further emphasized by the identification of the sitter in the larger portrait as Baron Maurice de Hirsch, a tireless supporter of Jewish immigration to Argentina, via his Jewish Colonial Organization, established in 1891.[2] The second portrait is thought to be that of the relative who has migrated to Argentina. Hirszenberg's work influenced a number of later Jewish artists including Marc Chagall, and Alfred Wolmark who specifically referenced *Sabbath Rest* in his own *Sabbath Afternoon* (see cat. 6), transposing the setting to London's Jewish East End.

Sabbath Rest is a key painting in the Ben Uri collection, and one of the earliest acquisitions, purchased in 1923 for £143 through subscription and the support, principally, of Moshe Oved (cat. 41). It was the opening exhibit in the first collection display when 'Ben Uri Gallery and Club' opened in May 1925 at 68 Great Russell Street, opposite the British Museum. It is one of six works by the artist in the Ben Uri collection.

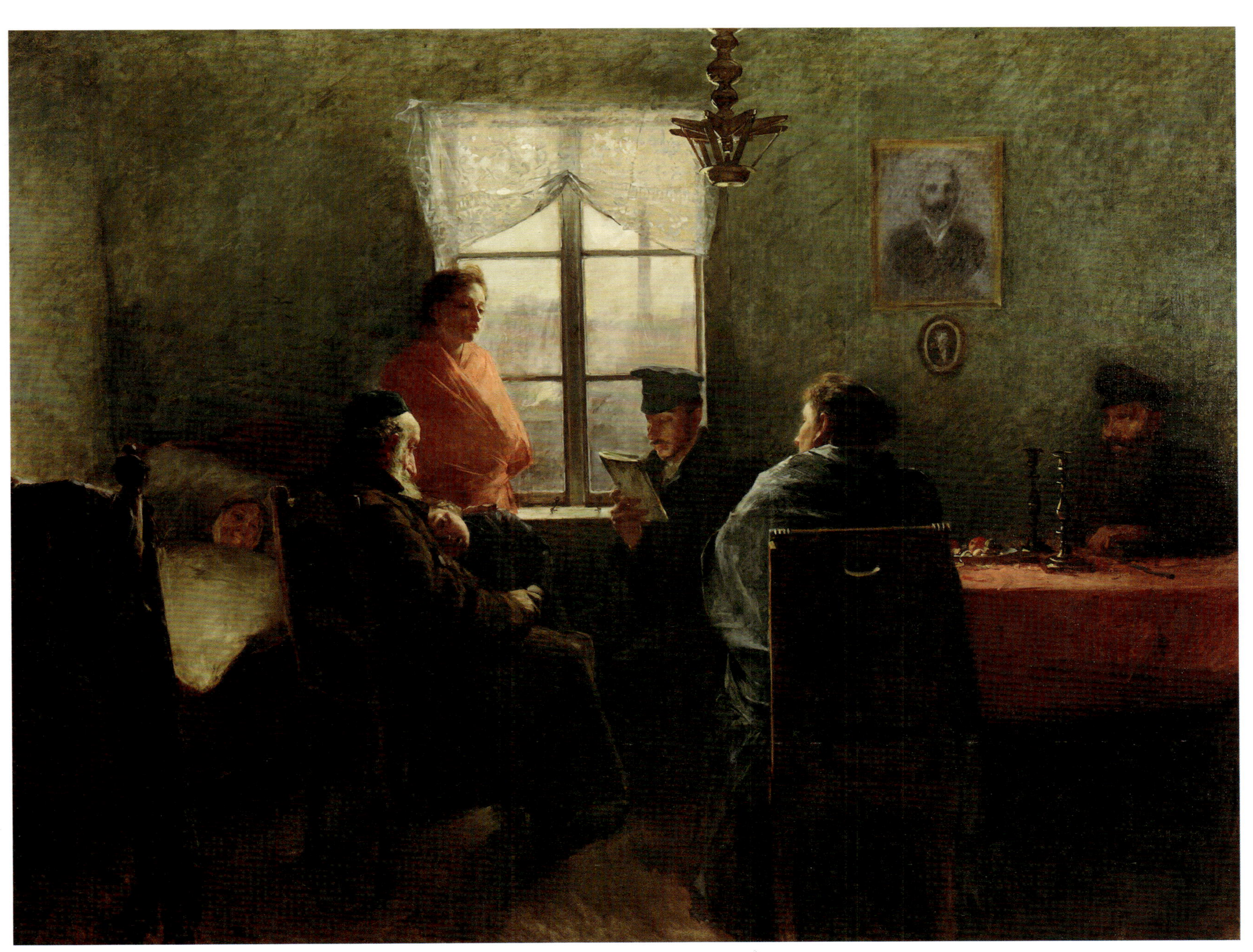

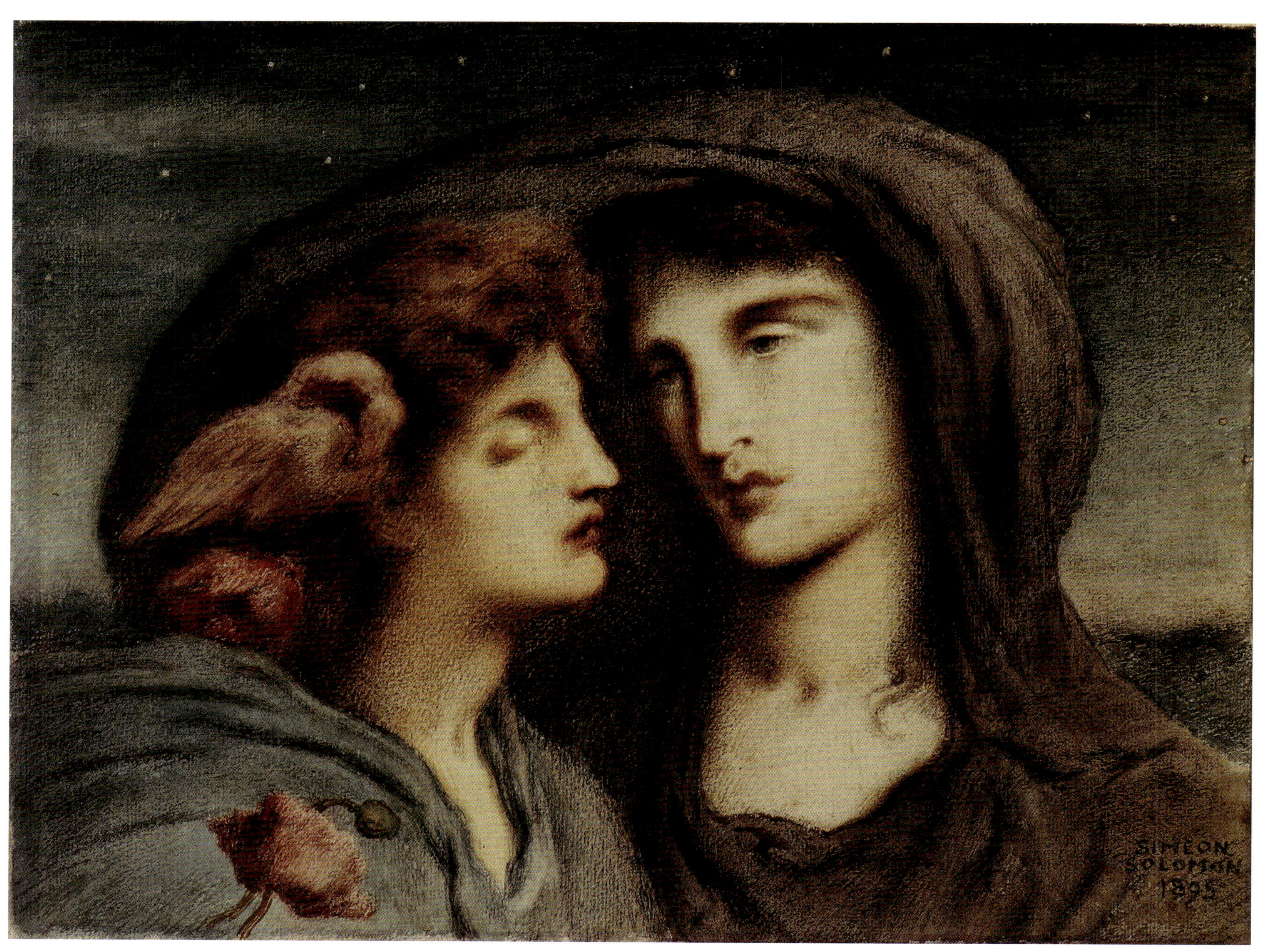

SIMEON
SOLOMON
1895

4

Night Looking upon Sleep her Beloved Child (II), 1895

SIMEON SOLOMON
(1840 London, England – 1905 London, England)

Watercolour and Charcoal
on paper
30 × 40.5 cm
Signed and dated (lower right)
'Simeon Solomon 1895'

Ben Uri Collection
Purchased with the assistance of
Moshe Oved, 1919

SELECTED EXHIBITION HISTORY
Love Revealed, Birmingham Museum
& Art Gallery; Ben Uri, London; Villa
Stuck, Munich, 2005–06; *Homeless &
Hidden*, Ben Uri, London, 2008;
Apocalypse, Osborne Samuel, London,
2010

Around 1857–8 Simeon Solomon was introduced to Dante Gabriel Rossetti and joined the Pre-Raphaelite circle, soon becoming a favourite of the group, especially with Edward Burne-Jones, who called Solomon the 'greatest artist of them all'. For a period he enjoyed the support of a number of wealthy patrons and Pre-Raphaelite collectors. Among their wider circle Solomon was also influenced by Algernon Swinburne and Walter Pater, key exponents of the Aesthetic movement. Following three trips to Italy in the 1860s, Solomon changed his style and subject matter concentrating on classical Renaissance imagery often shot through with a languid eroticism and exploring same-sex desire.

This delicate watercolour is closely tied up with the mystical, dreamlike atmosphere of Solomon's prose poem, *A Vision of Love Revealed in Sleep*, which he published in 1871, dedicated to his friend Burne-Jones. Solomon's late heads often represent abstract themes, such as Night, Love and Death and this is one of many reworkings. The two heads, Night and Sleep, with their distinctive classical features, are physically close, but do not look directly at one another. Night wraps them both protectively in her cloak, while looking upon her child Sleep with her closed eyes. Night's own expression is dream-like, with just a hint of suffering.

Swinburne wrote of Solomon's subjects:

There is a questioning wonder in their faces, a fine joy and a faint sorrow, a trouble as of water stirred, a delight as of thirst appeased. Always a feast or sacrifice, in chamber or in field, the air and carriage of their beauty has something in it of the strange: hardly a figure but has some touch, though never so delicately slight, either of eagerness or of weariness, some note of expectation or of saiety, some semblance of outlook or inlook; but prospective or introspective, an expression is there which is not pure Greek, a shade or tone of thought or feeling beyond Hellenic contemplation; whether it be oriental or modern in its origin, and derive from national or personal sources. This passionate sentiment of mystery seems at time to "o'er inform its tenement" of line and colour, and impress itself even to perplexity upon the sense of the spectator.

After his death, Solomon's work began to be reassessed. In 1906 two memorial exhibitions were held in London at the Royal Academy and the Baillie Gallery, and in 1908 Julia Ellsworth Ford published *Simeon Solomon: An Appreciation*. In 2005–6 Birmingham Art Gallery mounted an international retrospective, which toured to Ben Uri.

This work is one of 13 acquired in 1919 through the auspices of Moshe Oved (cat. 41), among the earliest art works to enter the collection. Solomon's career had ended in disgrace after he was prosecuted for homosexual activity. Oved's championing of Solomon's work was therefore important in the artist's rehabilitation.

5

Self-portrait with Candles, *c.*1906

LILY DELISSA JOSEPH

(1863 London, England – 1940 London, England)

Oil on canvas
105.5 × 59.5 cm

Presented by of Mrs. Redcliffe
Salaman 1948

SELECTED EXHIBITION HISTORY
*Festival of Britain Anglo-Jewish
Exhibition 1851-1951*, Ben Uri, London,
1951; *The Ben Uri Story*, Phillips,
London, 2001; *Homeless and Hidden*,
Ben Uri, London, 2008; *Fragmented
Mirror: Exhibition of Jewish Artists,
Berlin, 1907*, Tel Aviv Museum of Art,
Israel, 2009

FOOTNOTES
1   There are two candles to represent
the fact that the command to keep
Shabbat holy appears twice in the
Torah, (the first five books of Moses).
They are traditionally kindled by the
woman of the house to mark the
formal beginning of Shabbat about
twenty minutes before sundown. The
day will have been spent in
preparation since no work can be done
once Shabbat has started. It is
customary for the whole family to
then eat together on Friday evening.

Born Lily Solomon in 1863, Lily Delissa Joseph was the younger sister of the artist Solomon J Solomon (cat. 18), who may have encouraged her to paint. She also trained at the Ridley School of Art and the Royal Academy becoming a portrait, landscape and interior painter. She later married the architect Delissa Joseph, who built two of her brother Solomon J Solomon's studios.

Deeply involved in the women's suffrage movement, Delissa Joseph was famously unable to attend her own Private View at the Baillie Gallery, London in 1912 after being detained at Holloway Gaol 'on a charge in connection with [the] Women's Suffrage Movement'. One of the first women to own and drive a car, she also learnt to fly aeroplanes when in her fifties. A committed member of the Jewish community, she was involved in many charitable ventures. In 1911 she met the young poet Isaac Rosenberg (cat. 13) while painting at the National Gallery (she depicted its interior in a number of works). She employed him briefly as a tutor to her children and her sister Mrs. Henrietta Lowy did the same, before introducing him to their wealthier friend Mrs Herbert Cohen (fig. 4), who sponsored his studies at the Slade School of Art.

Lily Delissa Joseph was also religiously observant and well-known for her musical voice in the communal singing at the Brook Green synagogue in Hammersmith – she had also been active in its establishment. In *Self-Portrait with Candles*, one of three works in the Ben Uri collection, she shows herself in modest dress and with her head covered.[1] She holds the two

Shabbat candles which are traditionally kindled by the woman of the house about twenty minutes before sundown to mark the formal beginning of the Sabbath on Friday evening. The work combines her interest in portraiture and interiors, and is influenced by her admiration for Rembrandt, particularly in the use of light and shadow. It also shows her characteristic use of a limited palette of white, cobalt blue and rose or orange madder.

This is one of three works by Lily Delissa Joseph in the Ben Uri Collection.

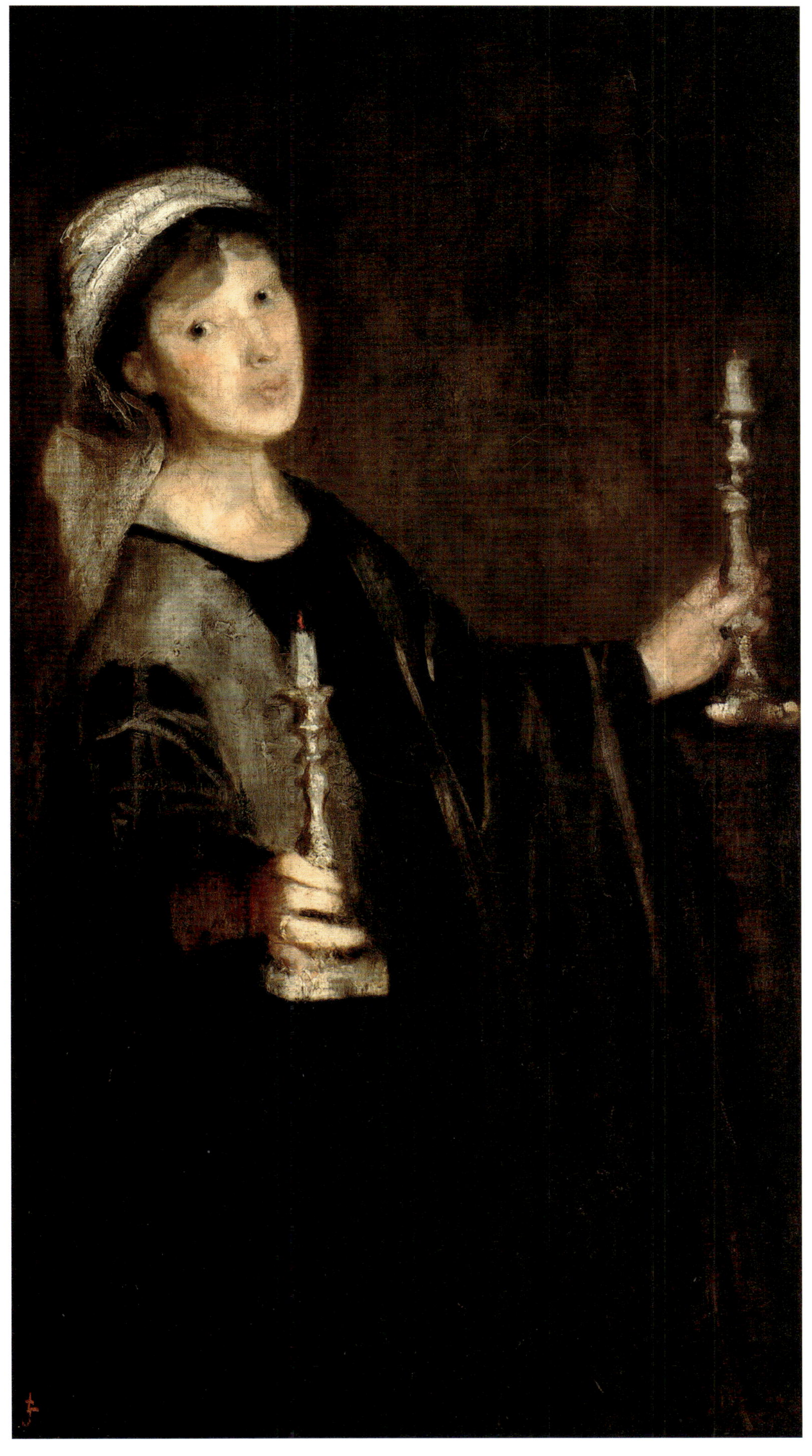

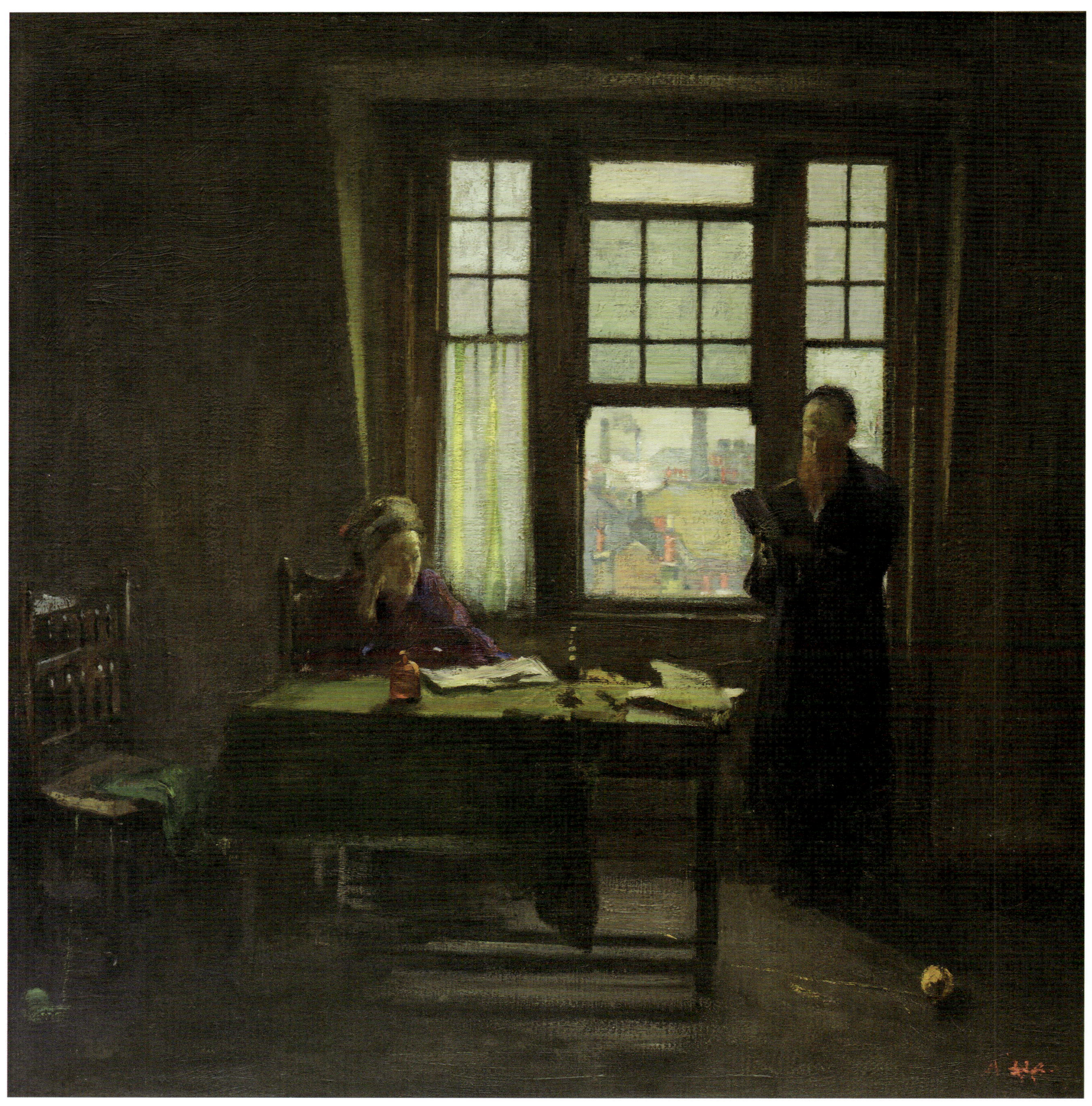

6

Sabbath Afternoon, *c.*1909–10

ALFRED WOLMARK

(1877 Warsaw, Poland – 1961 London, England)

Oil on canvas
77.5 × 77.5 cm

Ben Uri Collection
Acquired in 2013 with the assistance of
the HLF, the V&A Purchase Grant
Fund and the Art Fund

SELECTED EXHIBITION HISTORY

Ben Uri Story, Phillips, London, 2001;
Re-discovering Wolmark, Ben Uri,
London, 2004; *Recent Acquisitions,*
Ben Uri, London, 2013

FOOTNOTES

1   Alfred Wolmark, *The Times*, 1961.

2   See Richard Cork's essay in this
volume.

'From Eastern Europe to the East End and back again,' Alfred Aaron Wolmark declared, 'I am very much a product of this country'.[1] Born in Warsaw in the late 1870s, he came to England with his family in 1883 as part of the early wave of eastern-European Jewish migration. The family eventually settled in the more affluent neighbourhood of Tredegar Square, Bow, where Wolmark remained for three years before setting up his own studio in Kilburn. Wolmark's years in the East End – then the heart of the immigrant Jewish community – and his two lengthy sojourns in Poland, between 1903 and 1906, had a huge visual (as well as spiritual) impact on his early work. For the first 10–15 years of his career he produced a remarkably consistent and mature body of paintings on Jewish subjects in the manner and spirit of Rembrandt, 'the only painter,' he later remarked, 'who ever […] influenced him'. Then, in July 1911, after an artistic epiphany while on honeymoon in Concarneau, Brittany, Alfred Wolmark jettisoned his earlier methods in favour of the 'New Art', embarking upon a pioneering 'colourist' path for the next two decades of his working life.

Sabbath Afternoon is a key transitional work showing a new handling of paint and touches of a lighter palette as Wolmark began to move towards modernism. Familiar with the work of Samuel Hirszenberg's from his time in Poland, he undoubtedly references the older artist's *Sabbath Rest* (1894, cat. 3) in his own Sabbath painting, but transposes his subjects to a typical East End setting. To underline their Orthodoxy, Wolmark shows his couple absorbed in their Sabbath studies, including important details of Jewish religious observance, such as the *Bessamim* (ceremonial spice tower) on the table. Yet the focus has shifted from interior to exterior and from domestic to industrial, as the sun setting over the city's smoking chimneys is glimpsed through the window behind. It is not the interior or its inhabitants but the brilliantly lit, urban townscape beyond which provides the focus for the composition, identifying Wolmark with a modernist motif typical of his Camden Town contemporaries.

A pioneer as a painter of both the Jewish community in London's East End and as an early modernist, Wolmark has been called the 'father' of the Whitechapel Boys.[2] He was the only artist to be included in both the Whitechapel Art Gallery's 1906 *Jewish Art and Antiquities Exhibition* and in David Bomberg and Jacob Epstein's 'Jewish Section' at the 1914 exhibition *Twentieth-Century Art: A Review of Modern Movements*. Closely associated with the Ben Uri for many years: he was Vice-President from 1923–56, and in 1925, together with Solomon J Solomon (cat. 18), presided over the official opening of the Ben Uri's first gallery in Great Russell Street.

Wolmark is one of the best-represented artists in the Ben Uri Collection which holds 27 of his works, and curated the retrospective *Alfred Wolmark: A Pioneer of British Modernism* in 2004.

7

Portrait of Mrs. Ethel Solomon in Riding Habit, 1909

ALFRED WOLMARK

(1877 Warsaw, Poland – 1961 London, England)

Oil on canvas
89.6 × 69.9 cm
Signed (centre right) with
monogram and dated '09'

Ben Uri Collection
On loan from the executors of Mrs.
Ethel Solomon 1988

SELECTED EXHIBITION HISTORY
Homeless and Hidden, Ben Uri,
London, 2008

FOOTNOTES

1   Zangwill was a member of the
group of London Jewish intellectuals
known as the 'wanderers of Kilburn',
that also included Solomon J Solomon
(cat. 18), and later formed the core of
the Maccabeans and the Jewish
Historical Society of England.

Wolmark's striking portrait of Mrs Ethel Solomon shows his work at a key transitional moment between his early Rembrandtesque manner and dark palette and his notable conversion to colour after 1911. Against a putty-coloured background, he uses a bolder, looser paint handling, picking out his young sitter's fresh complexion, which contrasts with her fashionable black and white riding attire, offset by her mustard-yellow gloves. Wolmark uses her dramatic pose as a compositional device to indicate her strong character. The portrait also relates specifically to Wolmark's own later series of single-figure works including *The Fencer* (*c.*1914, current whereabouts unknown), which repeats the emphatic hand-on-hip gesture, and the *Portrait of Dottie Konstam* (aka *Mrs. Alfred Kohnstamm*, 1915, Private Collection), in which his female subject holding her parasol echoes the strong diagonal of Mrs Solomon grasping her riding crop. The work is boldly signed with an early version of Wolmark's monogram.

Born in Edgbaston, the daughter of a draper, Mrs Ethel Solomon (née Cohen, 1888–1985), went on to become a highly influential figure. In 1920 she became Chair of the Women's Federation of British Zionists and in 1939 she and her husband established Whittinghame Farm School to educate German and Austrian refugee children. Between 1943 and 1966, she was also Chair of Ben Uri.

Wolmark executed many portraits of Jewish sitters including a head of the writer Israel Zangwill (1925, Ben Uri Collection), known as the 'Jewish Dickens'. The Ben Uri Collection also holds 13 of the 14 illustrations that formed frontispieces to the multi-volume edition of Zangwill's work published in 1925,[1] and an equally striking head-and-shoulders portrait of Mrs Herbert Cohen, which was presented to the collection by Mrs Ethel Solomon.

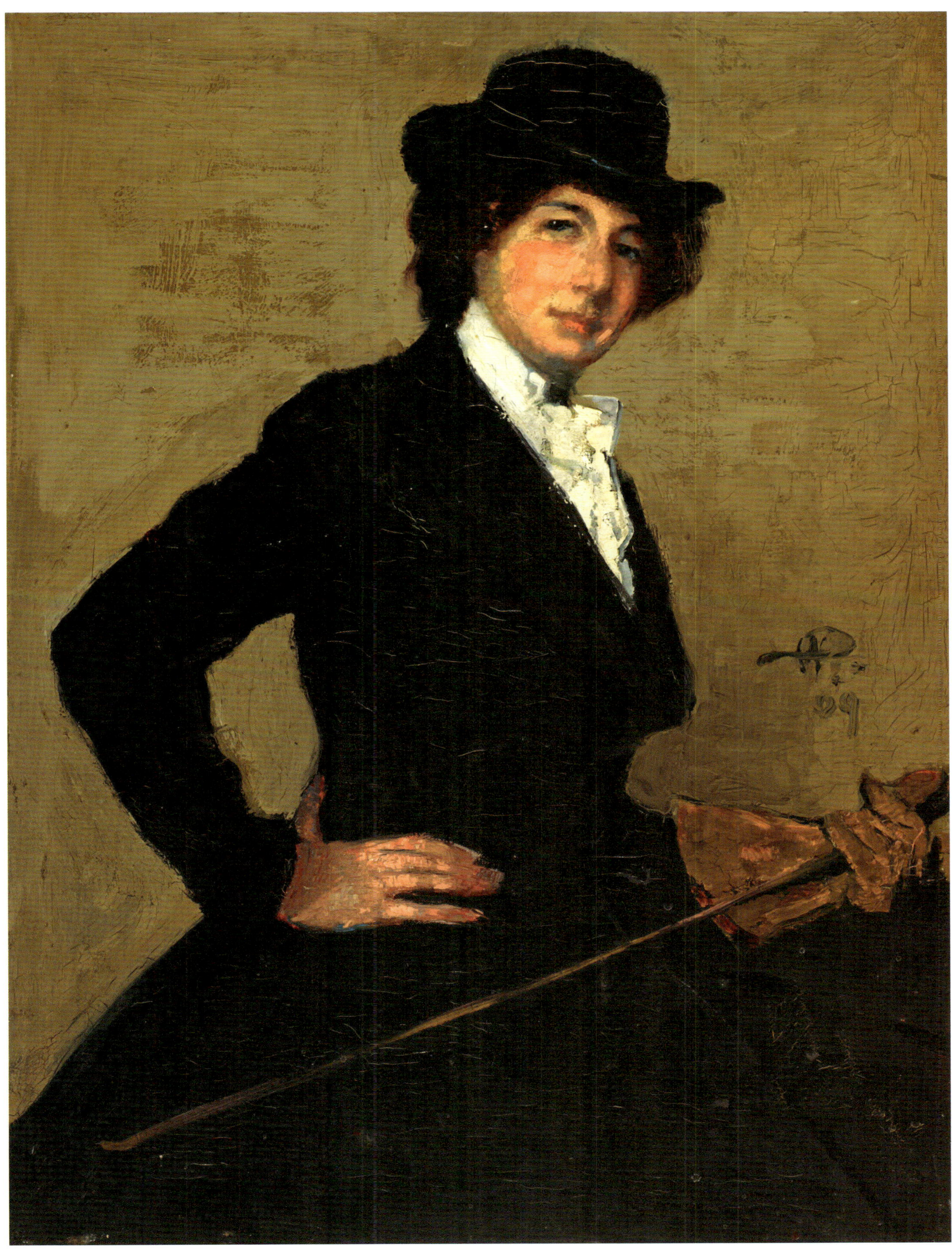

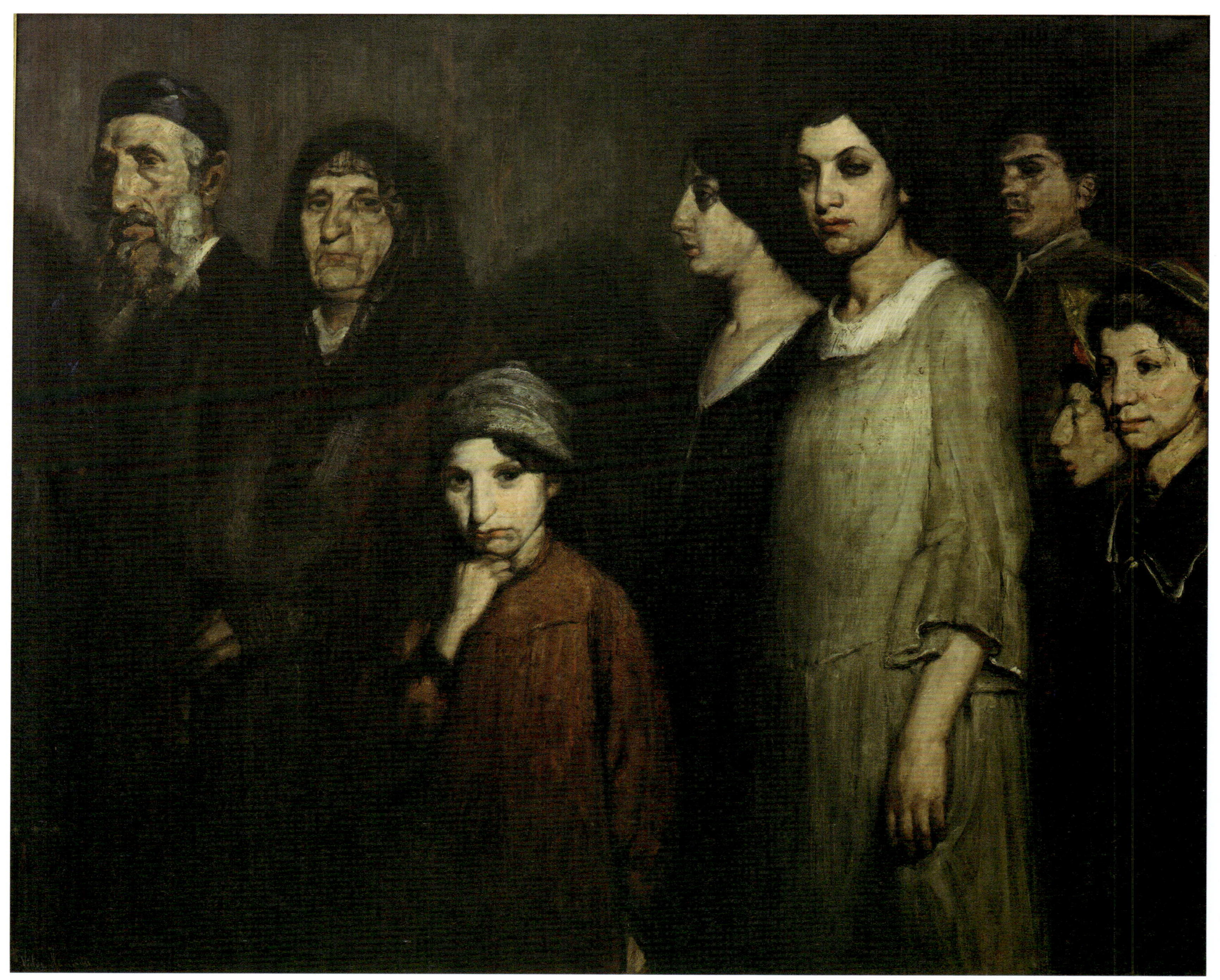

The Emigrants, *c.*1910

VICTOR HAGEMAN

(1868 Antwerp, Belgium – 1940 Belgium)

Oil on canvas
122 × 155 cm
Signed (lower left) 'Victor
Hageman' and inscribed (verso)
'Descendants Israelites'

Ben Uri Collection
Presented by the Trafalgar Gallery,
London, 2013

SELECTED EXHIBITION HISTORY
Contemporary Art, Royal Museum of
Fine Arts, Antwerp, Belgium, 1928, as
'Jewish Family'

Belgian artist and art teacher Victor Hageman was born and raised in Antwerp and trained at the Academy alongside Vincent Van Gogh, whom he recalled as a 'disheveled [*sic*], nervous, and restless man who fell like a bomb on the Academy of Antwerp, overwhelming the director, the drawing master, and the students'. A socially-conscious realist painter, Hageman specialized in studies of migrants and particularly, of his Russian-Jewish neighbours. The distinctive, dark-haired young woman facing outwards (on the right of the canvas) also sat for at least two further separate studies. Painted on a monumental scale, *The Emigrants* depicts three generations of one family gathered at the point of exile, their emotive expressions capturing the trauma of forced migration. In 1928 Hageman exhibited this work in Antwerp under the title 'Jewish Family', while an inscription on the reverse of the canvas reading 'Descendants Israelites' specifically references Jewish exile. Another painting of the same title is in the Museum in Antwerp, and further works by Hageman on this theme can be found in the museums of Brussels, Namur and Ghent.

The painting originally belonged to the Speth family in Antwerp, owners of the Red Star Line which arranged for many Jewish emigrants to travel to America.

Racehorses, 1913

DAVID BOMBERG

(1890 Birmingham, England – 1957 London, England)

Black chalk and wash on paper
41.5 × 66.2 cm
Signed and dated (lower right)
'D. Bomberg 1913'

Acquired at Sotheby's in 2004 with assistance of the Art Fund, the HLF and the MLA/ V&A Purchase Grant Fund, The Julius Silman Charitable Trust, Pauline and Daniel Auerbach, Sir Michael and Lady Morven Heller and anonymous donors

SELECTED EXHIBITION HISTORY
The London Group, London; Chenil Gallery, London, Whitechapel Art Gallery, London, all 1914; *Homeless and Hidden*, Ben Uri, London, 2009; 'The Whitechapel Boys', the Archive Gallery, Whitechapel Art Gallery, London, 2009; *Apocalypse*, Osborne Samuel, London, 2010; *Recent Acquisitions*, Ben Uri, London, 2013

In May 1914, David Bomberg exhibited this extraordinary chalk-and-wash drawing among his five exhibits in the 'Jewish Section' of the Whitechapel Art Gallery's exhibition *Twentieth Century Art: A Review of Modern Movements*, which he co-curated with Jacob Epstein. Simultaneously, his friend John Rodker (a racing enthusiast) reproduced it as a frontispiece in *The Dial Monthly*, explaining that it was set in a paddock at a race meeting, that the two figures on the front right of the composition were bookies, those to their left spectators, and that the style was 'cubist'. He also felt it necessary to add, 'It is not intended to be comic'. Executed in 1913, when Bomberg was only 22 and approaching the height of his youthful powers, *Racehorses* is a key transitional work, which demonstrates his absorption and understanding of the contemporaneous European avant-garde, skilfully reworked into a drawing of startling power and originality.

Even before he became a student at the Slade School of Art, inspired by Roger Fry's seminal Post-Impressionist exhibition in 1910–11, Bomberg had begun to employ a shallow picture space and to simplify his forms. By 1913 he had started to produce specifically 'Cubist compositions' including one featuring the wooden 'donkey' on which students sat to sketch in the Slade life class – and which bears a close resemblance to Bomberg's stiffly-jointed racehorses. Bomberg's understanding of Cubism was enhanced by his visit to Paris in 1913 and he had been exposed to Futurism. Indeed, the 1910 Futurist Manifesto with its explanation that 'a running horse has not four legs, but twenty, and their movements are triangular' could have directly inspired his racehorses. The rigidity of Bomberg's figures also suggests a fascination with mechanisation that Bomberg shared with the nascent Vorticist movement. This was reflected in the manifesto that accompanied his first solo show at the Chenil gallery, London, in July 1914, where he explained that his object was 'the construction of Pure Form'. However Bomberg also combined modernist techniques with allusions to older processes: the close-grained texture of the picture is reminiscent of woodcuts, and monochrome colouring akin to that in photography of the day. He would have been familiar with Eadweard Muybridge's famous photographs of the 'animal in motion', and his racehorses also neatly illustrate what Muybridge himself noted in his 'Prelude to Analyses', that 'during very rapid motion by a good horse, the aggregate of the body preserves a nearly horizontal line.'

Like Bomberg's other innovative works, *Racehorses* was generally viewed with hostility and incomprehension when first exhibited. The *Jewish Chronicle* called his racehorses 'Opposed to all that is rational in art'. However, the work marks Bomberg's transition from aspiring student to recognised radical and, in the coming year, acted as a springboard for the experiments that have earned him a lasting place in British modernism. This is one of 14 works by Bomberg in the Ben Uri Collection.

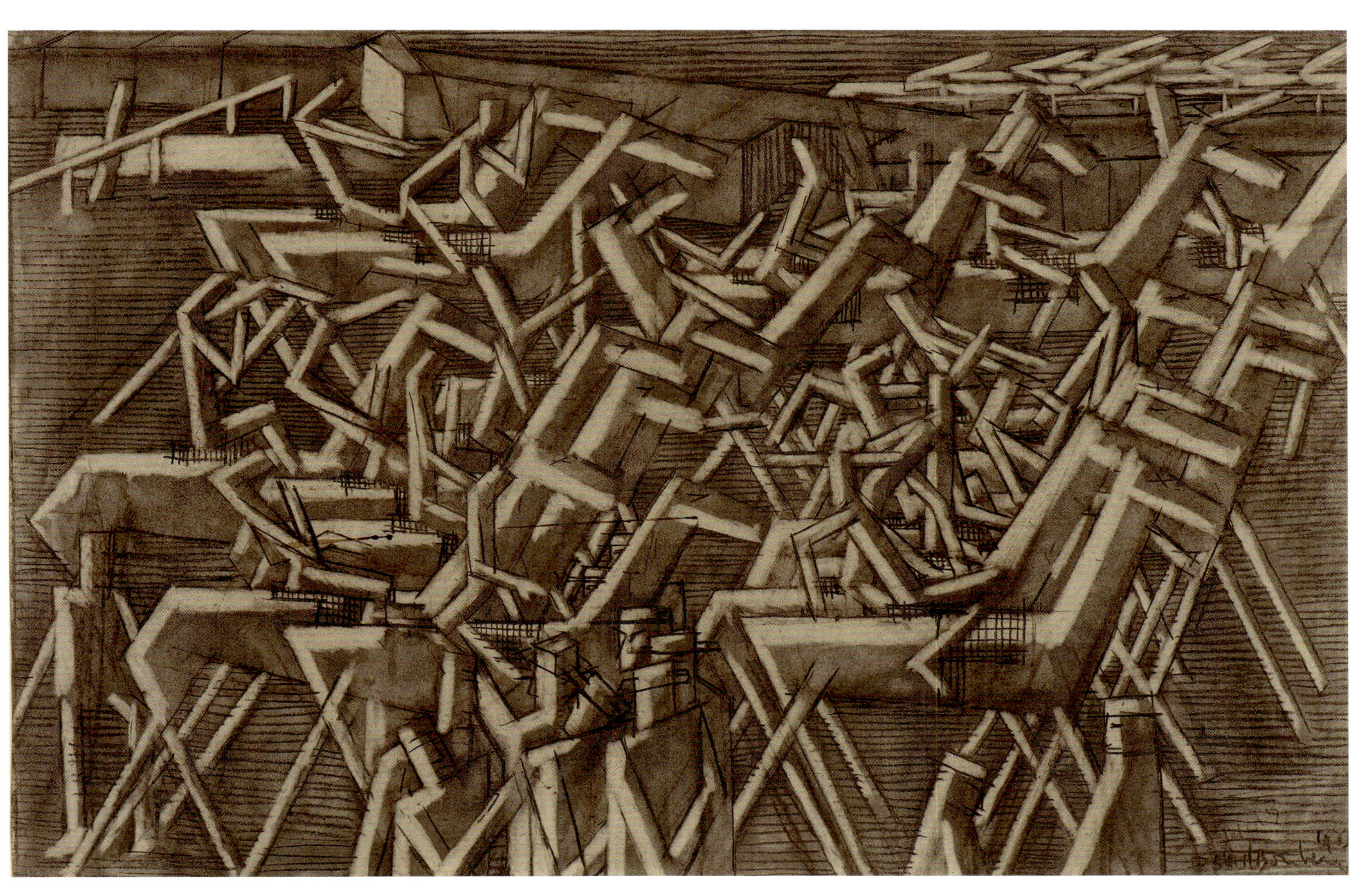

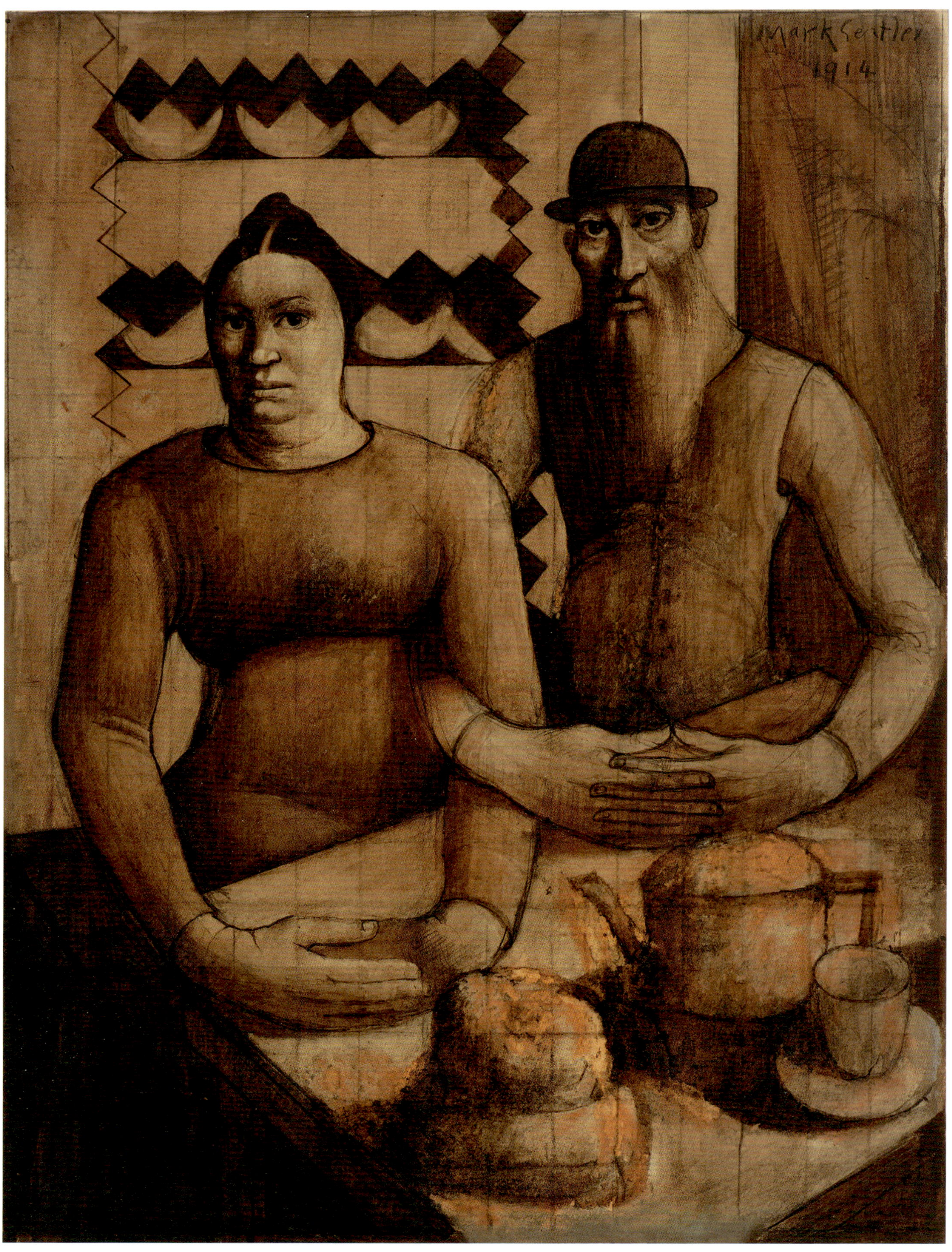

Mark Gertler
1914

10

Rabbi and Rabbitzin, 1914

MARK GERTLER

(1891 London, England – 1939 London, England)

Watercolour and pencil
on paper
48.8 × 37.6 cm
Signed and dated (upper right)
'Mark Gertler 1914'

Ben Uri Collection
Acquired in 2002 by private treaty
through Sotheby's with the assistance
of the Art Fund, HLF, V&A/MLA
Purchase Grant Fund, Pauline and
Daniel Auerbach, Sir Michael and
Lady Morven Heller, Agnes and
Edward Lee, Hannah and David
Lewis, David Stern, Laura and Barry
Townsley, Della and Fred Worms and
anonymous donors

SELECTED EXHIBITION HISTORY
New English Art Club, London 1915;
Exhibition of British Art, Vienna, 1927
(as *Mann & Frau*); *The Immigrant
Generation*, New York, Jewish
Museum, 1983 (45); *Mark Gertler:
Paintings and Drawings*, London,
Camden Arts Centre and tour, 1992;
Mark Gertler: A New Perspective, Ben
Uri, London, 2002; *The Whitechapel
Boys*, Whitechapel Art Gallery, 2009;
Muirhead Bone and his Contemporaries,
the Fleming Collection, London, 2009

Mark Gertler was born in a slum lodging house in Spitalfields in 1891, the fifth and youngest child of Austrian-Jewish immigrant parents 'trying their luck' in London. Repatriated to their native Przemysl in Galicia the following year, the family lived on the brink of starvation after the departure of Gertler's father, Louis, to search for work in America until they were reunited in London's East End in 1896, less than a mile from where Mark had been born. Following an unhappy apprenticeship at Clayton and Bell stained-glass makers, and a brief training at the Regent School Polytechnic, Gertler entered the Slade School of Fine Art (1908–11), aided by a loan from the Jewish Educational Aid Society – the first and youngest Jewish working-class student of his generation to do so. His spectacular progress – he twice won the Slade scholarship and left with another from the British Institution – encouraged further 'Whitechapel Boys' including David Bomberg (cats. 9, 16 and 30), Jacob Kramer (cat. 14) and Isaac Rosenberg (cat. 13) to follow in his footsteps.

Three years out of the Slade, Gertler's work became increasingly experimental. *Rabbi and Rabbitzin*, executed on the eve of the First World War, captures the tension between the traditional way of life depicted and the incipient warfare which threatens to overwhelm it. The concentrated, almost claustrophobic domestic interior with the scrubbed kitchen table and simple meal typify Jewish East End life of the period. The simplification of the figures and the still life objects seen from different viewpoints reflect Gertler's awareness of Cézanne, while the treatment of the dresser and crockery shows the influence of Cubism. The presence of a grid (common Slade practice for squaring up the picture for transfer to canvas) indicates that Gertler planned a painting of the composition. A companion drawing, *Rabbi and Rabbitzin with Fish*, is in the British Museum.

The focus of the work is the relationship between the man and wife – without the title we would not know they are Rabbi and Rabbitzin – yoked together and anchored to their spartan surroundings. Their huge eyes increase their emotive appeal, while their enlarged hands, as in Gertler's *Portrait of the Artist's Mother* (1913, Glynn Vivian, Swansea), indicate suffering and a life that has known hardship. The picture, as a contemporary reviewer noted, also evokes the wider history of the Jewish diaspora: 'A man and a woman with all the history of an oppressed people behind them […] the incisive and unflinching design […] controlled without loss to their humanity'.

This work is one of 11 Gertlers in the Ben Uri Collection.

II

Circular Design for Ben Uri Art Society, 1915

LAZAR BERSON

(1882 Skopichky, Russia (now Skapiškis, Lithuania) – 1954 Nice, France)

Pen and coloured inks on paper
44 cm diameter
Verso: inscribed 'D. Simkovitz'

Ben Uri Collection
Presentedby D. Simkovitz 1915

SELECTED EXHIBITION HISTORY
Homeless and Hidden, Ben Uri, London, 2008; *Apocalypse*, Osborne Samuel, London, 2010; *From Russia to Paris,* Ben Uri, London, 2012; *Soutine, Chagall and the School of Paris*, Jewish Museum, Manchester, 2013

Lazar Berson was born in 1882 in the village of Skopichky, Russia (now in Lithuania). Little is known about his early life, although he probably spoke Yiddish at home and received a traditional Jewish religious education. At the turn of the century, he studied painting in St Petersburg, where he was influenced by the Jewish cultural renaissance and the renewed interest in Russian and Jewish folk art and craft.

Berson took these ideas to Paris, where he continued his studies, probably as a student under Professor Cormon at the École des Beaux-Arts. Later, Berson described studying 'together with a prayer quorum of Jewish children', referring to the large number of mostly eastern-European Jewish émigré artists then working in Paris. Between 1911 and 1912 he exhibited at the Salon d'Automne alongside Marc Chagall (cat. 40), Léon Bakst (fig. 16), Moise Kisling and Jules Pascin, and lived at *La Ruche* (the beehive), at the same address as the sculptor Jacques Lipchitz (fig. 24). In contrast to other École de Paris artists who embraced modernist styles, Berson maintained the decorative approach to traditional folk art and sought to develop a specifically Jewish type of art.

Following the outbreak of the First World War, Berson moved to London, where he set up a portrait studio and wrote articles for Jewish and Yiddish newspapers, espousing his uncompromising Jewish nationalist, Zionist and fierce anti-assimilationist views. In 1915, he realised his long-held ambition of forming a society for Jewish art when he founded 'The Jewish-National Decorative Art Association (London) "Ben Ouri"', in Whitechapel. In 'the Ben Uri studio' in West London he brought together a number of East End artisans, who together with the jeweller Moshe Oved (cat. 41) worked on a series of decorative 'Jewish' designs on wooden plates and bowls. In addition, Berson produced the *Ben ouri albom,* 'one of the worlds' first Yiddish art albums', printed in 1916 by the Ukrainian-born Hebraist Israel Narodiczky (1874–1942), as a fundraiser. By 1916, the Society had over 100 members and had organised many events and classes, but in September of that year, Berson left without warning for America, only resurfacing late in life in Nice, where he continued to work as a painter until his death in 1954.

This beautiful, intricate design executed in pen and coloured inks incorporates flowers, birds and animals with signs of the zodiac and Yiddish lettering marked Ben Uri's progress one year on. It may even have been a collaboration with Dovod Simkovitz, who presented it to the Ben Uri Collection in the year of its creation. It reveals the precision and pattern-making that characterised Berson's style, which was probably influenced by the *Machmadim* (Precious Ones), a textless Jewish art journal produced in Paris in 1912 by Isaac Lichtenstein and others. The circular design is one of a number of fine designs produced specifically to mark the birth of the Ben Uri and one of six works by Berson in the Ben Uri Collection.

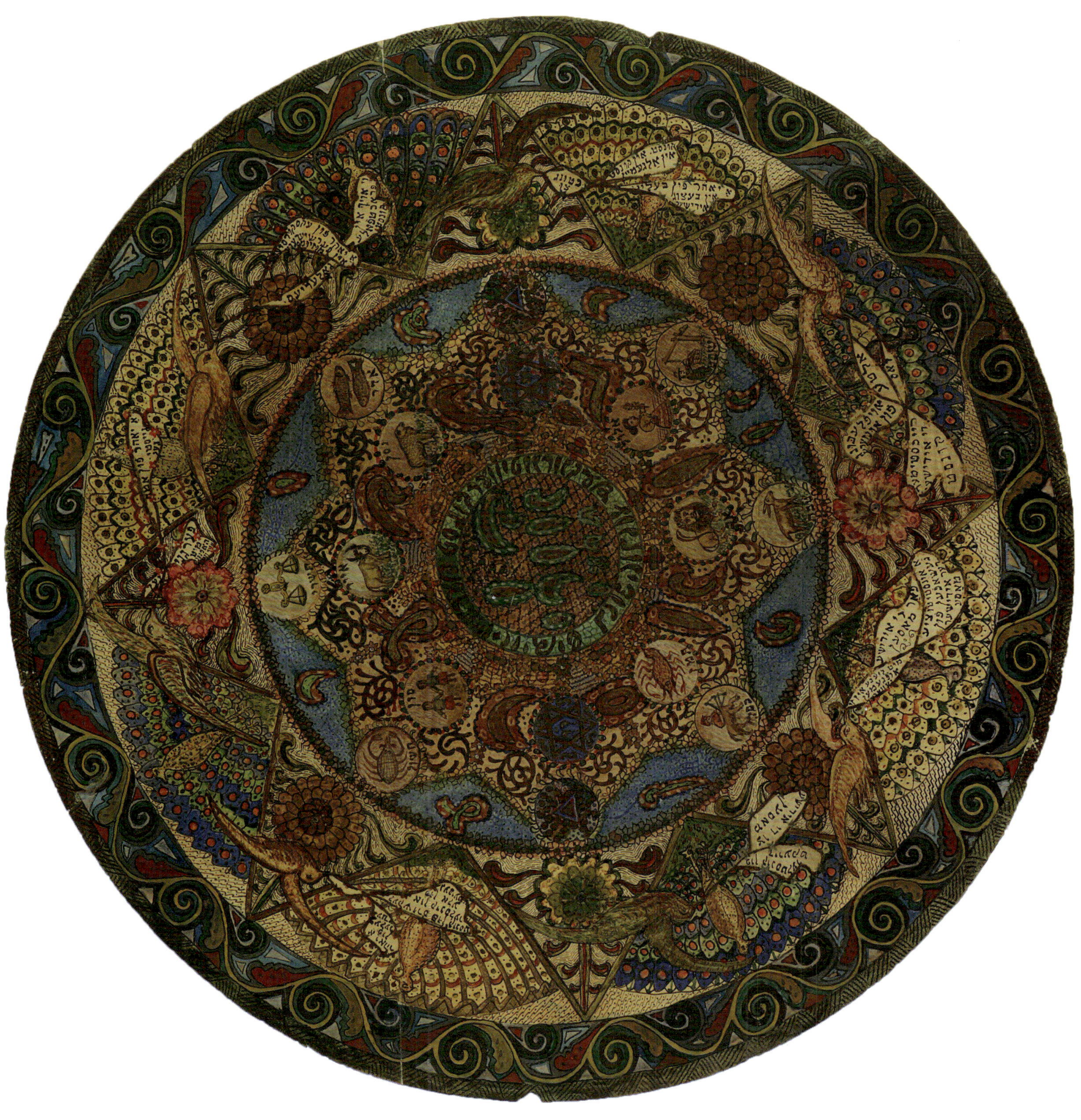

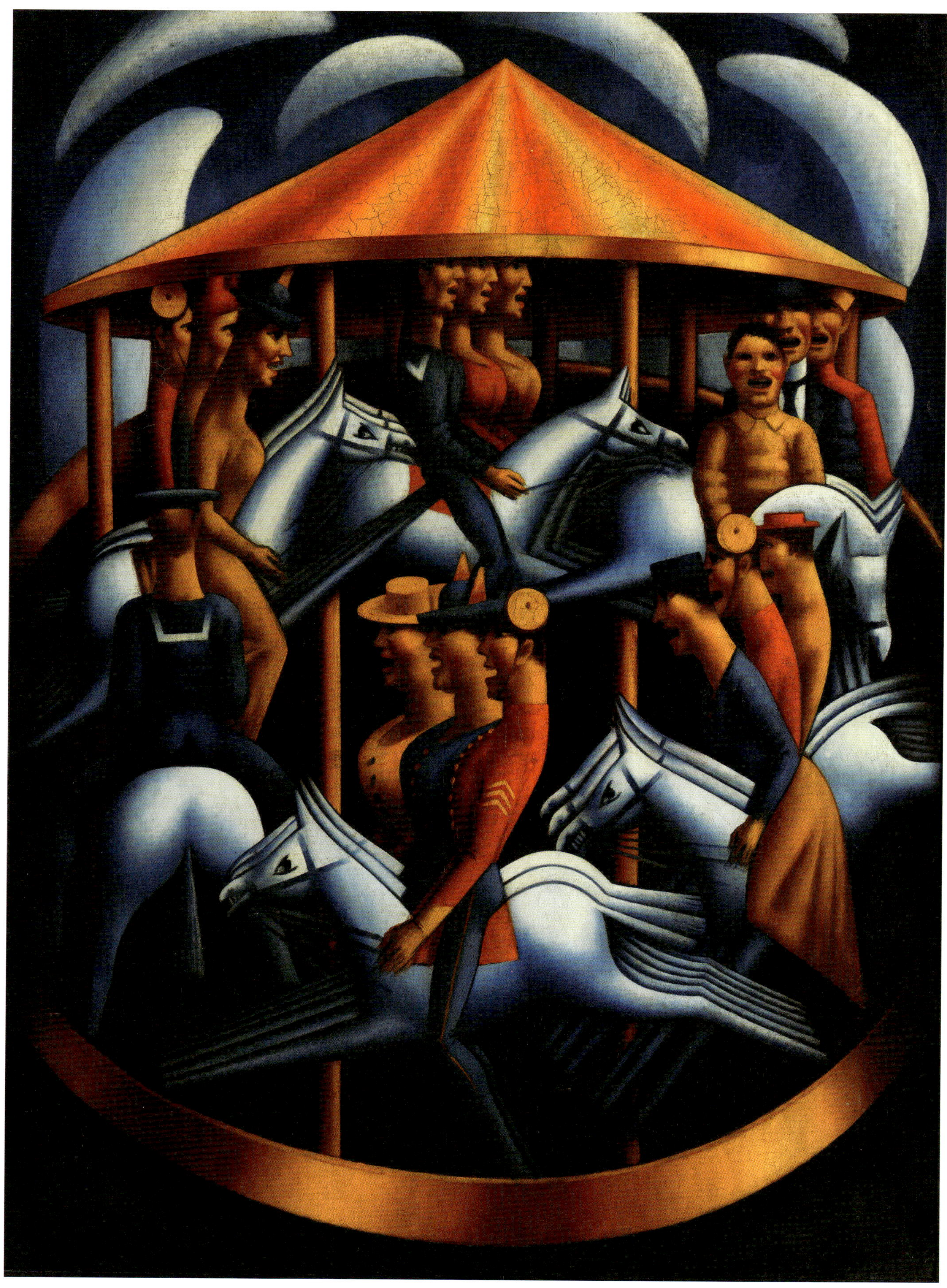

12

Merry-Go-Round, 1916

MARK GERTLER

(1891 London, England – 1939 London, England)

Oil on canvas
189.2 × 142.2 cm
Insribed (verso)
'Merry-Go-Round | 1916 |
Mark Gertler'

Tate
(formerly Ben Uri Collection;
sold to Tate 1984)

SELECTED EXHIBITION HISTORY
The London Group, Heal's, London,
1917; *The London Group Retrospective*,
London, 1928; *Mark Gertler*, Ben Uri,
London 1944; *Mark Gertler*,
Whitechapel Art Gallery, 1949; *L'Art
en Europe autour de 1918*, Council of
Europe, Strasbourg, 1968; *Mark
Gertler, the Early and Late Years*, Ben
Uri, London 1982; *British Art in the
20th Century, The Modern Movement*,
Royal Academy, London, 1987

FOOTNOTES
1   Noel Carrington ed., *Mark
Gertler: Selected Letters* (London:
Rupert Hart-Davies, 1965), p. 11.

2   D. H. Lawrence to Mark Gertler,
9 October 1916, cited ibid, pp. 129-130.

3   Lytton Strachey to Lady Ottoline
Morrell, 3 July 1916, cited Michael
Holroyd, *Lytton Strachey* (London:
Chatto and Windus, 1994), p. 369.

4   St John Hutchinson to Mark
Gertler, [c. November 1916], cited
Mark Gertler: Selected Letters,
pp. 128-129.

Completed in 1916 in the midst of the First World War, Gertler's *Merry-Go-Round* marks the peak of his early modernist period and captures his pacifist vision of the nightmare of conflict: the carousel is frozen in motion, the mouths of its riders (including uniformed soldiers, sailors and their sweethearts) opened in a long, unending scream, as they whirl forever, unable to stop or get off. The riders' thrusting chests echo those of their horses joined nose-to-tail, their outstretched hind legs resembling raised rifles as they rear and plunge with teeth bared. The carousel's vertiginous tilt tips it dangerously towards us, while bullet-shaped clouds rain down around it. Yet a series of strong verticals underpins the composition's tautly controlled structure: as Quentin Bell has observed, 'everything is held, as though within some whirling, metallic labyrinth by a system of ellipses and verticals',[1] underpinned by the strong palette of blue and black, offset by strident orange, mustard-yellow and red. D. H. Lawrence, in a long, perceptive letter, called the painting 'horrible and terrifying', concluding that in 'this contemplation of blaze, and violent mechanical rotation and complex involution, and ghastly, utterly mindless human intensity of sensational extremity', Gertler had 'made a real and ultimate revelation'.[2]

When unveiled at The London Group's sixth show in April 1917, *Merry-Go-Round* was greeted as 'sheer sensationalism', yet astonishingly, critics failed to detect its pacifist message. Lytton Strachey famously wrote that he 'admired it of course, but as for *liking* it, one might as well think of liking a machine-gun',[3] while Gertler's friend, the lawyer St John Hutchinson, predicted it would 'raise a tremendous outcry – the old, the wise, the professional critic will go mad with righteous indignation', causing them to 'write all sorts of rubbish about German art and German artists'.[4] Following the introduction of conscription in February 1916, Gertler presented himself at his local recruiting office, only to be refused on account of his Austrian parentage; when finally called up in March 1918, he was rejected as 'medically unfit'. Prevented by depression from fulfilling an Official War Commission, *Merry-Go-Round* remains Gertler's only painting in this genre. Unsold during the artist's lifetime, it was given by his family after his death to the Leicester Galleries, who presented it to Ben Uri in 1945. It remained a highlight of the collection until 1984 when it was sold to Tate to safeguard the gallery's future. Ben Uri has exhibited Gertler's work on numerous occasions including solo shows in 1944, 1982 and 2002.

13
Self-portrait in Steel Helmet, 1916

ISAAC ROSENBERG

(1890 Bristol, England – 1918 Fampoux, France)

Black chalk, gouache
and wash on paper
22.4 × 19.6 cm

Ben Uri Collection
Acquired in 2009 with the assistance
of the Art Fund, the MLA/V&A
Purchase Grant Fund and anonymous
donors

SELECTED EXHIBITION HISTORY
Whitechapel at War, Ben Uri, London;
Stanley & Audrey Burton Gallery,
University of Leeds, 2008; *Apocalypse*,
Osborne Samuel, London, 2010;
Recent Acquisitions, Ben Uri, London,
2013; *Screaming Steel*, Hatton Gallery,
Newcastle, 2014

Isaac Rosenberg was born in Bristol in 1890 and raised in great poverty in Whitechapel. Despite an early talent for drawing and writing, by the age of fourteen he was unhappily apprenticed to a firm of Fleet Street engravers. He took evening art classes at Birkbeck College, where he won many prizes, before following Mark Gertler (cats. 10 and 12) and David Bomberg (cats. 9 and 16) to the Slade School of Art (1911 – 14). Afterwards Rosenberg visited his sister in South Africa where he painted, wrote and lectured about art, before returning to England in 1915. After enlisting in the army in October 1915, he was sent to the Front in 1916.

Rosenberg often unable to afford models and his oeuvre includes many self-portraits. The earliest are slight and delicate in the melancholic Romantic tradition of Benjamin Robert Haydon's portrait sketches of the young Keats. Between 1912 and 1915, however, under the influence of the Slade, Rosenberg began to shed this persona in a series of leaner, bolder self-portraits which display a new bravura confidence and mark his transition to modernism. Unsentimental, yet poignant, *Self-Portrait in a Steel Helmet* is Rosenberg's final self-portrait and completes the series; it is also his final finished work as a painter. Drawn in the trenches in gouache and chalk on crumpled, poor quality brown paper, possibly salvaged from a parcel sent from home, its fragile state documents this important part of its history. The portrait appears to relate closely to a sketch made in a letter, entitled *Self-Portrait Sketch in Tin Helmet* (*c.*1916,

Imperial War Museum) of which Rosenberg joked to his family that it was 'The New Fashion boiler hat – the trench hat'.

This is one of two portraits by Rosenberg in the Ben Uri collection. The second, a portrait of former sweatshop worker and aspiring actress Sonia Cohen (fig. 8), with whom Rosenberg was in love, was mostly painted during several sittings in May 1915. He transformed Sonia, then pregnant with her first child by his friend and fellow Whitechapel writer John Rodker into a Whitechapel Madonna. According to their daughter Joan, who bequeathed this portrait, together with one of her father by David Bomberg (cat. 30) to the collection, Rosenberg also worked on Sonia's portrait during his final leave from the Front in 1917. He was killed while on patrol on 1st April 1918 at the age of 27. Despite publishing only two short collections of poetry during his lifetime, Rosenberg is now regarded as one of the finest War Poets of his generation. The exhibition, *Whitechapel at War: Isaac Rosenberg and his Contemporaries* (Ben Uri, 2008), which included both Rosenberg portraits, was the first to examine his art in the context of his Whitechapel peers.

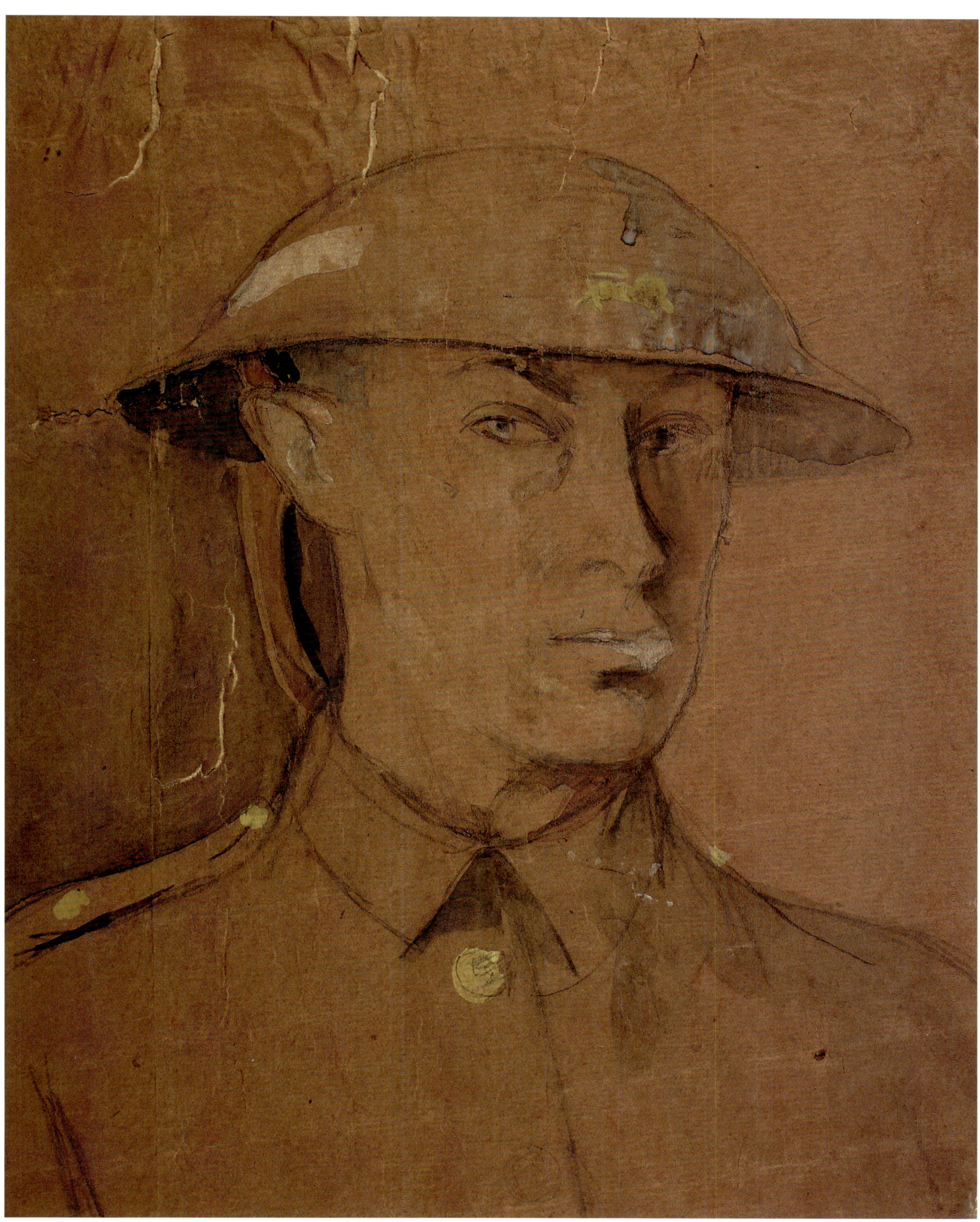

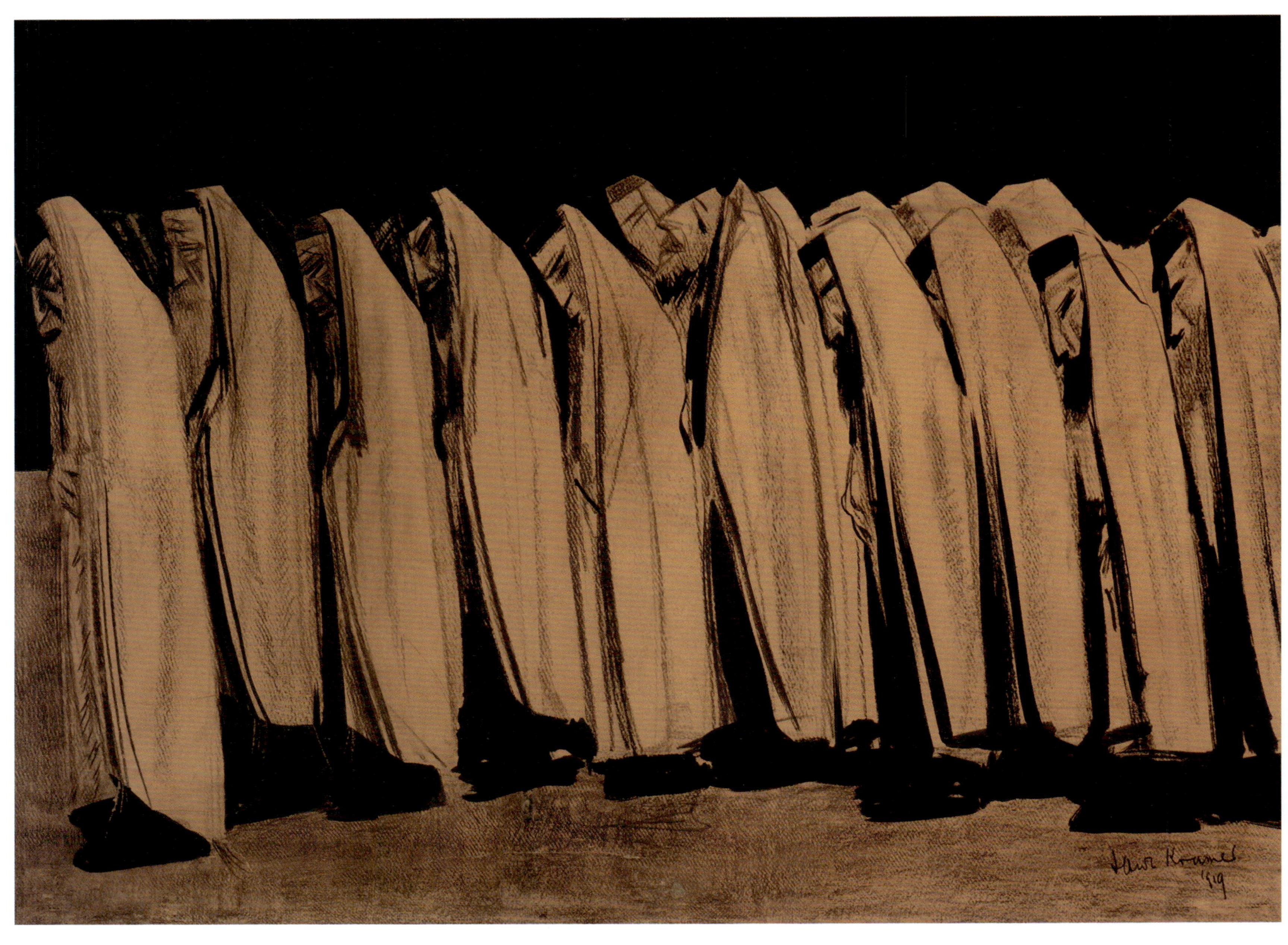

The Day of Atonement, 1919

JACOB KRAMER

(1892 Klincy, Russia – 1962 Leeds, England)

Pencil, brush and ink on paper
63.5 × 93 cm
Signed and dated (lower right)
'Jacob Kramer 1919
'

Ben Uri Collection

SELECTED EXHIBITION HISTORY
Festival of Britain Anglo-Jewish Exhibition 1851-1951, Ben Uri, London, 1951; *Jacob Kramer Reassessed*, Ben Uri, London, 1984; *The Tortoise and The Hare*, Ben Uri, London, 2003; Leeds University Gallery, 2003; *Apocalypse*, Osborne Samuel, London, 2010

The Day of Atonement is a study for a larger painting regarded as one of the most important in the Anglo-Jewish canon, gifted to Leeds Art Gallery by the local Jewish community in 1920 to mark Kramer's departure for London. These semi-abstract works, drawing on contemporary influences, including Cubism, Futurism, Vorticism and David Bomberg's own visual experimentation during the 1910s, audaciously fuse the subject of Jewish devotion during the most solemn day in the religious calendar with a new modernist vocabulary.

For Kramer, a Russian-born, Yiddish-speaking émigré, who attended art school in Leeds, the donation was further affirmation of his position within the modernist vanguard. He had first left Leeds in 1913, with support from his patron, Michael Sadler, modernist collector and Vice Chancellor of the University, and limited funding from the Jewish Educational Aid Society, to attend the Slade for one academic year. Despite his artistic talent and imposing physical presence, the year was marked by anxieties and financial hardship. Nevertheless, it provided entry to London's bohemian circles, alongside fellow 'Whitechapel Boys' Bomberg and Jacob Epstein, who included Kramer's work in the 'Jewish Section' in the 1914 Whitechapel Gallery exhibition *Twentieth Century Art: A Review of Modern Movements.*

After leaving the Slade, Kramer strove to achieve a spiritual quality in his art without jettisoning his modernist credentials, perhaps driven by a postwar mood of disillusionment. He had failed as a War Artist, spending a short time as a regimental librarian, a post facilitated by Herbert Read – hardly an experience on which to base a brave new art. In 1918 a design for a woodcut, entitled *The Day of Atonement,* appeared in the sole issue of the literary review *New Paths,* co-edited by Michael Sadleir, son of his patron. Here the procession was simplified to six angular figures; those at the front tilting their mask-like features upwards in poses that anticipate the painting. The text described Kramer as: 'far more essentially Hebraic in his outlook than Gertler, whose Jewish extraction seems over emphasised. Kramer is a grim bitter realist […] Kramer obtains the effect of Primitivism through a ruthless elimination of all that is unessential'.

Despite Ben Uri's early support (*Study in Black and Lemon* was donated by Moshe Oved in 1926 and Kramer exhibited regularly in the *Annual Exhibition of Works by Jewish Artists* from 1935–50), his subsequent career disappointed. Following a crisis of confidence, he returned north, eventually becoming known for his characteristic portraits of Leeds locals and notable visitors. A retrospective was held at Leeds Art Gallery in 1960. Twelve works by Kramer are held in the Ben Uri Collection.

Portrait of Joseph Leftwich, *c.*1919–20

CLARE WINSTEN

(née Clara Birnberg, 1892 Romania – 1984 England)

Oil on canvas
40.6 × 25.4 cm

Clare Winsten was born Clara Birnberg in 1892 in Romania, where her parents spent a decade after fleeing pogroms in their native Tarnopil, Galicia (now in Western Ukraine), before emigrating to England, *c.*1902, via Germany. They settled in London's East End in the heart of the Jewish community. Birnberg gained a scholarship to the Female School of Art, but was transferred to the Slade School of Art (1910–12) 'on the strength of her promise', arriving to find her fellow students 'seething' under the influence of Post-Impressionism, following Roger Fry's two seminal shows in 1910 and 1912. Joining two years after Mark Gertler (cats. 10 and 12), she predated the arrival of David Bomberg (cats 9, 16 and 30) and Isaac Rosenberg (cat. 13), both of whom painted her. She was also the lone woman among the 14 artists in Bomberg and Epstein's 'Jewish Section' at the Whitechapel Art Gallery's *Twentieth Century Art: A Review of Modern Movements* in May 1914. She shared with the nascent Vorticists a certain restlessness and dynamism in her active, struggling forms and bold palette, although she afterwards returned mainly to figurative work, particularly portraiture, later painting a number of well-known sitters including George Bernard Shaw.

Birnberg was a member of the Women's Freedom League, a vegetarian and a confirmed Pacifist, like her future husband Stephen Winsten, whom she married during the First World War. They were members of the No-conscription campaign and Stephen was imprisoned as a conscientious objector. Postwar they anglicized their names to Stephen and

Clare Winsten and embraced Quaker humanism. Along with other Whitechapel Boys, they also both contributed to *Voices: In Poetry and Prose*, a short-lived literary periodical (1919 –20) with pacifist leanings edited by journalist Tom Moult.

Joseph Lefkowich (Leftwich, 1892–1984) was born in Zutphen, Holland, of Polish-Jewish parents in 1892, and raised in Germany until the age of seven when the family emigrated to Whitechapel. He worked as a furrier, afterwards writing for the Yiddish daily, *Di Tsayt*, and became a founding member of the Whitechapel writers group, which included Isaac Rosenberg, Simy Weinstein and John Rodker. His 1911 diary (Tower Hamlets Local History Library) revisited in a memoir of the Whitechapel Boys for Ben Uri's 50th anniversary publication in 1965, is the foremost document on the history of the Whitechapel Boys.

Winsten executed a number of portraits of her fellow Whitechapel peers including Rosenberg, Leftwich, Winsten and Clara Klinghoffer (cat. 46) – a 'Whitechapel Girl' from the next generation, and also worked briefly alongside Amy Drucker (cat. 25) during her time at the Central School. This is one of five works by Clare Winsten in the Ben Uri Collection.

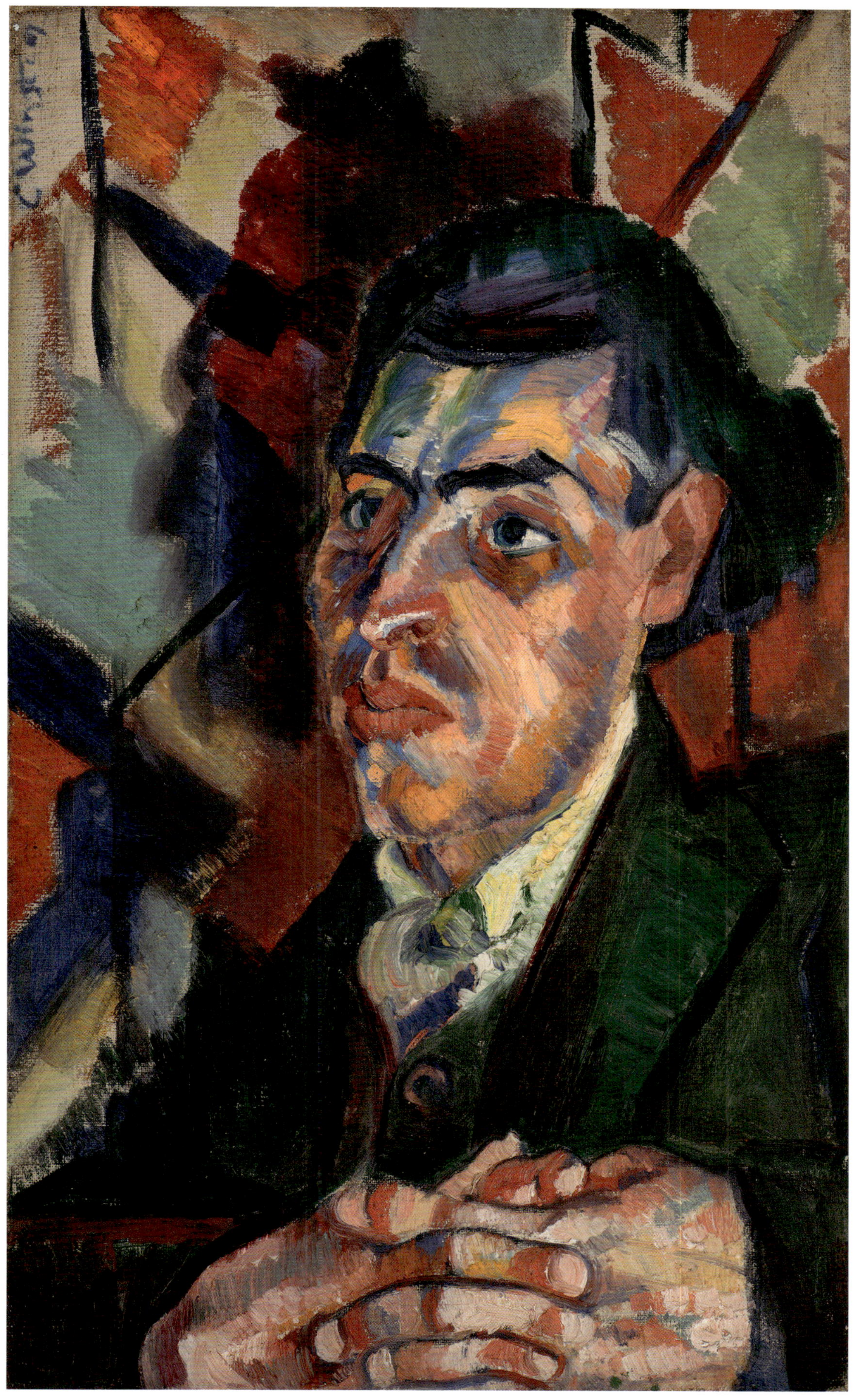

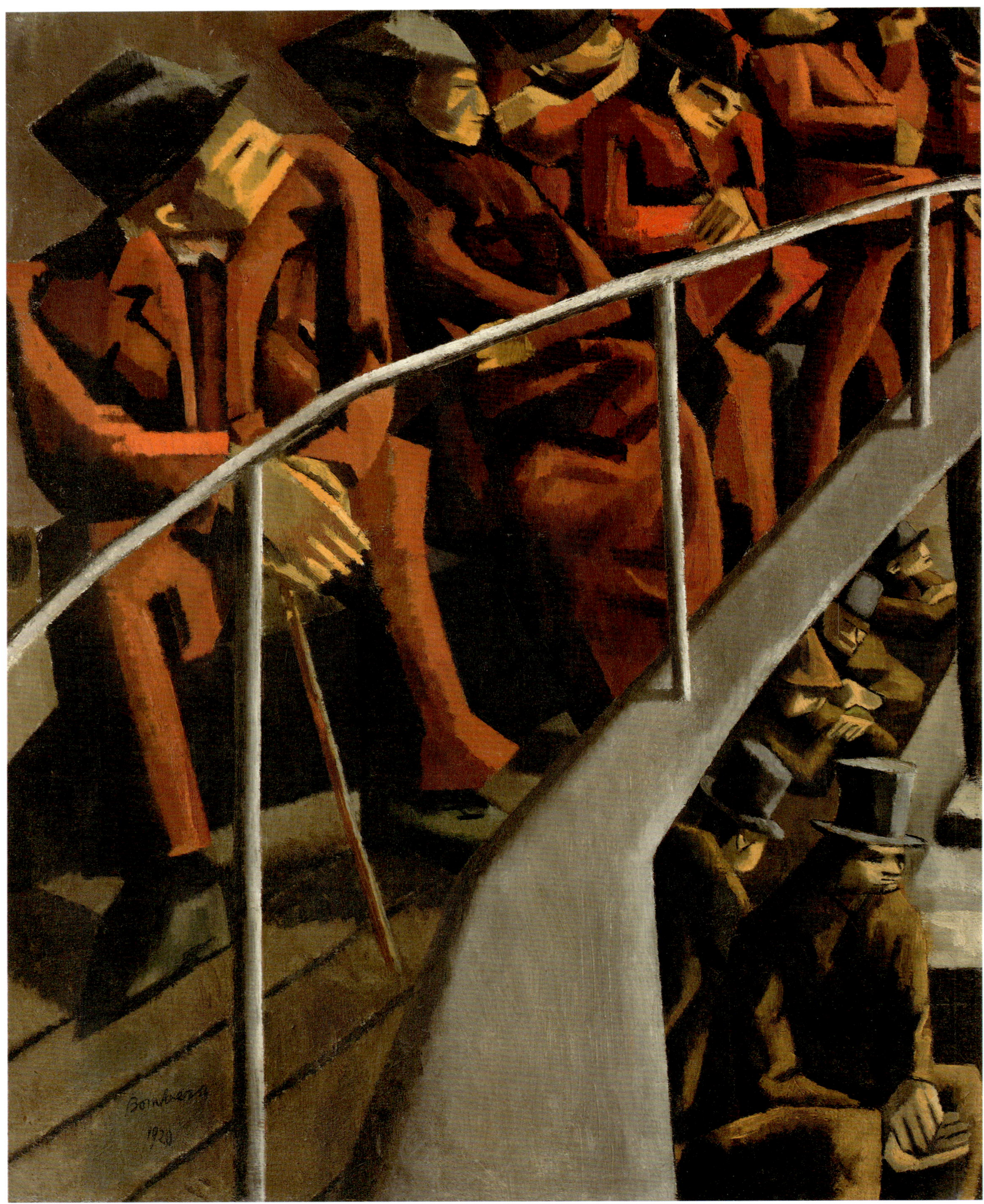

Bomberg
1920

16

Ghetto Theatre, 1920

DAVID BOMBERG

(1890 Birmingham, England – 1957 London, England)

Oil on canvas
74.4 × 62 cm
Signed and dated (lower left)
'Bomberg 1920'

Ben Uri Collection
Purchased direct from the artist, 1920

SELECTED EXHIBITION HISTORY
Opening Exhibition, Ben Uri, London,
1925; *Catalogue and Survey of Activities*,
Ben Uri, London, 1930; *Faces in the
Crowd - Picturing Modern Life from
Manet to Today*, Whitechapel Art
Gallery, London, 2004; *Uproar*, Ben
Uri, London, 2013

By the time he left the Slade in 1913, Bomberg had established a reputation as a leading member of the avant-garde. His work was admired by the Vorticist leader Percy Wyndham Lewis and he was among the non-members invited in 1915 to show work in the first Vorticist exhibition (although he was always careful to retain his independence). The previous year, in 1914, Bomberg had exhibited five works at The London Group (of which he was a founder member) and also held his first solo show at the Chenil Gallery, Chelsea. However his enlistment in the Royal Engineers (he later transferred to the 18th King's Royal Rifles) in November 1915 brought this audacious progress temporarily to a halt. In March 1916 he married his first wife, Alice Mayes, and shortly afterwards was sent to the Front. His harrowing experiences including the death of his brother eventually resulted in him shooting himself in the foot. Escaping court martial and temporarily invalided out, he was soon returned to active service. In 1918 Bomberg was commissioned by the Canadian War Memorials Fund to produce a painting of *Sappers at Work*. His first, severely abstracted version was woundingly rejected and although the second, more naturalistic version was accepted, the experience left Bomberg severely demoralized.

In *Ghetto Theatre*, set in Whitechapel's lively Pavilion Theatre, where the classics were performed in Yiddish, Bomberg returned to the subject matter and setting of a number of his earlier sketches. Possibly, he hoped to recapture something of his earlier exuberance. In contrast to his animated prewar theatre-goers however, these drably-dressed spectators with their mask-like faces and closed body language are indicative of his dismal, postwar vision. The hunched male figure (in the upper foreground) leaning wearily on a stick embodies his own personal disenchantment and the compressed space, cleaved by a bold and imposing balcony rail, echoes the claustrophobic tunnels of his wartime sappers. Only the bold sweep of red adds richness to an otherwise sombre palette. Painted on the eve of his departure from the East End, it reveals that for Bomberg, it was no longer a place of excitement and vitality. Yet elsewhere in a series of related Ghetto Theatre sketches, the artist's looser handling once again liberates his audience from their constraints.

In 1923, to escape poverty and neglect in England, Bomberg accepted a post with the Palestine Foundation Fund, who paid for his voyage in return for a number of works featuring Zionist reconstruction work. He remained in Palestine until 1927, travelling widely in the 1930s with the painter Lilian Holt, who became his second wife. *Ghetto Theatre* was one of Ben Uri's earliest purchases, acquired immediately after its showing at The London Group exhibition in 1920. Bomberg remained deeply involved with Ben Uri from this time onwards, including lecturing on 'Palestine Through the Eyes of an Artist' after his return to England in 1928. Among Bomberg's 14 works in the Ben Uri Collection are two pencil studies and one oil and pencil study for *Ghetto Theatre*, the latter gifted by his widow, Lilian, in 1959.

17

Shabbat Blessing, 1920

YITZHAK FRENKEL-FRENEL

(1899 Odessa, Russia (now in Ukraine) – 1981 Tel Aviv, Israel)

Watercolour, pen, ink and
brush on paper
17.6 × 23.5 cm
Signed and dated (lower right)
'Y. Frenkel Paris 20'

Ben Uri Collection

SELECTED EXHIBITION HISTORY
From Russia to Paris, Ben Uri, London,
2012; *Chagall, Soutine and the School of
Paris*, Jewish Museum Manchester,
2013

Yitshak Frenkel-Frenel was born in Odessa, Russia (now in Ukraine) in 1899, the great-grandson of Rabbi Levi Itzack of Berdichev. In 1917, he studied under the pioneering painter and theatrical designer Alexandra Exter (1882 – 1949) at the Art Academy of Odessa. Exter had spent the years 1908–14 in Paris, forging a link with the Western avant-garde and her work in this period was influenced by Cubism and Futurism. In 1919 Frenkel-Frenel emigrated to Mandate Palestine as part of the first wave of settlers of the Third Aliyah, setting up an artists' cooperative in Jaffa in 1920 and a studio in Herzliya. Later that year he travelled to Paris, where he enrolled at the École des Beaux-Arts and the Académie de la Grande Chaumière. During this productive period, he also studied sculpture at Antoine Bourdelle's studio, and painting under Henri Matisse, exhibited his work at the Salon des Indépendants and regularly frequented the café Le Dome in Montparnasse.

Frenkel-Frenel returned to Palestine in 1925 and opened the Masad and Eged studios of art, establishing and directing the painting studio of the Histradut School in Tel Aviv, where his students included Shimshon Holzman (represented in the Ben Uri Collection). He was also a mentor to Bezalel Academy of Art and Design, where Moshe Castel (represented in the Ben Uri Collection) was among the pupils. Frenkel-Frenel settled in Safed in 1934, co-founding the Artists' Colony in 1949. In 1973, a museum of his work was opened at his home and in 1979 he had a solo exhibition at the Musée de l'Orangerie, Paris. He died in Tel Aviv in 1981 and was buried in Safed.

In *Shabbat Blessing* and two related studies in the Ben Uri Collection, both entitled *Man with Torah*, all executed in Paris, Frenkel-Frenel reinterprets traditional Jewish subject matter with warmth and even humour, adopting a short-lived Cubist manner.

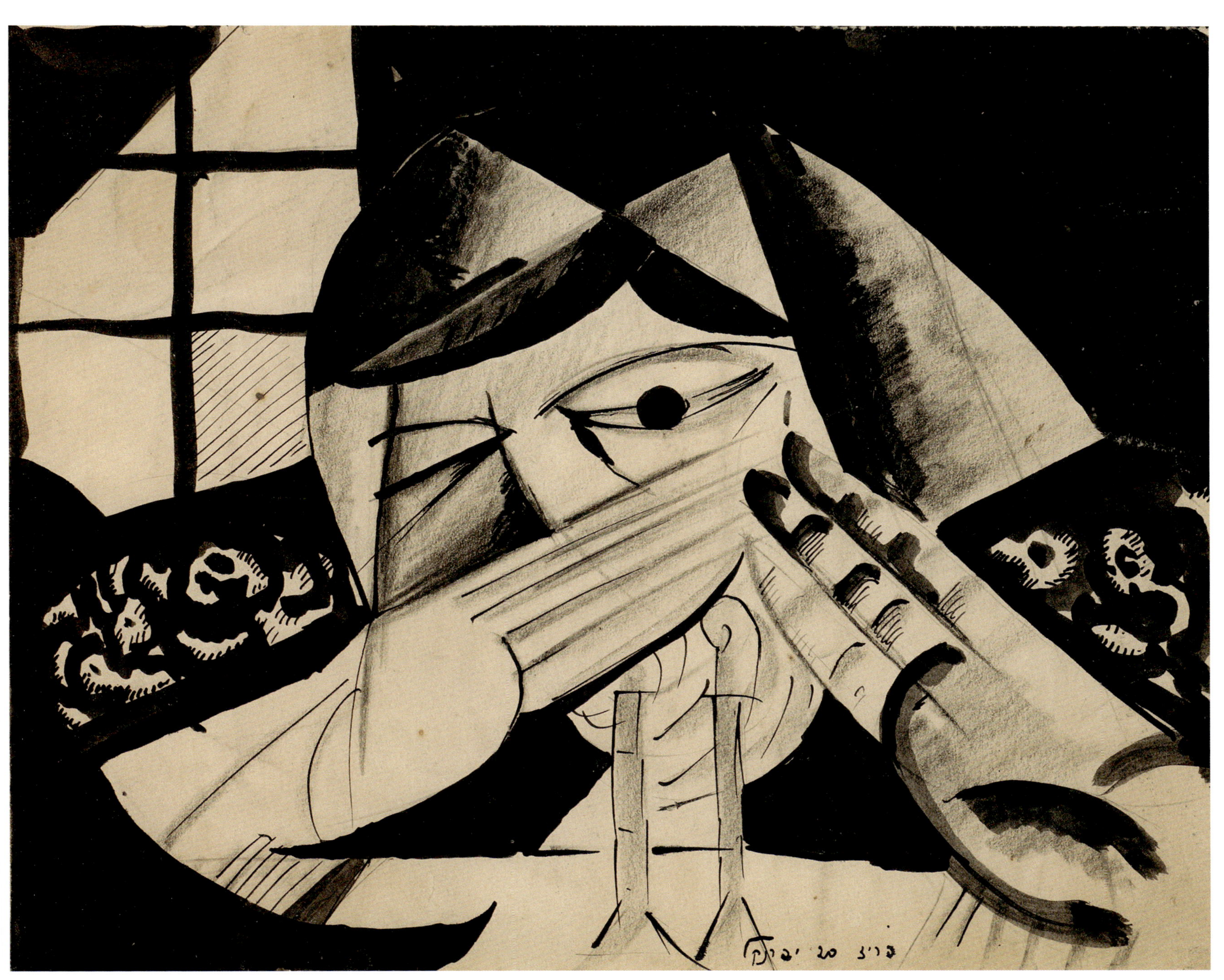

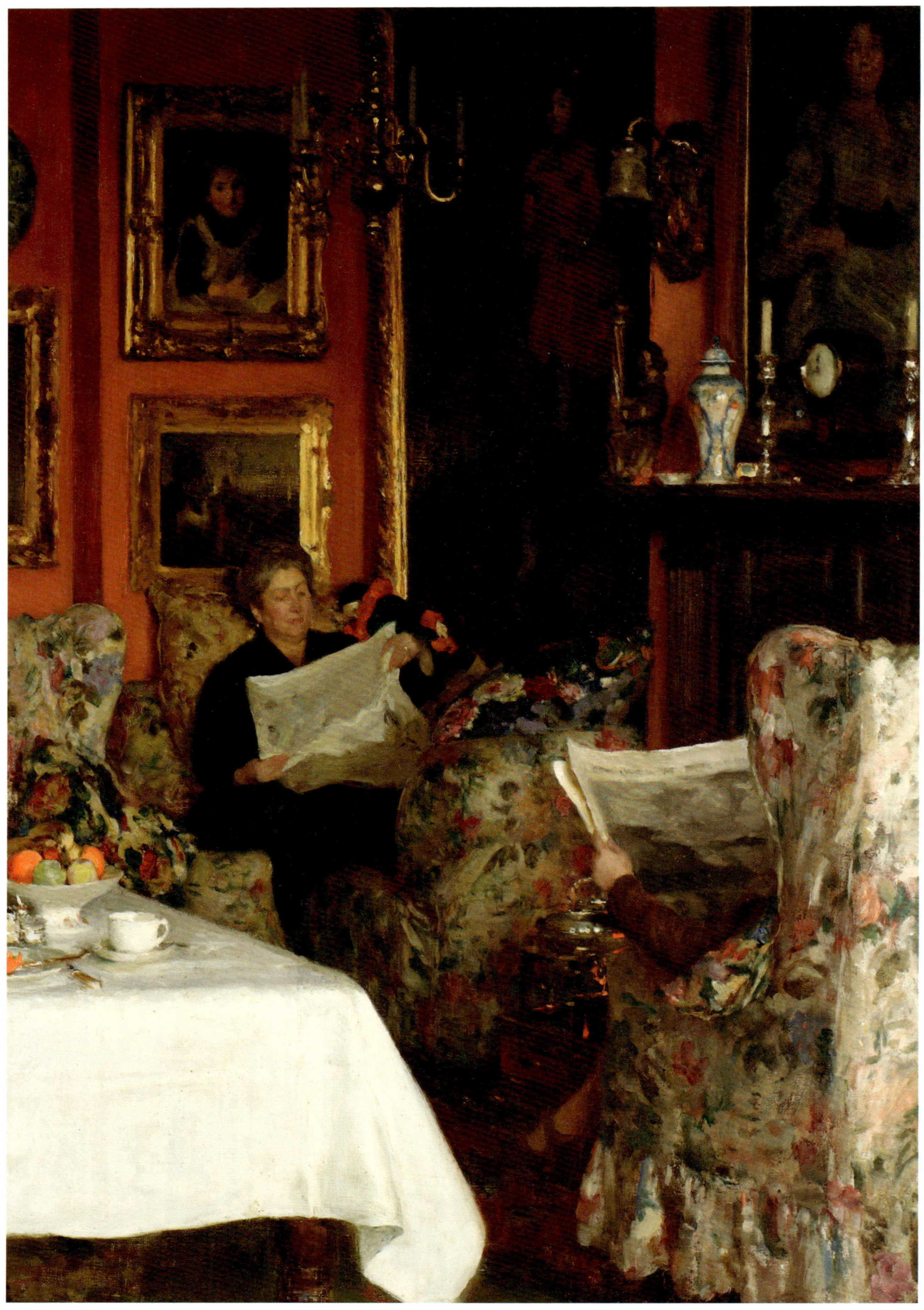

The Breakfast Table, 1921

SOLOMON J SOLOMON, RA

(1880 London, England – 1927 Birchington, England)

Oil on Canvas
69 × 50.5cm

Ben Uri Collection
Presented by Mrs Ronald Rubenstein
(the artist's daughter) 2002

SELECTED EXHIBITION HISTORY
Solomon J Solomon RA, Ben Uri,
London, 1990; *Apocalypse*, Osborne
Samuel, London, 2010

A fine painter in the Academic style, Solomon was a founder member of the Society of Portrait Painters and the first President of the Maccabeans, later the Jewish Educational Aid Society, which organised loans to help the majority of the Whitechapel Boys to attend the Slade School of Art. In 1906 Solomon became only the second Jewish Royal Academician and was President of the Ben Uri from 1924–26. Solomon was well-known for his historical and biblical works and for his society portraiture. His annual contributions to the Royal Academy Exhibition were hung in what came to be known as 'Solomon's corner.' Although a practising Jew, he rarely painted works with overtly Jewish themes, though he did make portraits of some of the leading Jewish figures of the day.

During the First World War Solomon pioneered camouflage work for tanks and aeroplanes, sometimes in the thick of the fighting, despite being 54 at the outbreak of hostilities. In addition, he also sculpted dummy heads to attract fire in order to locate snipers and developed hollow, metal and bark-covered Observational Post Trees, where lookouts could hide along the front line. After the war, he continued painting portraits until his death in 1927.

Solomon's richly-decorated interior of the family bungalow at Birchington, Kent (where his brother-in-law Delissa Joseph, had built him a second studio) depicts his wife Ella and youngest daughter Iris (later the Hon Mrs Ewen Montagu) in the comfortable intimacy of the breakfast room Iris is denoted only by her hand holding the newspaper and her dangling leg with its fashionable shoe. On the wall behind a selection of paintings by Solomon includes one of his older daughter, Mary, on her pony (the landscape is by another painter). Solomon's tasteful and opulent breakfast room reveals the extent of his identification with English life; the only reference to his Jewish origins is the two candlesticks upon the mantelpiece.

The Ben Uri Collection features six works by Solomon, including the magnificent portrait of Mary, *The Field: The Artist's Daughter on a Pony*, which was presented by his widow in 1937.

Bust of Jacob Kramer, 1921

SIR JACOB EPSTEIN

(1880 New York, USA – 1959 London, England)

Bronze
64 × 49 × 25 cm

Ben Uri Collection
Acquired at Bonhams in 2003 with the
assistance of the Art Fund, V&A
Purchase Grant Fund, Pauline and
Daniel Auerbach, Sir Michael and
Lady Morven Heller and anonymous
donors

SELECTED EXHIBITION HISTORY
Embracing the Exotic, Ben Uri,
London, 2006; *Homeless and Hidden,*
Ben Uri, London, 2008; *Apocalypse,*
Osborne Samuel, London, 2010

Jacob Epstein was born in 1880 to relatively prosperous Polish-Jewish émigré parents, in Manhattan's Lower East Side. He worked at a New York Bronze foundry and studied modelling at the Art Students' league (1901 –2), before sailing for Paris, where he studied for 18 months. In 1905 he moved to London and settled in Chelsea, received vital early backing from Jewish patrons, Alfred and Rudolf Kohnstamm, through his friendship with Alfred Wolmark (cats. 6 and 7). Between 1912 and 1914 he established important links with other 'Whitechapel Boys', particularly David Bomberg (cat. 9) and Mark Gertler (cat. 10).

From his first public commission for the British Medical Association's building in The Strand, Epstein's career was always mired in controversy, partly because of the uninhibited sexuality of his figures and his lasting interest in the non-Western (and often mixed-race) model. However, his portraiture was always highly prized. Epstein's head of Leeds-born painter Jacob Kramer (there are also casts at the Tate and Leeds City Art Gallery) captures his sitter's famous nervous energy and restlessness. Epstein wrote to Kramer to encourage him to come to London to sit for the portrait after November 1920. He later recalled that Kramer 'was a model who seemed to be on fire. He was extraordinarily nervous. Energy seemed to leap into his hair as he sat, and sometimes he would be shaken by queer trembling like ague. I would try to calm him so as to get on with the work'. Epstein scholar Evelyn Silber has cited the work as 'the portrait of one outstanding Jewish contributor to British modernism by

another [which] sees both close to the peak of their creative energies'.

Epstein was only finally accepted by the establishment five years before his death when he was knighted in 1954.

Ben Uri owns six works (the earliest dating from 1931) by Epstein, who was a noted Patron of the Society from 1936–37. He first exhibited in the *Opening of the Ben Uri Jewish Art Gallery and an Exhibition of Works by Jewish Artists* at Woburn House in 1934. Ben Uri subsequently held a number of retrospectives including an *Exhibition of Bronzes* in 1959; a *Centenary Exhibition* in 1980; and *Embracing the Exotic: Jacob Epstein and Dora Gordine* in 2006. A special Epstein day tour around London led by Richard Cork was also held on 19 August 2009 to mark the 50th anniversary of the artist's death.

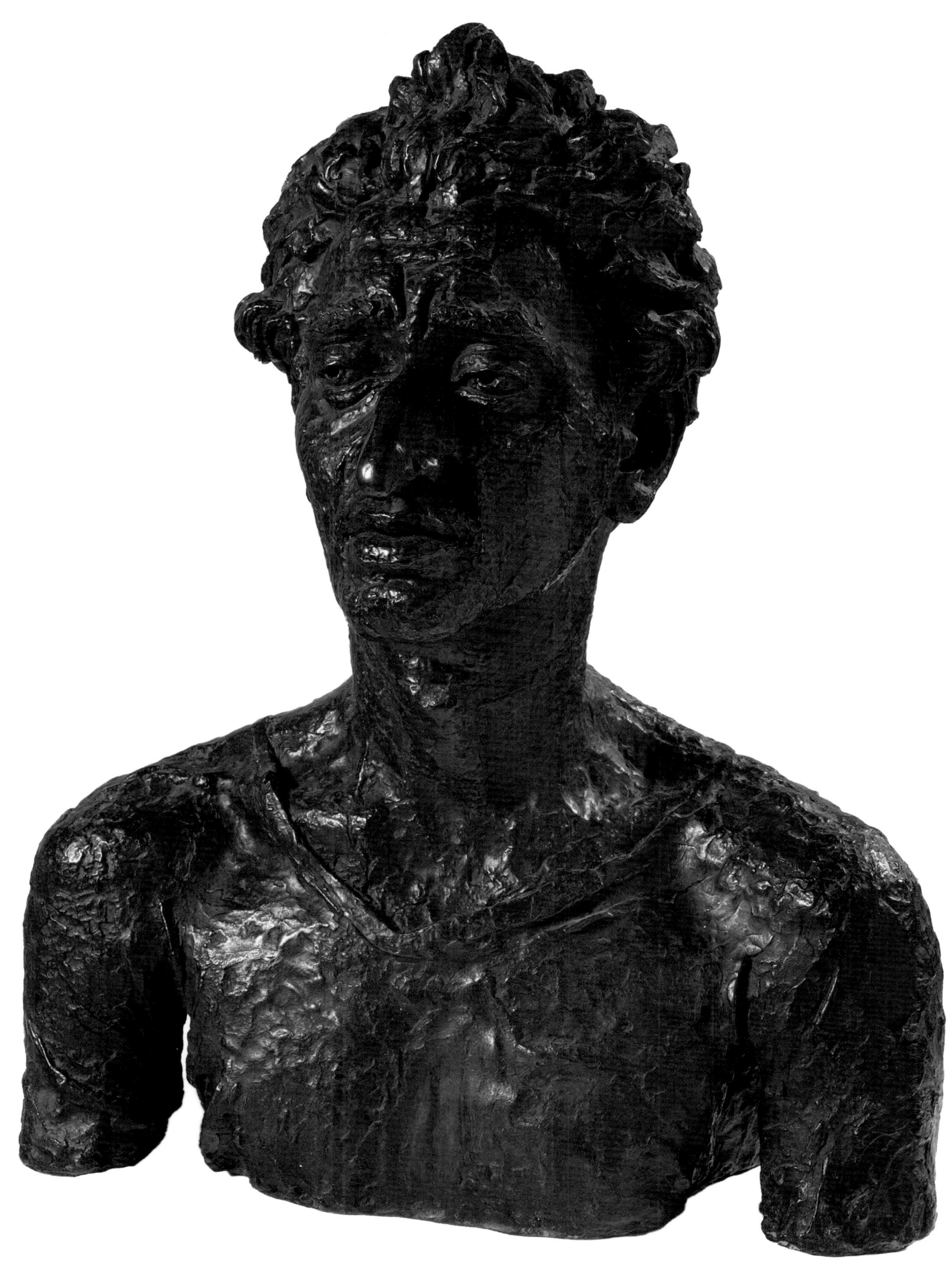

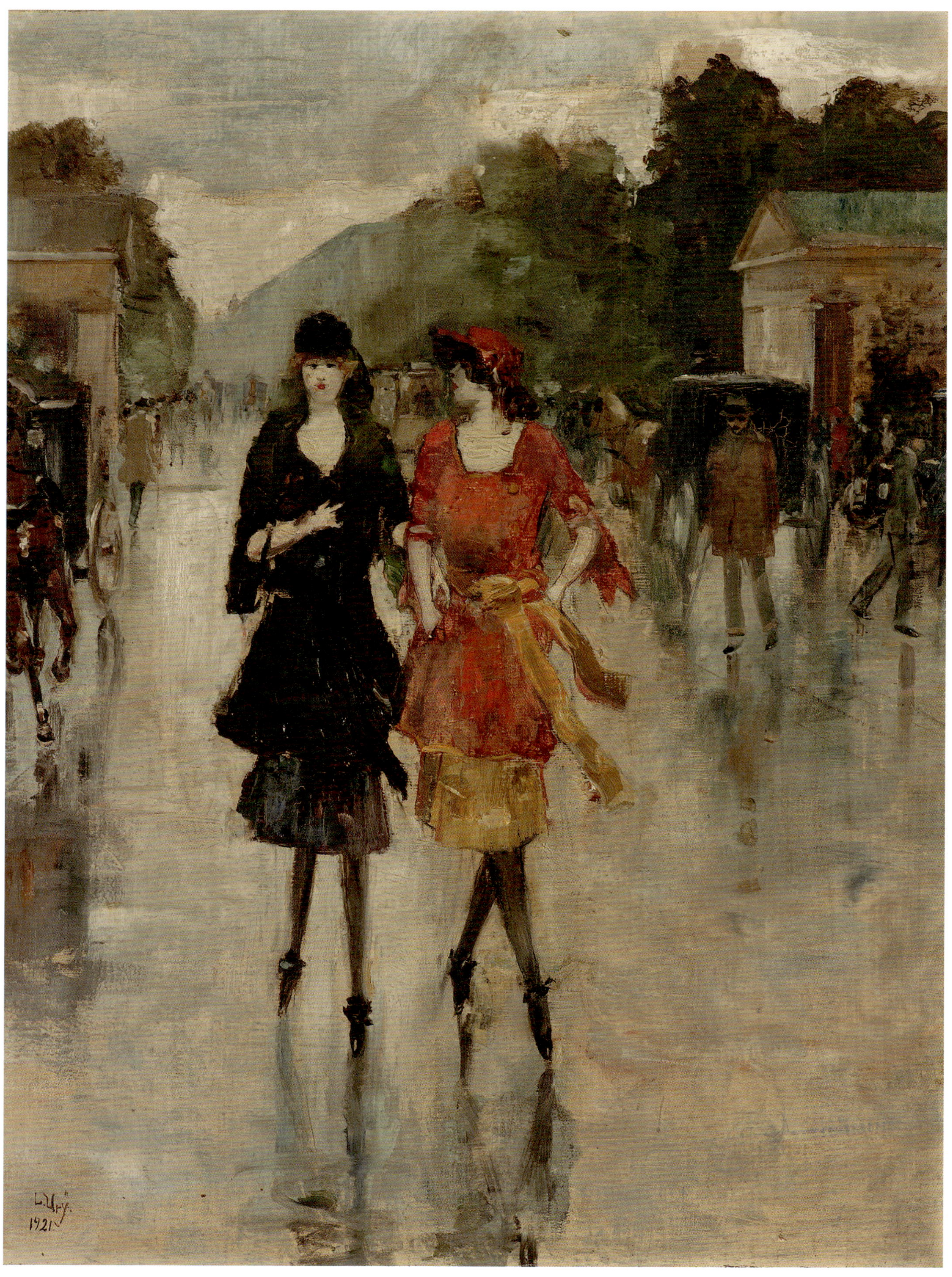

20

Berlin Street Scene, 1921

LESSER URY

(1861 Birnbaum, Prussia (now Międzychód, Poland) – 1931 Berlin, Germany)

Oil on canvas
63.2 × 48.1 cm
Signed and dated (lower left)
'L. Ury 1921'

Ben Uri Collection
Presented by Miss Stephanie Ellen
Kohn, 1990

SELECTED EXHIBITION HISTORY
Shtetl Scenes, Ben Uri, London, 1990;
Homeless and Hidden, Ben Uri,
London, 2008; *The Inspiration of
Decadence*, Ben Uri, London, 2012

Born in Birnbaum, in the then Prussian province of Posen, in 1861, Lesser Ury was initially apprenticed to a merchant before leaving to study painting, first in Düsseldorf and then in Brussels, Paris, Stuttgart and Munich; in Paris he developed a fascination with the modern metropolis and nocturnal urban life. He settled in Berlin in 1887, holding his first exhibition there in 1889. Despite a hostile reception, Ury was championed by the artist Adolph von Menzel and was subsequently awarded the Michael Beer prize by the Berlin Academy, which enabled him to visit Italy. In 1893 he joined the Munich Secession (a group of progressive artists), but returned to Berlin in 1901 and exhibited with the Berlin Secession in 1915 and 1922, when, during a display of 150 of his paintings, Uri was honoured as 'the artistic glorifier of the capital' by the mayor of Berlin.

Set in the Charlottenburg district, this is one of Ury's many Impressionistic Berlin street scenes, which are typically set either at night or in the rain. Framed by distinctive classical architecture and accentuated by vivid splashes of colour, the angular shapes of two fashionably dressed young women contrast strongly with the muted background and the horse-drawn carriages which evoke an earlier era. Our focus is cleverly drawn to the two women by the artist's sparing use of red highlights within a mainly sombre palette – in the dress of one and the dash of lipstick of the other.

Lesser Ury died in Berlin in 1931. Shortly afterwards a major memorial exhibition was held at the National Gallery and he is now regarded by critics as perhaps the first German artist to portray life in the modern city. As well as urban landscapes, he also explored Jewish subject matter in his art, although these works were less well received critically both during his lifetime and posthumously. This is one of four works by the artist in the Ben Uri Collection.

21

Portrait of a Girl, 1922

LUDWIG MEIDNER

(1884 Bernstadt, Germany, now Bierutów, Poland – 1966 Darmstadt, Germany)

Charcoal on paper
68.5 × 50.5 cm

Ben Uri Collection
Presented by Cyril J. Ross, 1950

SELECTED EXHIBITION HISTORY
Ludwig and Else Meidner, Ben Uri,
London, 2002; *Homeless and Hidden*,
Ben Uri, London, 2008; *Forced
Journeys*, Ben Uri, London; Douglas,
Isle of Man; Birkenhead, 2009–10

FOOTNOTES
1   including Dadaist Kurt Schwitters,
Expressionist Erich Kahn, engraver
Hellmuth Weissenborn and art
historian Klaus E Hinrichsen, who
subsequently documented their
cultural activities.

Ludwig Meidner was born in Bernstadt (now Bierutów, Poland) and studied in Breslau, Berlin and Paris. Apprenticed unsuccessfully as a stonemason, he then worked as a fashion illustrator, producing realistic if uninspired views of Berlin. In 1912 he began the *Apocalyptic Landscapes* series anticipating the carnage and destruction of the First World War and exhibited with *Die Pathetiker* group in Herwarth Walden's influential gallery, *Der Sturm*. An avowed pacifist following military service, Meidner paitned Jewish religious and mystical works, Rembrandt-inspired self-portraits, and portraits of leading expressionists, Dada writers and poets. This drawing, from the Weimar period, is typical of Meidner's powerful, graphic, expressionist style.

With rising anti-Semitism in Berlin, he and his family moved to Cologne in 1935, where he worked as a drawing teacher at a Jewish school. In 1937 he was included in the infamous 'Degenerate Art' exhibition. Immigrating to England in August 1939, he was interned from 1940–41: first at Huyton Camp, Liverpool, and then in Hutchinson on the Isle of Man, which was known as the 'artists' camp' for its roster of notable artist-internees.[1] His wife, Else, his former pupil and a painter in her own right, became a domestic during this period.

Fellow internee, artist Hellmuth Weissenborn (1898–1982) noted that of the 2,000 men in Hutchinson – 'Germans, Austrians and a few Italians, people of all social circles' – 90% were Jews'. Hence, for the devout Meidner, internment developed into a positive experience. Compared to the poverty and isolation of exile, it was a safe, religiously tolerant and intellectually stimulating environment, providing Kosher food and the means to continue drawing, such that, prior to his release, Meidner even asked to stay on.

Despite receiving little recognition as an artist, Meidner remained in London after the war, taking odd jobs and dependent on support from the émigré community – particularly art historian J. P. Hodin. Participating in some Jewish artistic circles, he unsuccessfully attempted to establish a Jewish art society with fellow émigré Jankel Adler (cat. 22). Meidner also joined the Ohel Club in Gower Street organised by émigré brothers Alexander and Benjamin Margulies for Jewish refugee intellectuals. Josef Herman (cat. 36) recalled artist members including Adler, Marek Szwarc, Bloch and Bomberg. Alexander Margulies also provided a conduit to the Ben Uri Art Gallery, where he became Chairman, and where Meidner exhibited *Memorial to Death* and *In a Concentration Camp*, his haunting response to the Holocaust, in the exhibition *Subjects of Jewish Interest* in December 1946. In late 1949 his sole exhibition in exile was a joint Ben Uri show with Else, a show whose limited success he likened to a 'second-class funeral'.

Meidner finally returned alone to Germany in 1953 to renewed acclaim and awards. A joint retrospective of work by husband and wife was held at Ben Uri in 2002. Meidner's second work in the Ben Uri Collection, a fine portrait of *Lilo Gwosdz*, was presented by the sitter in 2007.

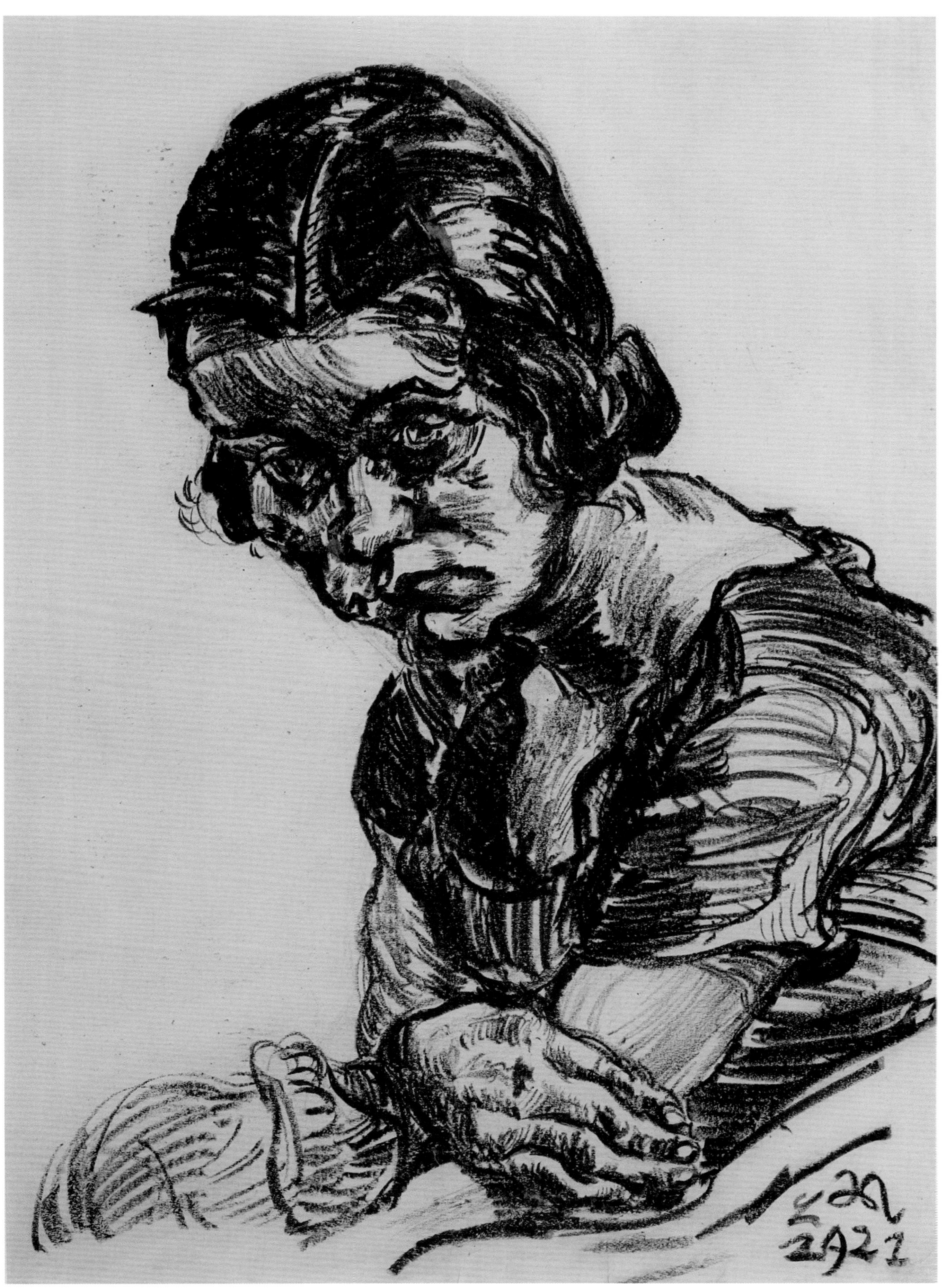

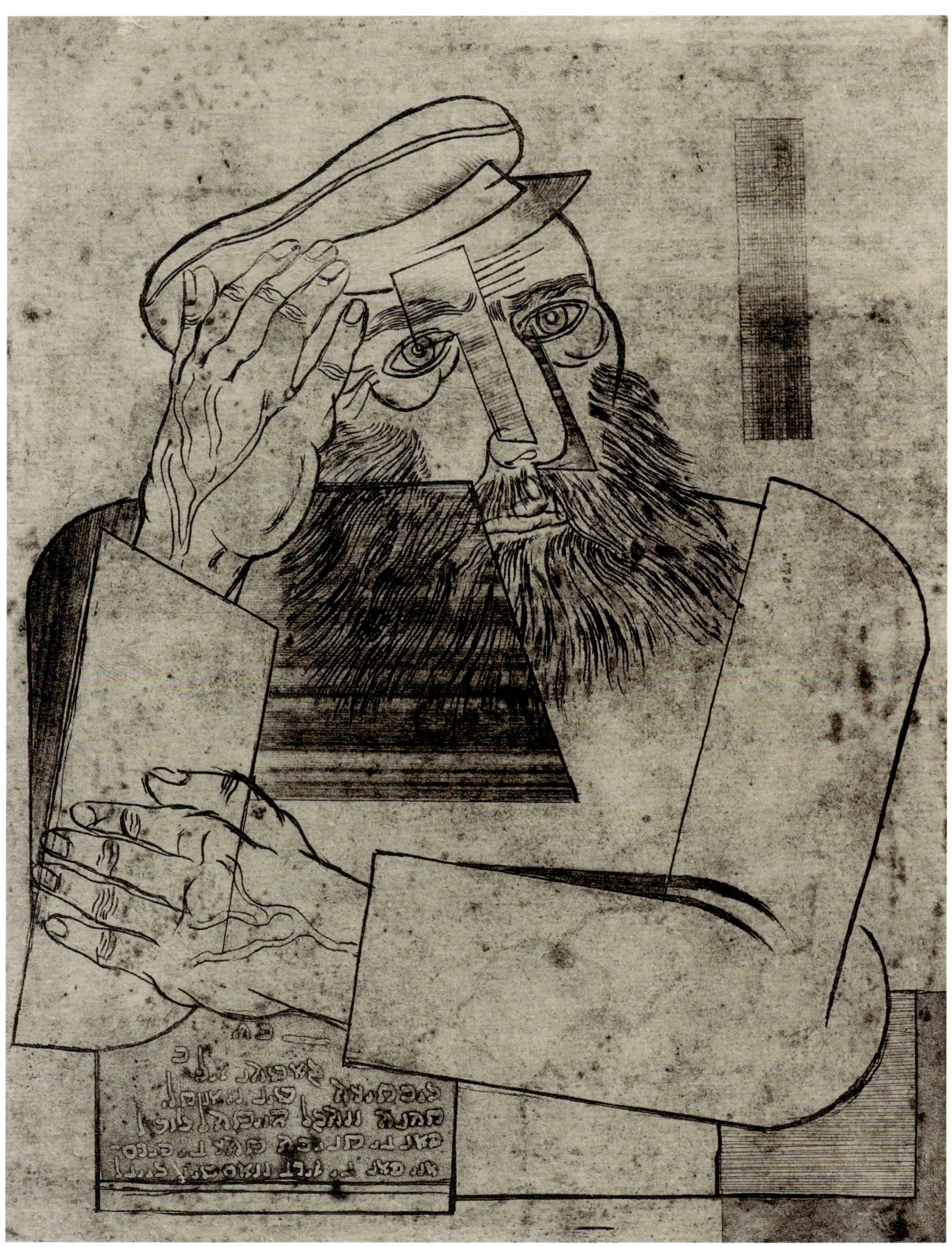

22

Ein Jude, *c.*1926

JANKEL ADLER

(1895 Tuszyn, Poland – 1949 Aldbourne, England)

Etching on paper
44.5 × 34.7 cm

Ben Uri Collection
Purchased from Peter Gidal and his
mother 2008

SELECTED EXHIBITION HISTORY
Homeless and Hidden, Ben Uri,
London, 2008; *Apocalypse*, Osborne
Samuel, London, 2010; *From Russia to
Paris*, Ben Uri, 2012; *Chagall, Soutine
and the School of Paris, Jewish Museum
Manchester*, 2013.

FOOTNOTES
1   See Sarah MacDougall ed., *Josef
Herman: Warsaw, Brussels, Glasgow,
London, 1938–44* (London: Ben Uri,
2011).

2   'Rev. Goldstein will sing Yiddish
folk songs. At this opportunity, the
Society will present A. Michaelson
with a bronze bust, created by
Melnikoff as a token of appreciation
for his good work as Chairman of the
Society for the last 13 years. The
famous Jewish artist Jankel Adler, who
is now in London, will also be present
at the festive evening.' Ben Uri
Archive: Box 3.

Jankel Adler was born in 1895 in Tuszyn, near Łódź, into a large orthodox Jewish family. He studied engraving in Belgrade in 1912, then art in Barmen and Düsseldorf until 1914. Adler returned to Poland in 1918, becoming a founder-member of Young Yiddish, a Łódź-based group of painters and writers dedicated to the expression of their Jewish identity. During the First World War he was conscripted into the Russian army, but resettled in Germany in 1920, notably meeting Marc Chagall (cat. 40) in Berlin, before returning to Barmen. In 1922 Adler moved to Düsseldorf, joined the Young Rhineland circle, became friendly with Otto Dix and helped found *Die Kommune* and the International Exhibition of revolutionary artists in Berlin. His Planetarium frescos in 1925 were highly successful and he exhibited widely. In 1931, at the Düsseldorf Academy, he formed an important friendship with Paul Klee, who had a profound influence on his style.

In 1933 Adler was forced to flee Nazi Germany at the height of his success after his work was declared 'degenerate' – he was later included in the infamous *Entartete Kunst* (Degenerate Art) exhibition in 1937. His arrival in Paris can be seen as part of a 'second wave' of artists from Russia, who were drawn west to Germany, then to France, though Adler continued to travel widely until 1937, when he worked with the printmaker Stanley William Hayter at *Atelier 17* in Paris. He also met Picasso, who became the second major influence on his style. Adler joined the Polish Army upon the outbreak of the Second World War and was evacuated to Scotland in 1940,

where he was demobilized owing to poor health. In Glasgow he and Josef Herman (cat. 36) – whom he had known previously in Poland – became members of the influential Glasgow New Art club founded by J. D. Fergusson.[1] Adler moved to London in 1943, sharing a house with 'the two Roberts', the painters Colquhoun and MacBryde, whose style he greatly influenced; he died at Aldbourne in Wiltshire in 1949.

Adler's etching, *Ein Jude*, is one of five works in the Ben Uri Collection, which also holds the plate for this work. It was probably created in 1926 on the artist's second visit to Paris and brings clean lines and a modernist technique to a beautifully executed traditional subject. In *Portrait of a Woman* Adler employs a a sombre palette and a bold, expressive style showing the influence of Picasso. His mixed media *Still Life* was acquired in 1937 after his arrival in London and a press cutting in the archives suggests that the Society anticipated the attendence of this 'famous artist' at a 'festive' event in the autumn of the same year.[2]

23

Self-portrait, 1927

MAX LIEBERMANN
(1847 Berlin, Germany – 1935 Berlin, Germany)

Oil on canvas
48 × 38 cm
Signed and dated (upper right)
'Liebermann 27'

Ben Uri Collection
On long term loan from the Zondek
Legacy through the good offices of the
Board of Belsize Synagogue 2002

SELECTED EXHIBITION HISTORY
Apocalypse, Osborne Samuel, London,
2010; *The Inspiration of Decadence*,
Ben Uri, 2012

This self-portrait by the German-Jewish artist Max Liebermann was painted in 1927 when the artist was in his eighties. Born in Berlin, he spent a formative period in Paris, then moved to Munich in 1878, before returning to Berlin in 1884. He became a leading figure in German Impressionism and was one of the founders of the Berlin Secession in 1889, of which he became the first President. A decade on, as one of the dominant figures in the German art scene, he was considered one of the establishment figures against whom the German Expressionists revolted.

Portraiture was an integral part of Liebermann's repertoire, however in this late work he relinquished the vivid colour palette usually associated with the work of the Impressionists. Instead, his use of earthy colours testifies to the influence of the French Barbizon School during the 1870s. The majority of his portraits represent seated sitters in a three-quarter-length pose, but here his decision to adopt a bust-length pose allows him to engage more directly with the viewer.

After the National Socialists came to power in Germany in 1933, Liebermann was obliged to resign as President of the Prussian Academy; he died two years later in 1935. In 1943, his wife, fearing Gestapo interrogation, committed suicide. In a chilling quirk of history, the Liebermann's villa and studio at Wansee, a suburb of Berlin, was located next door to the house in which senior officials of the party gathered on 20 January 1942 to implement the Final Solution to 'the Jewish question'.

The Ben Uri collection holds four other works by Max Liebermann: a sketch and three etchings.

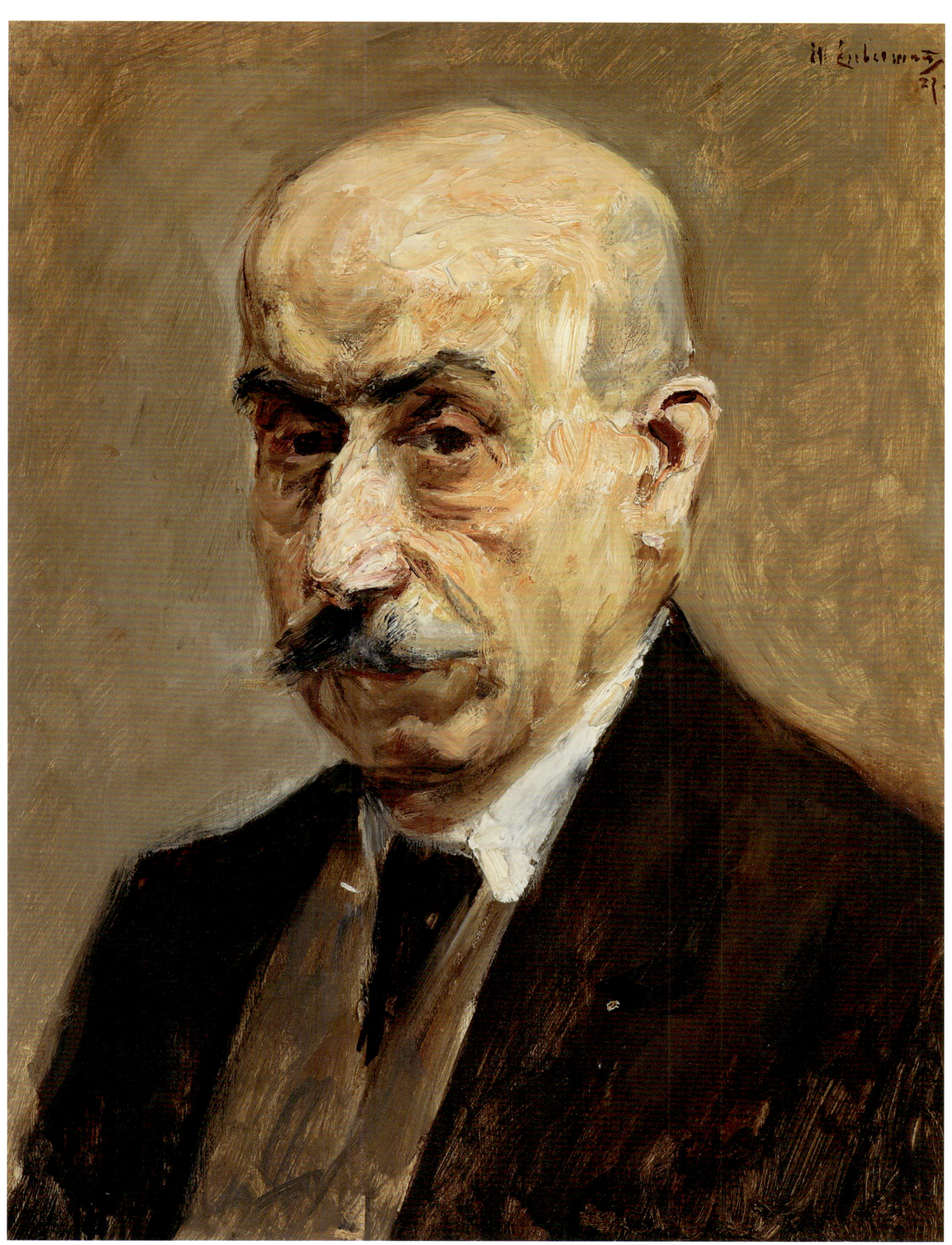

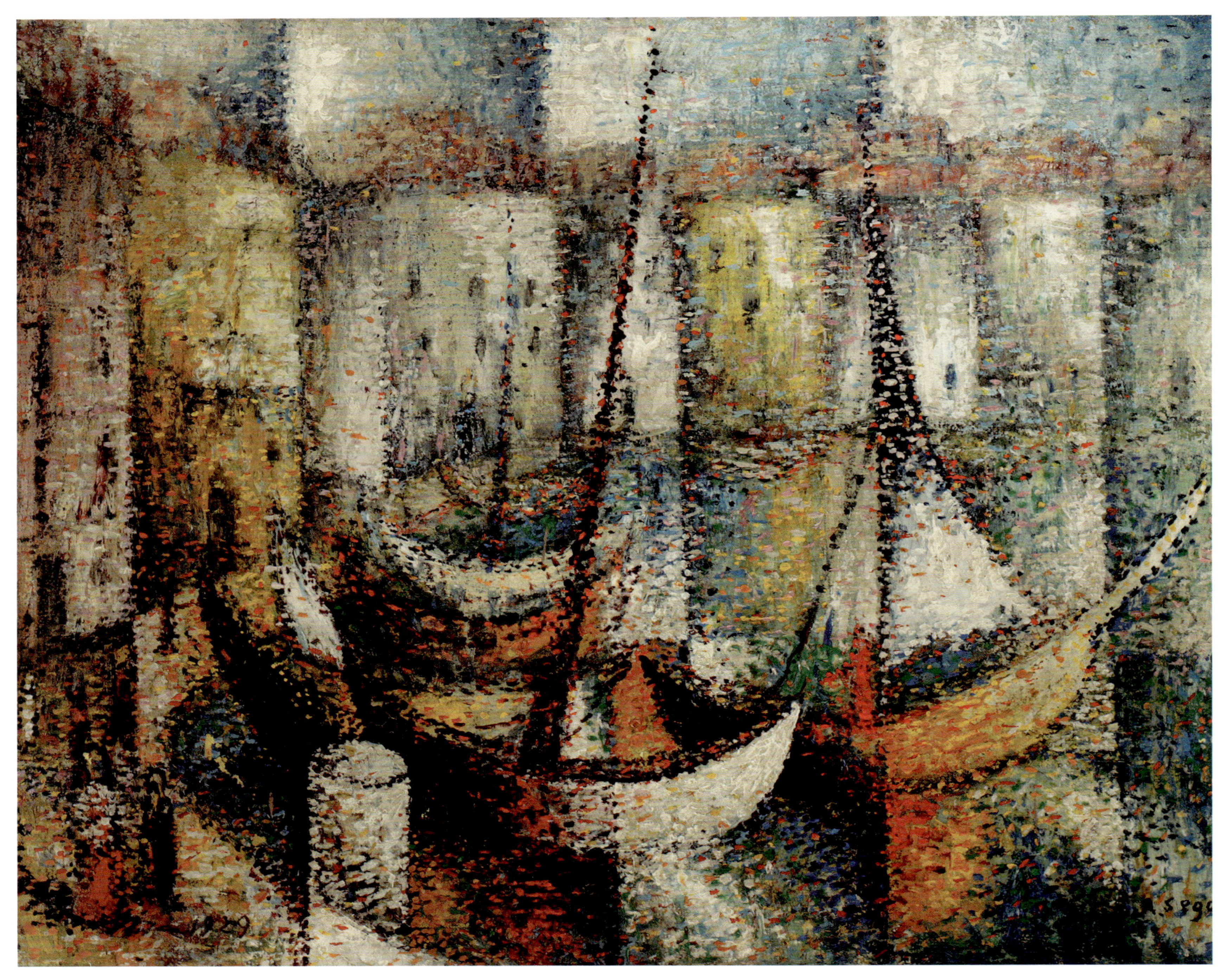

Halen, La Ciotat (Harbour Scene), 1929

ARTHUR SEGAL

(1875 Iași, Romania – 1944 London, England)

Oil on canvas
68.5 × 88.3 cm
Signed (lower right) 'A Segal'

Ben Uri Collection
Acquired prior to 1959

SELECTED EXHIBITION HISTORY
Homeless and Hidden, Ben Uri,
London, 2008; *Forced Journeys*, Ben
Uri, London, Douglas, Isle of Man
and Birkenhead, 2009–10

Arthur Segal was born in Romania in 1875 and left school early to study painting first at the Berlin Academy (1892), then in Munich (1896), Paris and Italy (1902–3), initially working in an Impressionist manner. He settled in Berlin in 1904, exhibiting with the leading Expressionist groups, *Die Brucke* and *Der Blaue Reiter*, becoming one of the leaders in 1910 of the New Berlin Secession group of progressive artists established in opposition to the Impressionist Secession founded by Max Liebermann (cat. 23).

In 1914, together with his family, Segal sought refuge in Switzerland, where he exhibited with the Dada group at the Cabaret Voltaire, Zurich. Here he began to make optical experiments in his painting, developing a distinctive type of prismatic Cubism. Afterwards he returned to Berlin where he ran his own painting school between 1923 and 1933 (declining a teaching post in the New Bauhaus, Dessau in 1925). Following the rise of Nazism, Segal was forbidden to paint and moved first to Mallorca and then, in 1936, to London. Despite a brief period in internment in Hutchinson, the so-called 'Artists' Camp', in Douglas on the Isle of Man in 1940, Segal again established his own Painting School in London for both professionals and amateurs together with his wife, Ernestine, and daughter, Marianne, which he ran between 1937 and 1944. Interested in painting as a therapy for mental illness, Segal corresponded with many psychoanalysts and psychiatrists and had the support of Sigmund Freud.

La Ciotat is a port in the Provence-Alpes-Côte d'Azur region in France. Painted in 1929, Segal's dazzling image of a peacetime harbour shimmering in the sunlight gives no hint of the darker future. His artistic experiments sought to break with a single point of focus or dominance in painting and here he combines his knowledge of Impressionism (as a means of representing light) with his individual and striking variant of Cubism, dividing his canvas into eight carefully constructed and balanced schematic fields.

For He Had Great Possessions, 1932

AMY J. DRUCKER

(1873 London, England – 1951 London, England)

Oil on canvas
49 × 60 cm
Signed and dated 1932

Ben Uri Collection
Presented by Dr Geoffrey Konstam
1952

SELECTED EXHIBITION HISTORY
*Memorial Exhibition of the Works of
Amy J. Drucker*, Ben Uri Art, London,
1952; *Homeless and Hidden*, 2008

The painter, etcher, miniaturist, lithographer, woodcut engraver and teacher, Amy Julia Drucker was born in London in 1873, although her origins are obscure. She trained at both St John's Wood and Lambeth Schools of Art (the latter aimed at artisans who wished to earn a living from art), afterwards maintaining a studio in Bloomsbury, before travelling to Paris. Drucker also travelled extensively in the Far East, South America and in Abyssinia (Ethiopia), where she painted a life-size portrait of the Emperor, and spent several months in Palestine in 1920. During the First World War she served in the Land Army and during the Second worked as a factory hand and night-watchman. Between 1889 and 1939 she exhibited regularly all over England, including at the Royal Academy, specialising in atmospheric paintings of London (particularly East End) life. In 1906 she exhibited a well-received painting, fittingly entitled *The Aliens* at the Whitechapel Art Gallery's *Jewish Art and Antiquities* exhibition, which had been largely conceived in response to the 1905 'Aliens Act' designed to limit foreign immigration rights. She was also included (outside the 'Jewish Section') in 1914 in the exhibition *Twentieth-Century Art: A Review of Modern Movements*, when her work was hung between that of 'Whitechapel Girl' Clare Winsten (cat. 15), with whom she studied sculpture at the Central School, and the Vorticist Helen Saunders.

For He had Great Possessions, possibly a later reworking of *The Aliens*, depicts a migrant family, probably newly-arrived in England, seeking work and shelter; the presence of a barrow boy locates it in the East End. This single family unit is emblematic of the vast wave of eastern-European Jews escaping persecution and financial hardship who fled to Britain before, during and after the Second World War. However, the date also suggests that they are economic migrants, victims of the 1930s 'slump'. The title invokes the biblical story in which a man refuses to part with his earthly riches in exchange for spiritual enlightenment, the subject of a well-known single figure painting by G. F. Watts (1894, Tate). However, Drucker's painting suggests that although the father is not materially wealthy, the members of his family are nonetheless his 'great possessions'.

A striking figure with a strong profile and a highly individual way of dressing, Drucker often wore a cape and a broad-brimmed black hat and was never without a multi-coloured Mexican bag slung from her left shoulder. Following strong sales from her 1952 memorial exhibition, the Ben Uri Arts Committee (7 April 1952) decided to purchase *For He Had Great Possessions*; however, the work was subsequently acquired and presented by Dr Geoffrey Kohnstamm (a patron of Alfred Wolmark). She has four further works in the Ben Uri collection. After her death an annual prize of £10 was twice awarded to a promising young Jewish artist in her memory. The first recipient was Henry Sanders (1952); the second and final prize went to Alfred Harris (1954).

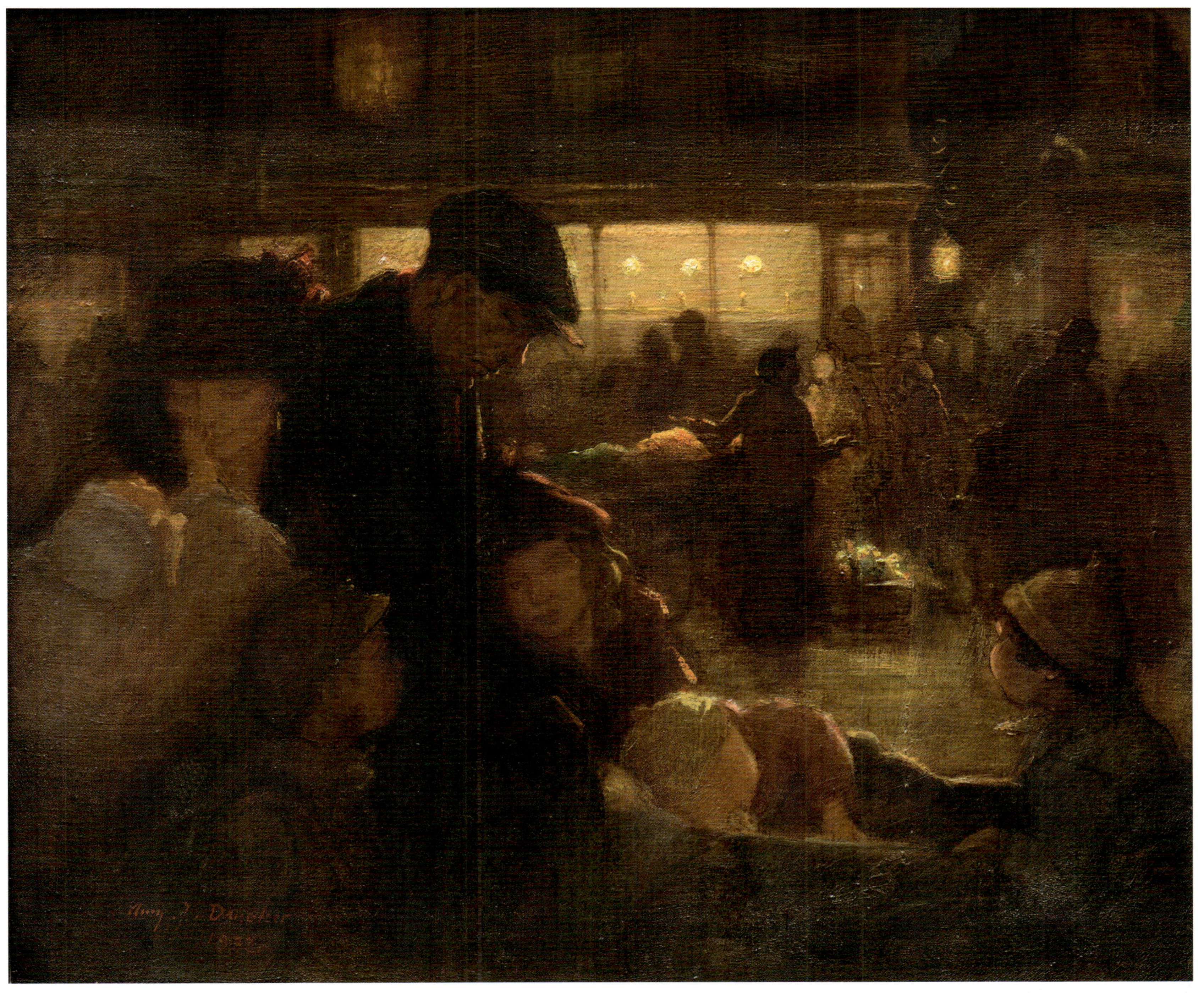

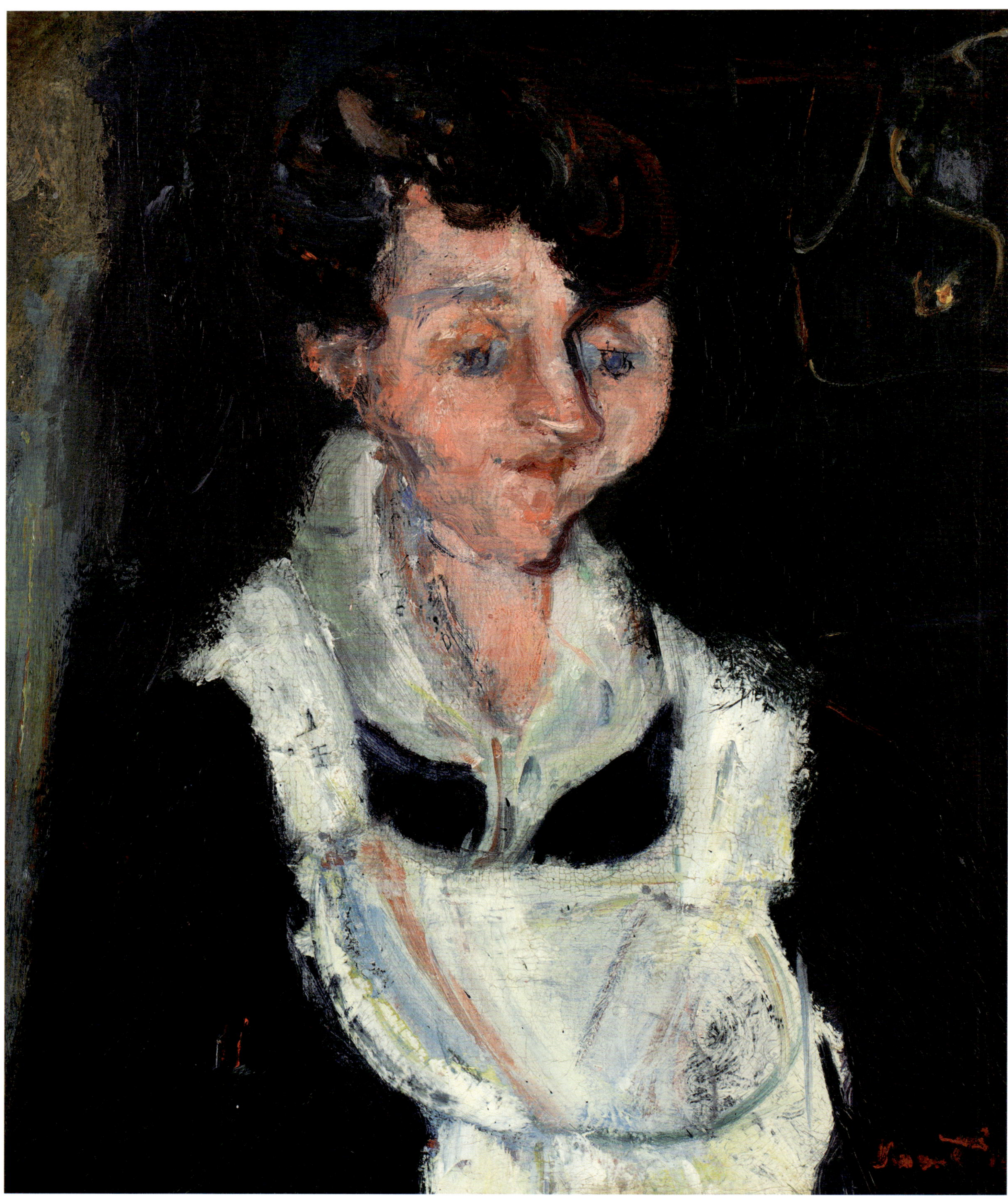

26

La Soubrette (Waiting Maid), *c.*1933

CHAÏM SOUTINE

(1893 Smilovitz, Russia (now Smilavichy, Belarus) – 1943 Paris, France)

Oil on canvas
46.5 × 40.5 cm
Signed (lower right)
'Soutine'

Ben Uri Collection
Acquired in 2012 with the assistance of the HLF, the Art Fund, the V&A Purchase Grant Fund, Miriam and Richard Borchard, Sir Harry and Lady Djanogly, Patsy & David Franks, Sir Michael and Lady Morven Heller, Joan and Lawrence Kaye (USA), Laura and Lewis Kruger (USA), Agnes & Edward Lee, Simon Posen (USA), The Marc Rich Foundation (Switzerland), Anthony Rosenfelder & family in honour of Marilyn, Jayne Cohen and Howard Spiegler (USA), and Judit & George Weisz

SELECTED EXHIBITION HISTORY
Catalogue des Tableaux Modernes, Hotel Drouot, Paris, 1937 as 'Jeune Servante'; *The Tragic Painters*, Alex, Reid & Lefevre Ltd., London, 1938, as 'La Soubrette'; as 'Waiting Maid', Arts Council, London, 1963; *From Russia to Paris: Chaïm Soutine and his Contemporaries*, Ben Uri, London, 2012; *Soutine, Chagall and the School of Paris*, Jewish Museum, Manchester, 2013

Chaïm Soutine was born to a poor Jewish family, the tenth of eleven children, in the shtetl of Smilovitz, and drew from an early age. He studied at the School of Fine Arts, Vilna (1910 – 13), and in the Atelier Cormon at the École des Beaux-Arts, Paris (1913–15), becoming closely associated with the group of foreign-born, predominantly Jewish artists, known as the 'École de Paris'. The majority including Marc Chagall, Isaac Dobrinsky (fig. 22), Jacques Lipchitz (fig. 24) lived and worked together in great poverty in the studios known as La Ruche ('the Beehive') near the old Vaugirard slaughterhouses of Montparnasse. In 1915 Lipchitz introduced Soutine to Amedeo Modigliani with whom he developed a strong friendship.

During the First World War Soutine enlisted in the work brigades but was soon dismissed on health grounds, having developed the stomach problems which would later kill him. His oeuvre includes a series of powerful, visceral landscapes and an important series of Rembrandt-inspired beef carcasses painted in a characteristic, expressionistic style. The American collector Albert Barnes bought a significant amount of Soutine's work in 1923, affording him financial stability for the first time. He held his first solo exhibition at the Galerie Bing, Paris in 1927. In 1928 Waldemar George published the first monograph on Soutine as part of 'les artistes juifs' series; Elie Faure's followed a year later. From then Soutine worked mainly in Paris, spending the summers near Chartres with his patrons Marcellin and Madeleine Castaing.

In *La Soubrette* Soutine focuses on a single subject against an unadorned background, an anonymous, working-class figure in uniform painted with typically expressive and tactile brushwork. Originally known, more accurately, as *Jeune Servante* (a Soubrette is a character derived from operetta), the title was changed when the work was offered for sale in London in 1938 in a show entitled *The Tragic Painters* at Alex, Reid & Lefevre Ltd., when it was also dated to *c.*1925. Working direct from the life, Soutine captured an expression somewhere between weariness, wariness and submission, but drew attention to the maid's inner life by emphasising her individuality. His virtuoso paint handling illuminates her white apron with a dazzling display of colour. This portrait relates to Soutine's series of powerful character studies of pastry cooks, choirboys, boot boys, bell-boys and maids, dressed in the uniforms of their professions, in exaggerated poses ranging from awkwardness to arrogance. From the 1930s Soutine's figure paintings became less frenzied and more meditative. After 1941, using a false identity card, he sought refuge from occupied Paris in Touraine, but in 1943, suffering from a rapid decline in health, returned to Paris and died during an operation for perforated stomach ulcers.

La Soubrette was unveiled in 2012 at the exhibition, *From Russia to Paris: Chaïm Soutine and his Contemporaries*. It is one of only seven Soutines in British museum collections.

27

Shtetl, 1934

CHANA KOWALSKA

(1907 Włocławek, Poland – 1941 Auschwitz, Poland)

Oil on canvas
45 × 60 cm

Ben Uri Collection
Presented by Mrs Moshe Oved, 1962

SELECTED EXHIBITION HISTORY
From Russia to Paris, Ben Uri, London, 2012; *Soutine, Chagall and the School of Paris,* Jewish Museum, Manchester, 2013

Chana Kowalska was born in 1907 in Włocławek, Poland. Her father, a rabbi, senator and Zionist, made their home a meeting point for intellectuals, and the Yiddish writer Sholem Asch wrote his first book there. Kowalska began drawing at the age of 16, but at 18 became a school teacher. In 1922 she moved to Berlin, where she met her future husband, the writer Baruch Winogora.

Kowalska later moved to Paris and settled in Montparnasse, borrowing the studios of her friends to paint. She was actively involved in the Paris *Kultura-Liga* and in Jewish communist circles, and also worked as a journalist and wrote about painting in Yiddish journals including *Presse Nouvelle* and the daily *Le Journal de Paris.* She held the post of Secretary of the Jewish Painters and Sculptors Association and participated in the 1937 Jewish Cultural Congress. During the Second World War, she was involved in the French Resistance with her husband; arrested by the Gestapo they were either shot, or deported and then killed, in 1941.

Despite Kowalska's naïve style of painting, her strong lines, bold colours and simplified figures often disguise a more complex message in which a series of contrasting images are linked both literally and symbolically. In *Shtetl* – the traditional Jewish village or small town with a tightly-knit community that was common throughout eastern Europe before the Holocaust – Kowalska conjures up an archetypal scene with, at its centre, villagers gathering round the water pump. Nevertheless, the horse-drawn cart winding up a street lined with traditional, single-storey houses (a motif also used in her painting *The Bridge,* Ben Uri Collection) warns of a fast-disappearing way of life. Pavements and streetlights signal approaching modernisation and a church in the distance underlines the presence of the wider community. Many of Kowalska's paintings recall her homeland and their folk-like quality, bright palette and unnatural perspective have affinities with the work of Chagall. This is one of two works by Kowalska in the Ben Uri Collection.

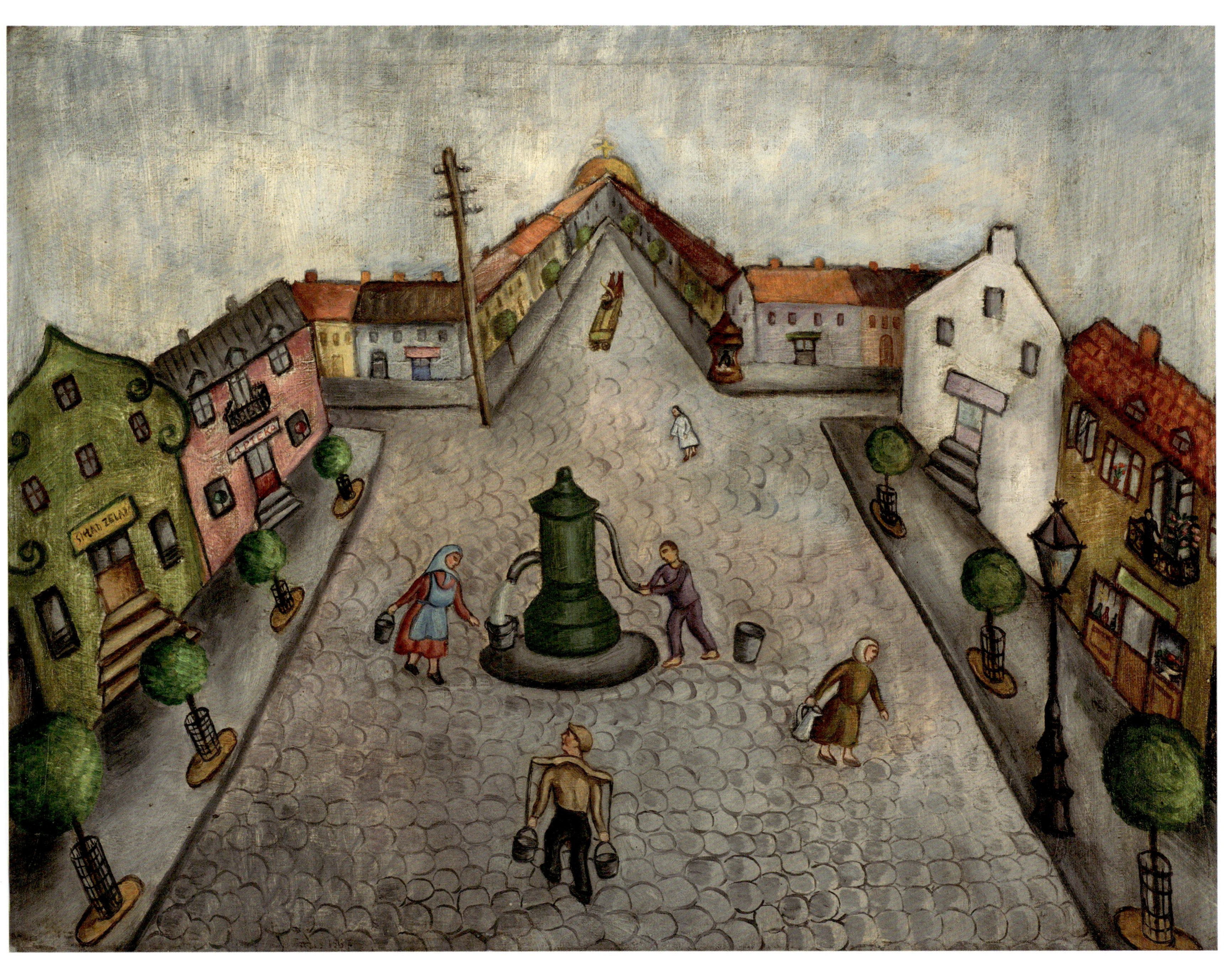

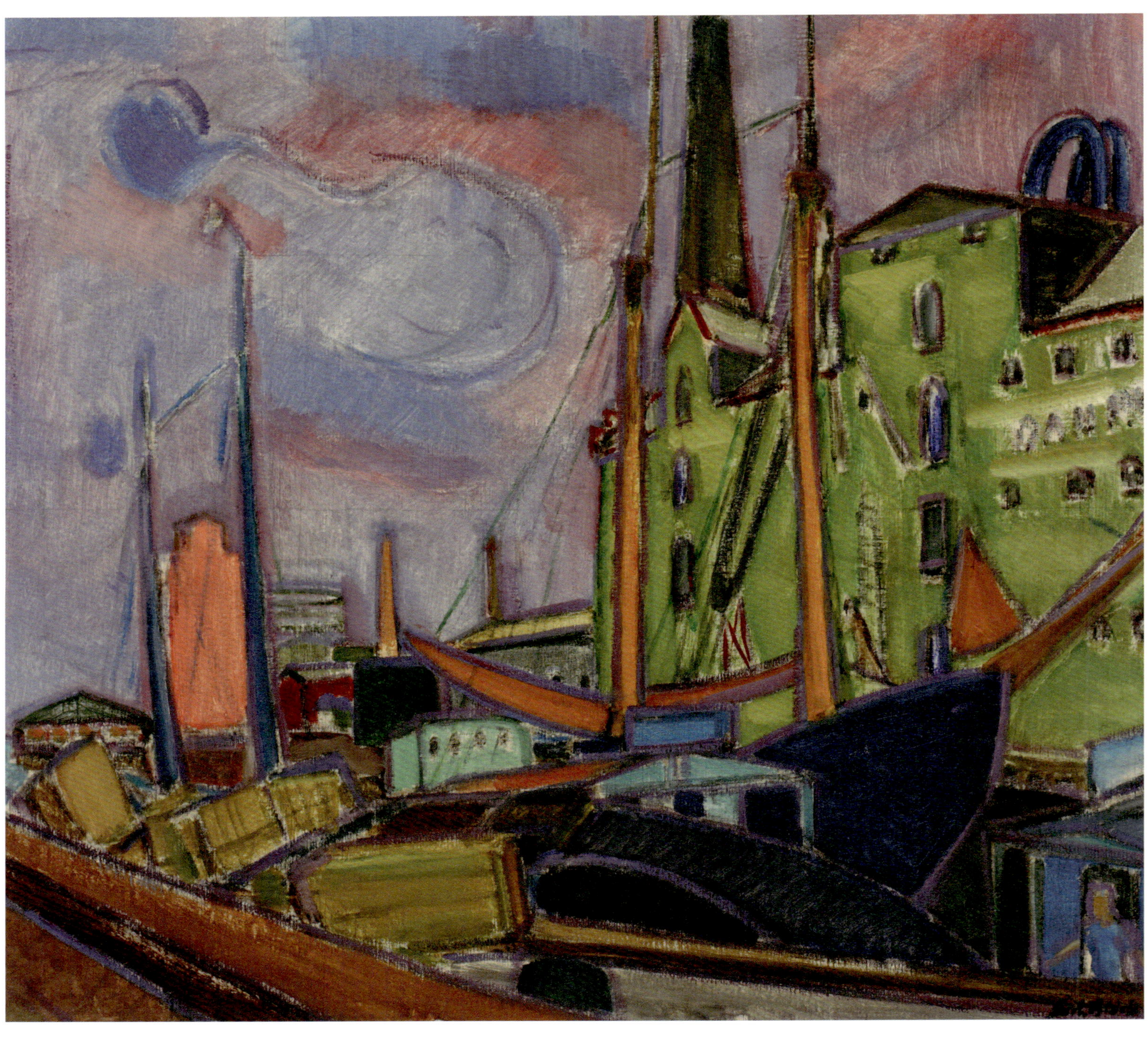

Svendborg Harbour, Denmark, 1934

MARTIN BLOCH

(1883 Neisse, Prussia (now Nysa, Poland) – 1954 London, England)

Oil on canvas on board
69 × 79 cm
Signed (lower right)
'Martin Bloch'

Ben Uri Collection

Martin Bloch initially trained as an architect and later studied drawing in Berlin under Lovis Corinth, exhibiting at the Paul Cassirer Gallery. He held his first solo exhibition in Berlin in 1911, travelled to Paris and Spain, then returned to Berlin to co-found a painting school. After fleeing via Denmark, Bloch settled in London, opening a second painting school with Australian painter Roy de Maistre (1894–1968). He exhibited in the controversial *Exhibition of Twentieth-Century German Art* at the New Burlington Galleries in 1938 and held his first solo London show at the Lefevre Gallery in 1939. Between 1940 and 1941 he was one of many 'enemy aliens' interned, first at Huyton Camp, Liverpool, then briefly on the Isle of Man. In later years, his fluid style of painting and spontaneous use of colour inspired his students at the Camberwell School of Arts and Crafts. A regular exhibitor with Ben Uri, he held a joint exhibition with Josef Herman (cat. 36) at Portman Street in 1949 and a memorial exhibition was curated by Ben Uri in 1963. His work also featured in Ben Uri's *Festival of Britain Anglo-Jewish Exhibition 1851–1951 Art Section*, an adjunct to the main *Anglo-Jewish Exhibition* held at University College.

This claustrophobic depiction of boats in a crowded harbour, a classic symbol of exile, was painted during the artist's brief stay in Denmark after he fled Nazi Germany in 1934. Despite the traumatic experience of flight, it is full of energy and colour. Drawing on his German expressionist roots, Bloch pares down form into simple shapes and conveys emotion through the use of heightened purples, greens and mustard yellows. The compression of the perspective into a single, suffocating plane jams the boats against the harbour and creates a distinct uneasiness. This is one of three works by Bloch in the Ben Uri Collection.

The Lecture (aka Letter to an Anti-Semite), 1935

GEORGE GROSZ

(1893 Berlin, Germany – 1959 Berlin, Germany)

Pen and ink and
watercolour on paper
55 × 45 cm
Signed (with ink,
lower right) 'Grosz'
Titled (with pencil, lower right)
'Letter to an Anti-Semite'

Ben Uri Collection

Presented 2013 by Sally, Richard and
Andrew Kalman in honour of their
late father Andras Kalman

Georg Ehrenfried Gross was born in Berlin in 1893, studying at the Dresden Academy (1909–11), Berlin's School of Arts and Crafts (1912–14) and the Atelier Colarossi, Paris (1913). He served twice during the First World War: having enlisted in 1914, he was discharged on medical grounds, rejoining in 1917 and again being discharged as unfit. In 1916 he changed his name to George Grosz to indicate his admiration for American life and culture and from 1917–20 was a prominent member of the German anti-Bourgeois Dada movement. Postwar Grosz channeled his fierce anti-militarism into satirical, politically excoriating works, and was repeatedly prosecuted on the grounds of obscenity and blasphemy. In 1933, only days before Hitler's accession to the Chancellorship of Germany, Grosz moved to New York to avoid persecution and to take up the offer of a teaching post. In his absence, he was stripped of his German citizenship and a number of his books and portfolios were destroyed.

The lecture is one of two works in the Ben Uri Collection that commemorate the brutal death of Grosz's friend, the radical Jewish writer and anarchist Erich Mühsam (1878–1934), a long-time critic of successive German political regimes, who was tortured and murdered in Oranienburg concentration camp. To the National Socialists, Mühsam, as a Jew, was the definition of everything worth hating – even though, according, to Grosz, he was 'actually a completely harmless, idealistic anarchist'. Grosz shows only Mühsam's head, brutally shorn and branded and with a noose around his neck

(Mühsam's wife was informed that he had hanged himself); beneath him a copy of the Talmud has been speared by a dagger. A thuggish officer grasping a knuckle-duster, his face red and contorted with rage, points to the image on a lecture board while his audience slavers with anticipation or appreciation. Both these works are part of a larger disturbing series commemorating the writer (see also *The Interrogation*, 1938 (cat. 33)) created in America although Grosz later largely abandoned his satirical work for landscapes and still-lifes. In 1937 Grosz's work was included, in his absence, in the infamous 1937 'Degenerate Art' exhibition that opened in Munich before touring throughout Germany and Austria. He became a naturalised American citizen in 1938 and published his autobiography, *A Little Yes and a Big No* in New York in 1946, but, disillusioned with the 'American Dream', he returned to postwar Berlin in 1959 and died shortly afterwards.

This work (together with *The Interrogation*) was unveiled at a special ceremony at Ben Uri in Boundary Road, St John's Wood, London on 30 January 2013. This marked the 80th anniversary of the day on which Adolf Hitler succeeded to the Chancellorship of Germany in 1933 and the donation to the museum by Sally, Richard and Andrew Kalman in memory of their late father, Andras Kalman (1919–2007). He was a Hungarian émigré, who came to the UK to study in 1939 and later founded the Krane Calman Gallery, and whose own immediate family perished in the Holocaust.

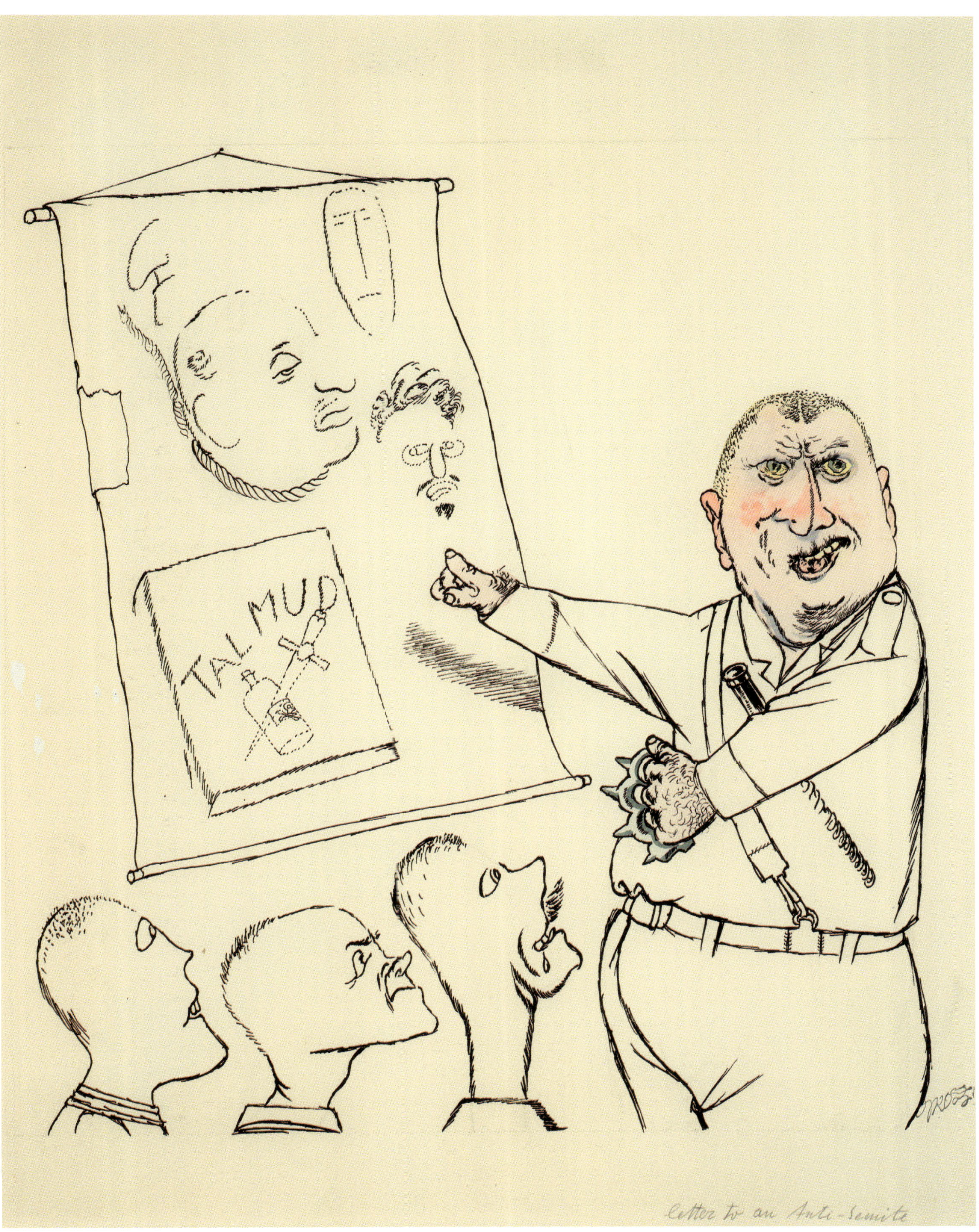

letter to an Anti-Semite

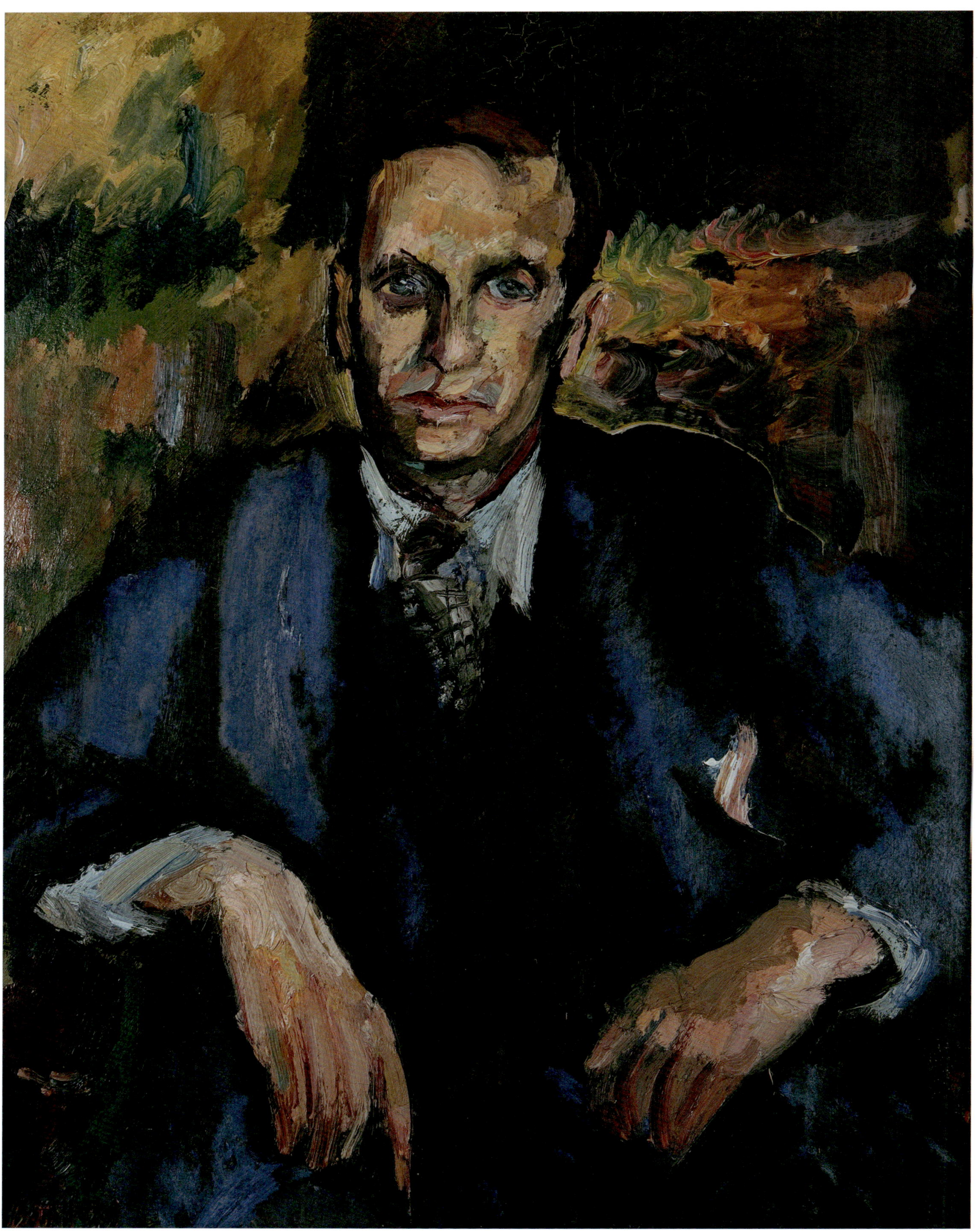

Portrait of John Rodker, *c.*1936

DAVID BOMBERG

(1890 Birmingham, England – 1957 London, England)

Oil on canvas
71.5 × 57 cm
Signed (lower left) 'Bomberg'

Ben Uri Collection
Presented by Joan Rodker, 2008

This portrait depicts Bomberg's close friend and fellow 'Whitechapel Boy', the modernist poet, essayist and publisher John Rodker (1894–1955). Bomberg designed a semi-abstract cover for the writer's first collection of poems in 1914, based on studies of Rodker's girlfriend Sonia Cohen performing a dance as a member of Margaret Morris's famous troupe. Rodker reciprocated with reviews of Bomberg's art, including one of *Racehorses* (1913, cat. 9) in *The Dial Monthly* in May 1914. During the First World War, Rodker went on the run, sheltering with the poet R. C. Trevelyan, but was eventually captured and imprisoned in Dartmoor. He later explored this experience in his account, *Memoirs of Other Fronts*, published anonymously in 1932. One of his many publishing projects included the short-lived Ovid Press (1919), which brought out work by the modernist poets T. S. Eliot, Wyndham Lewis and Ezra Pound.

Bomberg painted Rodker's portrait during a period of critical neglect when he turned largely to himself, his family and close friends as subjects. It was donated to the Ben Uri Collection by the sitter's daughter, Joan Rodker, in 2008. Bomberg's realistic approach to Rodker's portrait illustrates his move away from his earlier sharp-edged Vorticist treatment of the figure and towards a more painterly style. He uses broad, expressive brushstrokes and the pink and green flesh tones of the face, reminiscent of Cézanne, are offset by the rich blue of Rodker's suit.

Bomberg's correspondence from the early 1930s (University of Texas at Austin) reveals the enduringly close friendship of the two men, as well as Rodker's later efforts to obtain financial assistance for Bomberg (including a 1954 reply from 10 Downing Street indicating that the artist had not been awarded a civil list pension). Despite support from a small number of collectors in Britain, Bomberg's financial anxieties were acute. He remained a prominent member of The London Group, to whom he submitted a revolutionary set of proposals suggesting affiliation with the Anti-Fascist Allied Artists' International Association (AIA), but this, like his subsequent plans to re-organise the Ben Uri, was emphatically rejected. 'The Jewish artists are starving,' he wrote in 1938, 'none of us can work, most of us receive one form of charity or another – we can make a market for ourselves if we organise'. A recently uncovered letter from Ben Uri's treasurer Cyril J. Ross (24 June 1939) in Ben Uri's Archive refers to a number of 'upsetting letters' from Bomberg. Ross subsequently offered to either make a studio space available for the impecunious artist or to pay (at his own expense) the rent on Bomberg's existing studio. During the Second World War Bomberg was appointed an Official War Artist but only completed one commission, *Underground Bomb Store* (1942). Afterwards, he became a highly influential teacher, most notably at the Borough Polytechnic (1945–53), where he formed The Borough Group (1947–9), and the Borough Bottega (1953). Bomberg moved to Spain in 1954 and remained there until shortly before his death in 1957.

The Rt. Hon. Leslie Hore-Belisha, *c.*1937–39

ZEEV BEN-ZVI

(1904 Ryki, Poland – 1952 Jerusalem, Israel)

Bronze on marble base
44.5 × 31 × 40 cm

Ben Uri Collection
Gift

SELECTED EXHIBITION HISTORY
Selected Masterworks: Israeli, Modern and Contemporary Collection, Bonhams, London, 2011

Sculptor Zeev Ben-Zvi was born in Poland in 1904 and studied at the Academy of Art in Warsaw before immigrating to Palestine in 1924. After working for two years with Boris Schatz (1866–1932), founder of the Bezalel Academy of Arts and design in Jerusalem, Ben-Zvi taught sculpture at Bezalel from 1926–7, and continued to hold a teaching post there intermittently until his death. Ben-Zvi's early naturalistic style gave way to a more intense expression based on Cubist techniques and he became known for his portrait sculptures and his masks made from beaten copper. His work influenced a subsequent generation of sculptors.

Ben-Zvi lived in England between 1937 and 1939, featuring in Ben Uri's annual exhibition of 1937 and having a notable one-person exhibition at the Matthiesen Gallery in London in 1938. At this time he began to use more rounded forms and to minimise detail, as can be seen in his head of Lord Hore-Belisha. (Isaac) Leslie Hore-Belisha (1893–1957) became a Liberal MP in 1923 and helped to form the National Liberal Party in 1931 in support of the national coalition government. As Minister of Transport (1934–37), he gave his name to the 'Belisha beacon' on pedestrian crossings and was responsible for introducing the 30 mph speed limit. As British Secretary of State for War (1937–40), he instituted military conscription in the spring of 1939, a few months before the outbreak of hostilities, but lost his post in 1940.

During the 1940s Ben-Zvi's work became more abstract. His sculpture continued to feature in Ben Uri loan exhibitions, including the 1944 *Opening Exhibition* and the 1953 *Coronation Exhibition of Paintings and Sculpture*; the latter was characterised, according to the catalogue, as being 'European rather than British'. After his return to Jerusalem, he became a lecturer at Bezalel and created a monumental sculpture at *Mishmar Ha'emek* kibbutz, *In Memory of the Children of the Diaspora* (1947), which has been described as 'the apogee of Israeli monumental sculpture'. In 1953 he posthumously received both the Dizengoff Prize and the inaugural Israel Prize for Sculpture.

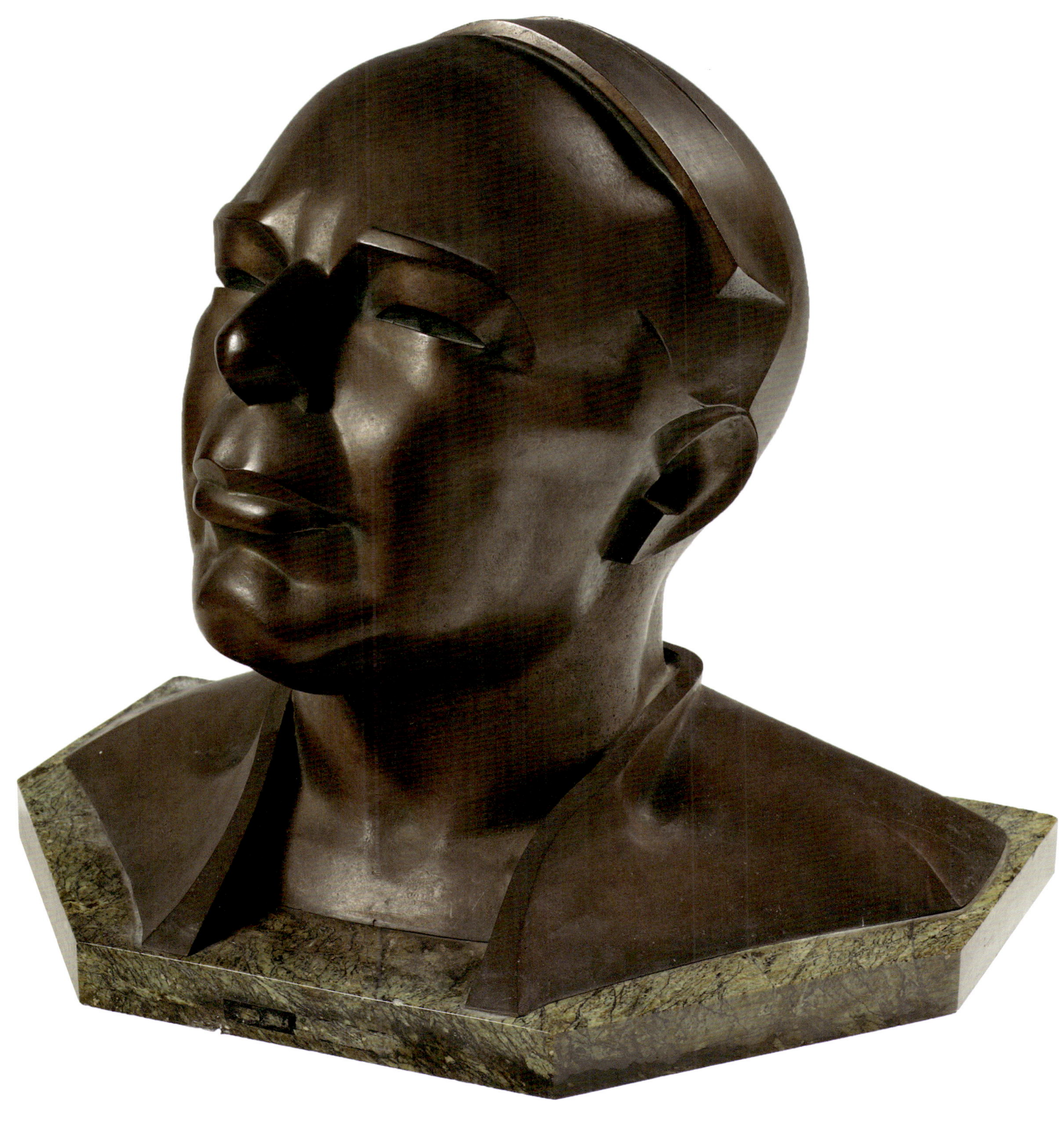

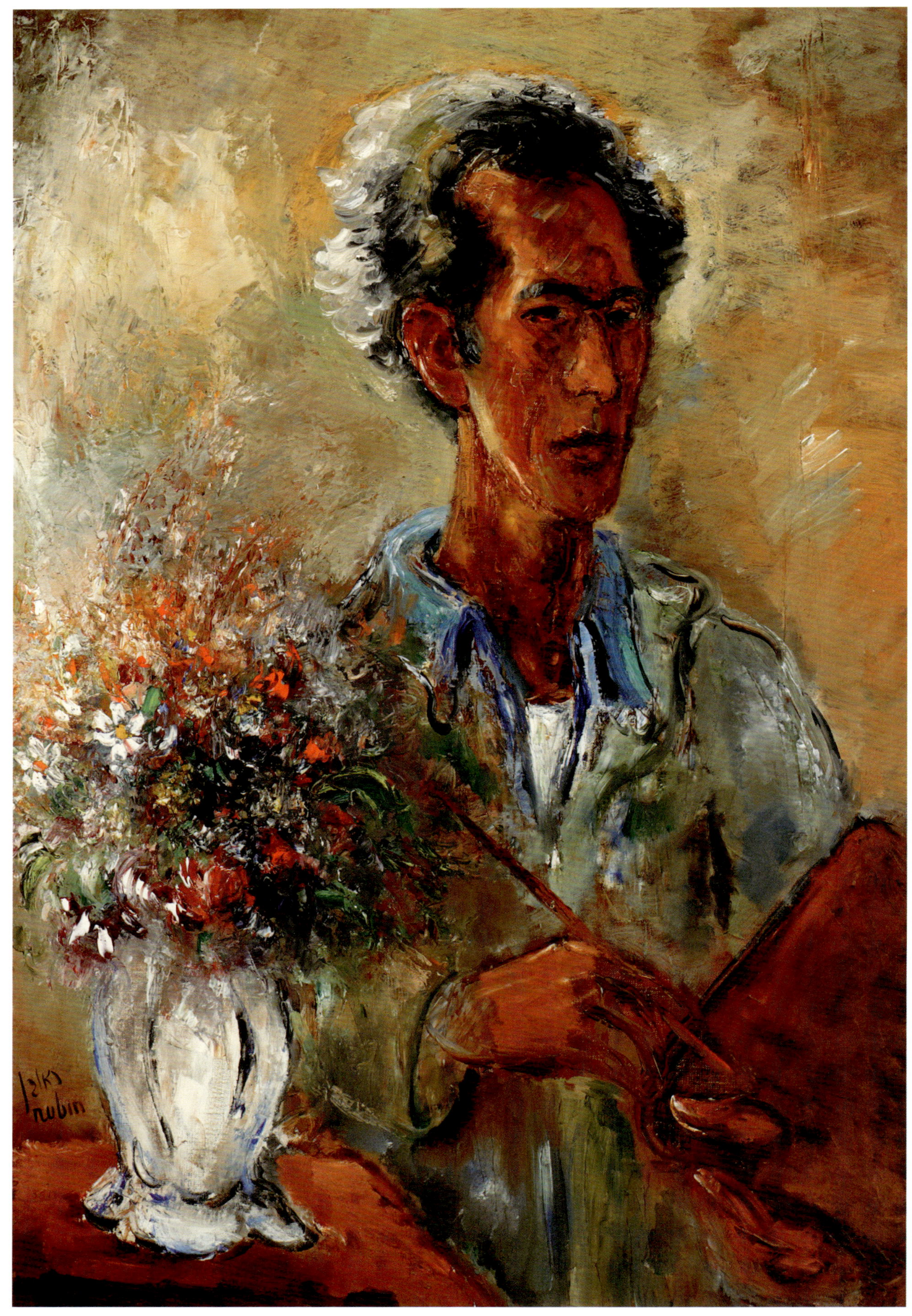
ראובן
rubin

Self-portrait, 1937

REUVEN RUBIN
(1893 Galati, Romania – Tel Aviv, Israel 1974)

Oil on canvas
91 × 63.5 cm
Signed (lower left) in English
and Hebrew 'Rubin'

Ben Uri Collection
Purchased

SELECTED EXHIBITION HISTORY
Arthur Tooth & Sons Ltd, London,
1938; *Opening Exhibition*, Ben Uri,
London, 1944; The Rubin House, Tel
Aviv, 1993; *Apocalypse*, Osborne
Samuel, London, 2010; Christie's
Reuven Rubin survey, London, 2013

Reuven Rubin was born in Romania in 1893 and studied at the Bezalel Academy of Arts and Design, Jerusalem in 1912 and afterwards in Paris and Italy. He returned to Romania from 1916–19. In 1921 he travelled to America, where his development so impressed Alfred Stieglitz, the photographer, publisher, dealer and pioneer of modern art in America, that he arranged an exhibition of Rubin's work at the Anderson Gallery, New York in 1922.

Rubin settled in Palestine in 1922 setting up a studio in Tel Aviv, where he developed a new naïve style and bold palette which reflected the optimism of the young Jewish community. In 1923 he moved to Palestine and worked on stage and costume designs for *Habimah* and other theatrical companies, co-founding the Association of Painters and Sculptors of Palestine in 1924. In the 1920s he and Nahum Gutman (also represented in the Ben Uri Collection) were among a group of young pioneering artists who painted works celebrating the renewed fertility of the land. Rubin also painted the Jewish figures of Safed and Jerusalem, local flowers, fruits and lyrical Palestinian landscapes. Between 1948 and 1950 he served as the first official Israeli diplomatic envoy (minister) to Romania. His autobiography, *My Life – My Art*, was published in 1969.

The Rubin House, Tel Aviv houses a collection of the artist's paintings. This fine self-portrait from the late thirties, employing a bold handling and a colourful palette, was exhibited there in 1993 and was a highlight of the Christie's *Reuben Ruvin Survey* held in March 2013 to celebrate the 120th anniversary of the artist's birth and the 30th anniversary of the Rubin House. It shows Rubin displaying a painterly style and returning to greater realism following a decade in which he had been strongly influenced by the School of Paris, particularly Modigliani, and, during the early thirties the naïve style of Henri Rousseau.

The Interrogation, 1938

GEORGE GROSZ

(1893 Berlin, Germany – 1959 Berlin, Germany)

Watercolour and ink on paper
46 × 59 cm
Signed l/r: *grosz*
Inscribed in Berlin dialect: 'un kannste uns ma wat komisches vortanzen Jenosse, det haste doch so scheen in Moskau jelernt'/ 'And, can't you dance something entertaining for us comrade, you learned this so beautifully in Moscow, indeed'

Ben Uri Collection
Acquired in 2010 with the assistance of the Art Fund, the MLA/V&A Purchase Grant Fund, Sir Michael and Lady Morven Heller, Judit and George Weisz, Agnes and Edward Lee, and The Montgomery Gallery, San Francisco

By 1938 the satirical artist George Grosz was in exile in New York, having fled days before Hitler's accession to power in order to escape prosecution. Grosz had trained at the Dresden Academy and later at the school of the Museum of Decorative Arts in Berlin, but was also greatly influenced by graphic artists including William Hogarth and Honore Daumier and by popular art forms including grafitti. From 1916 he began to paint in oils and his lithographs featured regularly in books and magazines. He served twice during the First World War (the first time as a volunteer), and was twice discharged for medical reasons. This experience only sharpened his political conscience resulting in a series of bitingly satirical works that were particularly critical of militarism, corruption and hypocrisy. A prominent member of the Dada movement, he also became the leading exponent of the *Neue Sachlichkiet* (New Objectivity) movement and established an international reputation that led to an invitation to teach in New York.

In *Interrogation*, the second of the two works in the Ben Uri collection referencing the murder of Grosz's friend, the writer and anarchist Erich Mühsam, the artist depicts the scene with characteristic savagery underlined by the casually brutal attitude of the torturers and the free-flowing blood. The work may also reference the experience of another friend, Dr. Hans Borchardt, who had been imprisoned in Dachau and Sachsenhausen before escaping. The drawing also relates thematically and compositionally to a number of Grosz's works from the 1930s, including *After the Questioning* (also known as *They Couldn't Get Anything More Out of Him*), a watercolour in which a prisoner is shown being dragged from a room. The German-American philosopher Hannah Arendt later observed that Grosz's cartoons 'seemed to us not satires but realistic reportage: we knew those types, they were all around us'. The composition and iconography also invoke comparison with Piero della Francesca's *Flagellation of Christ*, underlining Mühsam's martyrdom. Yet although his face is recognizable in a number of these works, Mühsam's name never appears: as Juergin M Judin has observed, 'For him, the fate of Erich Mühsam represented the fate of all victims of the Nazi regime'. Both these works are part of a larger disturbing series commemorating the writer, five of which (including a version of *Interrogation*) were included in Grosz's final political portfolio, *Interregnum*, published in America in 1936.

This work, together with its companion piece, was unveiled at a special ceremony at Ben Uri on 30 January 2013 marking the 80th anniversary of Hitler's accession to the Chancellorship of Germany and the donation to the museum of *The Lecture* (cat. 29) by Sally, Richard and Andrew Kalman in memory of their late father, Andras Kalman (1919–2007), a Hungarian émigré who came to the UK to study in 1939, later founding the Krane Calman Gallery, and whose own immediate family perished in the Holocaust.

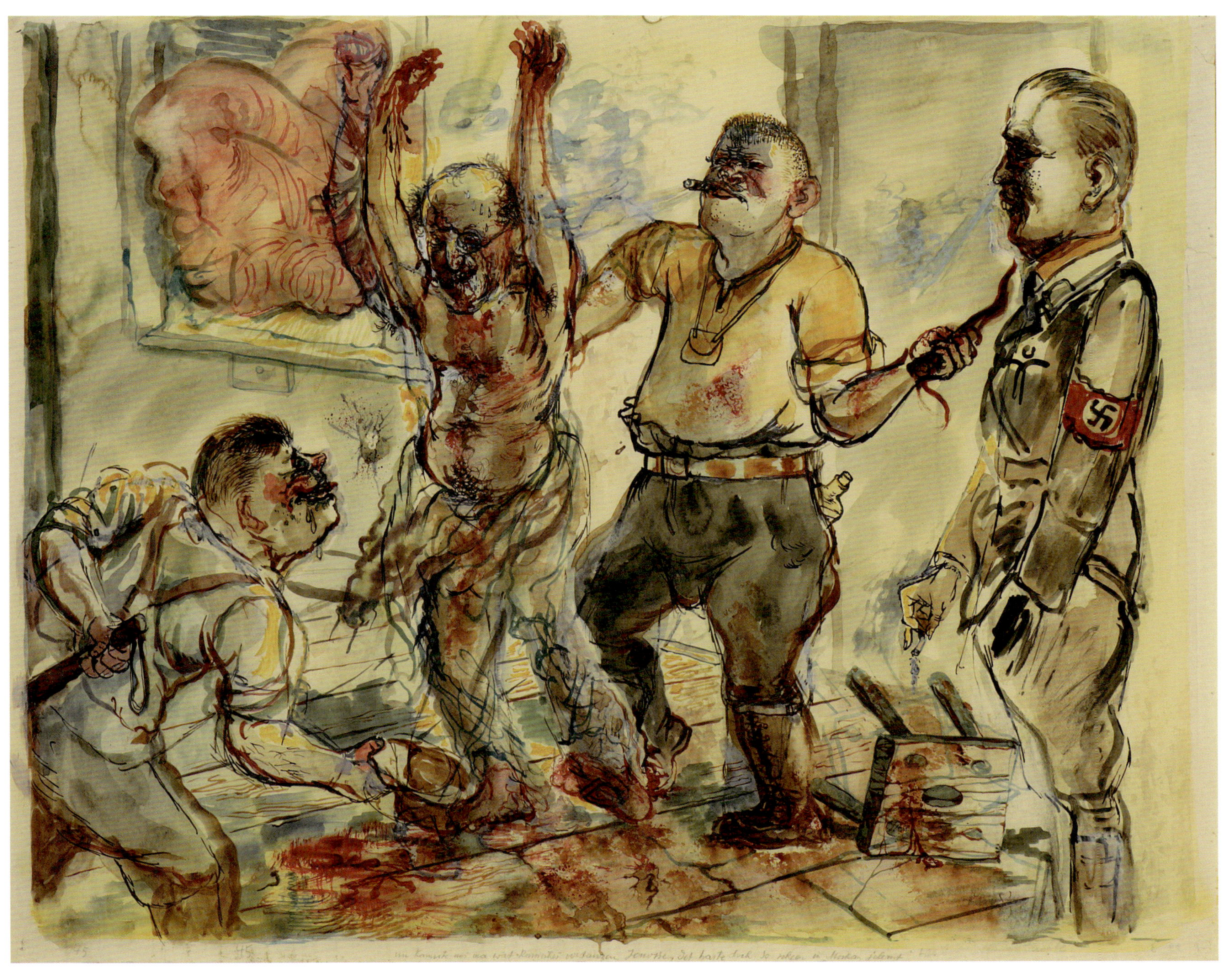

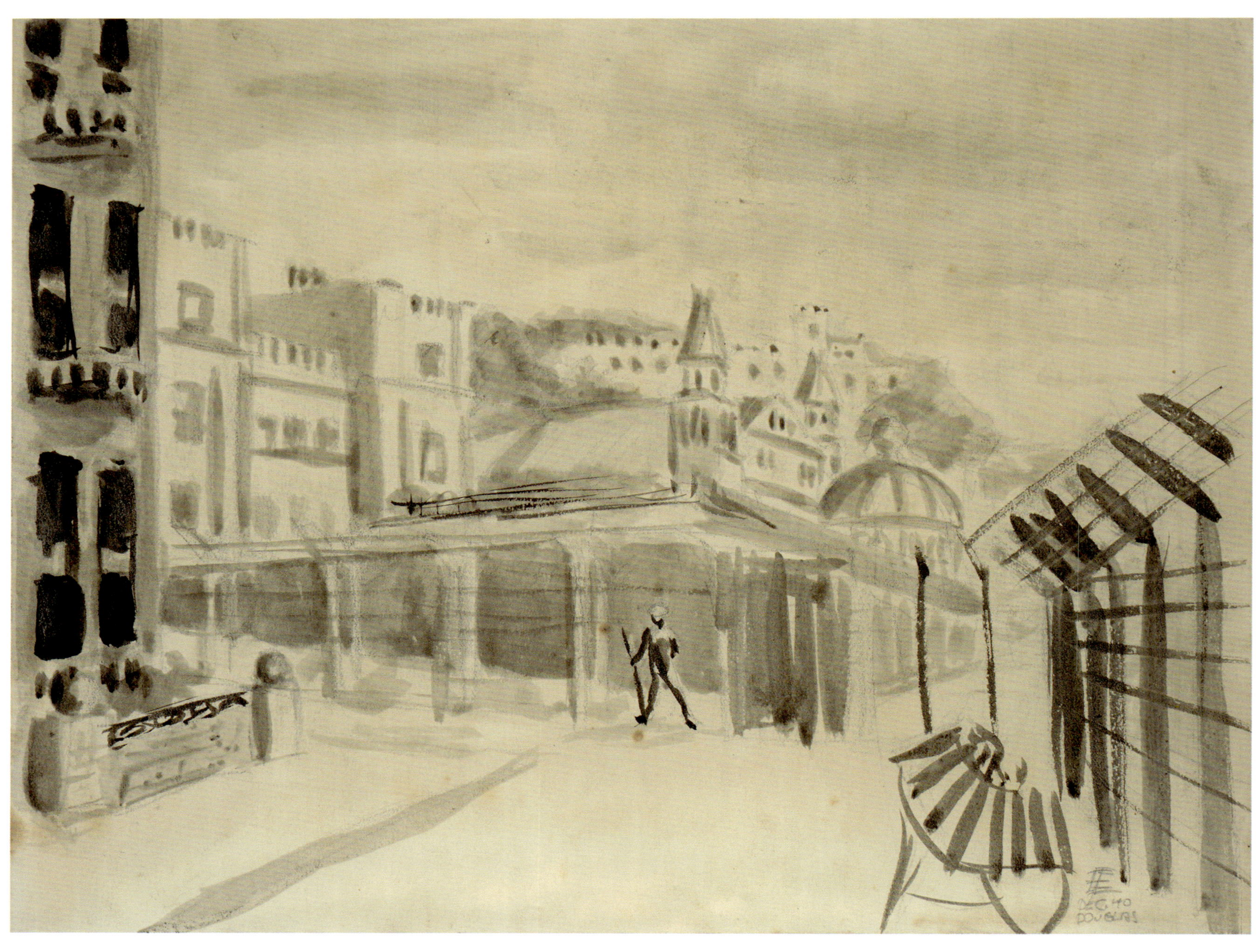

34

Commemorative piece with 29 signatures, 1940
Verso: Internment in Douglas, 1940

ERNST EISENMAYER

(b. 1920 Vienna, Austria – lives Austria)

Watercolour, graphite, pen and
ink on paper
30.3 × 22.8 cm

Ben Uri Collection
Purchased and presented by David
and Eva Wertheim, 2013

FOOTNOTES

1   See Jennifer Powell and Jutta
Vinzent, *Art and Migration Art Works
by Refugee Artists from Nazi Germany
in Britain* (Birmingham: George Bell
Institute, 2005), p. 7.

2   Category A ('dangerous enemy
aliens), category B ('friendly enemy
aliens') and category C ('friendly aliens
and refugees from Nazi oppression');
most Jewish refugees fell into B and C
categories; most artists into C.

3   At its peak, in August 1940, the
Isle of Man was home to *c*.14, 000
men, women and children in eleven
separate camps. Most men were
housed in the Douglas area, which
comprised Hutchinson, Onchan,
Palace, Metropole, Central
Promenade, Sefton, Granville and
Falcon Cliff Hospital, together with
Peveril Camp in Peel, and Mooragh
Camp, Ramsey. Around 1,000 women
were housed in Port Erin, and a
further 3,000 in Port St. Mary, which
together made up Rushen Camp.

Between 1933 and 1945 whether for religious, political or artistic reasons, over 300 painters, sculptors and graphic artists fled into exile or immigrated to Britain during the period of National Socialism in Europe.[1] Following Hitler's appointment as Chancellor in January 1933 and the foundation of the *Reichskulturkammer* (the Reich Chamber of Culture) – to which all professional artists and designers had to belong – all Jews, Communists, Social Democrats and 'avant-garde' artists were effectively banned from working in Germany.

Following the outbreak of war in September 1939, attitudes towards German-speaking émigrés in Britain hardened. Home Office tribunals re-categorised refugees,[2] and in response to Churchill's order to 'collar the lot', transit and internment camps were established on the mainland, the Isle of Man[3] and across the Commonwealth. Eisenmayer, a 19-year-old Jewish refugee fleeing Nazi persecution, had just reached England after being released from Dachau concentration camp, where he had been imprisoned for repeated attempts to escape from Nazi-controlled Austria. Like many so-called 'enemy aliens', he was then interned on the Isle of Man.

After Dachau, Eisenmeyer recalled that captivity in British hands was 'at times, a bit of a lark', with trips to the cinema, football matches, a choir and a camp 'university' offering art classes. For artists, continuing professional practice was certainly possible. Admirably resourceful, they dug up clay for sculpture, ground brick dust with linseed oil or olive oil from sardine cans to make paint, saved brown parcel paper and toilet paper for drawing, and pulled up lino for linocuts which were run through a mangle. Sitters were readily available amongst fellow internees; the most notable portraitist was Dadaist, Kurt Schwitters, whose realist paintings are highlights of internment art, contrasting with his *Merz* sculptures, assembled from camp junk, porridge, lino and paint.

Despite Eisenmayer's affirmation: 'I don't go along with the presentation by some artists of the clichéd barbed wire […] We were bloody lucky on the Isle of Man, unlike the millions in German concentration camps', this drawing, accompanied by 29 internees' signatures, commemorating camp friendships, clearly depicts the wire being triumphantly torn apart by a youth, beneath which appear the words 'Jungend Siegende Jungend' ('Youth Victorious Youth'). On the reverse is a topographical view of Douglas camp, a row of seaside boarding houses, guarded and enclosed by wire, with the town's distinctive architecture clearly visible beyond.

After release Eisenmayer moved to London, establishing his reputation as a painter, then from the mid–1960s, as a sculptor, living in Italy for a period from 1976. In 1962 Ben Uri held a solo Eisenmayer exhibition at Berners Street, and his painting *Strip Poker* closed Ben Uri's 2010 exhibition *Forced Journeys* which toured to Douglas and Birkenhead to mark the 70th anniversary of the establishment of the Manx internment camps. His work has recently undergone a critical reassessment.

35

Girl Behind Barbed Wire, *c.*1940

ALFRED LOMNITZ

(1892 Hessen, Germany – 1954 London, England)

Watercolour on paper
36.5 × 27 cm

Ben Uri Collection
Presented by Cyril J. Ross

SELECTED EXHIBITION HISTORY
Forced Journeys, Ben Uri, London;
Douglas, Isle of Man; Birkenhead,
2009–10

During the 1930s a growing number of Germans and Austrians immigrated to Britain, other European countries and the United States, driven both by adverse economic conditions and increasing political and racial persecution under the Nazi regime. By September 1939, the number of German-speaking émigrés in Britain amounted to an estimated 70,000 – among them a significant number of academics, artists and designers.

At the outbreak of war, former German and Austrian citizens resident in Britain were declared 'enemy aliens'. After an initially cautious approach, the fear of invasion and resulting media agitation led to the internment of the majority of male and a number of female 'aliens' during the early summer of 1940. Mainland transit camps were set up, from which internees were transferred to more permanent camps across Britain and the Commonwealth. Huyton, a recently completed housing estate outside Liverpool, temporarily housed artists including Alfred Lomnitz ('Lom'), Martin Bloch (cat. 28), Walter Nessler and Samson Schames.

Lom had worked as a painter and commercial artist prior to leaving Germany in 1933 and continued this dual career in England. Within a year of his release an autobiographical account of his internment was published by Macmillan in 1941, '[…] the first account of life in an English internment camp for aliens', with a striking cover design of a figure silhouetted against coils of barbed wire. The tone of the synopsis and the title itself, *Never Mind, Mr Lom* (apparently the cheery parting given by

Lom's charlady as he was escorted from home by two detectives, leaving behind his mother and schoolboy son), suggests a very British attitude to internment, a condition to be borne stoically and to be turned to its best advantage. Indeed, Lom described Huyton as a place where '[…] every corner of the camp is a potential picture'. Furthemore, '[…] the quietness of life and absence of any external distraction gave a splendid opportunity for more concentrated work than would have been possible in the normal way of life.' Given a room to paint in by the Company Captain, Lom describes making a collapsible easel from salvaged wooden posts and door hinges, using a piece of slate as palette and, at least initially, working with watercolours and cartridge paper brought from home. When the paper ran out he used newspapers to paint on, describing the satisfying effect of applying watercolour over type and images.

Little is known of Lom's career post-internment, though the onset of Parkinson's curtailed his artistic activities. He received particular support from Cyril J. Ross, Ben Uri's treasurer, who provided studio space and employment within his furrier business, Swears & Wells, and bequeathed a number of artworks to Ben Uri following Lom's death in 1954. These include *Girl behind Barbed Wire*, undated but clearly inspired by internment. Ben Uri held a retrospective in 1954, but Lom's reputation remained largely ignored until the 1980s when John Denham, who featured his work in a solo and group show. Ben Uri has 28 works by Lomnitz.

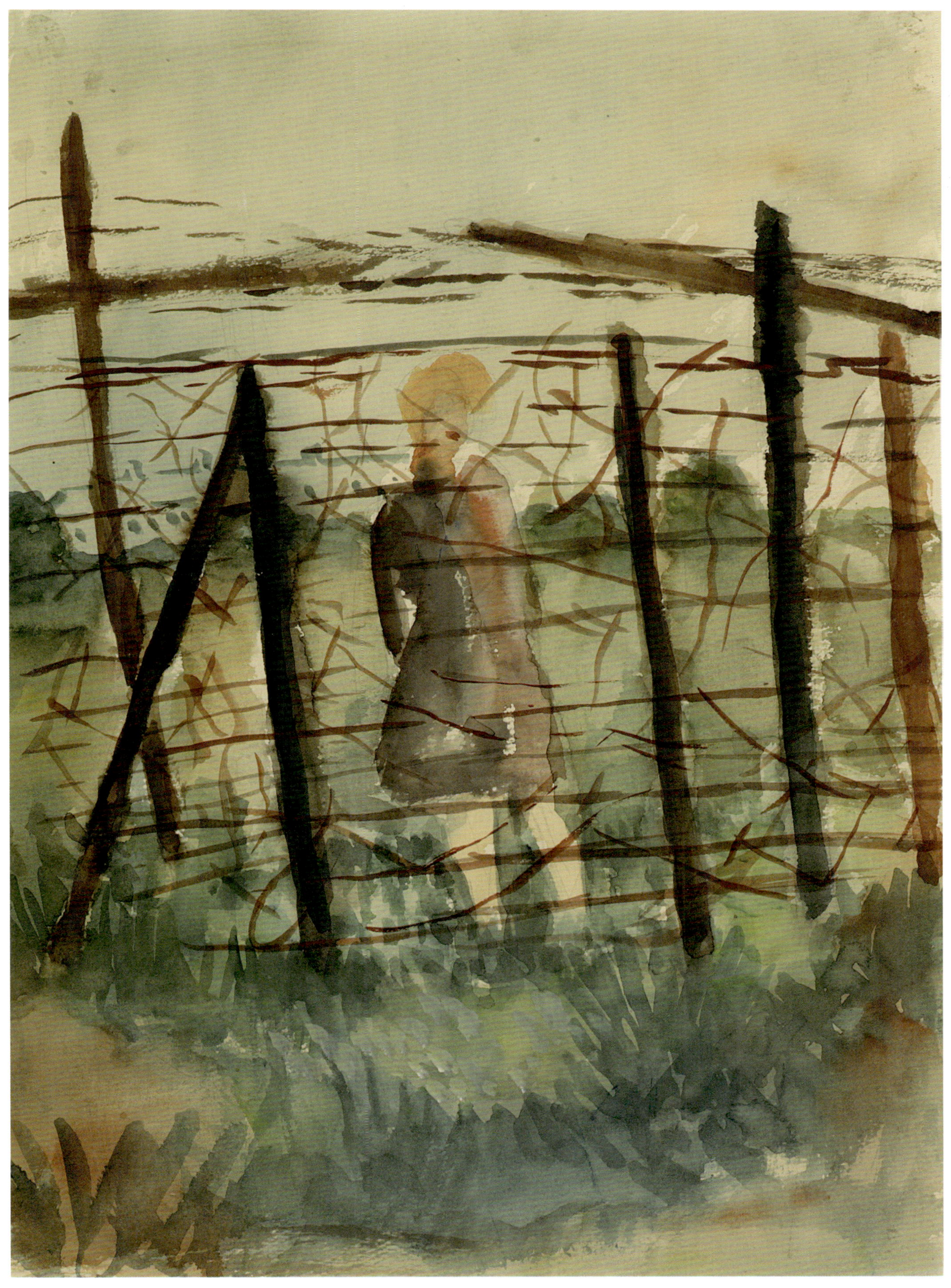

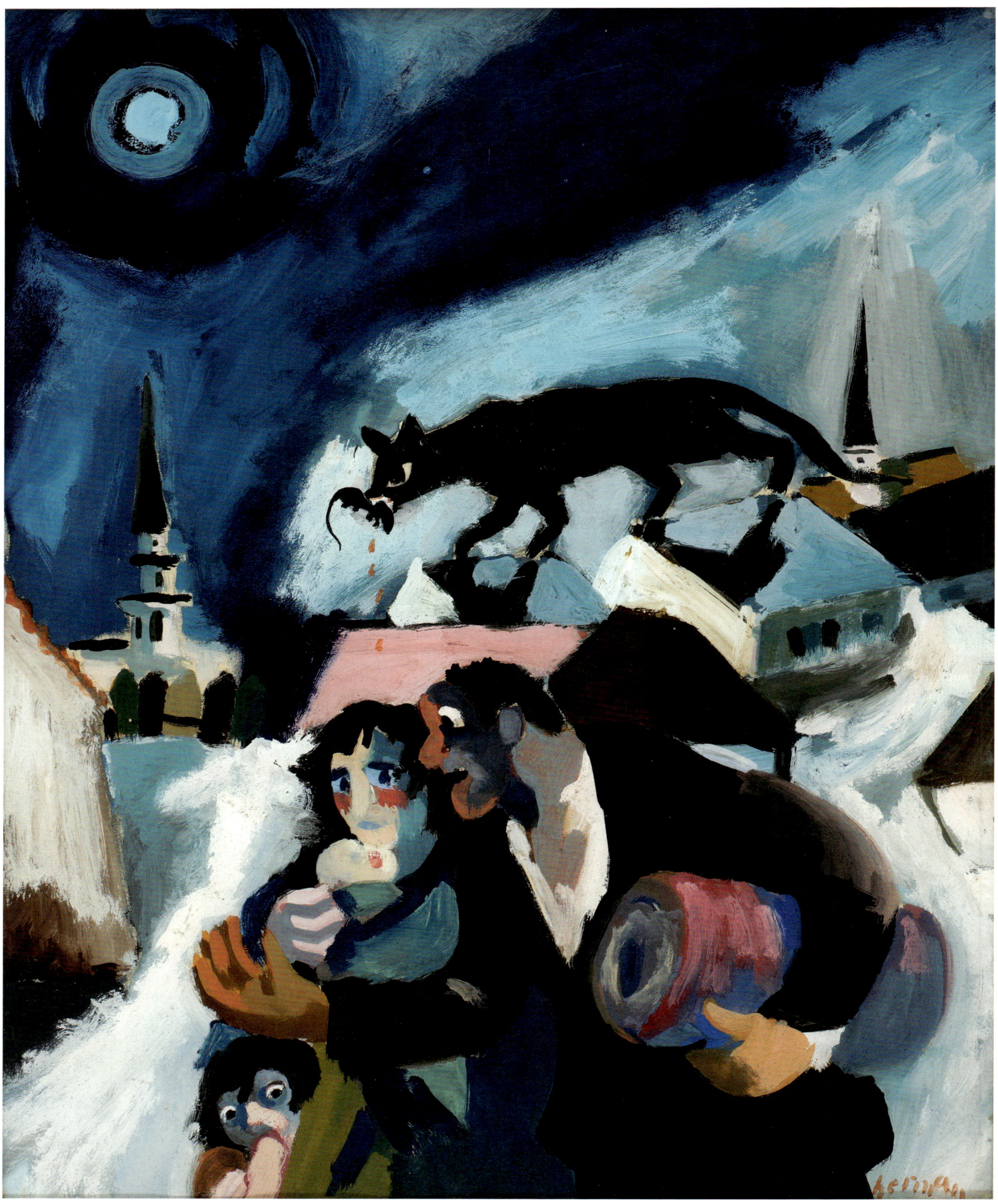

36
Refugees, *c.*1941

JOSEF HERMAN, RA

(1911 Warsaw, Poland – 2000 London, England)

Gouache on paper
47 × 39.5cm
Signed and titled on the reverse
of backing board: 'Refugees by
Josef Herman'

Ben Uri Collection
Purchased with the kind assistance of
the ACE/V&A Purchase Grant Fund
and the Art Fund 2014 via Conor
Macklin of the Grosvenor Gallery

SELECTED EXHIBITION HISTORY
Connell and Sons, Glasgow, 1941;
Aitken Dott, Edinburgh, February-
March 1942; *Cultural Connections: A
Celebration of Scottish-Jewish Art and
Life*, Maclaurin Art Gallery, Ayr, 2013

Josef Herman was born into a poor Jewish working-class family in Warsaw in 1911. He worked as an apprentice typesetter and graphic artist before briefly training at the Warsaw School of Art (1930–32), establishing a life-long interest in portraying working people. He co-founded the left-wing artistic group, 'the Phrygian Bonnet' in 1934. In 1938 amid rising anti-Semitism Herman fled to Brussels (1938–40), then following the German invasion of Belgium in May 1940, he fled again through France and England, settling in Glasgow (1940–43). There, together with Jankel Adler (cat. 22) and sculptor Benno Schotz, he contributed to a remarkable artistic renaissance spearheaded by the Scottish colourist J. D. Fergusson.In October 1941 Herman held his first UK exhibition in Glasgow; reprised in Edinburgh in 1942. In the same year he learned through the Red Cross that his entire family had perished in the Warsaw Ghetto. He had already begun the powerful, nostalgic body of work on Jewish themes, the *Memory of Memories* series, sketched quickly and fluidly from memory or imagination and this now darkened to include works referencing pogroms and the destruction of the Ghetto. In 1943 Herman moved to London, holding his first London exhibition (Reid and Lefevre Gallery) with the then little-known L. S. Lowry, and the 'Memory of Memories' series concluded.

Refugees is a rare, important early painting, thought lost for over 60 years. Herman destroyed the majority of work from this period in 1948, considering it too influenced by Chagall. Blue was the dominant colour of Herman's Glasgow years, used as a nostalgic evocation of a lost Warsaw with its moonlit spires. Like much of Herman's Glasgow work, this painting draws strongly on his eastern European Jewish heritage and themes. However the refugees also represent the wider displacement of peoples uprooted and forced into exile by the upheavals of the Second World War. The family's unknown fate is symbolized by the cat with a mouse dangling from its jaw. The treatment of the figures reflects Herman's admiration for Käthe Kollwitz, while the fearful child with her hand in her mouth is reminiscent of Goya. Ben Uri holds eight works by Herman including the early pen-and-ink sketch *Musicians*, *c.*1940–43 and a portrait drawing of the Yiddish poet, *Avram Stencl*. In 2011 it mounted the largest exhibition to date of Herman's work from this rare period.

During the summer of 1944, on a chance visit to the Welsh mining village of Ystradgynlais Herman experienced an artistic epiphany and made his home among this close-knit, hard-working community for the next 11 years, establishing his reputation with dignified and empathetic portrayals of miners, which remain his best-known works. He held numerous solo and joint exhibitions, including one at Ben Uri with fellow émigré painter, Martin Bloch, in 1949 and another with Lowry and Nehemiah Azaz (Wakefield City Art Gallery, 1955) and retrospectives in London (1956; 1980) and Glasgow (1975). Awarded the OBE in 1981, he was elected a Royal Academician in 1990. Ben Uri holds 10 works by Herman in the Collection

37
Crucifixion, 1942

EMMANUEL LEVY

(1900 Manchester, England – 1986 London, England)

Oil on canvas
102 × 78 cm
Signed and dated (lower right):
'Emmanuel Levy 1942'

Ben Uri Collection
Acquired at Bonhams through the
generous assistance of the members of
the Board of the Uri Gallery 2004

SELECTED EXHIBITION HISTORY
Cross Purposes, Mascalls, Kent; Ben
Uri, London, 2010; *Highlights of the
Ben Uri Collection*, Ben Uri, London,
2007; *Apocalypse*, Osborne Samuel.
London, 2010; *Made in Manchester:
the Art of Emmanuel Levy*, Jewish
Museum Manchester, 2014–15

Emmanuel Levy, like Jacob Kramer (cat. 14), was one of a small group of Jewish artists, whose families, fleeing persecution, restrictive legislation and economic hardship settled in the north of England as part of the wider Jewish migration to Britain at the close of the nineteenth century.

The son of Russian-Jewish immigrants, he was born in Hightown, Manchester, the area immortalized by the Jewish writer Louis Golding in his best-selling novel *Magnolia Street* (1932), which Levy later adapted as a radio play. His father was the beadle at the Great Synagogue, Cheetham Hill and Levy attended the local Jews' Free School, before studying at Manchester School of Art under Adolphe Valette (*c*.1918) together with L. S. Lowry, as well as at St Martin's School of Art in London, and in Paris. He returned to Manchester for his first solo show in 1925. In 1928 Levy was appointed a special instructor in life drawing at Manchester University School of Architecture, recommended by Valette, whom he succeeded, and gave popular public demonstrations in portrait painting. From 1929, for several years, he was Art Critic for *Manchester City News* and the *Evening News*. Indeed, his 60-year career was so closely associated with his native city that Lord Ardwick described him as 'a Manchester man through and through'. But', he continued, 'there is nothing provincial or even distinctly English in his work. He is a citizen of the world'.

Although he experimented with Cubism and Surrealism, Levy abandoned these styles in favour of naturalism, specializing in figurative work exploring the human condition. His *Crucifixion*, a personal protest against Jewish persecution in mainland Europe during the Nazi era, is probably his most powerful work in this genre. Here, Levy has used Christ as a symbol for the suffering of the Jews. From the nineteenth century onwards, Christ had been variously depicted as a preacher, scholar, mystical visitor or a victim of anti-Semitism by Jewish artists, including Maurycy Gottlieb, Wilhelm Wachtel and Marc Chagall. Levy draws on both Jewish and Christian imagery to present Christ as an orthodox Jew with his *Tallit* (prayer shawl) and prayer phylacteries. The label 'Jude' in blood red above and the rows of white crosses (traditionally marking Christian graves) symbolise the many Jews who were being killed at the time. Religious iconography was a dominant theme in Levy's work, and his *Two Rabbis with Scrolls of the Law* (Ben Uri Collection) employs a similar pared-down modern style and bold patterning to illustrate the joyous Jewish festival of *Simchat Torah*. Levy's central theme, however, was always the human condition.

He held six solo exhibitions in Manchester between 1925 and 1963, with further solo shows in London, including at Ben Uri (1953, 1978 and 1989), where his work was also shown from 1935 onwards in numerous group shows. The Ben Uri Collection holds 13 works by Levy including a portrait drawing of fellow Jewish artist Horace Brodzky.

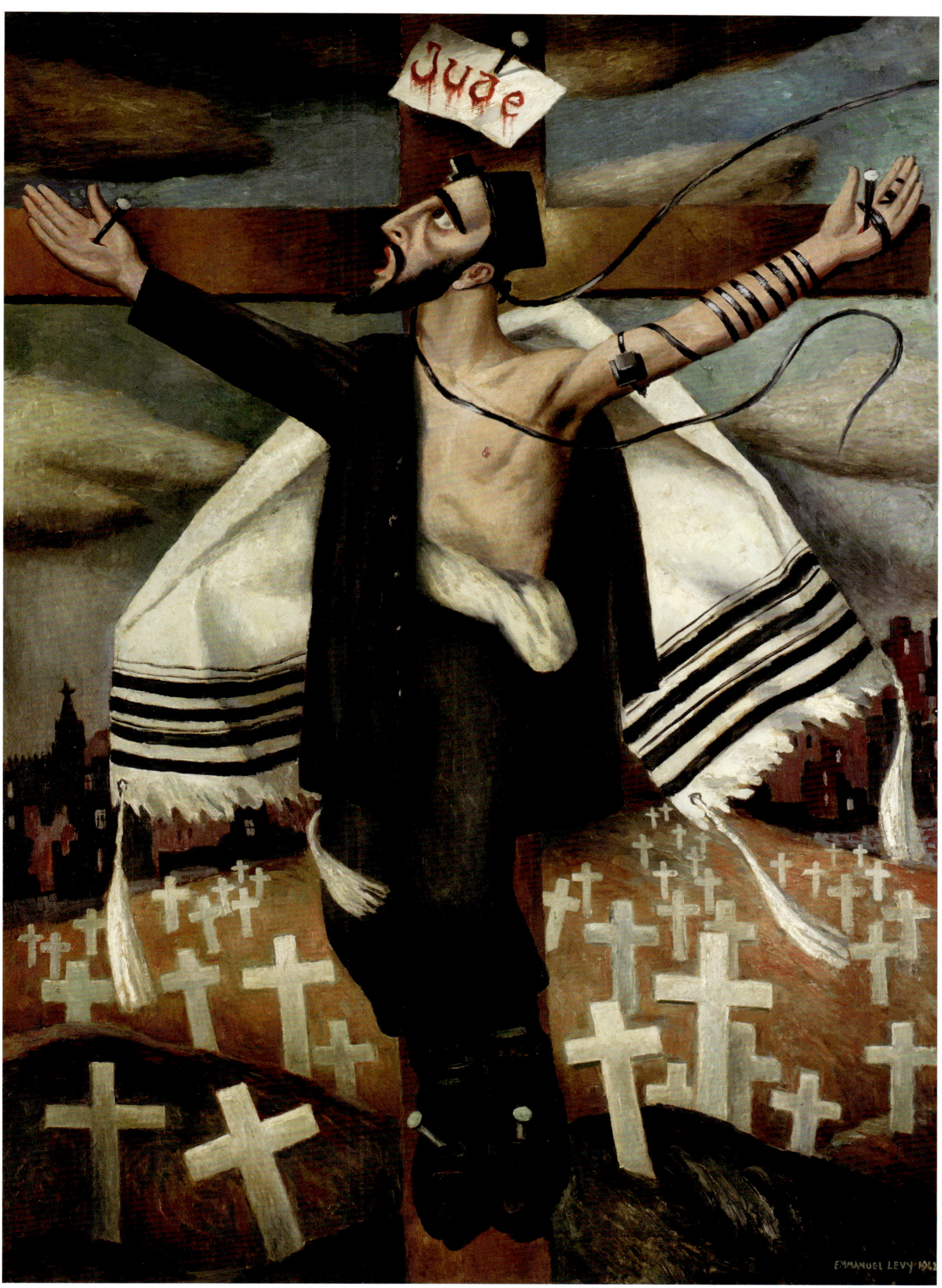
Jude
EMMANUEL LEVY 1942

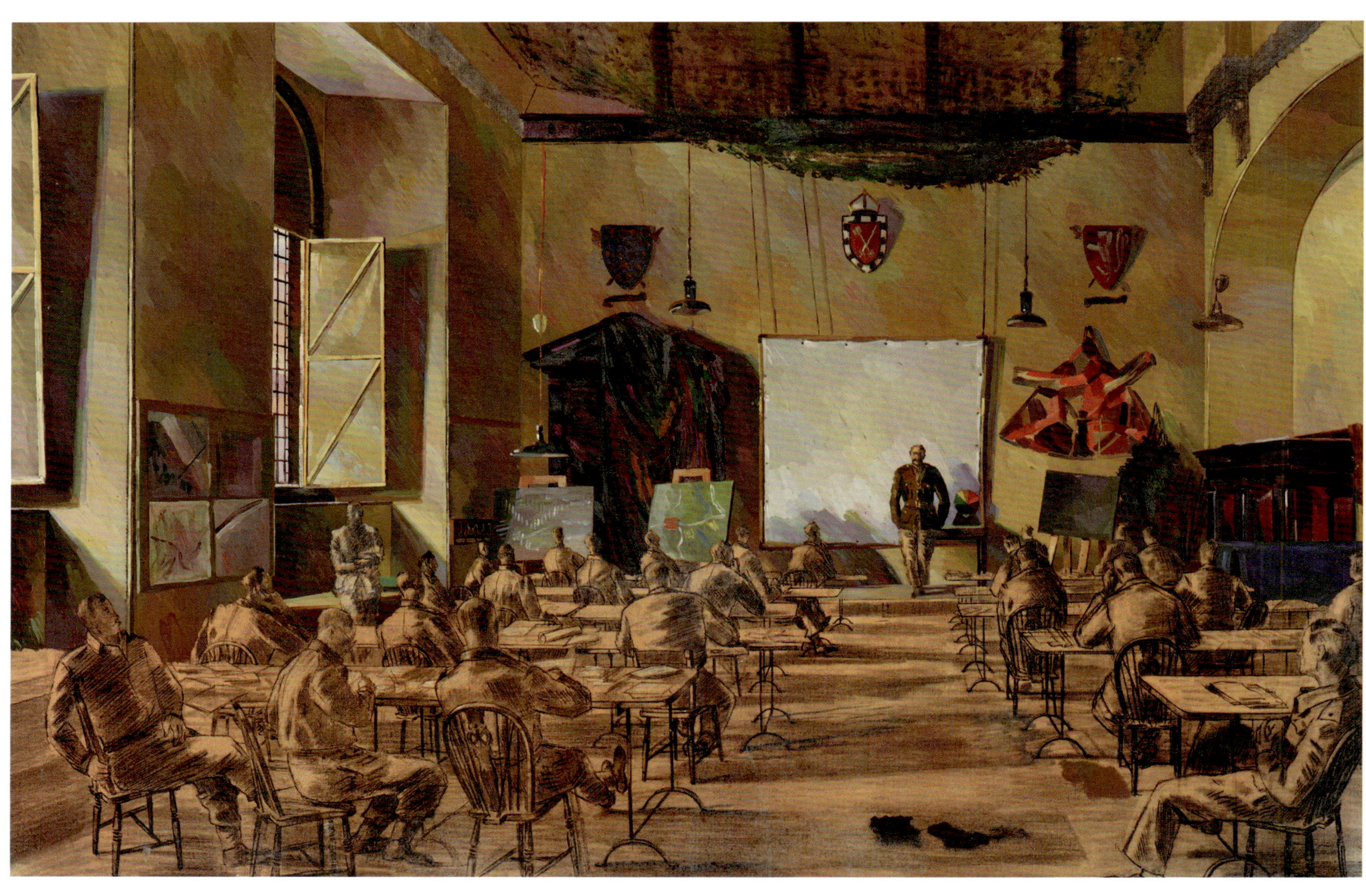

D-Day Preparations / The Briefing, 1944

BARNETT FREEDMAN

(1901 London, England – 1953 London, England)

Oil on canvas
59 × 90 cm

Ben Uri Collection
Presented by the artist's son Vincent
Freedman in 2010

FOOTNOTES
1   Barnett Freedman CBE, 'No
Starving Artists', *Jewish Chronicle*,
18.4.1947, Ben Uri Archive: Loose
Cuttings, 1947–50: PR/02/04.

This unfinished painting was commissioned while Barnett Freedman was working as an Official War Artist during the Second World War and documents Allied preparations for D-Day in the War Room of the Portsmouth Army Base. Freedman was made a War Artist in 1940, serving first with the British Expeditionary Force in France (alongside illustrators Edward Ardizzone and Edward Bawden), and then with the Admiralty until 1946, when he was awarded the CBE for his war work. This included large-scale paintings, portraits of entire ships' crews and a lithograph of the 15-inch Gun Turret in HMS Repulse. After the war, he became a TV and radio personality and was a supporter of Ben Uri, opening the 1946 collection exhibition and addressing an audience in 1947 on the subject of 'The Artist To-day', claiming that 'for the first time in history there was no such thing as a starving artist', either in painting, music or literature.[1] His work was also included in the 1948 Spring exhibition. Freedman was made a Royal Designer for Industry in 1949.

Barnett Freedman was born in London's East End to Russian-Jewish immigrant parents. Between the ages of nine and thirteen, he was confined by ill health to the London Hospital and worked afterwards as a signwriter, stonemason's assistant and architect's assistant, latterly attending evening classes at St. Martin's School of Art. Through the intervention of Sir William Rothenstein he won the London County Council Scholarship and studied at the Royal College of Art (1922–25) under Paul Nash, himself an Official War Artist during

both wars. In 1928 Freedman became a still life instructor at the RCA and later taught at the Ruskin School of Art, Oxford, under Albert Rutherston (Rothenstein's younger brother). He held his first exhibition at the Bloomsbury Bookshop in 1929 and his realist style in this period is linked to that of the Euston Road School. Freedman afterwards became well-known for his commercial illustration and poster work for notable clients, such as the London Underground, and carried out a number of commissions in this post including designing publicity for Shell, the BBC and the General Post Office and Ealing Films. In 1935 he designed the George V Silver Jubilee postage stamp.

Freedman also became a successful and prolific book illustrator and book jacket designer. His illustrations include work for Faber and Faber, such as Siegfried Sassoon's *Memoirs of an Infantry Officer* (1931), The Folio Society, and the Baynard and Curwen Presses. Using pen and chalk for reproduction by line blocks for black and white and auto-lithography for colour, Freedman developed an immediately recognisable style. He also became a distinguished letterer and typographer.

This is one of eight works in the Ben Uri Collection, seven of which were presented by the artist's son, Vincent Freedman, in 2010. A companion piece, *Soldiers in Town*, 1944 (also unfinished) depicts off-duty Allied soldiers walking through a Northern French town. The seemingly relaxed atmosphere with children playing around them perhaps anticipates the end of the war.

Terezin-Theresienstadt (Children on the way to Auschwitz), 1945/66

LEO HAAS

(1901 Opava, Austro-Hungarian Empire – 1983, Berlin, East Germany)

Drypoint and aquatint on paper
24 × 30 cm

Ben Uri Collection
Presented 1987
Selected exhibition history
Graphics, 1966, Ben Uri, London.

FOOTNOTES
1   An exhibition of *Ink and Wash Drawings Done in Terezin Concentration Camp by Bedřich Fritta (1907-1944)* was shown by Ben Uri in 14 Portman Street from 26 September – 5 November 1948.

Leo Haas studied in Karlsruhe and Berlin between 1919 and 1922, influenced by German expressionism and the works of Goya and Lautrec. From 1925–38 he worked in Vienna and Opava as an illustrator, painter and book-designer. He was arrested in 1939 for helping German communists to cross the border illegally and sent into forced labour. In September 1942, Haas was deported to the Theresienstadt (Terezin) ghetto, located in the main fortress of the town in northwest Bohemia.

In advance of a high profile visit by the International Red Cross in June 1944, the ghetto was to be recreated as a so-called 'model' community housing middle-class Jews, and to be used for propaganda purposes by the Nazis. Noted for its rich cultural life, the ghetto falsely presented a positive impression to the visiting delegation which only saw pleasant surroundings, a children's opera, freshly painted, uncrowded accommodation, and fake cafés and shops. In reality, about a quarter of the mainly Czech Jewish inmates died in the terrible conditions and many others were deported to extermination camps in the East.

As an artist, Haas was assigned to the Technical Department to illustrate propaganda material. However, this also enabled him to secretly record the true conditions in the ghetto, creating over 400 drawings inspired by real and terrible events. Following the Red Cross visit, Haas and his fellow artists were accused of smuggling out 'gruesome' art, arrested and tortured. In October 1944 Haas was transported to Auschwitz and a month later to Sachsenhausen, where he was assigned to counterfeiting currency as part of 'Operation Bernhard', a scheme to destabilize the British economy. In February 1945, the counterfeiters were transported to Mathausen and then to Ebensee, where they were finally liberated by the Americans.

After the war, Haas returned to Terezín, where he retrieved some 400 of his hidden artworks. Settling in Prague he worked as a newspaper editor and caricaturist, was reunited with his wife and adopted the son of his friend Bedrich Fritta (also an artist imprisoned in Terezin), who had died in Auschwitz.[1] Haas moved to East Berlin in 1955 as a university art professor and also worked in the film industry.

This powerful and haunting image, one of ten printed after the war using the original plate created during the Holocaust, depicts a scene in which children are led away by an armed guard and a hooded figure, whose faces are obscured and turned away from the viewer. In the background a mass of schematic faces press against barred windows. The contrast in light and deeply etched dark tones adds to the terrifying mood, the small stature of the children emphasised by the large scale of the two adult figures. Their features are hardly individualised, barely distinguished by gender, creating a sense of a generalised horror, even though Haas himself would have experienced these terrible and specific events on a daily basis. Ben Uri holds 10 works by Haas in the Collection. *Yad Vashem* in Jerusalem holds 21 of the artist's portraits.

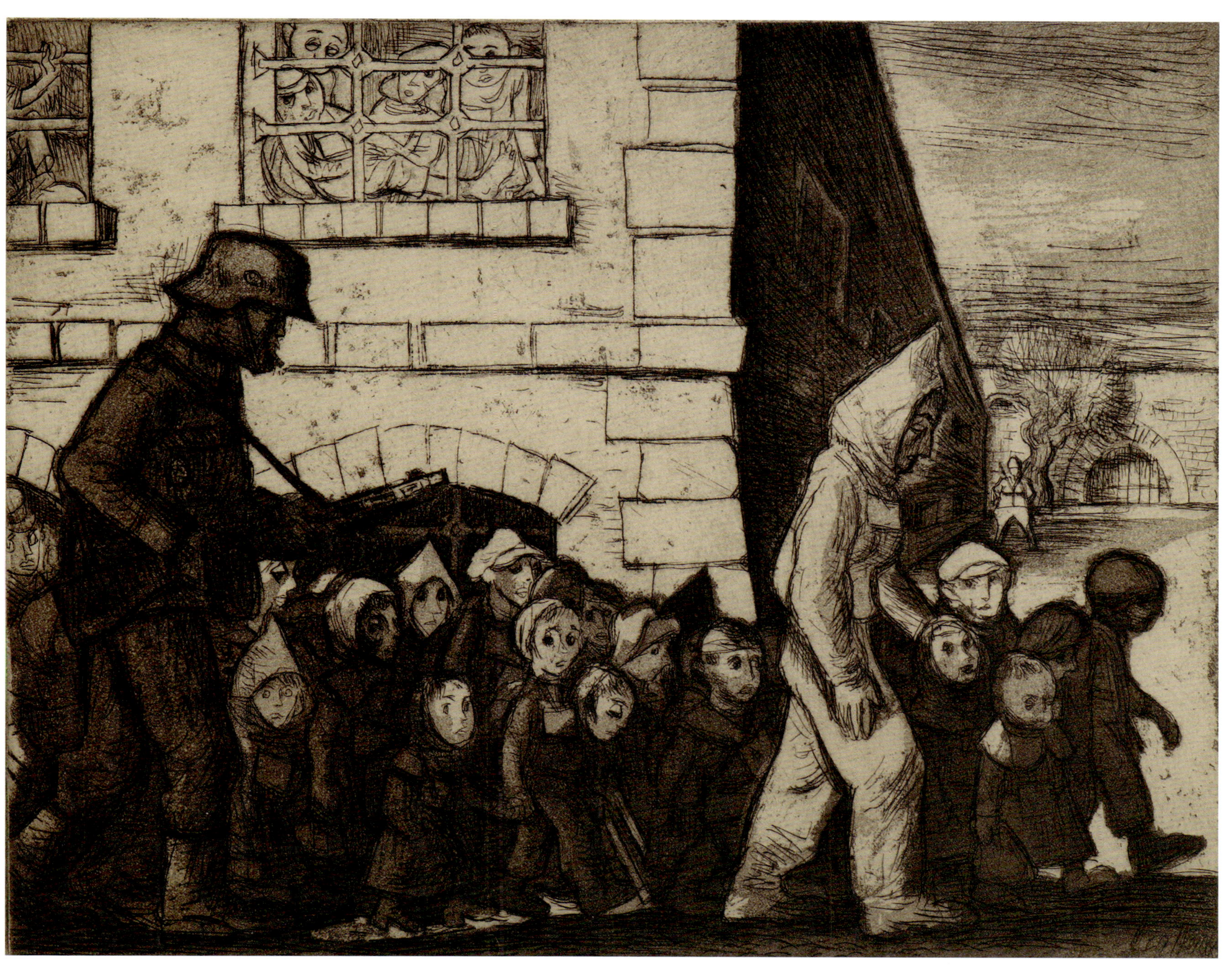

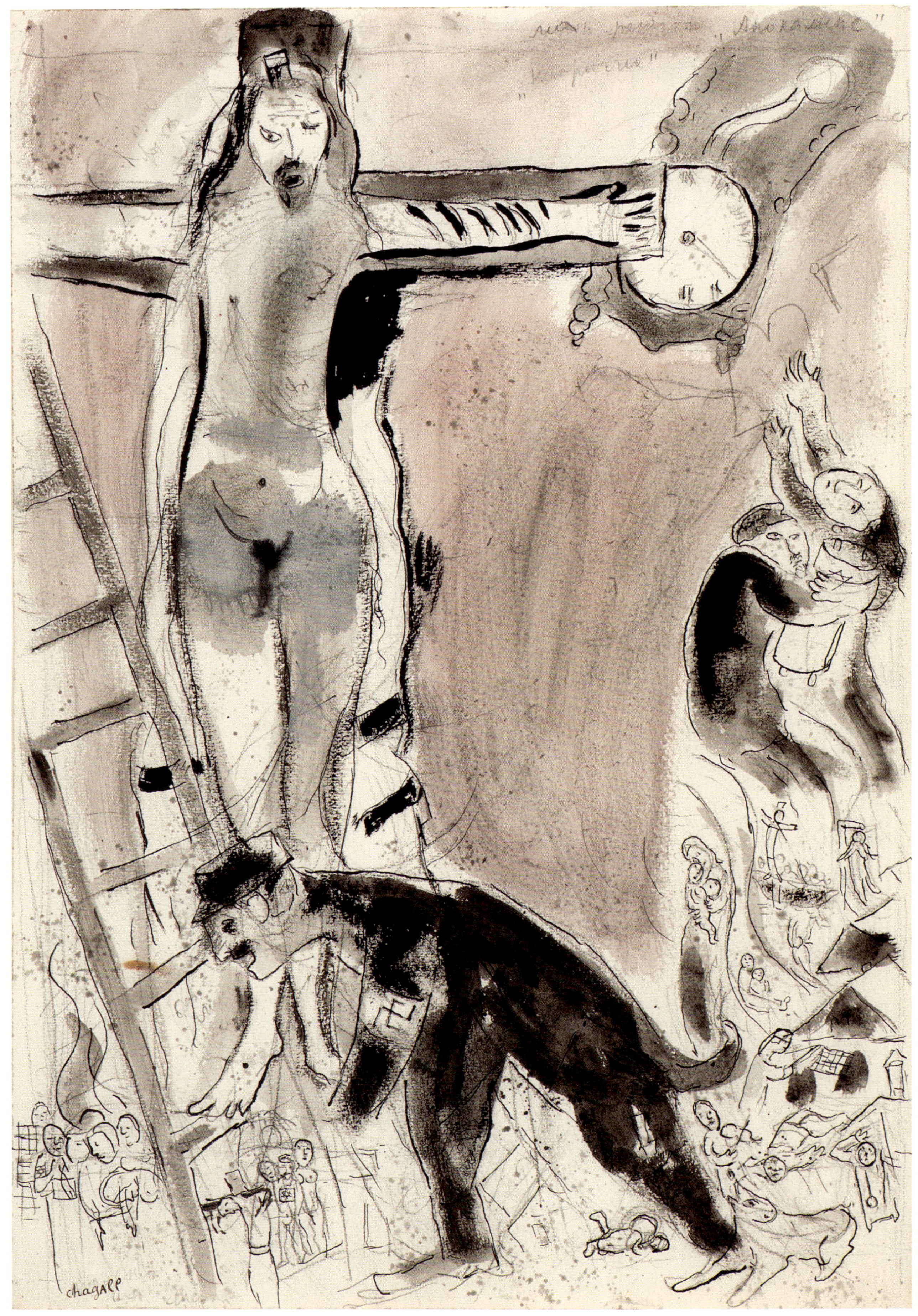

40

Apocalypse en Lilas, Capriccio, 1945

MARC CHAGALL

(1887 Vitebsk, Russia – 1985 Saint Paul de Vence, France)

Gouache, pencil, indian wash ink and indian ink on paper
51.2 × 36.3 cm
Signed (lower left): 'Chagall'

Ben Uri Collection
Acquired in 2009 suppported by Miriam and Richard Borchard, Sir Michael and Lady Morven Heller, and an anonymous donor, and benefitting from the advice of Lionel Pissarro and the Art Fund.

SELECTED EXHIBTION HISTORY
Apocalypse, Osborne Samuel, London, 2010; *From Russia to Paris: Chaïm Soutine and his Contemporaries,* Ben Uri, London, 2012; *Soutine, Chagall and the School of Paris* Manchester Jewish Museum, 2013; *Chagall retrospective*, New York, 2013, Milan, 2014, Brussels, 2015

Chagall was born in 1887 in the town of Vitebsk, Russia (now in Belarus), attending a traditional Jewish school and a Russian high school, before moving to St Petersburg in 1907. There he studied at the Imperial School for the Protection of the Fine Arts, and later at the Zvantseva School, led by Léon Bakst (fig. 16). In 1910, Chagall arrived in Paris, where he settled at La Ruche, meeting Jewish artists including Amedeo Modigliani and key figures in French modernism such as Guillaume Apollinaire and Robert Delaunay. Chagall's first solo exhibition took place at Der Sturm Gallery in Berlin in 1914. That same year, war broke out while Chagall was visiting his family in Russia, preventing his return to Paris. Following the Bolshevik Revolution in 1917, Chagall was appointed Fine Arts Commissar for his home province of Vitebsk, but in 1922 left for Berlin, where his work was published by the periodical *Der Sturm*. He returned to Paris in 1923, becoming a French citizen in 1937 and remaining until 1940

During the Second World War Chagall sought refuge in New York, where a major retrospective was held at The Museum of Modern Art in 1946. In 1948 he returned to France, settling in the south-eastern village of Saint-Paul-de-Vence in 1952. In later life, Chagall produced stained-glass schemes for churches including the chapel at Tudeley, Kent.

This important gouache, ink and pencil study was probably executed in April 1945 during Chagall's exile in New York. It is thought to be the first work he produced following a period of mourning for his late wife, Bella (who had died suddenly in September 1944). Created in direct response to seeing the horrors of the extermination camps revealed through newspapers and Pathé newsreels, Chagall's hermaphrodite Jewish Christ symbolises both male and female victims of the Holocaust. Previously, Chagall's crucifixions had symbolised the Nazi's Jewish victims in order to remind Christians that Christ was a Jew. However, here the artist alludes to the Holocaust for the first time. The clock in the top right of the study is missing a hand, commemorating the start of the apocalypse. Below, a series of complex and horrific scenes uncover the extent of Jewish suffering, among them another crucifixion, a hanging and a boatload of refugees. Chagall revisited the work in 1947 when considering an oil painting on the Apocalypse theme.

One of two works by Chagall in the Ben Uri Collection, *Apocalypse en Lilas, Capriccio* was unveiled at a special exhibition to mark its acquistion, at Osborne Samuel in Mayfair in 2010, with a new text by Chagall expert Professor Ziva Amishai-Maisels. Chagall's work was first exhibited at Ben Uri in 1934 and has since been shown on numerous occasions including *Chagall and his Circle* (2006) and *From Russia to Paris: Chaïm Soutine and his Contemporaries* in 2012, reconfigured as *Soutine, Chagall and the School of Paris* at Manchester Jewish Museum in 2013 simultaneous to the major Chagall show at Tate Liverpool. Most recently, it was loaned to the important Chagall retrospective in, New York (2013), Milan (2014) and Brussels (2015).

41
Chanukiah with Doves, *c*.1949

MOSHE OVED
(Edward Goodack, aka Edward Good, 1885 Poland – 1958 London)

Moshe Oved (aka Edward Good) was an émigré writer, sculptor, and founder of the antique jewellery shop *Cameo Corner*. He left his native Poland in 1903 and settled in London's East End, where he initially worked as a watchmaker. Oved was a founding member of the Ben Uri Society and a great supporter of Yiddish culture, holding an honorary office within Ben Uri from 1915–56 and always maintaining that its main goal should be to collect pictures and open a gallery. The collection in these years was influenced by his taste as he helped to fund and facilitate the acquisition of a number of important early works by artists including Simeon Solomon (cats. 2 and 4), Jacob Kramer (cat. 14), David Bomberg (cat. 16) and Samuel Hirszenberg (cat. 3). Oved was a great character, who presided over *Cameo Corner* in Museum Street in flowing purple robes regaling his customers – among whom Queen Mary was a regular – with well-honed anecdotes – and building a reputation as a recognised authority on cameos, antique watches and clocks. In 1919 David Bomberg produced a limited edition of boldly designed posters advertising 'Cameo Corner', one of which is in Ben Uri's archive collection. Anecdotal evidence suggests that in 1933 Oved sold the Mozaic Faberge Egg to King George V for £250 pounds, possibly as a gift for Queen Mary's birthday.

Oved's first book in Yiddish, *Aroys fun Khaos* (Out of Chaos, 1918), was followed by *Lebns Lide*r (1924). In *Visions and Jewels* (1925), a collection of 124 autobiographical stories and short tales, he wrote about Nahum Sokolow, Max Nordau, Sholem Asch and Jacob Epstein (cat. 19), who all came to speak at Ben Uri, among many others. *The Book of Affinity* (1933) was a deluxe production with original colour lithographs by Epstein; Oved also presented two busts by Epstein, *Professor Samuel Alexander* and *Shulamite Woman* (1935) to the Ben Uri, both in 1947. According to one story, it was while sheltering in the basement of *Cameo Corner* during the Blitz, that Oved first began modelling animal design rings to steady his trembling hands. He took up sculpting at the end of the war in his sixties and created a series of small bronze heads and a number of candlebra to commemorate the victims of the Holocaust. *Chanukiah with Doves* is one of 11 works by Oved in the Ben Uri Collection, which also includes a group of heads, designs for commemorative rings and a highly individual *menorah*. The Collection also includes a fine 1924 *Portrait of Moshe Oved* by fellow Pole Maurice Minkowski (1881–1930).

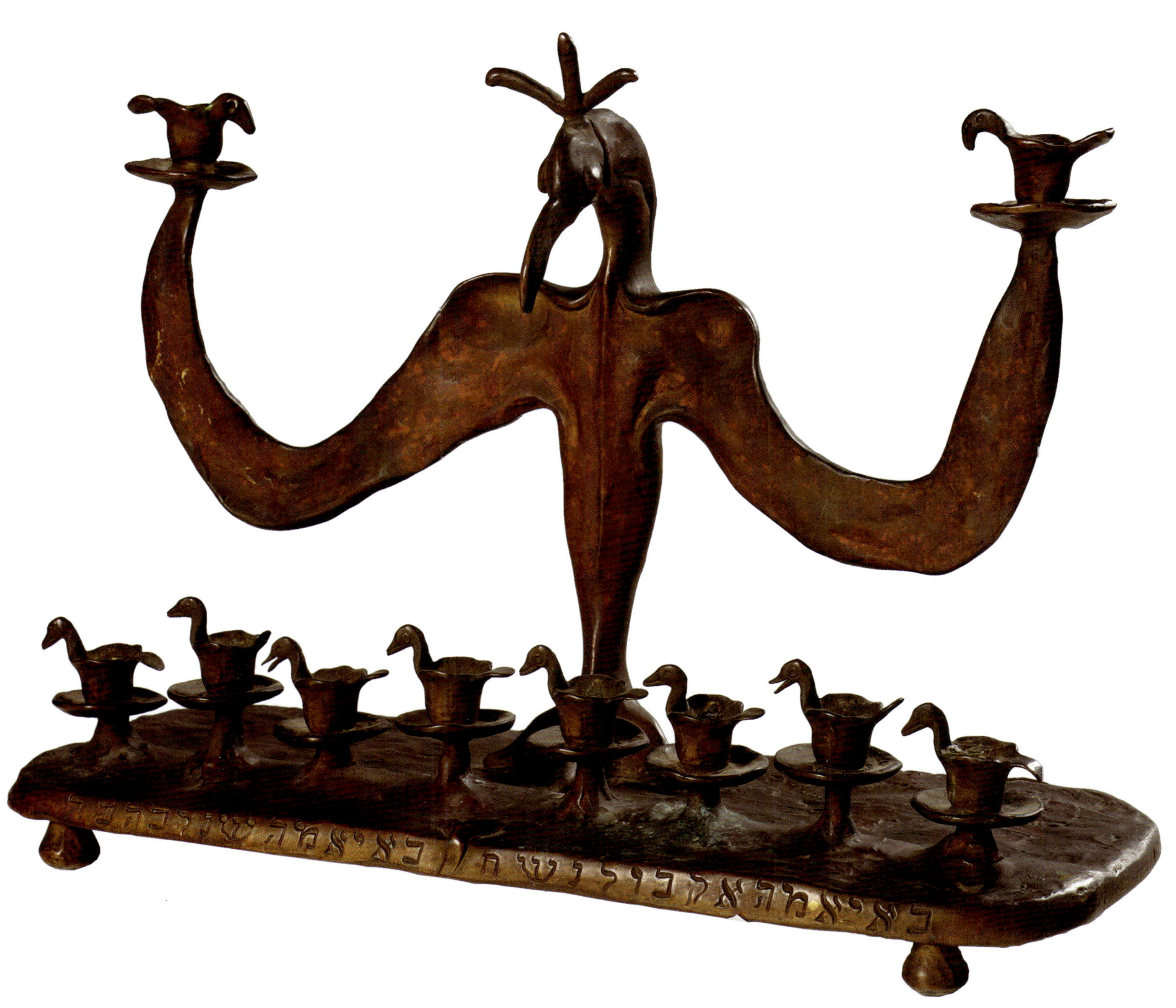

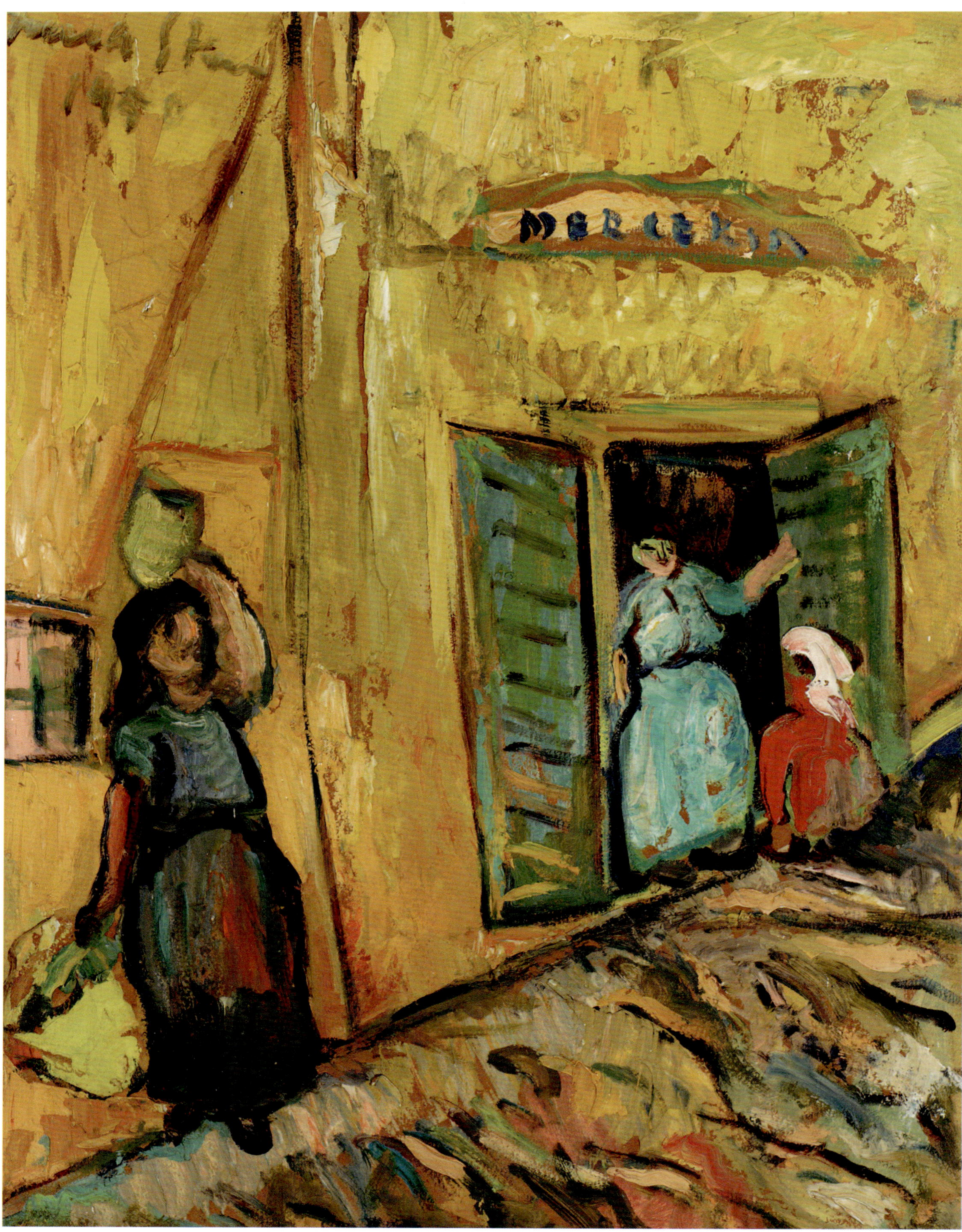

Summer Morning in Madeira (Mediterranean Scene), 1950

IRMA STERN

(1894 Schweitzer-Renecke, South Africa –1966 Cape Town, South Africa)

Oil on board
62 × 49 cm
Signed and dated (upper left):
'Irma Stern 1950'

Ben Uri Collection
Presented by Victor Rubens 1997

SELECTED EXHIBITION HISTORY
Highlights of the Collection, Ben Uri,
London, 2013

Irma Stern was born into a prosperous German-Jewish family in 1894 in the Transvaal in South Africa. The family retained strong ties with Berlin and its artistic culture, moving often between Germany and South Africa during her childhood. She later moved to Germany, where she studied art from 1913–20 associating with the Expressionists, particularly Max Pechstein, who mentored her. Her work was included in the Secessionist exhibitions of 1918 and 1920 and she was a founder member of the *Novembergruppe*. In May 1919 Pechstein helped arrange her first exhibition of 33 drawings at the Fritz Gurlitt Gallery, Berlin. Stern returned to South Africa in 1920, holding her first exhibition of self-styled 'modern art' in Cape Town in 1922. Her adherence to Expressionism, a strong but limited colour palette and exuberant, vigorous style together with her celebration of so-called 'primitive' African subjects was poorly received by provincial Colonial Cape Town society and the police were called after complaints of indecency. Nevertheless, Stern continued to create a large body of highly individualistic and forceful works on her wide travels throughout Africa and Europe and became a leading figure in modern South African painting. During the era of National Socialism she broke all ties with Germany, principally travelling in East Africa during the 1940s. Her wide circle of friends included the South African Yiddish writers Rakhmiel (Richard) Feldman (1897–1968) and Dovid Fram (1903–1988).

However Stern's celebrations of the natural African landscape and its people were actually carefully constructed, since she painted in the reserves, selecting her subjects and removing from them any sign of encroaching western civilization. Her love of the decorative also extended to an appreciation of textiles and she became a major collector of cultural artefacts, including oriental ceramics and African sculptures, which she displayed in her home and brought into her art. She often used fragments of Zanzibar doors to frame her paintings.

Summer Morning in Madeira is part of a late body of picturesque subjects which include harbours, markets, flower sellers, and harvest scenes across the Mediterranean and South Africa, in which Stern embraced a rich and sensual palette and painted in a somewhat looser, flatter style. Although as a colourist, Stern predominantly used oils, she also produced thousands of drawings, graphic works and monotypes, sculptures and ceramics, as well as writing and illustrating travel books inspired by her trips to Zanzibar and the Congo. Supported by her parents for much of her life, Stern did not rely on picture sales. Her marriage to her former tutor Johannes Prinz (1886–1942) in 1926 ended in divorce eight years later. After her death her Cape Town home became a museum housing her paintings and drawings as well as her collection of European, African and South American art.

Nude Standing, 1954

FRANK AUERBACH

(1931 Berlin, Germany – lives London, England)

Crayon on paper
55 × 37.6 cm
Signed and dated (lower left):
'Auerbach June 1954'

Ben Uri Collection

SELECTED EXHIBITION HISTORY
The Inspiration of Decadence, Ben Uri,
London, 2012

FOOTNOTES
1   *Twelve Contemporary Artists:
Archibald Ziegler, Alfred Harris, Claude
Rogers, Jacob Bornfriend, Morris
Kestelman, Frank Auerbach, John
Coplans, Kalman Kemeny, Josef
Herman, Alfred Daniels, Henry
Inlander, Fred Feigl* was held at Ben
Uri at 14 Portman Street, W1 from
7–28 July, 1958.

Born in Berlin in 1931 to an assimilated Jewish family, Frank Auerbach was sent to England for his own safety in 1939 and never saw his parents again. He attended Bunce Court, a co-educational boarding school at Lenham, near Faversham, Kent (relocated to Shropshire from 1940–45), founded by Anna Essinger, a German-Jewish educator influenced by Quaker principles, and staffed mainly by German-speaking refugees. It was here that he first exhibited his talent for drawing.

Afterwards, Auerbach settled in London and on the recommendation of the artist Archibald Ziegler (one-time chairman of the Ben Uri Arts Committee, whose wife had taught at Bunce Court) enrolled at St. Martin's School of Art (1948–52), where he met Leon Kossoff (cat. 45). Both joined the radical and 'exceptionally free' evening classes held by David Bomberg (cats. 9, 16 and 30) at the Borough Polytechnic (until 1954) and worked together capturing the devastated cityscape of postwar London. Auerbach also studied at the Royal College of Art, graduating in 1955 with a silver medal and first-class honours. His *Standing Female Nude*, c.1954, is one of two early art school life drawings (probably using the same model) in the Ben Uri Collection, which were almost certainly carried out at the Royal College and show the beginnings of Auerbach's distinctive vigorous and heavily worked style.

Auerbach had his first exhibition with Helen Lessore of the Beaux Arts Gallery in 1956, showing in a group show at Ben Uri in 1958[1], and taught, first at secondary schools, then, until 1968, one day a week at various art colleges, including the Slade. Auerbach has been represented by Marlborough Fine Art since 1965. He was included in 1976 in the group exhibition, *The Human Clay*, at the Hayward Gallery, organized by R. B. Kitaj, followed two years later by his inaugural retrospective sponsored by the Arts Council. He represented Britain at the Venice Biennale in 1986, winning the Golden Lion award jointly with Sigmar Polke. He has since exhibited widely in Europe, the USA and Australia.

Ben Uri holds 11 works by Auerbach including seven etchings of heads of his 'family' of familiar sitters ranging in date from 1985–90 and donated by the artist. Ben Uri has exhibited Auerbach's work in more than a dozen group exhibitions, either at the gallery or as loans, between 1956 and 2015.

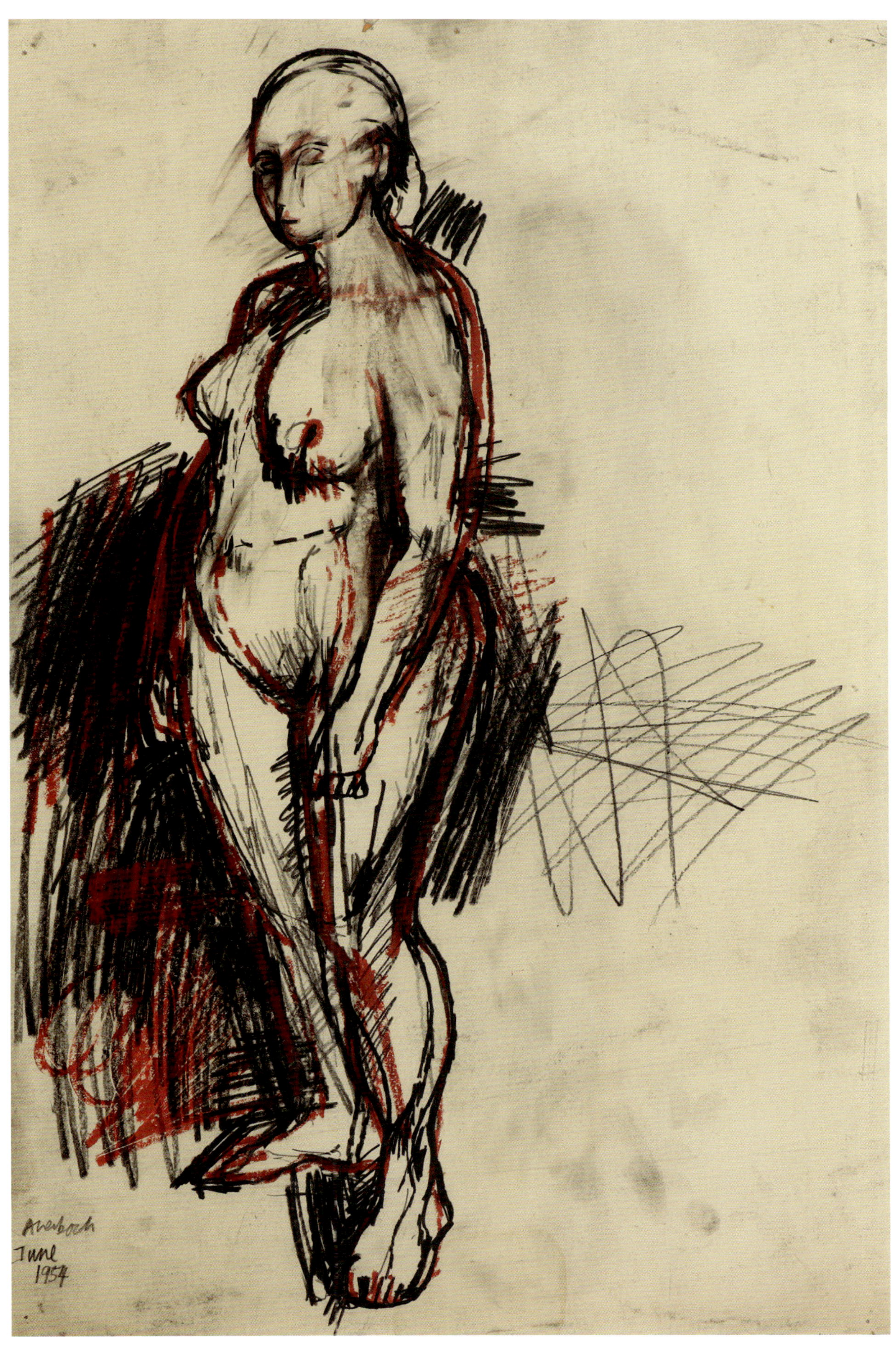

Averbach
June
1954

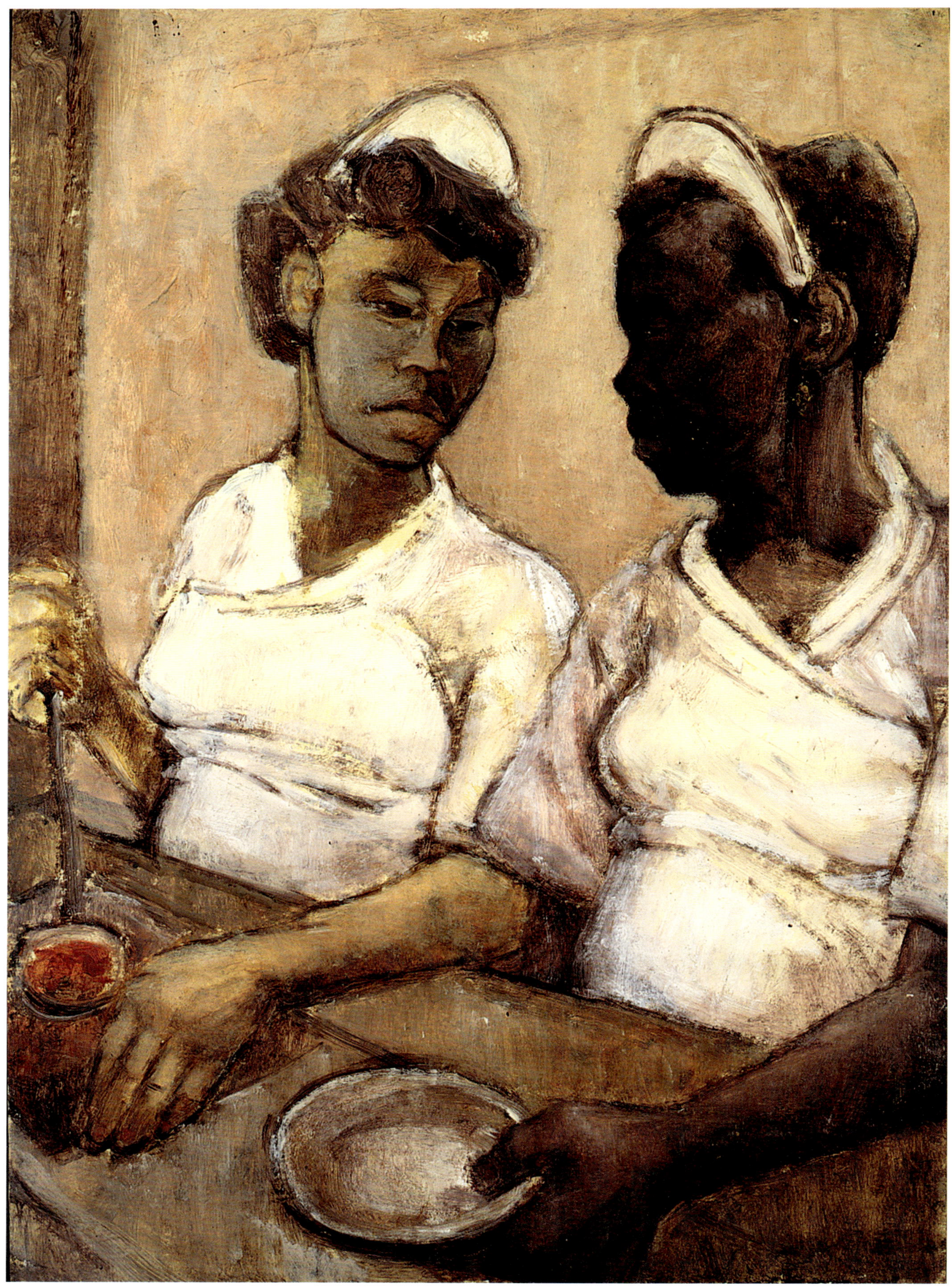

44

West Indian Waitresses, *c.*1955

EVA FRANKFURTHER

(1930, Berlin, Germany – 1959, London, England)

Oil on paper
76 × 55 cm

Ben Uri Collection
Presented by the artist's sister, Beate
Planskoy, 2015

SELECTED EXHIBITION HISTORY
Eva Frankfurther 1930–1959, Boundary
Gallery, London, 2001; *Forced Journeys*,
Ben Uri, London, 2009; *Refiguring the
50s*, Ben Uri, London, 2014-15

Eva Frankfurther was born in Berlin in 1930 into a cultured, assimilated Jewish family and arrived in England with her family in 1939. She studied at St Martin's School of Art (1946–51) alongside Frank Auerbach (cat. 43), Leon Kossoff (cat. 45) and Sheila Fell. In the holidays she travelled extensively in Europe, spent three summers in the USA and later, lived for several months in Israel. After graduating in 1951, disillusioned with the London art scene, she determined to earn her living by other means becoming an evening counter hand and washer-up at Lyons Corner House, Piccadilly, in order to concentrate on painting during the day. 'West Indian, Irish, Cypriot and Pakistani immigrants, English whom the Welfare State had passed by, these were the people amongst whom I lived and made some of my best friends,' she wrote. Employing loose brushwork and dry paint in a restricted palette, sparingly applied, she focuses on faces and postures in both single and small group portraits. Her subjects are observed with empathy and dignity, but rarely smile or engage the viewer. Although clearly modelled on individuals, they also serve as archetypes celebrating the stoicism and dignity of working people. Frankfurther's migrant Corner House workers also document the changing landscape of postwar Britain and provide a link to our own multicultural age. *West Indian Waitresses* further reflects the changes in consumerism that Lyons introduced postwar with self-service cafeterias, where counter staff portioned out standardized food from open *bains-marie* replacing the popular 'nippy' service.

Frankfurther's composition is so carefully arranged that her two waitresses appear to mirror one another: from the crossover tops of their distinctive Lyons uniforms to their outstretched arms and tilted heads with white peaked headdresses inclining toward one another, implying a close personal as well as professional relationship between them. The rose-coloured background is typical of the 'feminine' palette that indicates Frankfurther's instinctive sympathy for women. The strong verticals of the women's bodies and solid horizontals of their beam-like arms form a static framework counterbalanced by a series of strong diagonals. Their gestures are stilled, suggesting a rare quiet moment among the noisy, busy reality of restaurant life. Frankfurther lifts the scene from the frenzy of the everyday, suspending it for our contemplation.

This is one of four works by Frankfurther in the Ben Uri Collection and was shown with *Portrait of a Woman* in the survey exhibition, *Refiguring the 50s: Joan Eardley, Sheila Fell, Eva Frankfurther, Josef Herman and L S Lowry* (2014–15). Two drawings, *Old Woman* and *Elderly Jew of the East End*, also celebrate members of the poor but cohesive Jewish community among whom Frankfurther chose to live, away from her north London home. Frankfurther's work, *Stateless Person*, was included in Ben Uri's 1956 *Tercentenary Exhibition of Contemporary Anglo-Jewish Artists*, among others; and a memorial exhibition for her was held in 1962.

45
Portrait of N. M. Seedo, *c.*1957

LEON KOSSOFF

(1926 London, England – lives London, England)

Charcoal on paper
103 × 71 cm

Ben Uri Collection
Purchased 1987

SELECTED EXHIBITION HISTORY
Uproar, Ben Uri, London, 2013

FOOTNOTES
1 John Berger, 'The Weight', *New Statesman* (19 September 1959), pp. 352–354.

2 Ibid., p. 352.

3 See *1914–1964 Jubilee Exhibition: Fifty Years of British Art* (England: Humphries and Co Ltd., 1964), ill., b and w, fig. 158; see *Leon Kossoff: from the early years, 1957-1967* (New York: Mitchell-Innes & Nash, 2009), no.1, ill., col., p.19.

4 N. M. Seedo, *In the Beginning was Fear* (London: Narod Press, 1964), pp.335–38.

Initially trained at St Martin's School of Art, Kossoff also attended evening classes at Borough Polytechnic (1950–52) under David Bomberg (cats. 9, 16 and 30) with Frank Auerbach (cats. 43 and 57). He graduated from the Royal College of Art in 1956. Kossoff received critical acclaim during the 1960s following his first exhibited work in 1956; the Arts Council and Tate both acquired his work by 1963, when he was elected a London Group member, exhibiting for the third and final time with the Group in 1964. Ben Uri featured his work at this time in a group show with Sandra Blow, Henry Inlander, Helena Markson and Archibald Zeigler, held in spring 1968.

Kossoff has received recognition from the most notable critics of the day, including John Berger, who was impressed early on by the artist's 'shockingly thick' pigment and his '[…] equally heavily worked and very black' drawings,[1] observing that his 'brooding hunched up figures […] fit as tensely in their panels as mediaeval figures in their niches'.[2]

Portrait of N. M. Seedo bears a striking resemblance to *Seated Woman*, a 1957 oil painting, and a charcoal and conté drawing of the same title exhibited in Kossoff's second and third London Group exhibitions.[3] Heavily delineated with fluent thick black marks and depicted in three-quarters profile, N. M. Seedo sits with her hands together, and eyes downcast. The tubular arm-rest that portions off the bottom left corner is a compositional device that recurs in later works.

These three associated works are portraits of émigré Sonia Husid (1906–1985), known by her *nom de plume* N. M. Seedo. Possibly a distant relative of Kossoff's, she was an important model for the artist in this period. Seedo refers to their friendship in her semi-autobiographical account, *In the Beginning was Fear* (1964),[4] which also movingly describes her experiences of pogroms, fear and loss in Romania.

Seedo was also known in her own right in Britain as a Yiddishist. Born in Bessarabia and educated in Vienna, she was a member of the socialist Zionist youth group *Hashomer Hatzair* and the (then illegal) Romanian Communist Party before she settled in England in 1930. Seedo married fellow immigrant and Yiddish writer Y. I. Lisky (originally Yehuda Itamar Fuchs, official name Summer Fuchs) in London in 1935; they subsequently divorced and remarried in 1970. In the empathic work, *Portrait of N. M. Seedo*, Kossoff clearly conveys her strength through suffering.

This portrait is one of three works by Kossoff in the Ben Uri collection.

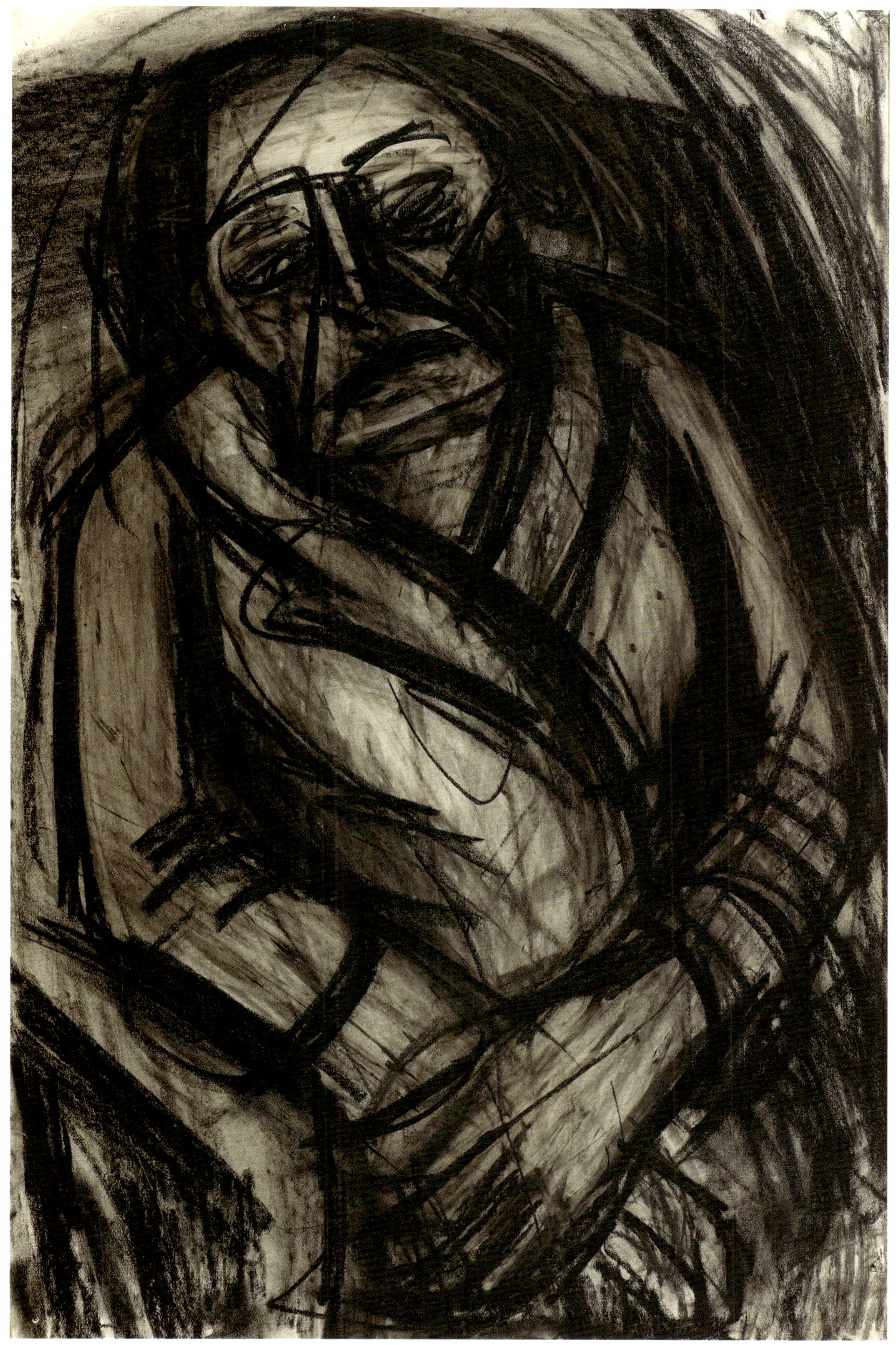

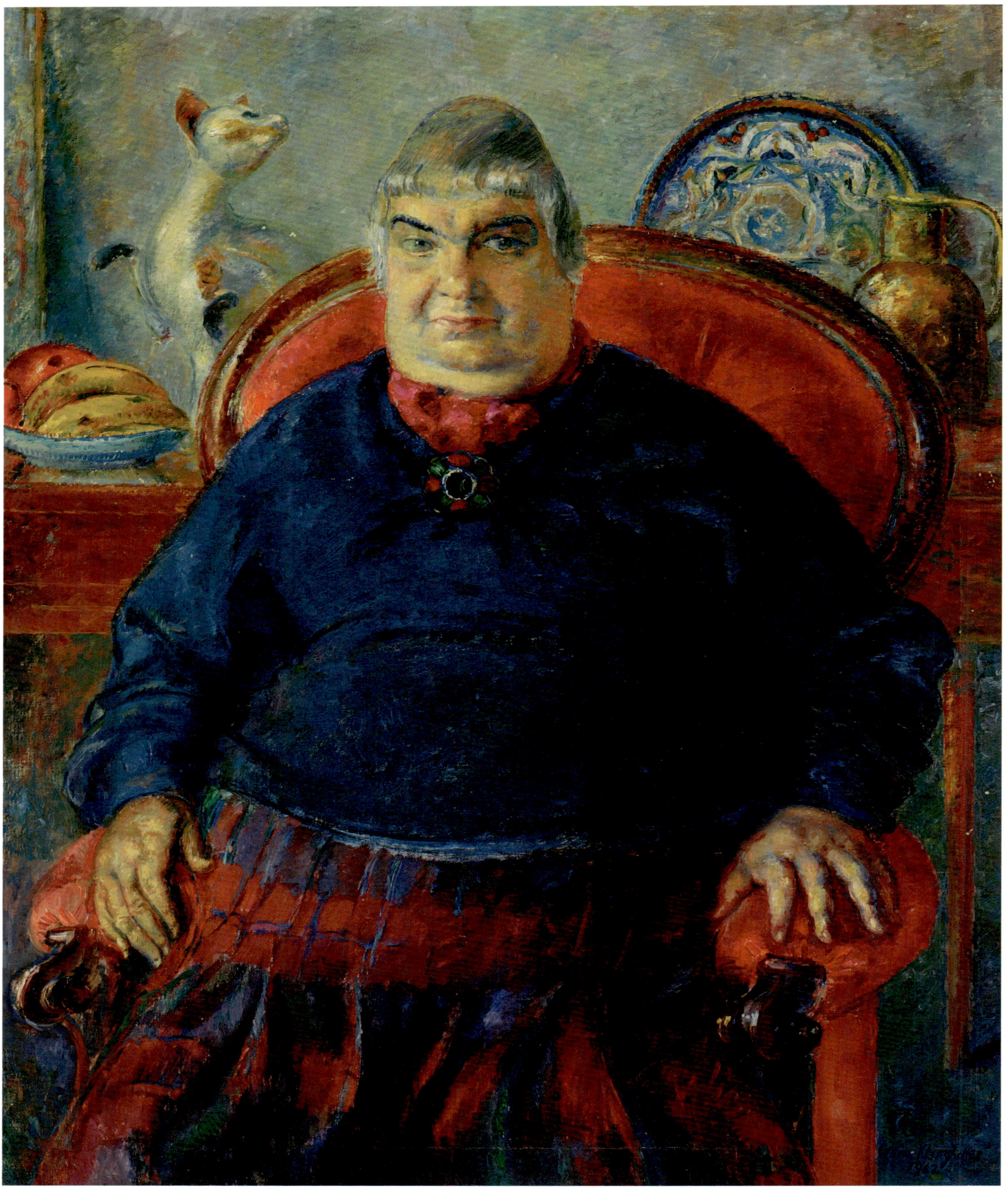

46

Portrait of Orovida Pissarro, 1962

CLARA KLINGHOFFER

(1900, Szerzezec, Austria – 1970 London, England)

Oil on canvas
102.2 × 86.8 cm
Signed and dated (lower right):
'C. Klinghoffer, 1962'

Ben Uri Collection
Purchased with assistance from the
National Art Collection Fund 1997

Austrian-born, Clara Klinghoffer grew up in East London, , taking art classes at the John Cass Institute in Aldgate, supported by her family who were not well-off but recognised her precocious talent. Holding her first exhibition at the age of nineteen, she quickly established a reputation as the new 'girl genius', earning a coveted place to study at the progressive Slade School of Art (1919–21) for two years. Championed by 'Whitechapel Boys' Alfred Wolmark (cats. 6 and 7) and Bernard Meninsky (fig. 7), her drawings, often studies of women and children, were frequently compared in the press to those of Raphael. The sculptor, Jacob Epstein (cat. 19) called her 'an artist of great talent, a painter of the first order. Her understanding of form places her in the very first rank of draughtsmen in the world'. Klinghoffer's sister, Rose, also sat for them both.

Klinghoffer can lay claim to being a later 'Whitechapel Girl'. She lived locally in Hackney until 1927, when she showed work in the Whitechapel Art Gallery exhibition of *Jewish Art and Antiquities*. She moved within East End Jewish and Yiddish social, literary and artistic circles, associating with a number of the Whitechapel Boys including Bomberg (cats. 9, 16 and 30) and Kramer (cat. 14).

In 1926 Klinghoffer showed at the prestigious Redfern Gallery, *Women of Today* praising her as 'one of the greatest English women painters'. She married Dutch journalist Joop Stoppelman the following year and they moved to Holland with their daughter in 1929. In 1939, aware of the imminent threat of German invasion, the family settled in America.

Klinghoffer subsequently split her life between London and New York, exhibiting with limited success in America during the 1950s and 1960s, her highly polished figurative works defiantly at odds with the prevailing trend towards Abstract Expressionism. In London, she showed with The London Group, New English Art Club and at the Royal Academy. In 1976 the Belgrave Gallery hosted a solo show.

Klinghoffer painted a number of celebrated sitters including Vivien Leigh as Shakespeare's Cleopatra, and her friends Lucien and Orovida Pissarro. Her striking portrait of Orovida, Camille's granddaughter, and herself an artist, presents Orovida as a series of ample forms including her rounded belly and face framed by her cropped pudding-basin hairstyle playfully echoed in the curves of the chair, the jug, plates, fruit and ornaments all forming a sinuous and slightly comical backdrop. The patterning of her kilt strikes a lone note of slightly controlled geometry.

Klinghoffer exhibited in Ben Uri's first Annual Open Exhibition in 1935, among a strong representation by émigré artists. In October 1996 her work was featured at Ben Uri in *Paintings Drawings and Sculpture by Austrian Artists Whose Lives Were Disrupted by the Holocaust*, part of the Festival of Austrian-Jewish Culture.[1] She is represented by six works in the Ben Uri Collection, all featuring single figures.

47
Invitation Card for Galerie Bing, Paris, 1964

SONIA DELAUNAY

(1885 Gradizhsk, Russia (now Ukraine) – 1979 Paris, France)

Poster paint on paper
14.7 × 12 cm
Signed and dated (inside):
'Sonia Delaunay 1964'

Ben Uri Collection

SELECTED EXHIBITION HISTORY
From Russia to Paris, Ben Uri, London,
2012; *Soutine, Chagall and the School of
Paris*, Jewish Museum, Manchester,
2013

Sonia Delaunay was born in 1885 in Gradizhsk, Russia (now Ukraine) and adopted by her maternal uncle at the age of five, taking his name (Terk). She grew up in St. Petersburg in an atmosphere of music and art, and learned several foreign languages, then moved to Germany to study drawing in 1903. In 1905, she travelled to Paris, studying at the Académie de la Palette, and discovering the work of Cézanne, Van Gogh, Pierre Bonnard, and Edouard Vuillard, as well as Matisse and Derain. In 1908 she married the German collector and art dealer, Wilhelm Uhde (1874–1947), whose Montparnasse Galerie Notre-Dame des Champs showed her first solo exhibition. Through Uhde, Sonia encountered many painters, including Picasso, Georges Braque, Maurice de Vlaminck, and Robert Delaunay (1885–1941). In 1910, Sonia divorced Uhde by mutual agreement and married Delaunay, with whom she had a son in 1911.

Together Sonia and Robert Delaunay pursued the use of abstract colour in painting and textile design. One of her first large-scale works was the painting of the Bal Bullier (1912–1913), a popular Parisian dance-hall. The Delaunays were ardent promoters of abstract art, became members of the Abstraction-Création group in 1931 and organized the first Salon des Réalités Nouvelles in 1939. In 1953 the Galerie Bing mounted a solo show, and her work was also included in exhibitions in Paris and Rome. In 1964 (following her donation of 117 works by herself and her husband), Delaunay became the first living female artist to have a retrospective at the Louvre. Delaunay also held her second solo show at the Galerie Bing, for which she designed a striking poster (fig. 23) and this signed invitation card employing bold colour and equally bold graphic forms.

In 1964 Delaunay formed a close friendship with the poet Jacques Damase and in July 1965 they collaborated on the book, *Rhythmes et Couleurs* (also in the Ben Uri Collection), which brings together Delaunay's abstract visual 'poetry', using circle and square motifs, with Damase's verbal rhymes. Throughout her career Delaunay used colour as an expressive language bringing about new 'poetic' combinations in abstract paintings and textile designs. Ben Uri holds six works by Delaunay in the Collection.

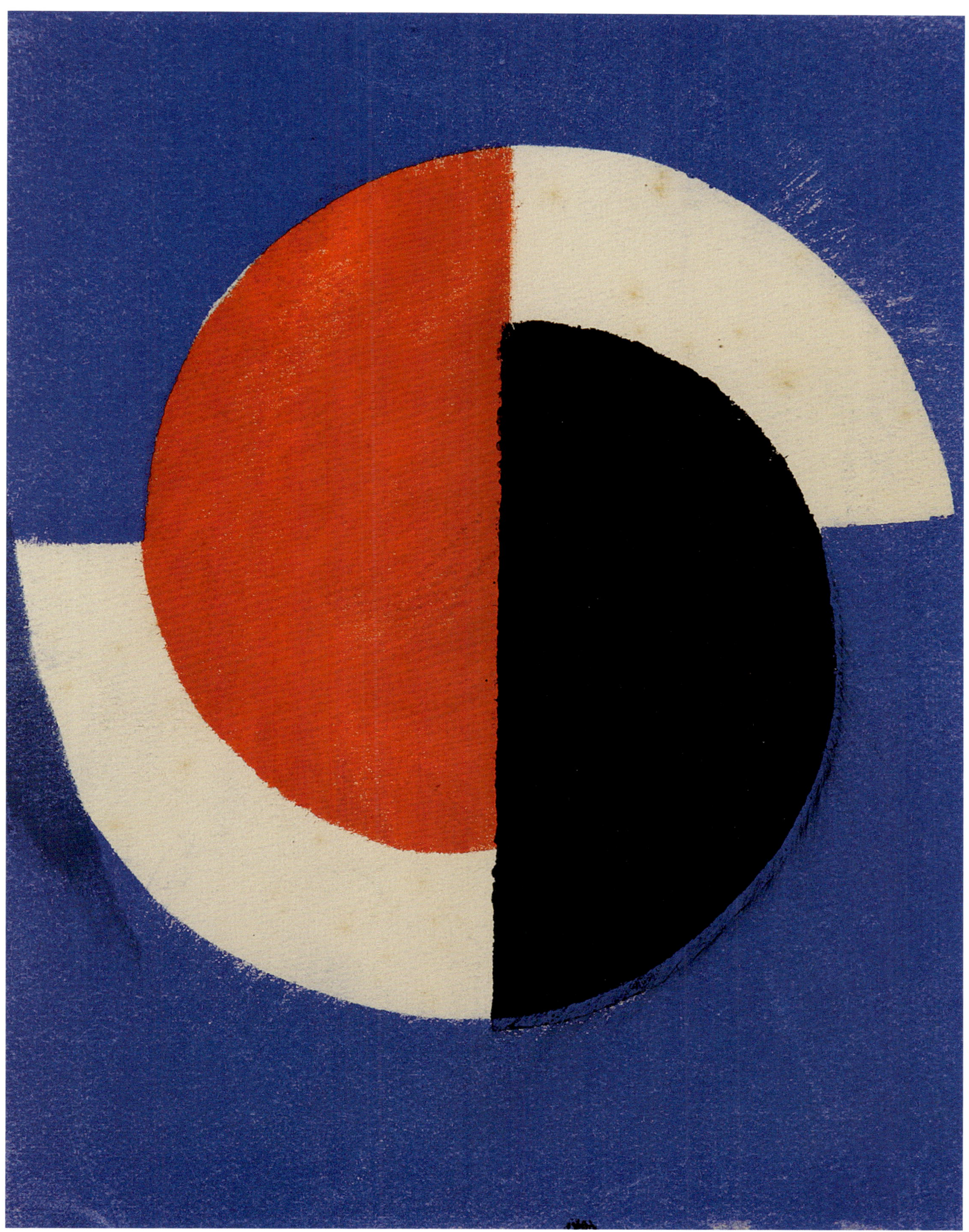

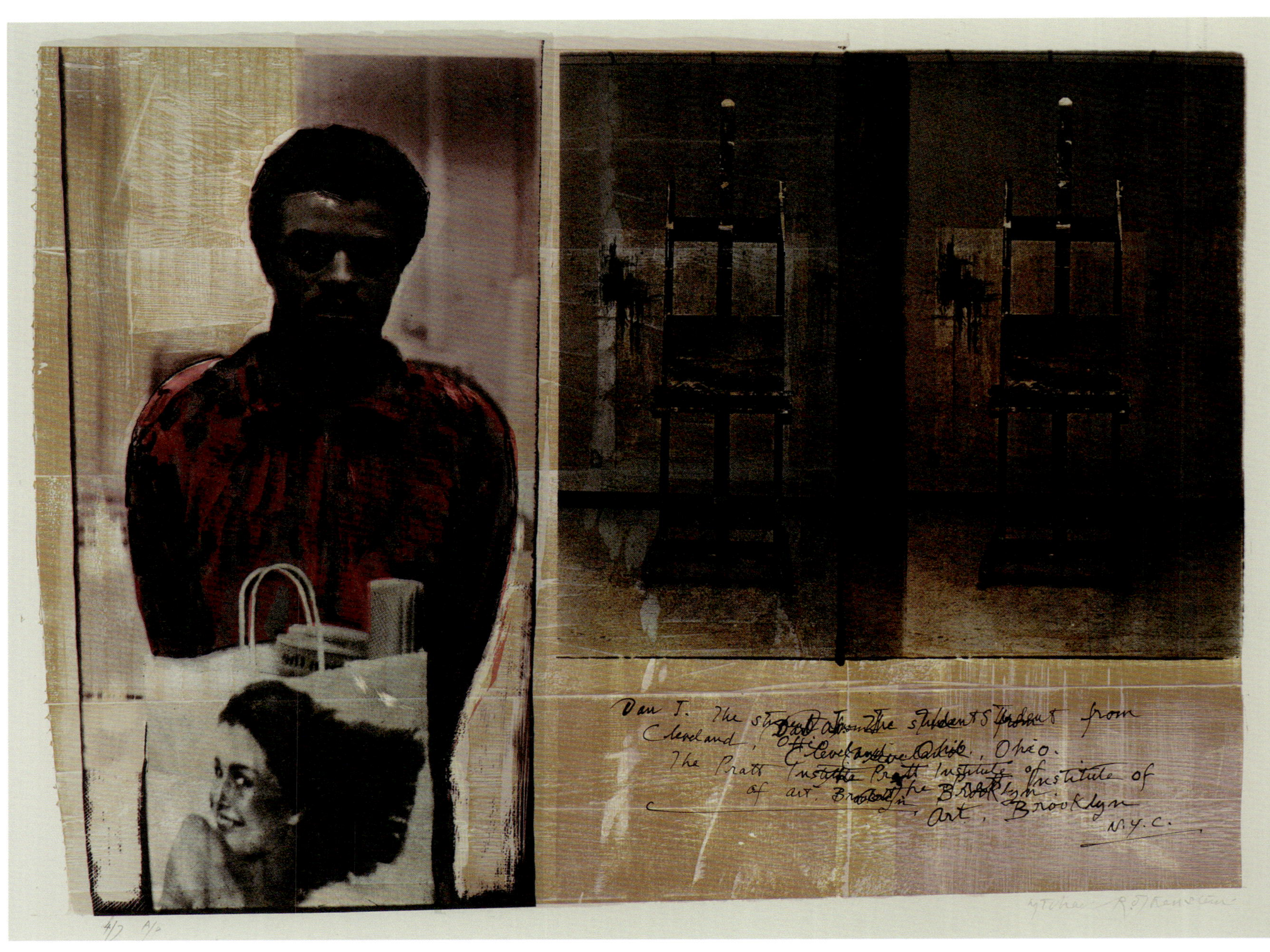

Dan T. The student from the students student from
Cleveland, Ohio. Cleveland, Ohio.
The Pratt Institute Pratt Institute of Institute of
of art, Brooklyn the Brooklyn Institute of
Art, Brooklyn
N.Y.C.

48

The Shooting of George Wallace, 1973

MICHAEL ROTHENSTEIN, RA

(1908 London, England – 1993 London, England)

Photographic silkscreen on paper
55.7 × 76.2 cm

Ben Uri Collection
Presented by Michael Rothenstein RA

Michael Rothenstein was born in 1908, the second son of the distinguished artist Sir William Rothenstein (1872–1945), Rector of the Royal College of Art, and grew up in a vibrant artistic household where visitors included Augustus John, Wyndham Lewis and Barnett Freedman (cat. 38); his elder brother John (1901–92) became a noted director of the Tate Gallery.

Home-schooled due to a lengthy childhood illness, Michael Rothenstein studied at Chelsea Polytechnic and the Central School of Arts and Crafts. During the late 1930s he concentrated on Neo-Romantic landscapes and in 1940 he was commissioned to paint topographical watercolours of endangered sites in Sussex for the *Recording Britain* project organised by the Pilgrim Trust. In the early 1940s he moved to the north Essex village of Great Bardfield, which developed an active artistic community. His first solo show was held at Redfern Gallery, London in 1942. During the postwar period, Rothenstein became increasingly fascinated by printmaking, enhanced by time spent working with Stanley Hayter at the renowned and progressive *Atelier 17* in Paris. From the mid-1950s, almost abandoning painting in preference to printmaking, he began working with linocut, silkscreen and etching, tending towards abstraction in the 1960–70s, the period of his greatest experimentation.

The Shooting of George Wallace clearly shows the influence of great American Pop artist/printmakers such as Andy Warhol and Robert Rauschenberg, with their repeated motifs, collaged photographic and popular images, often set within a larger grid-like composition. Lecturing extensively in America, Rothenstein would have been aware of the burgeoning Civil Rights movement and the dramatic assassination attempt in 1972 on Governor George Wallace, a staunch supporter of segregation, which left him paralysed and wheelchair-bound.

The young black man on the left of the image, whose hands we cannot see, conveys a sense of imprisonment, the colouring of his clothing reminiscent of prison uniforms, whilst the girl's smiling face on the carrier bag invokes mass media and billboard advertising. The angular forms of the easel to the right are ghostly reminders of the stark forms of the electric chair foregrounded in Warhols's prints and paintings of the same period.

Rothenstein's later prints of the 1980s are, by contrast, characterised by a more light-hearted mood, a vibrant palette and a repeated visual vocabulary of familiar, more domestic motifs, such as birds, flowers and vessels. Examples of which were included in Ben Uri's recent exhibition, *No Set Rules* (2015), bringing together selected works on paper from the Schlee Collection, Southampton and Ben Uri Collection, London.

Rothenstein taught for many years at Camberwell School of Art and Stoke-on-Trent College of Art; was elected an Associate of the Royal Academy (ARA) in 1977 and a Royal Academician (RA) in 1984. A retrospective was held at Stoke-on-Trent City Museum and Art Gallery in 1989. Ben Uri holds two works by Rothenstein in the Collection.

49
Untitled II, 1974

BERNARD COHEN

(b. 1933 London, England – lives London, England)

Gouache on paper
39.5 × 77.5 cm

Ben Uri Collection
Presented by Professor Bernard Cohen
1995

Cohen was born to an Orthodox Jewish family in 1933 in London, where he still lives and works. He studied at South West Essex Technical College in 1949 before training at St Martin's School of Art (1950–51) and the Slade School of Fine Art (1951–54), followed by a period in Paris in the mid-1950s. In 1958 he held his first solo exhibitions in Nottingham at the Midland Group and in in London at Gimpel Fils. He travelled to New Mexico for the first time in 1969, where he was excited both by the landscape and by Native American ritual dances. The Hayward Gallery hosted a retrospective in 1972. An influential teacher, with various positions at Ealing, Wimbledon and Chelsea Schools of Art, Cohen was appointed Professor and Director of the Slade School of Fine Art from 1988–2000.

Concerned with process in his art, Cohen is primarily known as an abstract painter, whose complex non-figurative forms have allowed him to express his responses to the world in rich and imaginative terms. His early work contrasted rigid, symmetrical shapes with loosely painted forms floating over, around or beneath them. From the mid-1970s, partly influenced by Abstract Expressionism, his works attempted to relate the process of painting to a range of social and religious rituals inspired both by his traditional Jewish upbringing and by the experiences from his travels. He has also produced an extensive body of prints, which currently employ densely layered, dazzling geometric patterns and motifs.

In this painting on paper, one of two in this volume (see cat. 54 for a companion piece, *Untitled (IV)*), Cohen – who describes himself as 'a storyteller and a creator of pictorial theatre' – contrasts different organic forms, delineated in black against white, and highlighted with red, to suggest a sense of change, evoking ideas such as cellular division and the process of evolution. The artist has said that through the combination of such shapes he hoped to create an overall image that was new and unique, imbued with different types of visual tension.

Five works on paper by Cohen are held in the Ben Uri Collection, where his work has been shown in exhibitions including *Jewish Artists at the Slade: Exhibition of Works from the Ben Uri Collection* (1992). In 1994–5 Ben Uri hosted a major survey exhibition *Bernard Cohen 35 Years of Drawing*, which toured to Norwich, Bristol and Birmingham and was opened in Dean Street by Sir Kenneth Robinson, the then Chairman of the Arts Council of Great Britain.

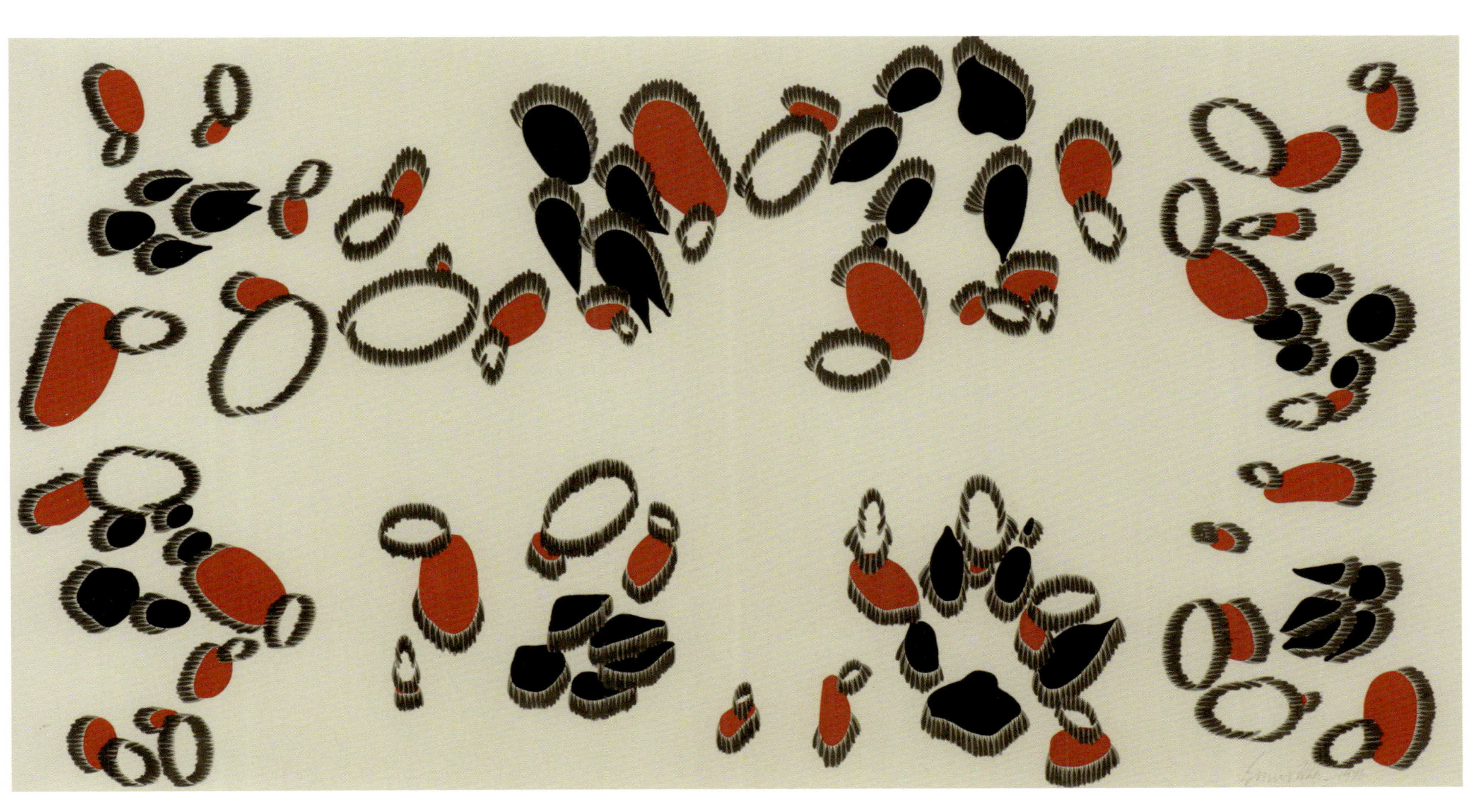

15 - 10 - 1978.

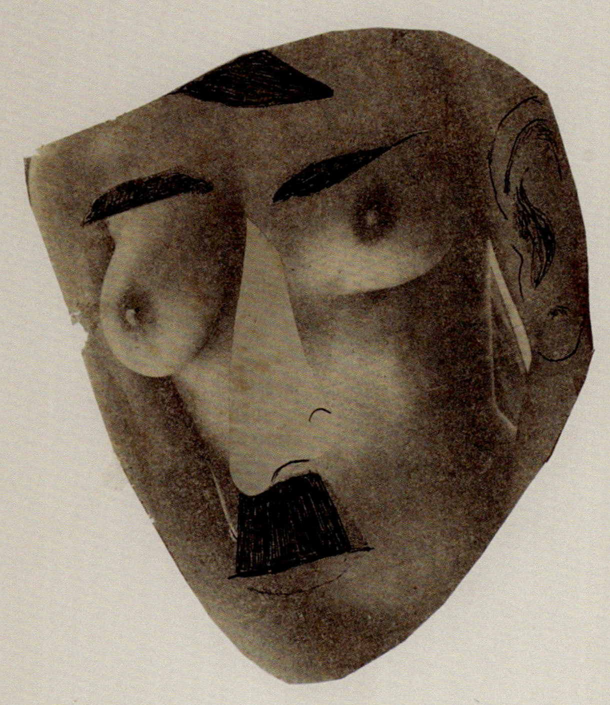

In the early nineteenth Century the world
was for about fifteen years ruled by a t uft, be-
sirous of power.

The twentieth Century has seen the rise
of the t uft _and_ moustache, when assump-
tion of power was for twelve fateful years accompanied by hatred and mass physical
destruction.

50
Caricature of Hitler, 1978

ARNOLD DAGHANI

(1909 Suceava, Romania –1985 Hove, England)

Pen and ink on newspaper
54 × 38 cm

Ben Uri Collection
Presented by Carole Grindea 1986

SELECTED EXHIBITION HISTORY
Drawings by Arnold Daghani, Ben Uri,
London, 1992

FOOTNOTES
1   Grindea and his wife Carole, a pianist, were part of Romania's avant-garde in exile in Britain. Following curtailed publication due to wartime rationing, ADAM reappeared in 1946, providing a vehicle for many literary figures and refugees (both Jewish and non-Jewish) from Nazi Europe. In 1985 numbers 455-467 were published in collaboration with King's College London. ADAM ceased publication in 1988. King's College London now houses the Adam Collection, Miron Grindea's personal library.

Artist, writer and Holocaust survivor Arnold Daghani grew up in Bessarabia prior to the Romanian annexation in 1918. He subsequently lived in Fascist-controlled Bucharest before moving to Czernowitz, under Soviet jurisdiction. Following the Nazi invasion, he and his wife, Anisoara, were arrested in 1942 and deported to the Mikhailowka labour camp in the Ukraine. Here he chronicled his experiences both in artworks and in a written diary which he managed to smuggle out during his escape to Budapest in 1943. After the war, Daghani lived variously in Israel, France, Switzerland and England. In 1947 Daghani published his experiences, first in Romanian, and subsequently in 1961 in English under the title *The Grave is in the Cherry Orchard*, in the ADAM (Arts, Drama, Architecture, Music) International Review. Originally founded in Bucharest, the magazine was edited in exile by Miron Grindea, Daghani's exact contemporary and fellow Romanian émigré.[1]

Daghani's collage, *Caricature of Hitler*, was made long after the Second World War in October 1978. Aged almost seventy and in poor health, the artist was restless and unsettled, dwelling on past events. Although he had produced art during his time in ghettoes and labour camps based on these experiences, many of these early works were lost during his subsequent exile and travels. Between 1960 and the late 1970s, Daghani worked constantly, writing and making simple sketches in preference to the physical and mental demands of more complex work. Incidents from the war, particularly the Jewish experience in the

Holocaust and representations of Hitler, recur frequently throughout this later body of work as a process of re-fixing unstable memory.

This powerful satirical portrait of Hitler comprises key collaged elements taken from newspapers: a cut-out of a woman's breasts has been cleverly and subversively transformed into the face of Adolf Hitler, to which a nose has been added, and a cartoon-like moustache, eyebrows and a tuft of hair have been inked in. Beneath the caricature a text equates the Dictator's distinctive hairstyle ('the rise of the tuft') and moustache as shorthand for the atrocities with which he is associated. With his savage wit, Daghani joins a roster of notable émigré caricaturists and political satirists, including George Grosz (cats 29 and 33), Victor 'Vicky' Weiss (fig. 36) and John Heartfield (1891–1968).

In 1992 Ben Uri held an exhibition of *Drawings by Arnold Daghani* in Dean Street, Soho to mark the 1991 publication of *The Seven Days of Schlemihl*, written and illustrated by the artist. Ben Uri owns 60 Daghani works including the *Love* print portfolio, comprising ten nudes executed in white on black, and more than 40 further works on paper dating from 1960 to the late 1970s, including views of Jerusalem and orthodox Jewish subjects, portraits and further caricatures referencing Hitler and the Holocaust. 6,000 of Daghani's works are also held in The Arnold Daghani Collection at the University of Sussex.

51

The Ghost Town, 1982

SHMUEL DRESNER

(1928 Warsaw, Poland – lives London, England)

Collage on paper
53 × 53 cm

Ben Uri Collection
Presented by the artist 1993

SELECTED EXHIBITION HISTORY
Homeless and Hidden, Ben Uri,
London, 2008

Samuel 'Shmuel' Dresner was born in Warsaw, Poland, in 1928. At the age of 12 he was forced into the Jewish Ghetto and afterwards held as slave labour in several concentration camps including Buchenwald and Theresienstadt. He came to England as a refugee in August 1945, with the help of the Central British Fund for German Jewry (now World Jewish Relief) and the agreement of the British government. He spent the years 1945–49 in sanatoria where he first began to paint, enrolling in 1949 at Heatherley School of Fine Art in London, under the tuition of Iain MacNab, and then, in 1953, at the Central School. In 1956 he moved to Paris to attend the André Lhote Academy, but later returned to London, where he continues to live and work. Between 1955 and 1981 he exhibited extensively including a number of solo shows including one at Ben Uri, Dean Street, Soho in 1975.

The Ghost Town is a collaged landscape comprising numerous pages of text ripped from books: one in English, one in Yiddish, then burned and arranged to overlap to suggest an area of 'land': plain pages at the top indicate the 'sky' and a circular piece of text represents the sun. There are no trees or discernible signs of life. The faded and burnt pages lend the image a sepia quality, much like an old photograph, apart from a few spots of purplish-red. The area of 'land' fills over two thirds of the paper, showing a jagged horizon high up on the page and positioning the viewer at a relatively low point, from which the landscape appears vast and dominating. Although the sun suggests a daytime setting, the absence of colour prevents us from knowing the season, but the charcoal tones and burnt areas give an impression of aridity: a parched landscape. Some of the fragments exhibit holes and scorch marks with the burns creating shadows and definition, particularly around the sun and the line of the horizon.

The first Nazi book burnings took place in 1933 and were a prelude to an era of state censorship in which any literature deemed unsuitable or against Nazi ideals was burnt in ceremonial displays of national 'cleansing'. Dresner directly references this by the use of pages from books, which he too has burnt. By including passages of Yiddish text, he is also drawing attention to the specific attack on Jewish culture, alluding not only to the texts that perished in the book burnings, but also to the fate of all those who lost their lives in the Holocaust. The subject of loss is underlined by the title 'The Ghost Town' which suggests an empty town, where not only the inhabitants have left, are missing, or deceased, but whole areas, such as the Warsaw Ghetto were destroyed. The torn pages can be seen to represent the crumbling buildings of such a place, once occupied by Jewish people, but now burnt and devoid of life. It serves both as an important historical record and also as a poignant *memento mori*. Ben Uri holds five works by Dresner in the Collection.

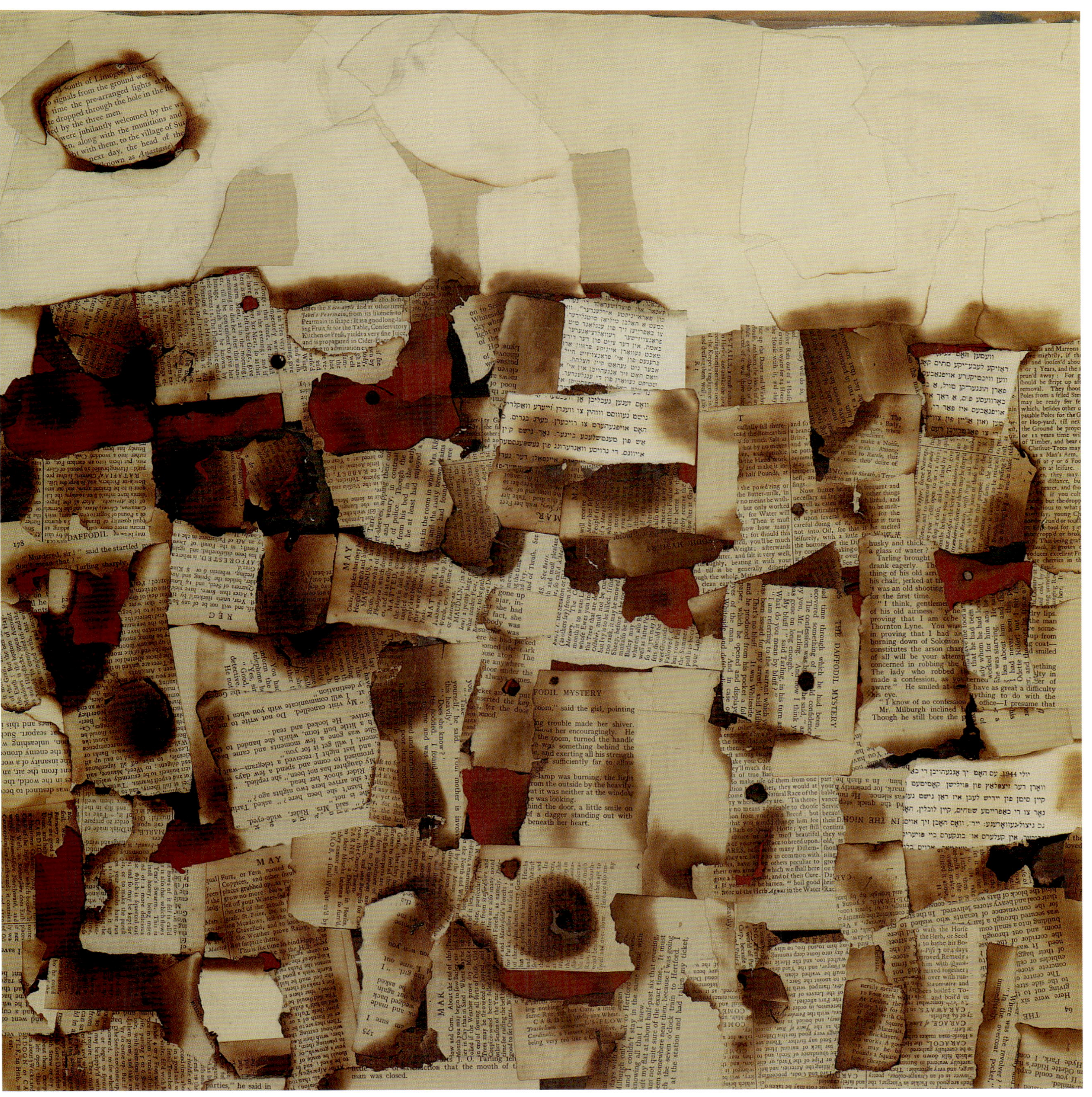

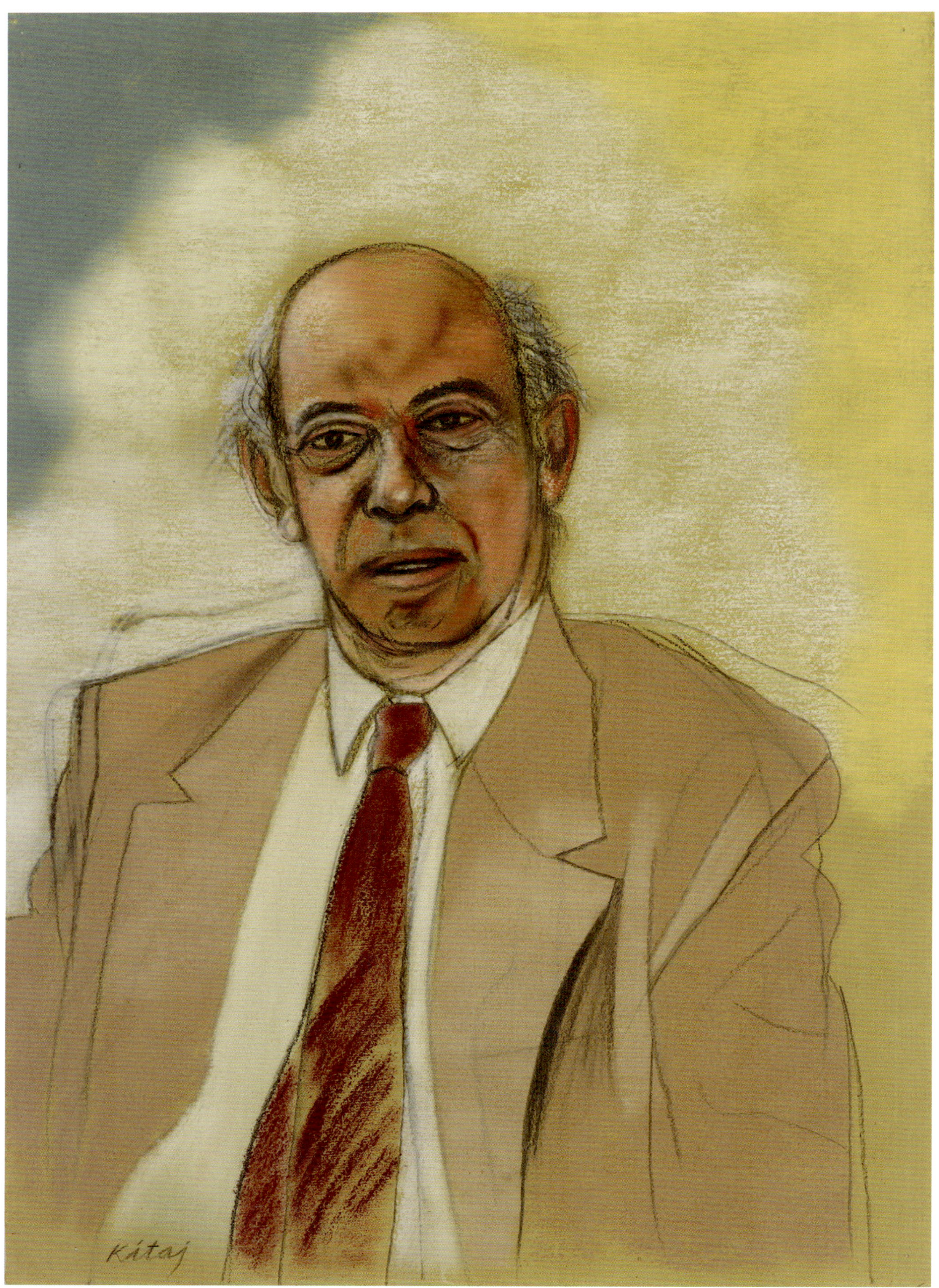

Kitaj

Sir Claus Moser, 1987

RONALD BROOKS (R. B.) KITAJ

(1932 Cleveland, USA – 2007, Los Angeles, USA)

Pastel on paper
77 × 57 cm

Ben Uri Collection
Presented by the artist through
Marlborough Fine Art, 2004

SELECTED EXHIBITION HISTORY
Apocalypse, Osborne Samuel, London,
2010; *Highlights from the Ben Uri
Collection*, London, 2012

Born in Cleveland, Ohio, USA, Kitaj studied at the Cooper Union Institute in New York in 1950–1 and 1952, and at the Academy of Fine Art, Vienna, following a period of travel in Central and South America as a merchant seaman. After moving to Britain he completed his art training at the Ruskin School of Art, Oxford from 1958–9, and at the Royal College of Art, London from 1959–61. His first one-man exhibition was held at Marlborough Fine Art, London in 1963. Kitaj held teaching posts in America during the 1960s and early 1970s, at the University of California at Berkeley and at Los Angeles, returning to London in 1972. His 1983 marriage to his second wife, the American artist Sandra Fisher (1947–94) is celebrated in his paintings *Cecil Court, London WC2 (The Refugees)* and *The Wedding*, both in the Tate Collection, which are rich with Jewish symbolism.

In 1976 Kitaj selected a group of works by British artists to form the core of an exhibition for the Arts Council of Great Britain, *The Human Clay*. The artists referred to by Kitaj in an accompanying essay were described as representing a School of London (much like the loosely connected *Ecole de Paris* with its significant number of Jewish exponents). This became a defining moment in British twentieth century art history, with the members of the 'School', gradually honed to an almost fixed 'core' of six or seven painters, including Michael Andrews (fig. 45), Frank Auerbach (cats. 43 and 57), Francis Bacon, Lucian Freud (fig. 38), Leon Kossoff (cat. 45) as well as Kitaj himself. As James Hyman notes

in his essay, 'The label 'School of London', despite the often-used prefix 'so-called', soon became the dominant framework for the presentation of postwar British figurative painting, despite the reservations of the artists themselves'. As both an insider and outsider, simultaneously at the heart of the contemporary British art establishment, and also an American Jew – personal identity and, latterly, a broader Jewish identity – are at the heart of Kitaj's later work. This subject is also addressed in print in his 1989 publication, *First Diasporist Manifesto*.

Kitaj was elected to the American Academy of Arts and Letters in 1982 and to the Royal Academy in 1985. However, in the wake of the savage response to his 1994 Tate exhibition by a number of British art critics, and the sudden death of his wife only weeks after its opening, Kitaj relocated to Los Angeles in 1997, where he remained debilitated by Parkinson's disease until his suicide in 2004.

This striking portrait of Claus Moser, Baron Moser, KCB CBE (b.1922), the distinguished German émigré statistician, is executed in Kitaj's characteristic dynamic and highly coloured figurative style and was originally commissioned by the Royal Opera House. It is one of two works by Kitaj in the Ben Uri Collection. Kitaj notably opened Ben Uri's *The Jewish Students Arts Festival* at Dean Street in 1991.

53

Torn Poster, London, 1990

DOROTHY BOHM

(b. 1924 Königsberg, East Prussia (now Kaliningrad, Russia) – lives London, England)

Photograph on paper
64 × 43.8 cm
Signed (lower right) 'Dorothy
Bohm'

Ben Uri Collection
Presented by the artist after her
exhibition, 2007

SELECTED EXHIBITION HISTORY
*Ambiguous Realities: Colour
Photographs by Dorothy Bohm*, Ben
Uri, London, 2007

FOOTNOTES
1   Cited Monica Bohm-Duchen
(introduction), *Ambiguous Realities:
Colour Photographs by Dorothy Bohm*,
Ben Uri: London, 2007), p. 4. All
quotations are from this source.

Dorothy Bohm has commented of her work:

The photograph fulfills my deep need to stop things disappearing. It makes transience less painful and retains something of the special magic, which I have looked for and found. I have tried to create order out of chaos, to find stability in flux and beauty in the most unlikely places[1]

Born into a Jewish family in Königsberg, East Prussia (now Kaliningrad) in 1924, Bohm was sent to England by her family in 1939 at the age of 14. As her father kissed her goodbye, he handed her his own Leica camera saying 'it may be useful one day'. During the Second World War, Bohm studied photography in Manchester and opened her own portrait studio at the age of 21. In the late 1940s her interest in outdoor photography was stimulated by frequent visits to the Swiss Lakes when she began to focus on photographing people un-posed and within the natural environment. Afterwards, she spent a year in Paris, before continuing to travel widely. Her early black-and-white photographs are in the tradition of the innovative humanist street photographers, Henri Cartier-Bresson, Manuel Álvarez Bravo and André Kertész, whom she knew and admired. When she began to work in colour in the 1980s she added a new sensuousness and tactility to her work. Focusing increasingly on easily overlooked details from the everyday world, she began creating complex, semi-abstract images in which the human presence is nonetheless always implicit.

Torn Poster, London (1990), a close-up photograph of a billboard hoarding is one of a series of works featuring torn posters, graffiti and other urban ephemera (Bohm often waits for such subject-matter to 'mature'). Here, the eroded and weather-ravaged poster in its distressed condition resembles a collage, dramatic in content and strongly-coloured. Although the original meaning is lost, each fragment hints at past events as both history and art history are layered including notably (lower left) one of the heads thrown back in agony from Picasso's *Guernica* (1937), expressing his horror at the bombing of the Basque capital by General Franco's German allies during the Spanish Civil War. This image is juxtaposed with the face of a woman wearing a soldier's helmet (upper right) – a disturbing intimation of conflict– offset by fragments of sky and landscape in between. It is part of a powerful group of works which represent, as Monica Bohm-Duchen has commented, 'a palimpsest of contemporary western culture which forcefully conveys its fickleness'. Bohm herself observes that she is keen to preserve a sense of mystery in her photographs: 'Sometimes I want a picture to ask why and not to be too easily deciphered and decoded because our lives are often like that.'

Dorothy Bohm has been instrumental in a number of important photographic initiatives including the co-founding of the Photographer's Gallery in 1971. *Torn Poster, London* was included in the 2007 exhibition of her work, *Ambiguous Realities: Colour Photographs by Dorothy Bohm* at the Ben Uri.

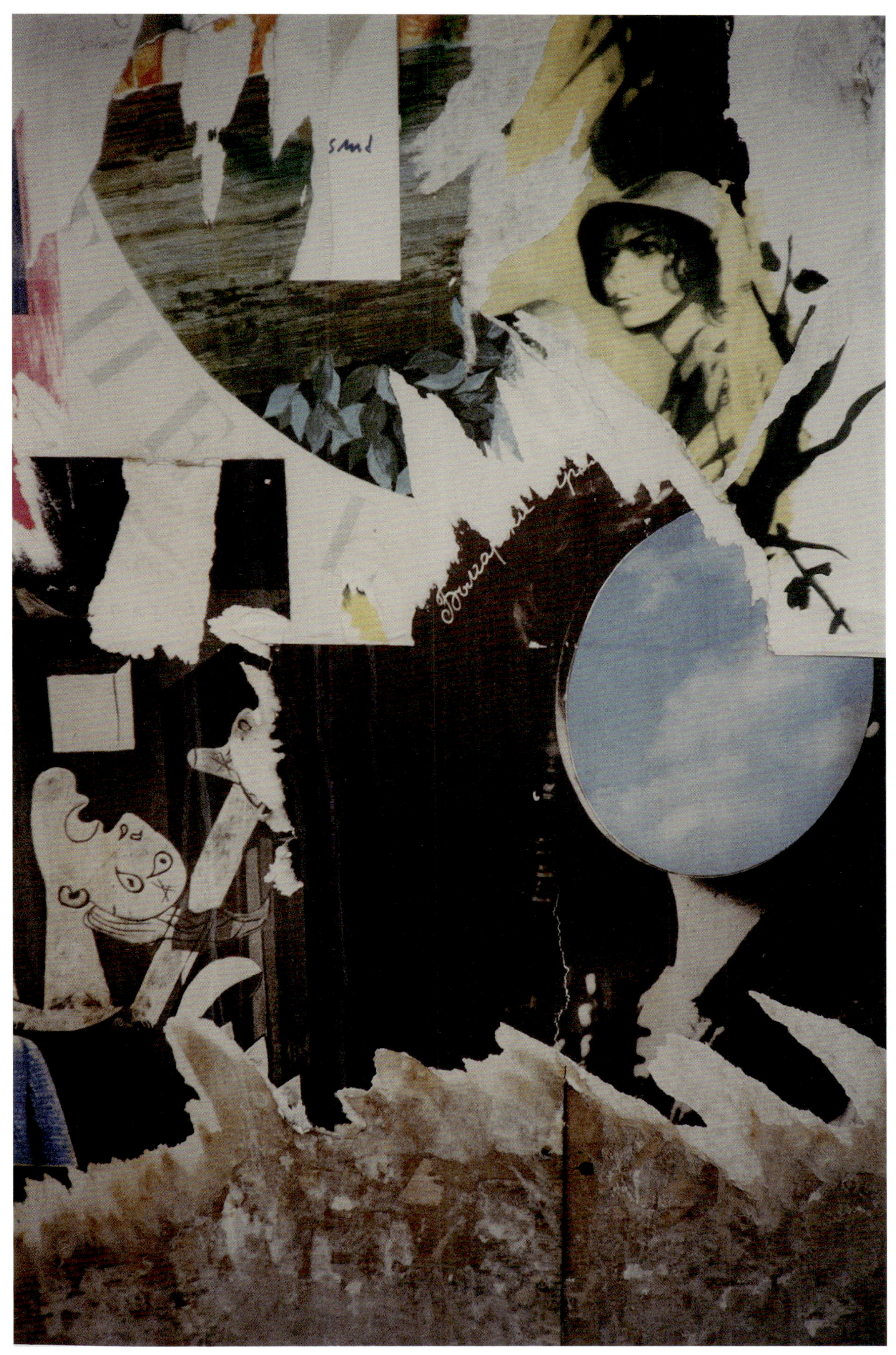

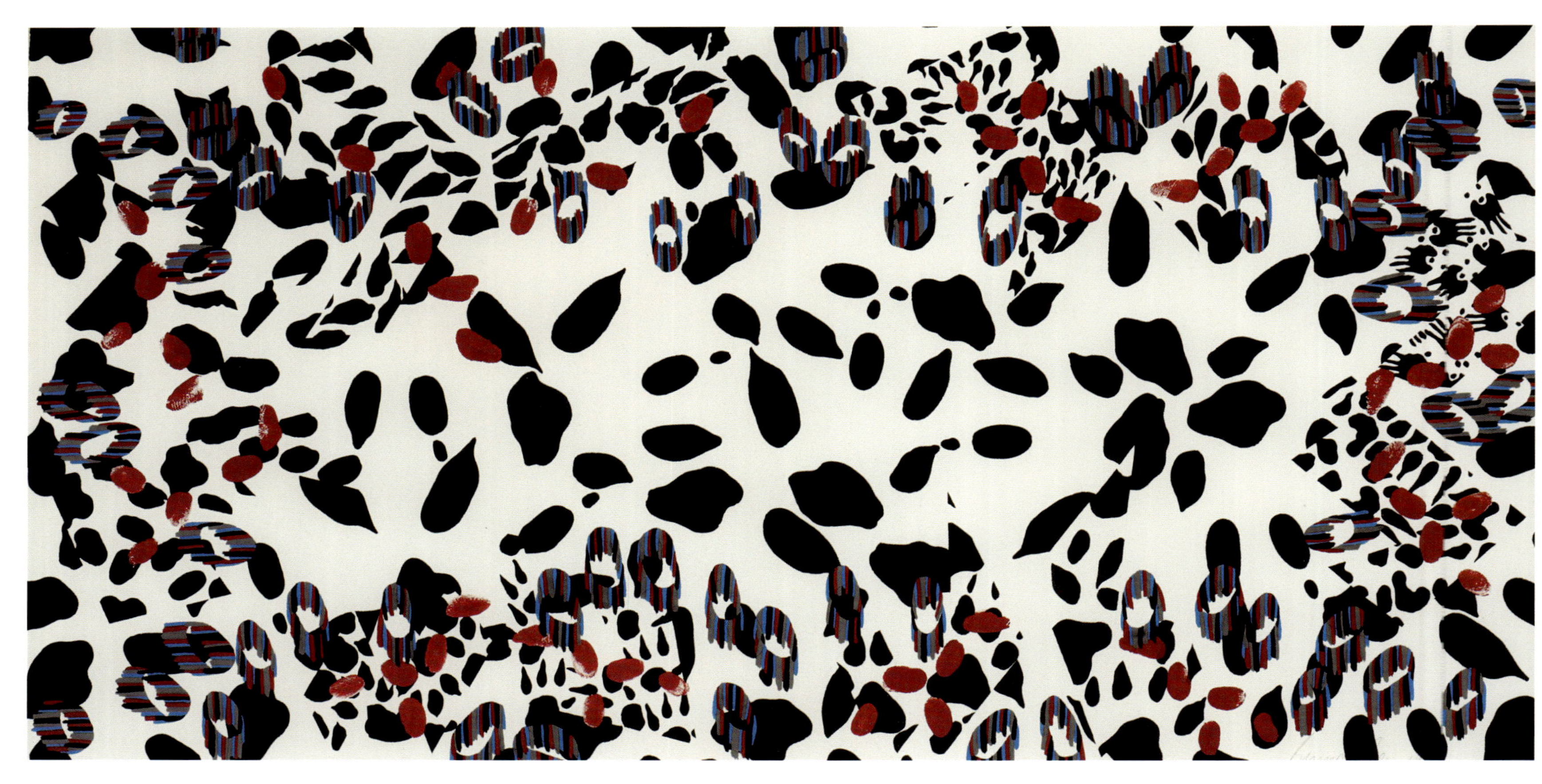

54

Untitled IV, 1970s

BERNARD COHEN

(1933 London, England – lives London, England)

Gouache on paper on board
38 × 76 cm

Ben Uri Collection
Presented by Professor Bernard Cohen
1995

Bernard Cohen was born to an Orthodox Jewish family in 1933 in London and still lives and works in the city. He studied at South West Essex Technical College in 1949 before training at St Martin's School of Art (1950–51) and the Slade (1951–54), followed by a period in Paris in the mid-1950s. In 1958 he held his first solo exhibitions in Nottingham at the Midland Group and in in London at Gimpel Fils. In 1969 he travelled to New Mexico for the first time. He held a retrospective at the Hayward Gallery in 1972 and, an influential teacher, has held various positions at Ealing, Wimbledon and Chelsea Schools of Art. Cohen was appointed Professor and Director of the Slade School of Fine Art from 1988–2000.

Cohen is primarily known as an abstract painter and printmaker, whose complex non-figurative forms have allowed him to express his responses to the world in rich and imaginative terms. His early work contrasted rigid, symmetrical shapes with loosely painted forms floating over, around or beneath them. From the mid-1970s, partly influenced by Abstract Expressionism, his works attempted to relate the process of painting to a range of social and religious rituals, inspired both by his traditional Jewish upbringing and by the experiences from his travels. He also sought to create various types of visual tension similar to those encountered in reality, in particular through the process of juxtaposition.

In this striking work on paper, part of a series of five related images (see the companion piece, *Untitled II*, cat. 49) Cohen contrasts a limited range of different dynamic forms in a spare palette of red, black and grey, to suggest a sense of the process of change. He has said that through the combination of such shapes he hopes to create an overall image that is simultaneously both new and unique In *Untitled IV*, Cohen explores ways of creating a spatial and pictorial experience. The dizzying combination of multiple forms, suggestive of both animal and human prints, stretching across the picture surface, creates a hypothetical ritual dance which unfolds before our eyes.

Five works on paper by Cohen are held in the Ben Uri Collection and he was included in the exhibition *Jewish Artists at the Slade: Exhibition of Works from the Ben Uri Collection* in 1992, alongside Frank Auerbach (cats. 43 and 57), David Bomberg (cats. 9, 16 and 30), Claude Rogers and Mark Gertler (cats. 10 and 12). In 1994 Ben Uri hosted a major survey exhibition, *Bernard Cohen 35 Years of Drawing*, which toured to Norwich, Bristol and Birmingham and was opened in Dean Street by Sir Kenneth Robinson, the then Chairman of the Arts Council of Great Britain.

55
Sir Norman Rosenthal, 1996

DANIEL QUINTERO

(1949 Málaga, Spain – lives Spain and USA)

Oil on canvas
157.5 × 91.5 cm

Ben Uri Collection
Presented by the artist 2013

SELECTED EXHIBITION HISTORY
Recent Acquisitions, Ben Uri, London,
2013

Daniel Quintero was born in Málaga, Spain in 1949. He spent much of his childhood in Málaga and in Melilla on the north coast of Africa. In 1959 he moved with his family to Madrid. He studied drawing and painting with the artist Amadeo Roca at the Roca Academy and in 1967 began studying at the Beaux Arts School in San Fernando where he was taught by the renowned Spanish realist painter Antonio López García. Quintero exhibited with Juana Mordó Gallery, Madrid, and, from 1975, has been represented by Marlborough Fine Art, London. In the mid-1970s he lived and worked in Cornwall and London, later spending time in Dublin. He returned to Spain in 1979 and now divides his time between Madrid and New York. Working within a predominantly realist tradition, his paintings and drawings (both portraiture and landscapes) are held in public collections throughout Europe and the USA.

This large, almost life-size portrait of curator and art historian Sir Norman Rosenthal was painted in 1996, mid-way through Sir Norman's 30 year-tenure as Exhibitions Secretary of the Royal Academy. Using light earthy tones, Quintero portrays his subject in a confident yet relaxed mood with a somewhat questioning air. It is believed to be the first portrait of this iconic and charismatic figure to enter a UK museum collection and was presented to the collection by the artist in 2013. Quintero's other portrait commissions include the King and Queen of Spain, and the Nobel Prize winner Severo Ochoa.

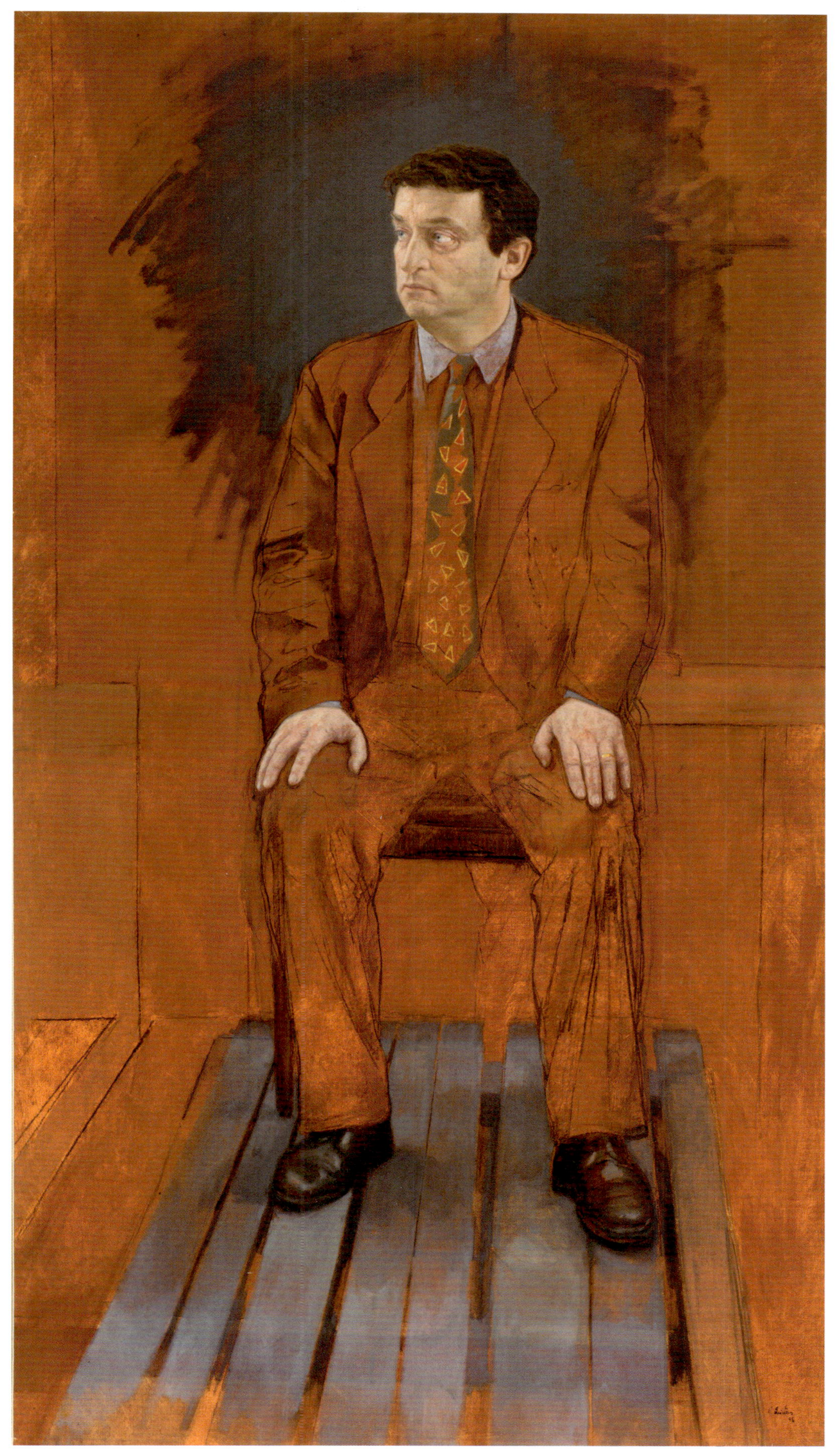

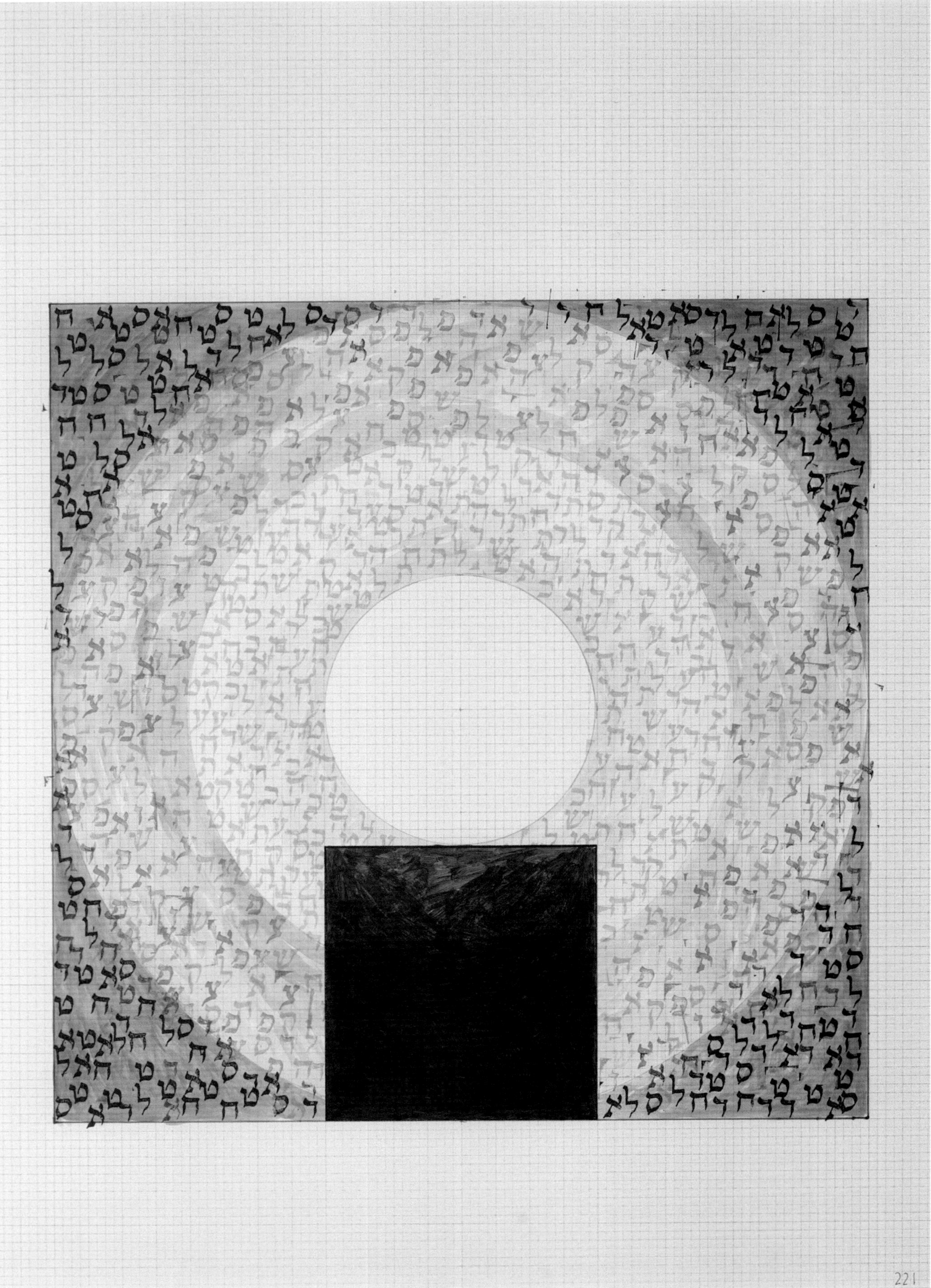

56

Big Bang, 2004

VITALY KOMAR

(1943, Moscow, Russia – lives USA)

and

ALEXANDER MELAMID

(1945, Moscow, Russia – lives USA)

Watercolour and pastel
on paper
101 × 75.5 cm

Ben Uri Collection
Presented by the artists 2004

SLECTED EXHIBITION HISTORY
IJAYA, Ben Uri, London, 2004

Although their co-authorship of artworks ceased in 2003–4, Komar and Melamid are two of the best known artists to emerge from the USSR in the late 1960s and early 1970s, as the founders in 1972 of the controversial *SotsArt*, a type of work which fused Russian Socialist Realism with elements of conceptual art, Western Pop Art and Dada. 'We are not just an artist. We are a movement' they famously declared, never precisely defining the role each played within the creation of any individual artwork. They both studied at the Moscow Art School from 1958–60 and the Stroganov Institute of Art and Design, graduating in 1967, the year in which they held their first joint exhibition. They subsequently joined the Moscow Union of Artists and took up teaching posts. However, the controversial nature of their works resulted in arrest in 1974 and both immigrated first to Israel in 1977, and then to New York, in 1978.

During the 1980s and 90s Komar and Melamid's repertoire expanded to include conceptual projects involving music, monumental sculpture, performance and even teaching elephants in Thailand to paint, often accompanied by publications to disseminate their ideas. *Symbols of the Big Bang*, referencing the very moment of the creation of the universe, was the duo's last major collaborative project in 2001–3, exhibited first in New York and then in Moscow. Here, the artists used a range of abstract, ancient and geometric symbols in a series of drawings and paintings, including the swastika, square and Star of David, to explore links between mysticism and science, creating 'The visual image of the beginning of our universe and our world'. Some of the works were intended to form the basis for designs for stained-glass, which the Russian authorities refused to allow.

This drawing, as with the whole series, is executed like a mathematical problem on graph paper, It overlays a sun-like element radiating outwards in concentric circles, with a sinister, brooding block-like form. On closer inspection, the surface is dappled with Hebrew letters, creating a dynamic surface suggesting the explosive moment of creation. *Big Bang* was the winning entry in the Painting and Drawing Section of Ben Uri's *International Jewish Artist of the Year Award* in 2004.

57

Mornington Crescent, Summer Morning II, 2004

FRANK AUERBACH

(1931 Berlin, Germany – lives London, England)

Oil on board
51 × 51 cm

Ben Uri Collection
Acquired in 2006 from Marlborough
Fine Art with the assistance of the
artist, Marlborough Fine Art, the Art
Fund, the V&A/MLA Purchase Grant
Fund, Pauline and Daniel Auerbach
and anonymous donors

SELECTED EXHIBITION HISTORY
Recent Acquisitions: 2001–2006, Ben
Uri, London, 2007; *Apocalypse*,
Osborne Samuel, London, 2010

This vibrant landscape is one of a number by the artist depicting Mornington Crescent, the area in Camden Town, north London, where he has lived and worked in a studio since 1954, when it was vacated by his artist friend and contemporary Leon Kossoff (and before him the Polish-Jewish émigré artist Gustav Metzger). It is painted with the distinctive heavy impasto which characterises Auerbach's work. In his portraits and nudes, as well as urban landscapes, Auerbach frequently returns to the same subject. Here, using a lively yellow and blue palette that contrasts with the earthy tones of his earlier urban scenes, he transforms the choking London traffic into a vigorous surge of pigment. The date '2004' scratched into the paintwork suggests the urgency and transience of both life and art.

A German-Jewish émigré with a focus on a particular 'home' location and a 'family' of familiar sitters, Auerbach's work has a particular resonance for the exploration of issues of identity and migration. As Auerbach himself has commented of his background: 'I wasn't British born, […] I didn't have a family and I didn't have anything to anchor me to whatever was going on'. *Mornington Crescent, Summer Morning II* combines the artist's focus on familiar architectural structures together with a sense of place. Auerbach deliberately restricts his landscape motifs, concentrating especially on London locations and foregrounding the area around his studio and its distinctive features, which include the landmark chimney.

This painting was acquired in 2004 to fill a longstanding gap in the Ben Uri collection and has since been exhibited on numerous occasions including for the day at Surrey Street Primary School, Luton, in the initiative 'Your Paintings: Masterpieces in Schools', in association with BBC & The Public Catalogue Foundation in October 2013 and featured on 'Front Row', BBC Radio 4.

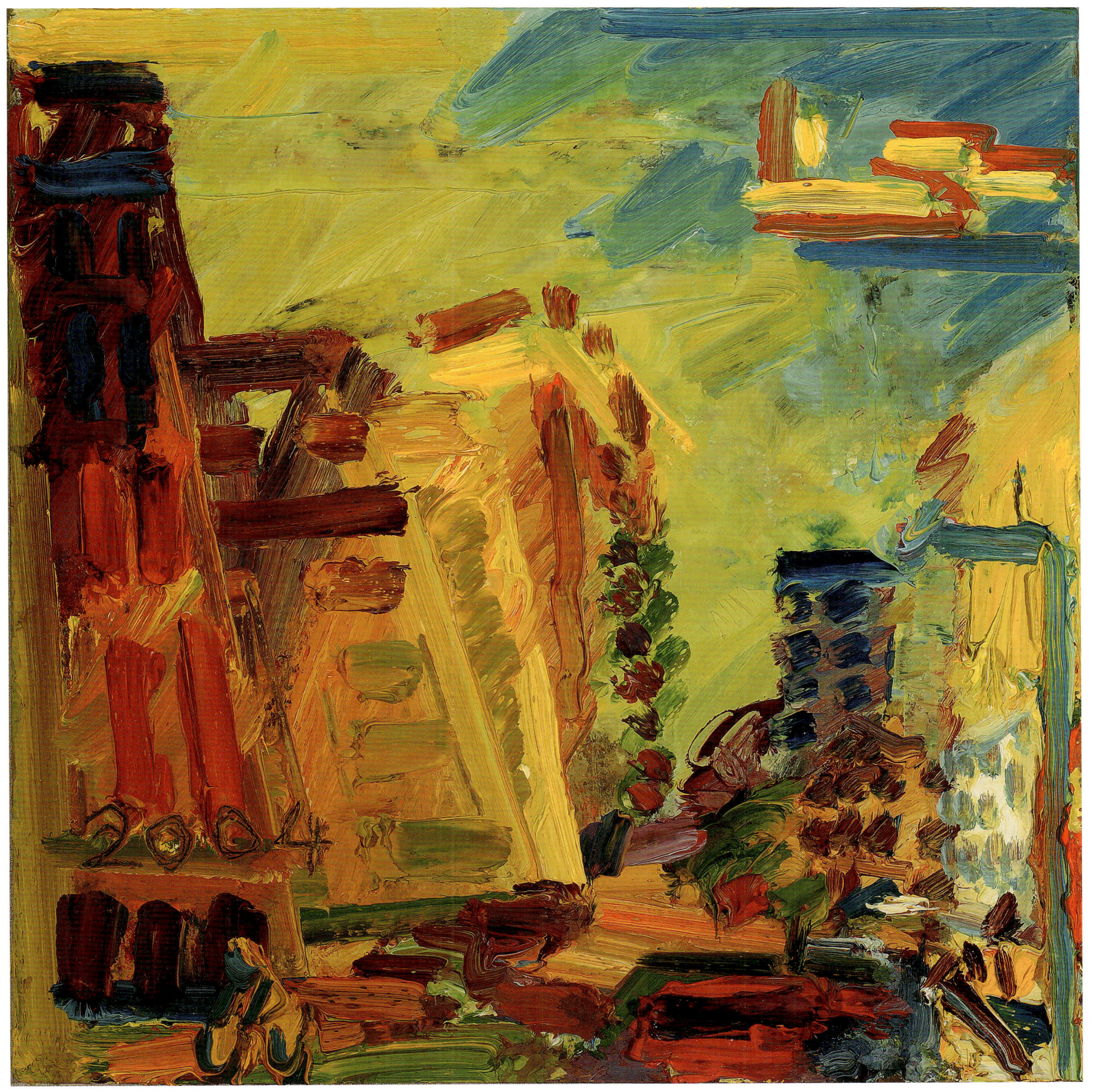

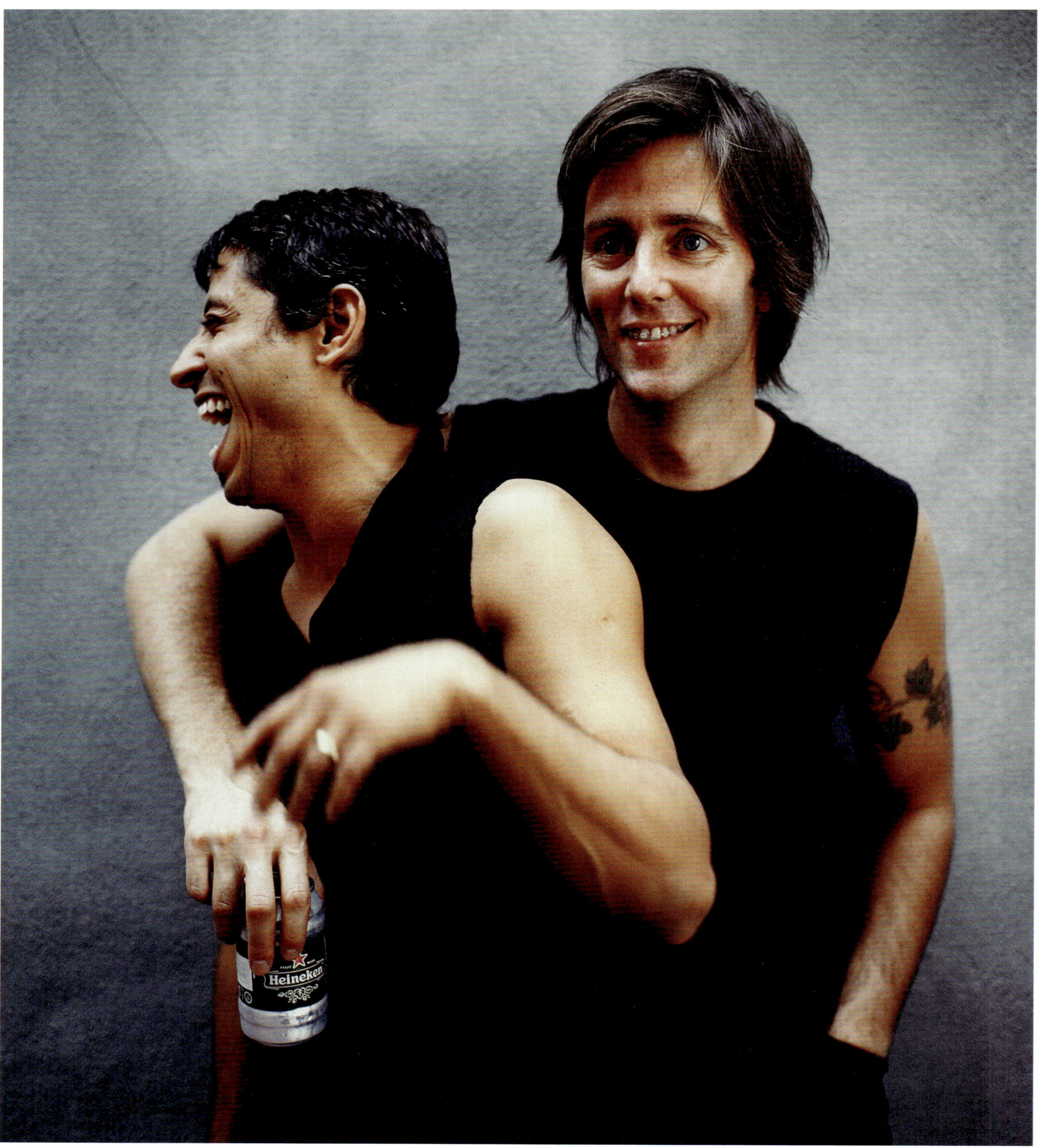

58
Michael and Elie, 2004

YAKI ASSAYAG

(1970 Jerusalem, Israel – lives USA)

Photograph on board
97.5 × 97.5 cm

Ben Uri Collection
Purchased with the generous support
of the V&A/MLA Purchase Grant
Fund, the artist and a philanthropist
who has requested anonymity, 2004

SELECTED EXHIBITION HISTORY
IJAYA, Ben Uri, London, 2004
(overall winning entry); *Apocalypse*,
Osborne Samuel, London, 2010

Photographer Yaki Assayag was born in Israel in
1970. *Michael & Elie* is part of a new series he
initiated after moving to Brooklyn and reflects
something of his and feelings about this new
location and its inhabitants. He writes of his
work:

I find portraits are the most interesting side of
photography as there are many ways to approach such
a dynamic and fascinating subject. It was self-portraits
that helped arouse the emotional feeling of standing in
front of the lens. I believe that the interaction between
the photographer and subjects could lead to a different
and more interesting result than if I came with my own
opinion of how the portrait should come out. The
more I interact with the subjects the more I understand
that there is no limit to what the camera can expose …

Ben Uri holds two works by Assayag in the
Collection.

59

Oh Jerusalem, 2005

OREET ASHERY

(1966 Jerusalem, Israel – lives London, England)

DVD (edition of 5), 4 minute
loop, original mini DVD

Ben Uri Collection
Presented by the artist 2006

SELECTED EXHIBITION HISTORY
Recent Acquisitions: 2001–2006, Ben
Uri, London, 2007; *Selected
Masterworks: Israeli, Modern and
Contemporary Collection*, Bonhams,
London, 2011

Born in Jerusalem in 1966, Oreet Ashery is a London-based interdisciplinary visual artist working in live art, video, 2-D image-making, installation and the internet. The work is process-based and context-specific; it investigates body politics and cultural anxiety, questioning notions of subjectivity and authenticity. She frequently produces work as a male character, including *Oh Jerusalem*, a single screen projection, looped black-and-white silent video for gallery viewing, in which the artist dresses up as both an orthodox Jewish man and an Arab man. The two characters alternate and perform an endless repetition of several acts: sitting on a chair, picking up a large paper cone, looking through the cone and 'discovering' Jerusalem and embracing the image of Jerusalem. The repetitions get faster and faster until the two characters merge into one another in their endless spirals. Their mannerisms are reminiscent of Keaton and Chaplin and, as such, refer to the history of film and representation, while simultaneously provoking the history of conflict.

Ashery exhibits, performs, intervenes and screens her work extensively, both in the UK and abroad, in both established public spaces including Tate Modern, the Pompidou Centre and the Freud Museum, and experimental locations including curators' bedrooms, a men-only religious celebration, the Qalandia checkpoint in the occupied West Bank, and a derelict fishermen's hut. Ashery is an AHRC fellow in the drama department at Queen Mary University, London.

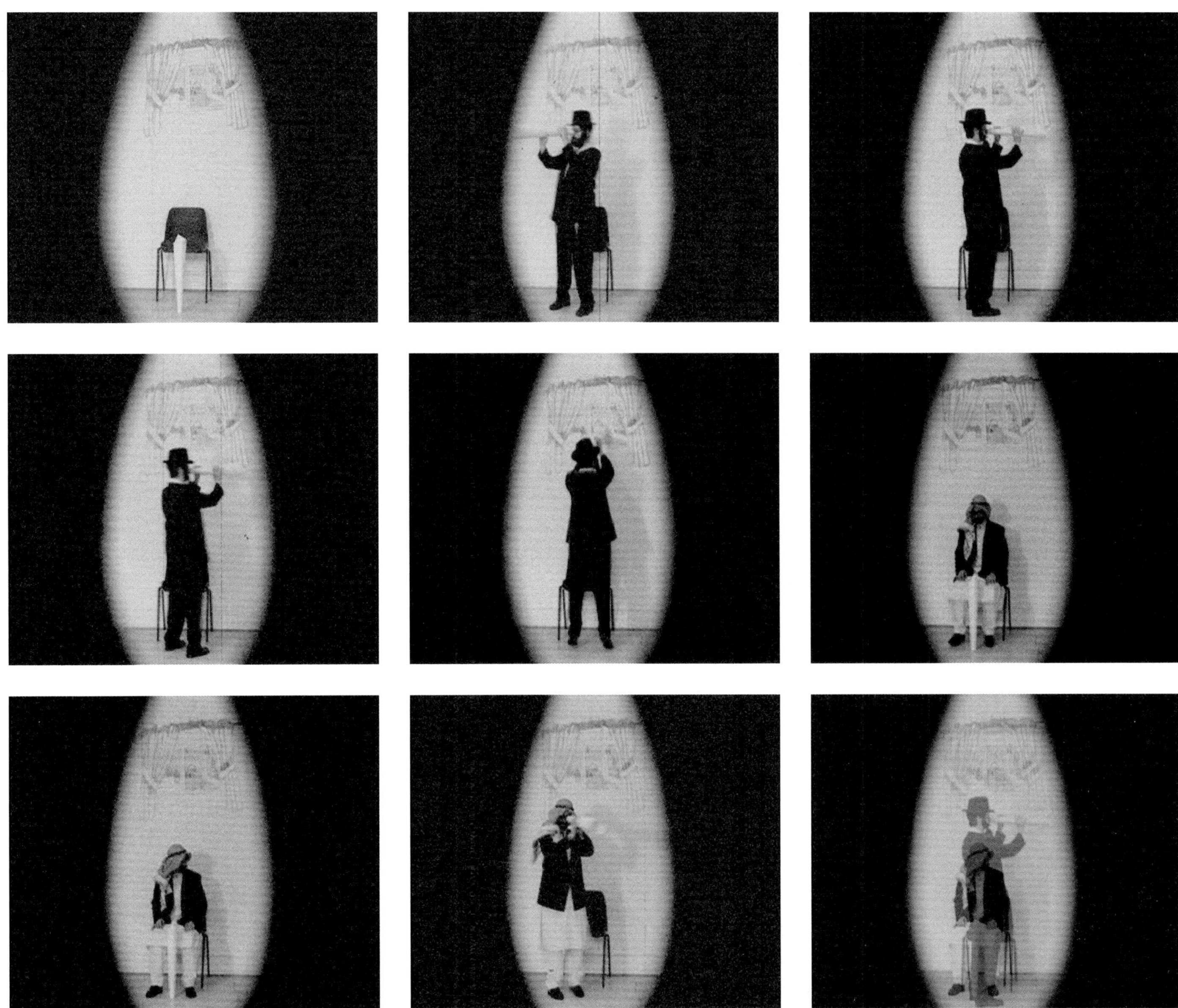

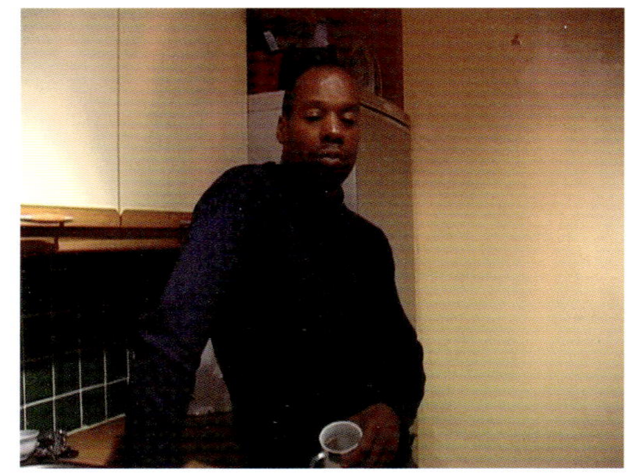
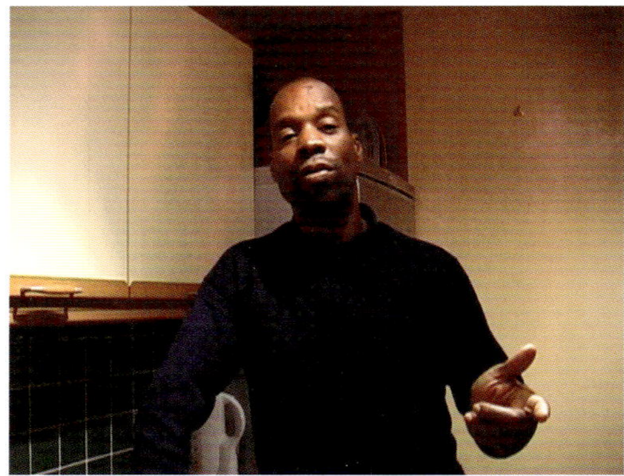
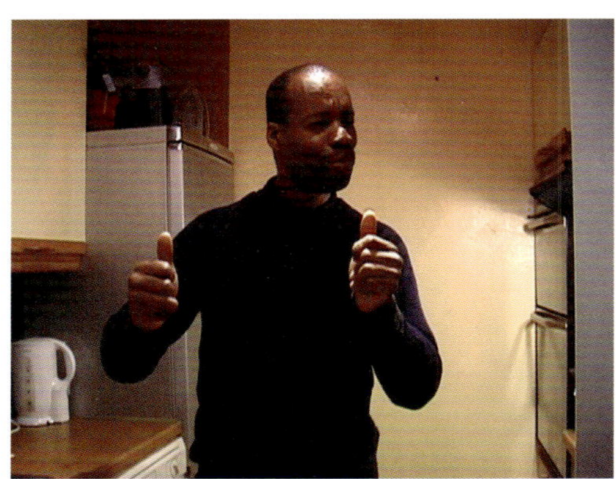
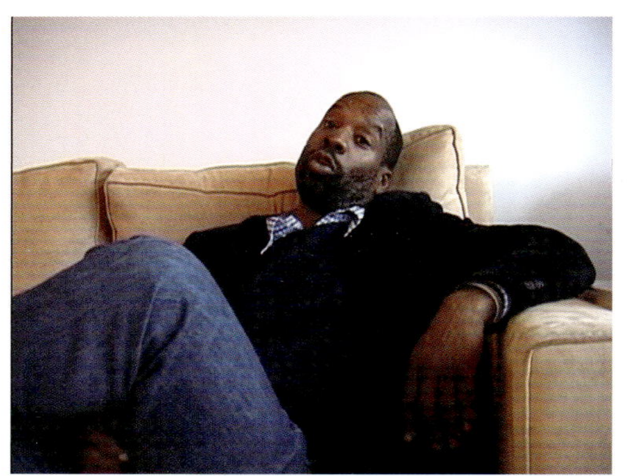
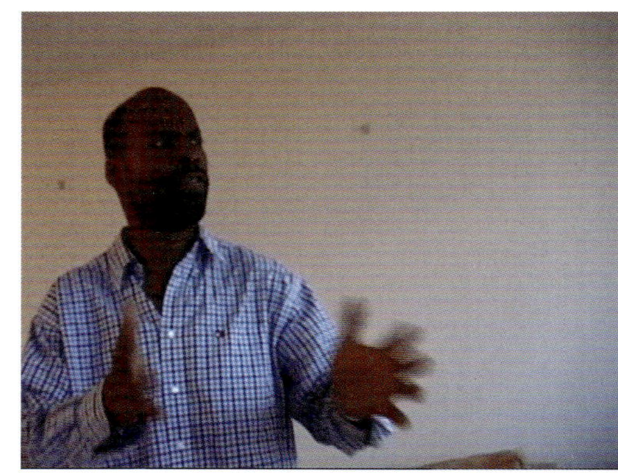
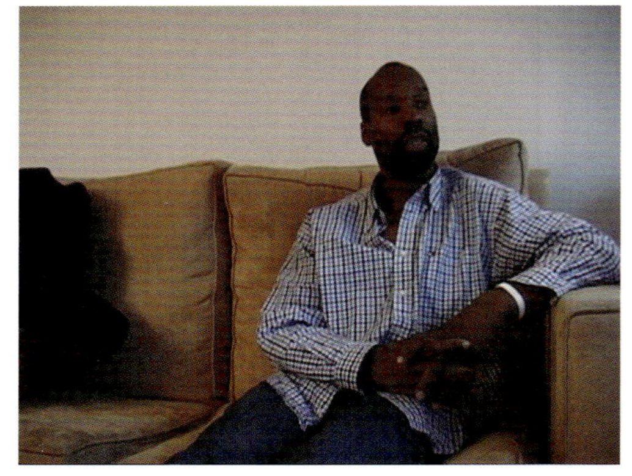
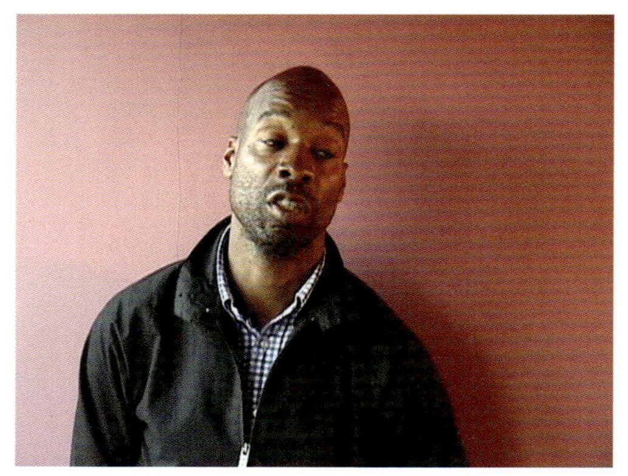
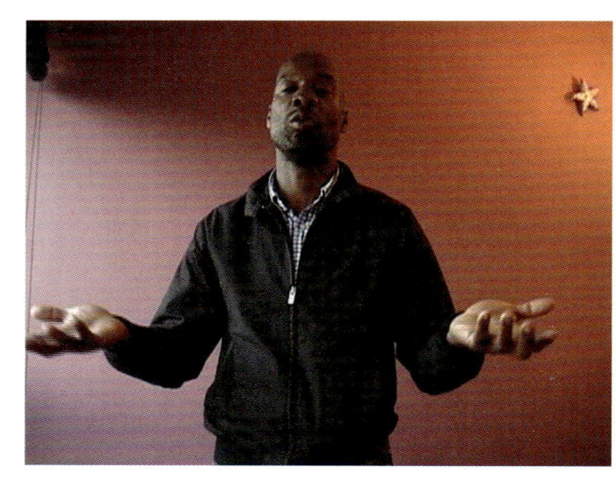
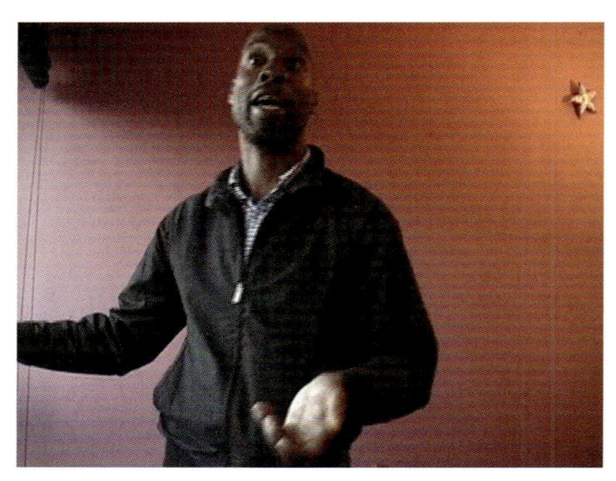
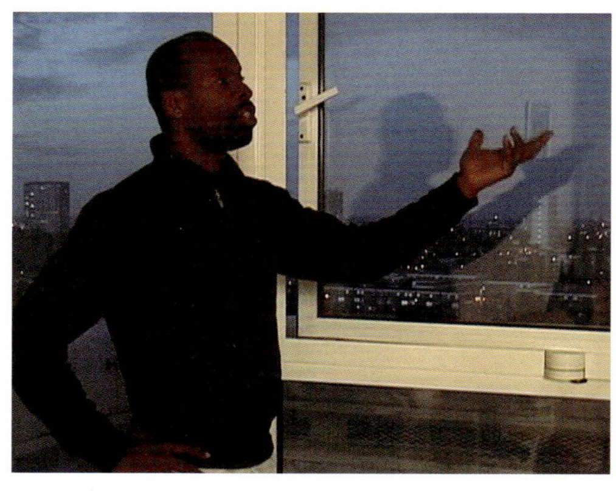
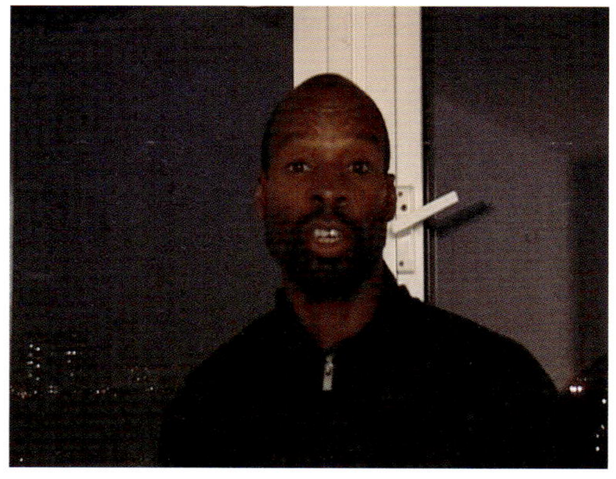
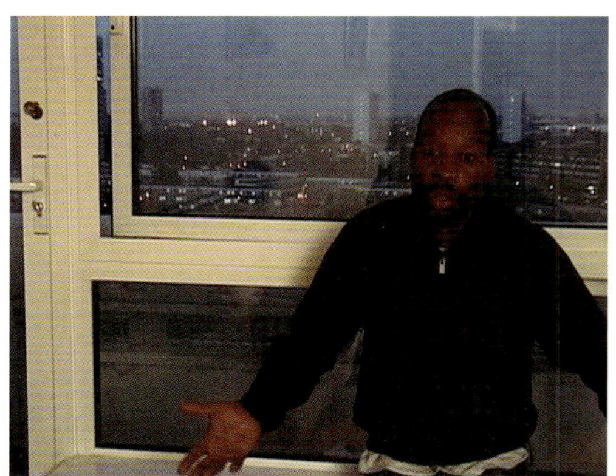

60

You're Joking, Aren't You?, 2005

RACHEL GARFIELD

(1963, London, England – lives London, England)

DVD, 4 × 2 min loop

Ben Uri Collection
Presented by the artist in 2006

SELECTED EXHIBITION HISTORY
Recent Acquisitions: 2001–2006, Ben Uri, London, 2007; Wisconsin Jewish Film Festival, 2008

Rachel Garfield studied for her MA at Central Saint Martins before completing her PhD at the Royal College of Art in London in 2003. Through her film and video portraits, Garfield explores the formation of subjectivity in relation to race, class and gender, as well as interrogating notions of authenticity and hierarchies of victim-hood. Although initially from a Fine Art background, Garfield sees her work as having an ongoing relationship with the traditions and concerns of avant-garde documentary film.

Garfield examines racial identity and the concept of the stereotype, as well as the complexities of how visibility – what we 'think we see'– affects our assumptions about who someone 'is'. *You're Joking, Aren't You?* is a series of vignettes in which actor Wayne Atkinson describes, in varying modes of address, and in different guises and domestic settings, everyday encounters involving racial prejudice. The first, told whilst standing in the kitchen is reminiscent of Frantz Fanon's *Black Skin White Masks*, and involves a lengthy rendition of a chance meeting with a child who calls him a 'nigger'. The subject of the second story is his engagement to a Portuguese woman whose belief it is that the African 'dilemma' (the extensive poverty and unrest associated with the myriad nations of the continent) is the fault of the Jewish people. The third vignette sees Atkinson standing in front of a red wall, describing seeing an 'Eastern European beggar' in London and being accosted by a black woman who confides in him her belief that the gypsies should be 'sent back' to where they came from. Garfield's protagonist notes wryly to the camera that these would have been the same kinds of comments made about her parents when they first arrived in Britain. *You're Joking* might also be seen as participating in a dialogue with *Portrait of Jason*, a 1967 documentary produced and directed by Shirley Clarke, featuring a gay, African-American hustler and aspiring cabaret performer, the film's eponymous narrator.

Garfield is Director of Postgraduate Studies at the University of Reading and a Visiting Fellow at the University of Newcastle in the Departments of Geography and Fine Art. In 2005 she curated the exhibition *Radical and Modest: Work, Leisure and the Everyday* at Ben Uri in St. John's Wood, juxtaposing work by Richard Billingham, Sonia Boyce, Jeremy Deller, Stephen Dwoskin and Chad McCail with works from Ben Uri's Collection by artists including David Azuz, David Bomberg, Josef Herman, Clara Klinghoffer and Jacob Kramer on the theme of working life and popular pastimes.

61

Perfect Match, 2006

NIRVEDA ALLECK
(1975, Mauritius – lives Mauritius)

Video: 6 minutes, 32 seconds

Ben Uri Collection
Presented by the artist 2014

SELECTED EXHIBITION HISTORY
Still Fighting Ignorance and Intellectual Perfidy: Video Art from Africa, Malmo Konsthall, Sweden; Motorenhall, Germany; Kunsthalle Sao Paulo, Brazil; Ben Uri, London, 2014

Born in 1975, Nirveda Alleck is a multi-disciplinary contemporary artist living and practising in Mauritius. She studied at Michaelis School of Fine Art, South Africa (BAFA 1997) and the Glasgow School of Art, Scotland (MFA, 2001). Formerly a lecturer in Art Education in Mauritius, Alleck has also worked as an Art Consultant at the Aapravasi Ghat World Heritage Site in Mauritius, and is currently lecturing part-time for the Master of Visual Arts course at the University of Mauritius. Alleck has participated in numerous international workshops in Namibia, South Africa, India, Lebanon, Mali and Mauritius, and taken up residencies at the Bag Factory Studios in Johannesburg as well as in Scotland, Reunion Island, Namibia, USA, Mali and Mauritius. She was awarded a Francis Greenburger Fellowship in 2011 to undertake a residency at Art OMI, New York. Alleck has also participated in many international exhibitions including: *Diplomatic Immunity* (New York, USA, 2001), *11th Triennale* (India, 2005), *Pan African Arts Festival* (Algeria, 2009), *Francophonie Games* (Beirut), *Arts Actuels Biennale* (Reunion Island, Mauritius) and *World Festival of Black Arts* (Dakar). In 2010, Alleck was a laureate at the *Dak'Art Biennale*, where she was awarded the Soleil d'Afrique Prize; she also participated again in 2012 winning an EMMA Award (Culture category).

Alleck's work is a combination of personal history fused with a more extended view of the world space in which we live and the psychological and sometimes romantic notions of existence and time. She often takes a 'felt' moment as a starting point, attempting to render certain intrinsic feelings into real situations and fusing the personal and the public into a whole. *Perfect Match* features two boxers – one male and one female – and the shadows they generate sparring against a changing sequence of backgrounds, interwoven with fragments of text in French and English. Alleck works with a range of media including paint, installation, video and sound. Most recently, she has been involved in implementing a major public art project in Mauritius.

In 2014 Togolese-French curator and producer Kisito Assangni toured *Still Fighting Ignorance and Intellectual Perfidy: Video Art from Africa*, a multi-national exhibition and a platform for critical thinking, researching and presenting African video art, to Ben Uri in London. The exhibition presented a selection of work by 21 contemporary African video artists, including Nirveda Alleck's *Perfect Match* (2006), and confronted some of the stereotypes that are still too often associated with African Art and its presentation in the West.

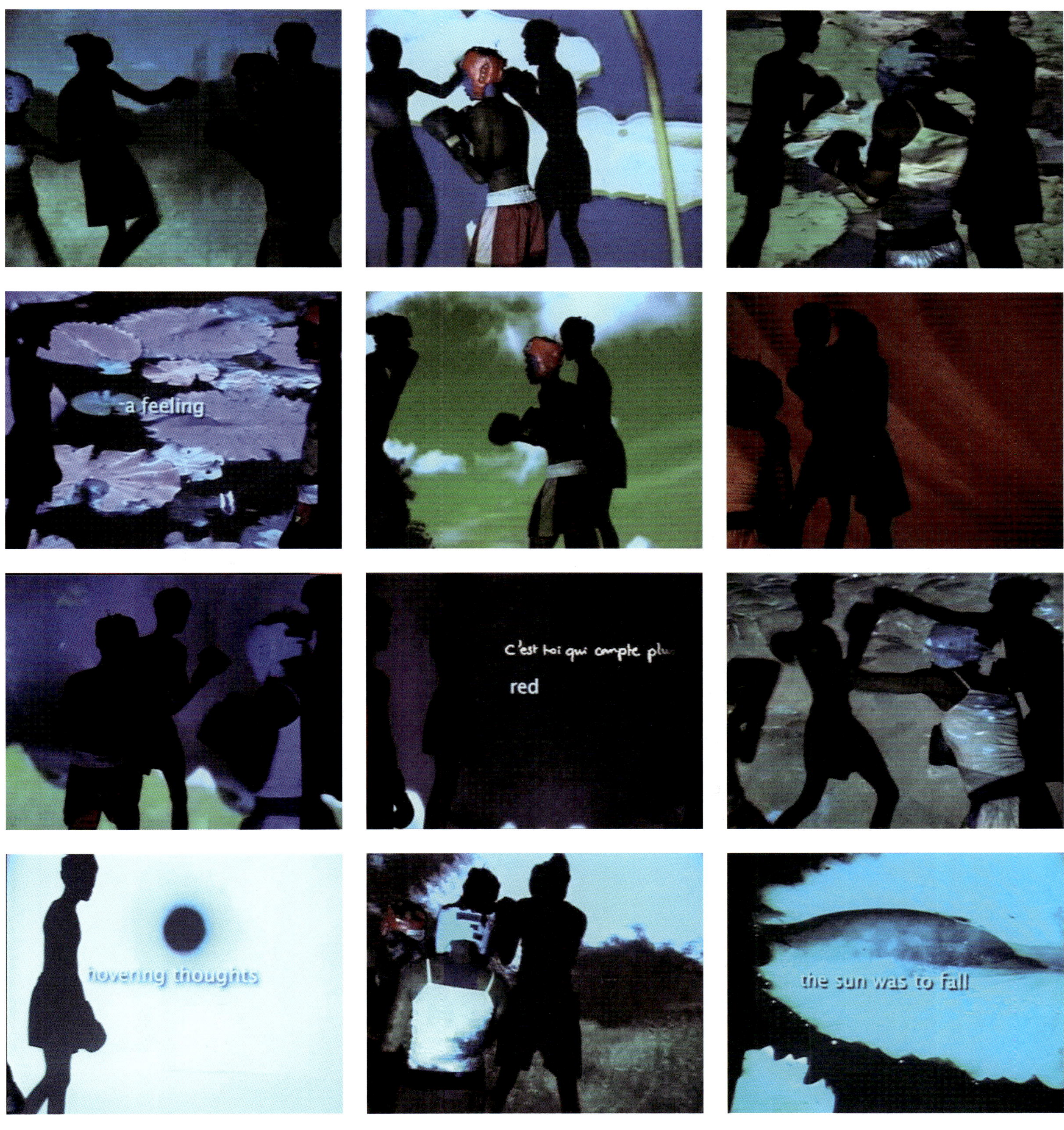
a feeling
C'est toi qui compte plus
red
hovering thoughts
the sun was to fall

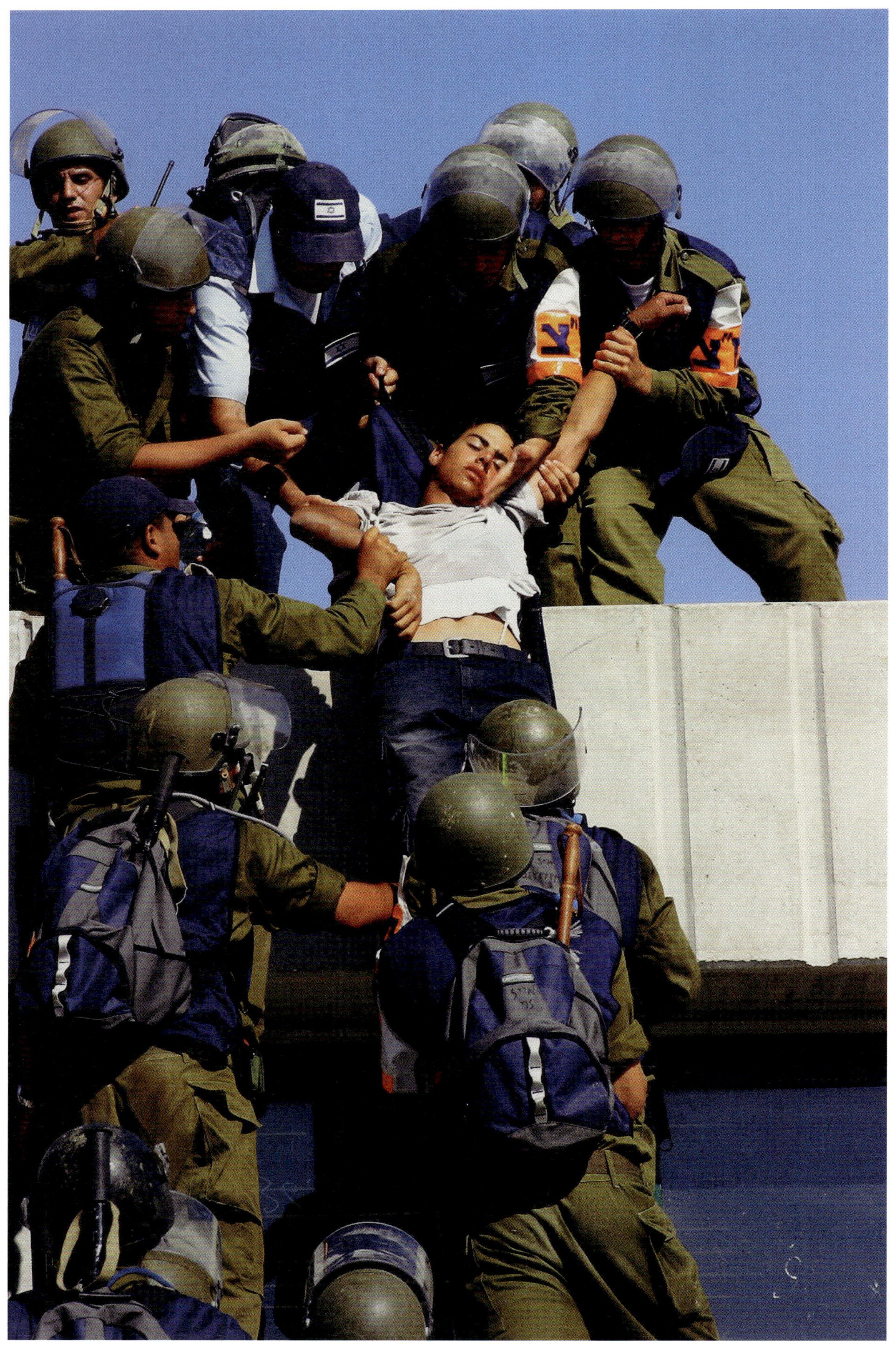

62

Homesh Evacuation #01 / Taken Down, 2007

NATAN DVIR

(1972 Nahariya, Israel – lives New York, USA)

Digital C-Type lambda print
mounted on aluminium
Edition 2/6

Ben Uri Collection
105 × 70 cm
Purchased from the artist, 2007
Overall winner: IJAYA 2007 and
recipient of the Annely Juda Prize

SELECTED EXHIBITION HISTORY
IJAYA, Christie's, London, 2007;
*Selected Masterworks: Israeli, Modern
and Contemporary Collection*,
Bonhams, London, 2011

Photographer Natan Dvir was born in Nahariya, Israel in 1972 and is based in New York. His work focuses on the human aspects of political, social and cultural issues. He graduated in Computer Science and Economics (BA, Tel Aviv University, 1995) and also gained an MA in Business Administration (1998), before he began his photography career, gaining an MFA in Photography from the School of Visual Arts (New York), after which he became a faculty member at the International Center for Photography (ICP). He photographs globally, represented by Polaris Images photo agency and Anastasia Photo gallery, specialising in editorial, documentary and commercial photography. His work has appeared in numerous publications including *Vanity Fair*, *Newsweek*, *Focus*, *Time Out*, *The New York Times*, *Wall Street Journal*, *The Times*, *Le Monde*, and *Le Figaro* among others, and he has exhibited internationally.

He has won international recognition and awards in competitions including PDN Photo Annual, USA (2012-13), International Photography Award, USA (2012), New York Photography Festival Award (2010), Critical Mass Top 50, USA (2013) and Picture of the Year Award in the Israeli press on several occasions. In March 2007 Dvir was 'Overall Winner' in Ben Uri's *International Jewish Artist of the Year Award*.

Dvir comments, 'The works are part of a long term project exploring various sides of Human Belief as it is reflected in scenes of conflict and religious nature. The intensity of belief driving people to extreme and sometimes surreal situations is reflected in the confrontations between the Israel security forces and Jewish settlers during the evacuation of Jewish settlements in the West Bank during 2005–6'. Dvir's main projects have been exhibited in numerous solo and group exhibitions in the United States, Europe, South America and Israel. Ben Uri holds three works by Dvir in the Collection.

63

Maternal Torah, 2008

JACQUELINE NICHOLLS

(1971 Nottingham, England – lives London, England)

Sinamay (lightweight millinery
fabric)
60 × 40 × 22 cm

Ben Uri Collection
Presented by the artist 2008

SELECTED EXHIBITION HISTORY
Schmatte Couture, Rivington Gallery,
London, 2008; *Apocalypse*, Osborne
Samuel, London, 2010

FOOTNOTES
1   Émigré exhibitors included Ernst
Eisenmayer (cat. 34), Hilde
Goldschmidt, Jacques Kupfermann
and Hans Schwarz.

Artist and educator Jacqueline Nicholls was born in 1971 in Nottingham and currently lives in London. Her work explores traditional Jewish concepts in non-traditional ways, using drawing, print, embroidery, textiles and clothing. She initially studied architecture, followed by Fine Art at the Byam Shaw School; London College of Printing, and the Prince of Wales Drawing School. She was a finalist in the Ben Uri's 2007 *International Jewish Artist of the Year Award*, shown at Christie's, London, and was one of the exhibitors in *Schmatte Couture* (2008), curated for Ben Uri at the Rivington Gallery, Shoreditch by contemporary artist Sarah Lightman, featuring 16 international contemporary artists dealing with issues surrounding clothing, memory, gender and identity. The location in Rivington Street was particularly apt as a once thriving centre where sweatshops employed waves of first generation immigrant communities – in turn, Jewish, Indian and Bangladeshi.

Maternal Torah (*Torat Imecha*), together with Nicholls' related work, *The Yeshiva Inside* (*Yeshiva Bifnim*), merges the forms of a corset and a *Sefer Torah* (scroll) cover. Jewish tradition sees the *Torah* as a feminine object. These corset/Torah hybrids explore this concept by highlighting the womanly aspects of the cover, as well as the beauty and constraints of *Halacha* (Jewish Law). *The Yeshiva Inside* is a 'pregnant' *Sefer Torah* cover, inspired by a Talmudic passage that describes a foetus being taught *Torah* in the womb; at birth, forgetting what it has learnt, it spends its life trying to remember. In the work, the mother's body has been transformed into a primal place of personal revelation.

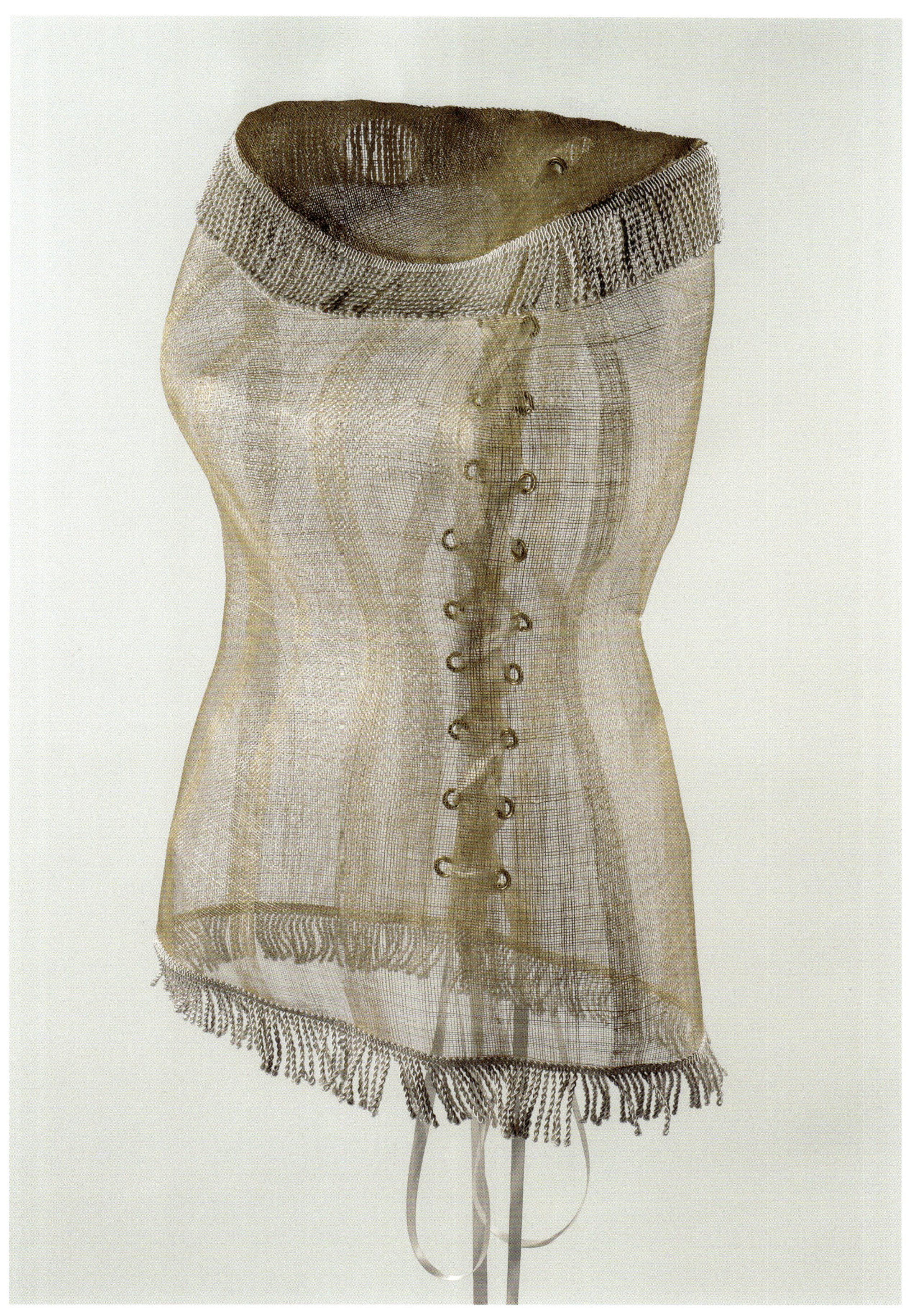

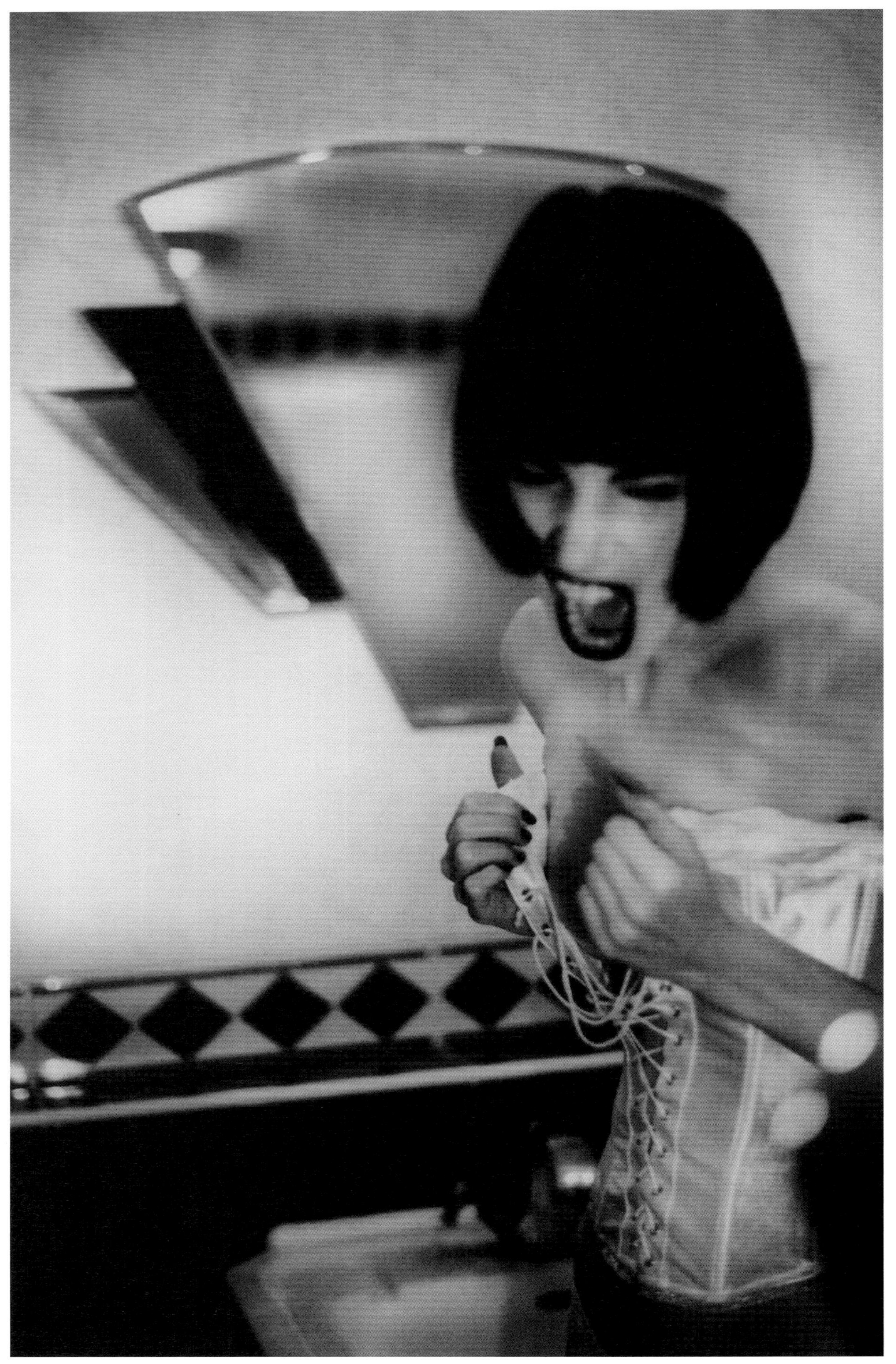

64

Rage, 2008

SOPHIE ROBERTSON

(1988 London, England – lives Sydney, Australia)

Digital photograph
69 × 45 cm

Ben Uri Collection
Presented by the artist

SELECTED EXHIBITION HISTORY
Schmatte Couture, Rivington Gallery, London, 2008; *Apocalypse,* Osborne Samuel, London, 2010; *The Anguish of being a Woman: Women Artists in the Ben Uri Collection,* online exhibition, Ben Uri, London, 2014

Sophie Robertson graduated from Central St. Martins with a degree in Fashion Photography in 2010. She has since worked on a number of projects including fashion shows and participated in exhibitions around the world. In 2012 she set up her own label designing digitally printed silk scarves.

Rage depicts a woman at her toilette, howling in anger as she struggles with the corset that defines and restricts her torso. A striking and highly stylised image, *Rage* comments on the anguish of being a woman. An intimate and seemingly candid expression of unbridled emotion, Robertson's subject might be seen to be responding to society's unnatural, unrealistic and in many ways harmful expectations of what a woman should be and should look like, and the pivotal role which clothing plays in fashioning the body.

Rage and its companion piece, *Release* (cat. 65), both featured in *Schmatte Couture* curated by Sarah Lightman for Ben Uri in 2008, addressing issues surrounding clothing, memory, gender and identity and featuring 16 international contemporary artists. The location in Rivington Street was particularly apt as a once thriving centre where sweat shops once employed waves of first generation immigrants from the Jewish, Indian and Bangladeshi communities.

65
Release, 2008

SOPHIE ROBERTSON

(1988 London, England – lives Sydney, Australia)

Digital photograph
70 × 52 cm

Ben Uri Collection
Presented by the artist

SELECTED EXHIBITION HISTORY
Schmatte Couture, Rivington Gallery, London, 2008; *Apocalypse,* Osborne Samuel, London, 2010; *The anguish of being a woman: Women Artists in the Ben Uri Collection*, online exhibition, Ben Uri, London, 4-31 March 2014

Sophie Robertson graduated from Central St. Martins with a degree in Fashion Photography in 2010. *Release* is her companion piece to *Rage* (cat. 64). Far from howling in rage, *Release* depicts Robertson's muse posing serenely, seemingly nude except for the many layered pearl necklace adorning her décolletage. Far more passive than her counterpart in *Rage*, Robertson's subject appears to accept her role simply as a beautiful object of desire.

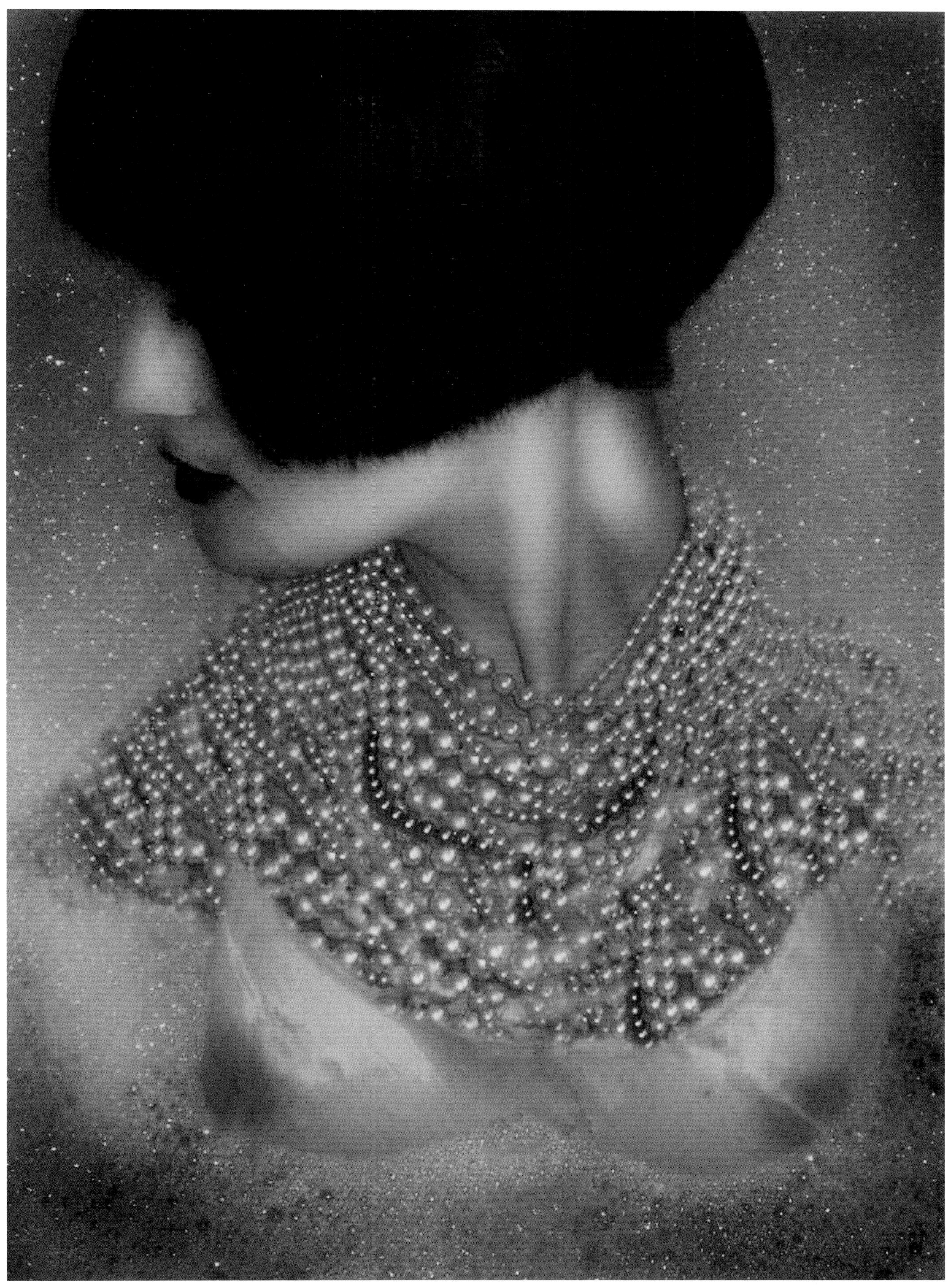

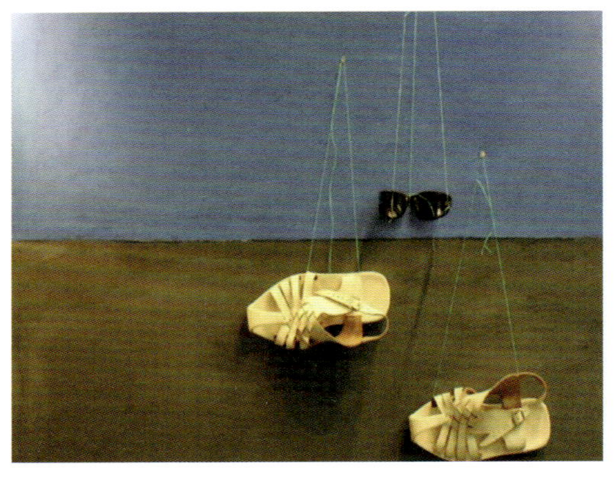
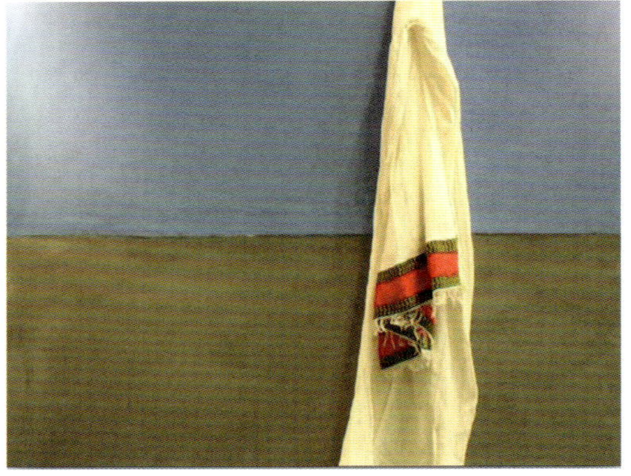
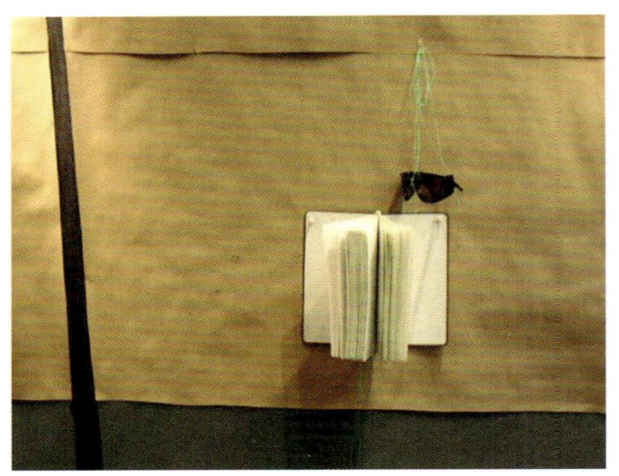
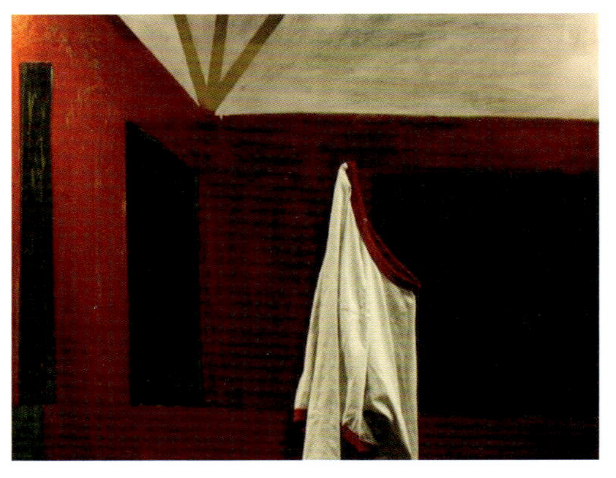
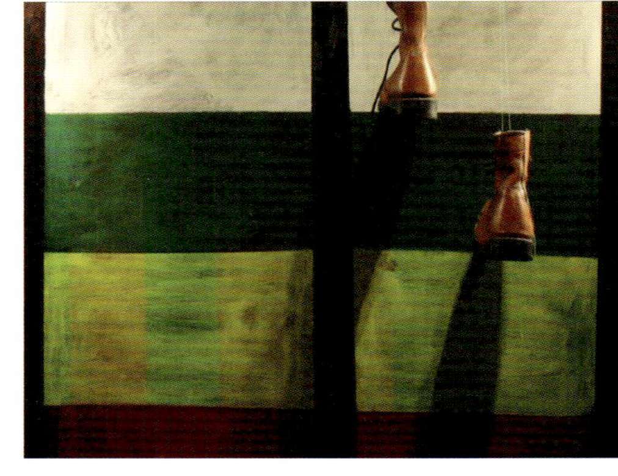
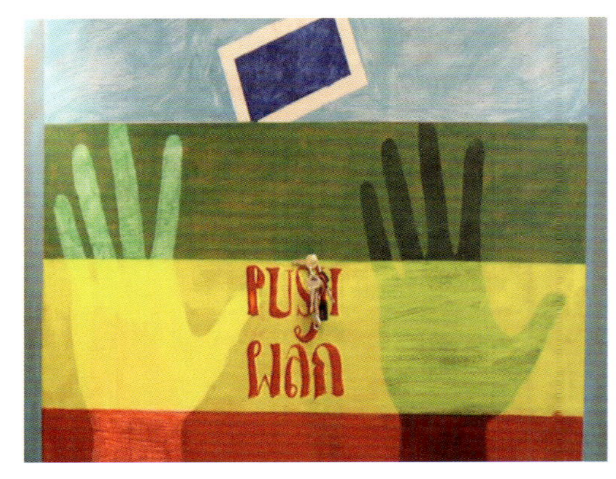

PUSH
WAN

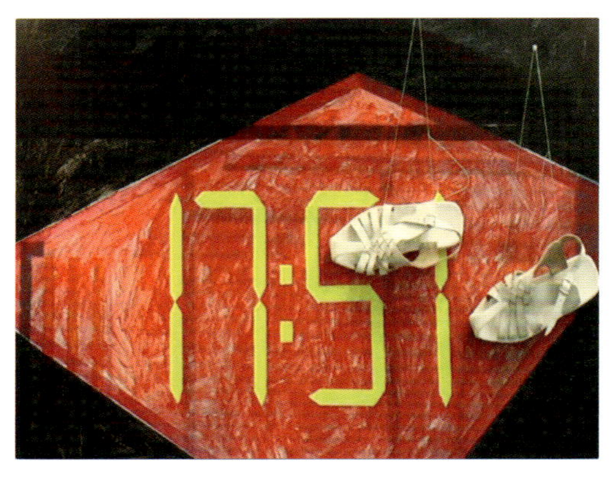

17:57

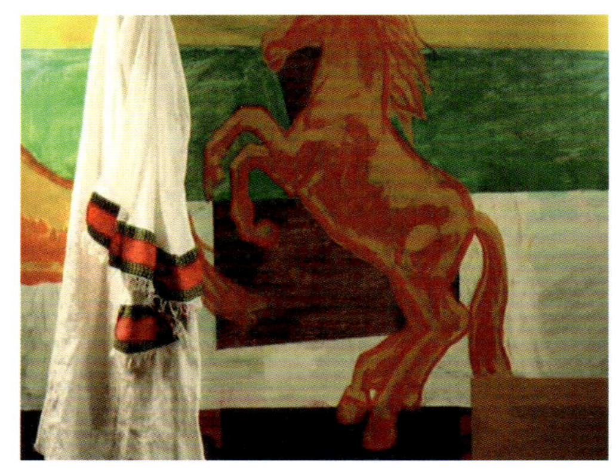
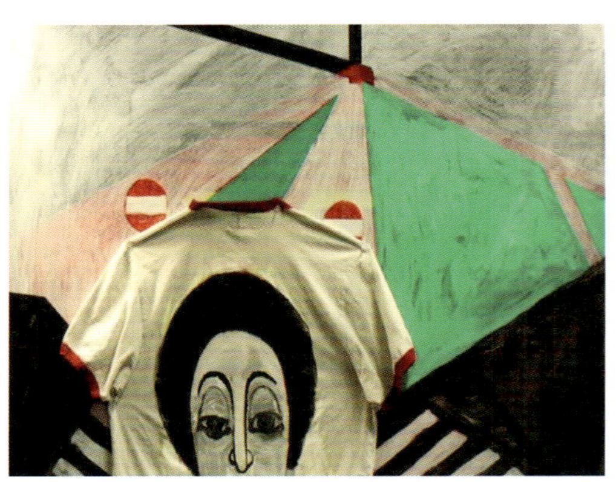
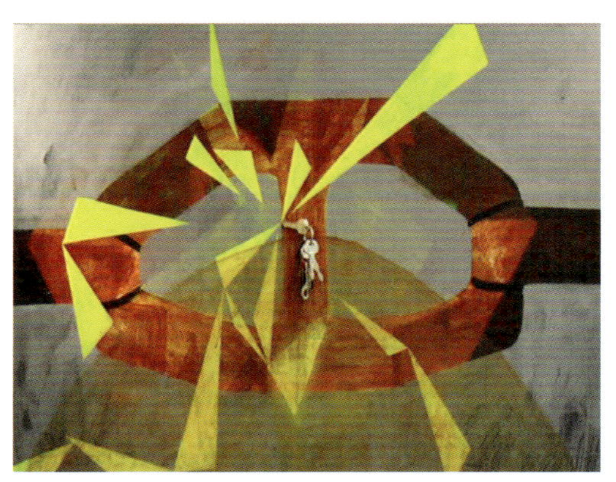
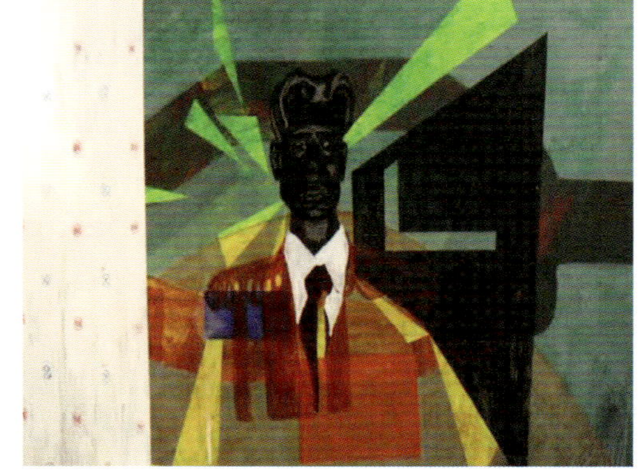
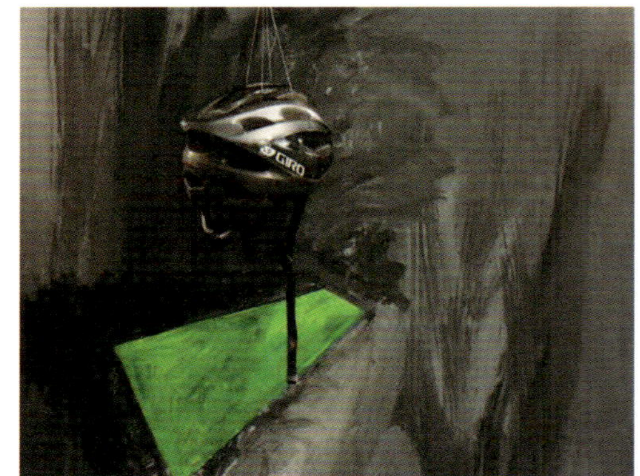

Gela 2, 2010

EZRA WUBE

(1980, Addis Ababa, Ethiopia – lives New York, USA)

Video: 1 minute, 57 seconds

Ben Uri Collection
Presented by the artist 2014

SELECTED EXHIBITION HISTORY
*Still Fighting Ignorance and Intellectual
Perfidy: Video Art from Africa*, Malmo
Konsthall, Sweden; Motorenhall,
Germany; Kunsthalle Sao Paulo,
Brazil; Ben Uri, London, 2014

Ezra Wube was born in 1980 in Addis Ababa, Ethiopia and moved to the United States at the age of 18. He received his BFA in Painting from the Massachusetts College of Art, Boston (2004), and his MFA from Hunter College, New York, NY (2009). His work encompasses video, installation, drawing, painting and performance. In 2003, he was awarded the Massachusetts Annual Black Achievement Award and held his first solo exhibition at the Dreams of Freedom Museum in Boston, Massachussetts. Upon graduation he was awarded a Dondis and Godine Travel Fellowship to carry out research in Ethiopia exploring folktales and traditional lore, resulting in his second solo show *Story Telling* (2006) at the United Nations in New York. He also participated in the *Ethiopian Millennium* art exhibition at the Blackburn Gallery, Howard University, Washington, DC (2007); and in 2008: *Reflections in Exile: Five Contemporary African Artists Respond to Social Injustice* at the South Shore Art Center, Cohasett; *Here to There* at the South Seattle Community College, Seattle, Washington, and *Abyssinia to Harlem and Back* at the Canvas Paper and Stone Gallery, New York. The following year he received the Pamela Joseph Art Scholarship while working on his MFA and exhibited in *The Happening: Kinetics as Art Object* (Rush Arts Gallery, New York); *MA selects MFA* (Hunter College, New York); *Freeze Frame* (throughout Miami, Florida) and the Bina Film Festival, New York; BAM (Brooklyn, New York, 2010). After completing his MFA, Wube was commissioned to direct and animate a television

advertisement for Standard Chartered Bank as part of a global campaign titled 'Here for Good'. He has also exhibited at MEIAC-Museum of Extramadura, Badajoz (Spain).

He has said of this work, '*Gela 2* defies singular categorization. Viewers witness a journey through the merging of past and present'.

In 2014 Togolese-French curator and producer Kisito Assangni toured *Still Fighting Ignorance and Intellectual Perfidy: Video Art from Africa*, a multi-national exhibition and a platform for critical thinking, researching and presenting African video art, to a number of international venues including Ben Uri. The exhibition presented a selection of works by 21 contemporary African video artists, including Wube's *Gela 2* (2010). In his catalogue introduction Assangni concluded that 'the project tells 'Africa's story by African new media artists as seen through the lens of the relation between tradition and modernity'.

Maquette for Visitor, 2010

DAVID BREUER-WEIL

(1965 London, England – lives London, England)

Bronze with brown patina
23 × 17.5 × 18.5 cm
AP

Ben Uri Collection
Presented by the artist 2010

David Breuer-Weil was born in London in 1965. His father, also an artist, was born in Vienna and fled to England after the *Anschluss*. A number of Breuer-Weil's early landscapes are set by beside Lake Holte in Denmark, where his maternal grandfather was killed in 1944. Breuer-Weil grew up in London and studied at St. Martins School of Art under Shelley Faussett (a former assistant to Henry Moore), afterwards attending Clare College, Cambridge. After graduating, he was awarded a bursary at Sotheby's, which he later referred to as 'the greatest art school in the world', and where he worked in many departments. His early 'Neracian' drawings – small enough to be stored in stamp albums – were based on an imaginary race that has consistently occupied the landscape of his art, though his later works are monumental in conception and execution. Breuer-Weil has also lived, worked and exhibited in Israel, the experience contributing to the development of light and colour in his work, as well as working as an art consultant for the Swiss dealers de Pury and Luxembourg. Breuer-Weil nonetheless rejects the commercial in art, writing of an earlier series of works known as *Project 3* that he wished to 'produce colossal, un-commercialized images of existential doubt'.

Breuer-Weil conceived the idea for the first Project in the early nineties, bringing it to fruition in the crypt of the Roundhouse, Camden Town, in 2001. *Project 2* followed two years later, held in the South Bank Bargehouse in 2003; and four years on, *Project 3* was a Ben Uri exhibiont held in a Covent Garden multi-storey car park in 2007. *Project 4* (2013), sited in the vaults at Waterloo, is Breuer-Weil's largest solo project to date and comprises around 130 works, including more than 70 large-scale canvases, sculptures, maquettes and drawings.

Breuer-Weil grew up in North London and lives near Hampstead Heath, a place he considers to be 'of great mystical power'. This mystical element is strongly alluded to in his work. The maquette for *Visitor* is the working model for Breuer-Weil's monumental head of the same title which was exhibited in *Beyond Limits – Sotheby's at Chatsworth House* in 2010. The tactile surface reveals the artist's fingerprints greatly enlarged in order to imply 'that a higher power has constructed and placed this unearthly figure in this suffocated position'. *Visitor I* relates closely to Breuer-Weil's *Philosopher* paintings, which also feature a large head creating a disturbance in the soil that surrounds it. Of these works, Breuer-Weil has stated that he wanted to express 'the immense potential power of thought'. He has commented of this piece:

By slightly submerging the image I wanted to suggest our connection with the earth. When installed in water, I wanted to give the impression of a figure with far greater potential than what you actually see, and I believe the reflections accentuate that effect. This work is a visual embodiment of thought. Every human being is largely hidden and secret.

Ben Uri holds three works by Breuer-Weil in the Collection.

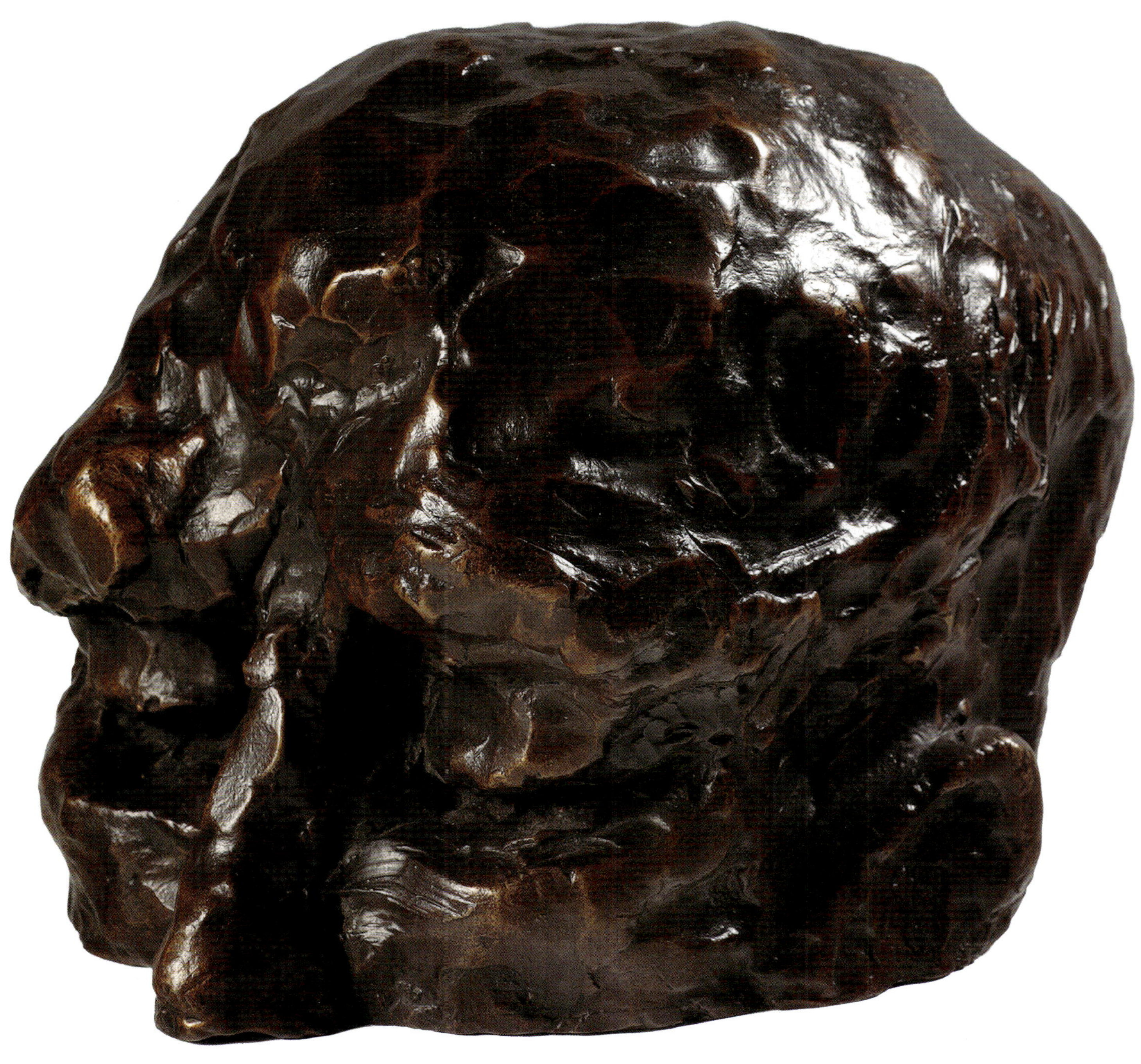

The
Whitechapel
Boys

Richard Cork

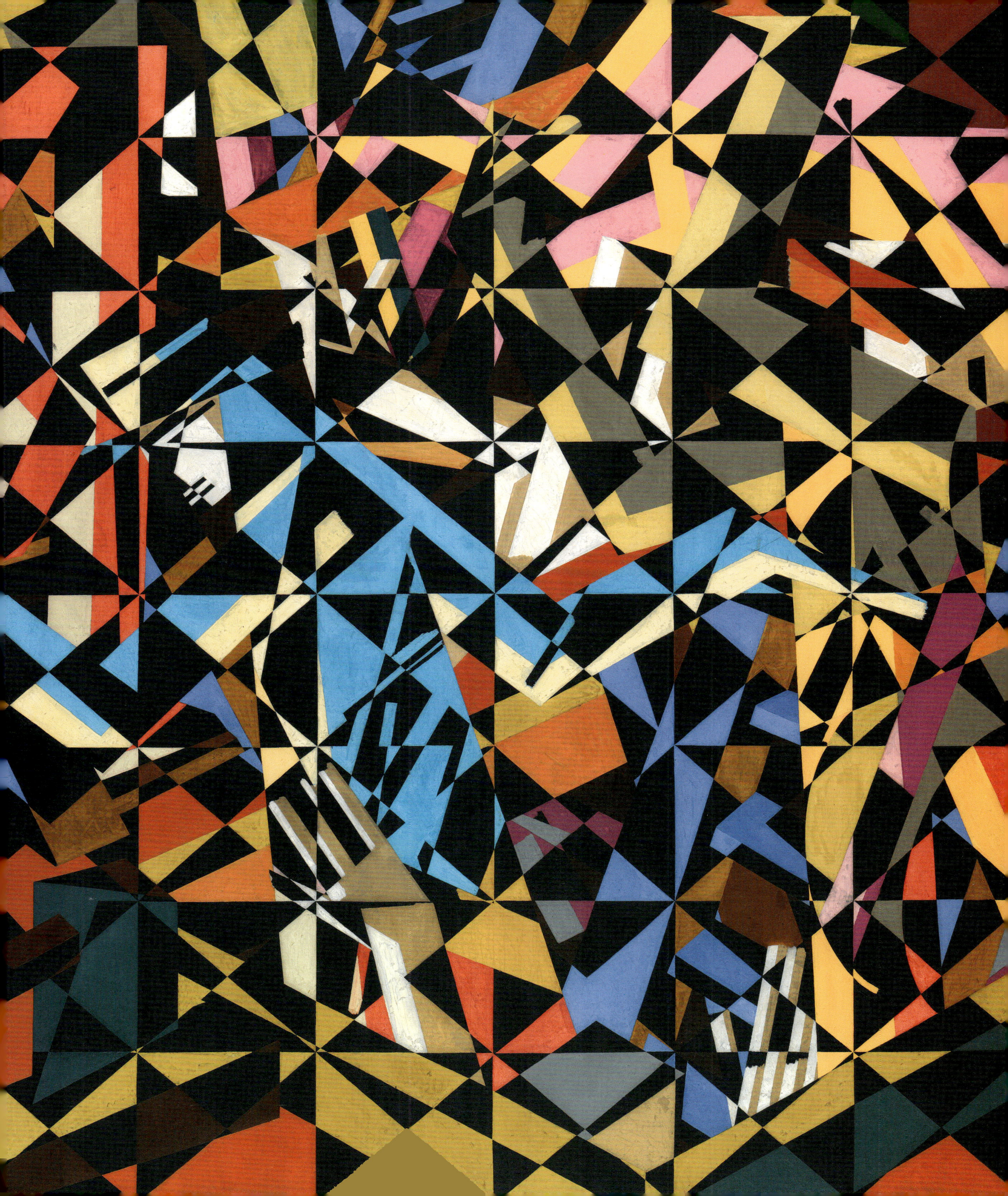

Fig. 1 *(previous page)* David Bomberg, *In the Hold* (detail), c.1913–14.
Tate

Fig. 2 The Slade School Picnic, 1912.
Private collection

Fig. 3 Alfred Wolmark, *In the Synagogue*, 1906.
Ben Uri Collection

As the twentieth century entered its first decade, most of the people who lived in the Whitechapel area of London were immigrants who had fled persecution in their native countries. Crowded into slum housing, and earning a precarious living as tailors, shoemakers and dock labourers, Eastern European Jews and Russian exiles struggled to cope with their fate as exiles. So the emergence, then, of several highly talented young artists from this stricken locale seems almost miraculous. Known as The Whitechapel Boys, they included David Bomberg, Mark Gertler and Isaac Rosenberg, all of whom succeeded in gaining places as students at the Slade (fig. 2) – far and away the most vital London art school during the restless years leading up to the First World War.

They must have taken heart from the example set by Alfred Wolmark, an older artist whose family had brought him to England from Warsaw in 1883. After an early period in Devon, the family moved to London's East End and settled in Tredegar Square, Bow, an elegant neighbourhood which reflected the fact that Wolmark's parents were not poor. Nor did they disapprove of his desire to study at the Royal Academy Schools. He soon became critical of the conservative teaching provided there, however, and established a studio at Aldgate to study the local people (*In the Synagogue*, 1906, fig. 3). Wolmark even went back to his native Poland for a year, savouring traditional Jewish life in Krakow. On his return to London he developed rapidly, and the painting *Sabbath Afternoon* (1909–10, cat. 6) shows his commitment to humble subjects in the East End. The vulnerability of immigrant Jewish life is sensitively conveyed here, but Wolmark was also adept at portraying the confidence and vitality of sitters as ebullient as *Mrs Ethel Solomon in Riding Habit* (cat. 7) and Mrs. Herbert Cohen (fig. 4).

Although Whitechapel was a tough area for most people, it became nourished by the arrival of

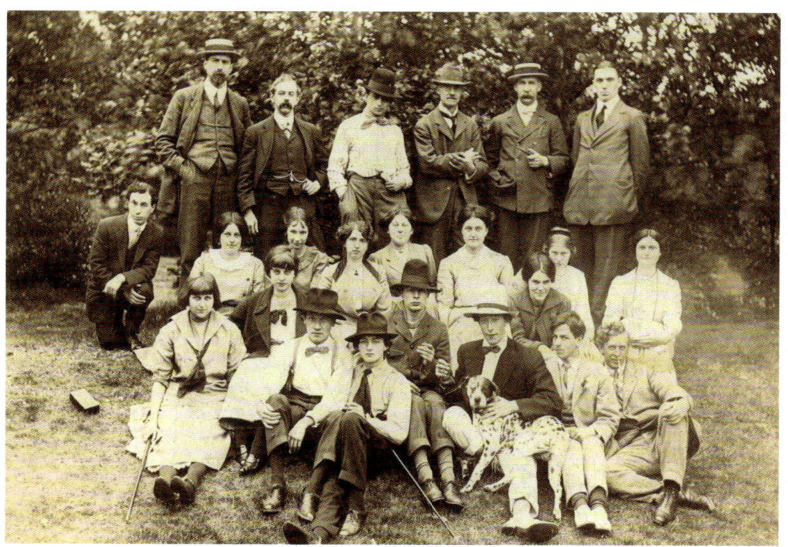

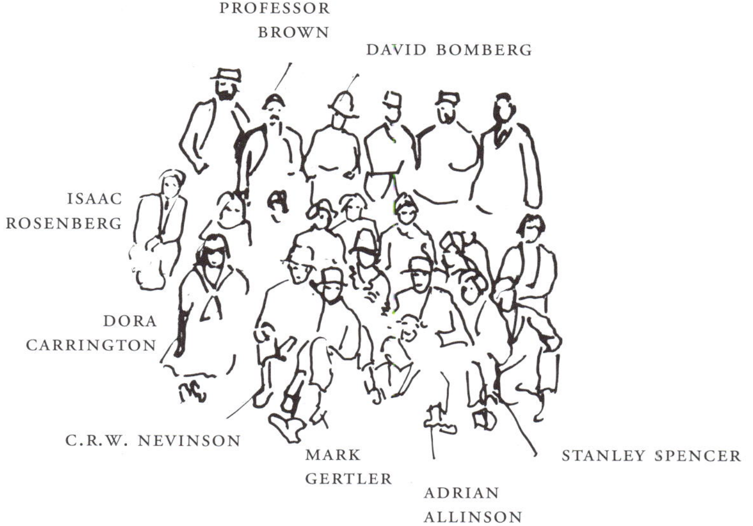

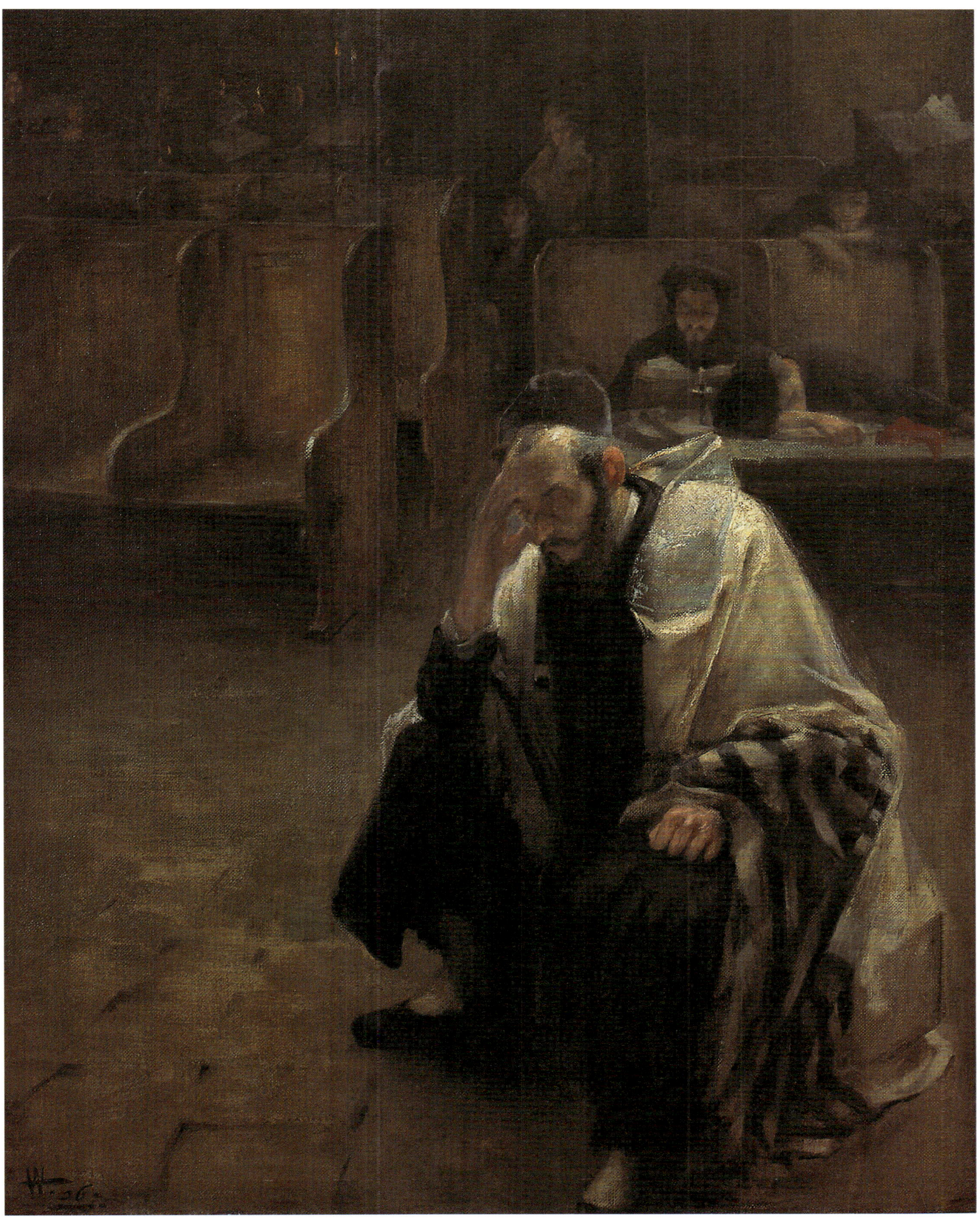

institutions as outstanding as the Passmore Edwards Library, which quickly became known as the 'University of the Ghetto'. Both the library and the Whitechapel Art Gallery, which opened in 1901, proved invaluable to the generation of young Jewish artists and writers who grew up in this beleaguered sector of the metropolis. Canon Samuel Barnett, who with his wife Henrietta had been instrumental in creating the gallery, protested in 1890 that East Enders:

[C]ertainly cannot afford time after work to clean themselves and travel to the West End, spend an hour in a gallery, return, and get enough sleep before next morning's early rising. Few, too, could afford a railway fare, which, though it may be small, often bears a large proportion to the weekly wage. If the mass of the people are to be interested in the life of the time as it is revealed through pictures, and if, too, the artists are to express the life of the time, galleries must be established where they may easily be visited.

The advent of the gallery and library meant an enormous amount to young people in the neighbourhood. The writer Joseph Leftwich (fig. 5), who was one of the Whitechapel Boys, told me how 'We used to mooch around the streets of Whitechapel completely wrapped up in our own misery; we didn't care where we were going because walking and talking were all we could do.'[1] They thus cherished the ability to meet at these new institutions, where intelligent and ambitious East Enders would delight in arguing about how to revolutionise the culture of the period. Leftwich remembered that Bomberg in particular was becoming 'very "blasty" – pugnacious is too mild a word. He wanted to dynamite the whole of English painting.'[2] But Bomberg also valued the opportunity for exercise and curative massage offered at Schevzik's,

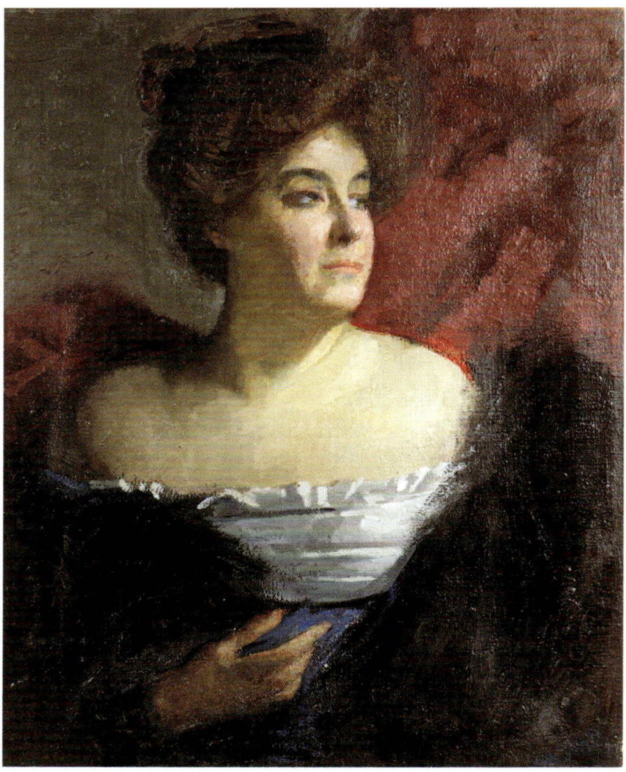

the Russian Vapour Baths opposite the synagogue in Brick Lane. A. B. Levy recounted how:

[I]n the courtyard to the extensive and dilapidated rest rooms and tiled baths you are informed that you can get here the "Best Massage in London: Invaluable Relief for Rheumatism, Gout, Sciatica, Neuritis, Lumbago, and Allied Complaints. Keep fit and well by regular visits." The orthodox of the East End certainly looked fit as they emerged from the gates of Schevzik's after their regular eve-of-Sabbath visit, displaying pink cheeks and stroking soft beards. Some of them, to continue cooling off, would drop in at the shop of Moshe the Scribe, a few doors away, to exchange shool [sic] gossip or listen to the latest record of American Cantor, Yossele Rosenblatt.[3]

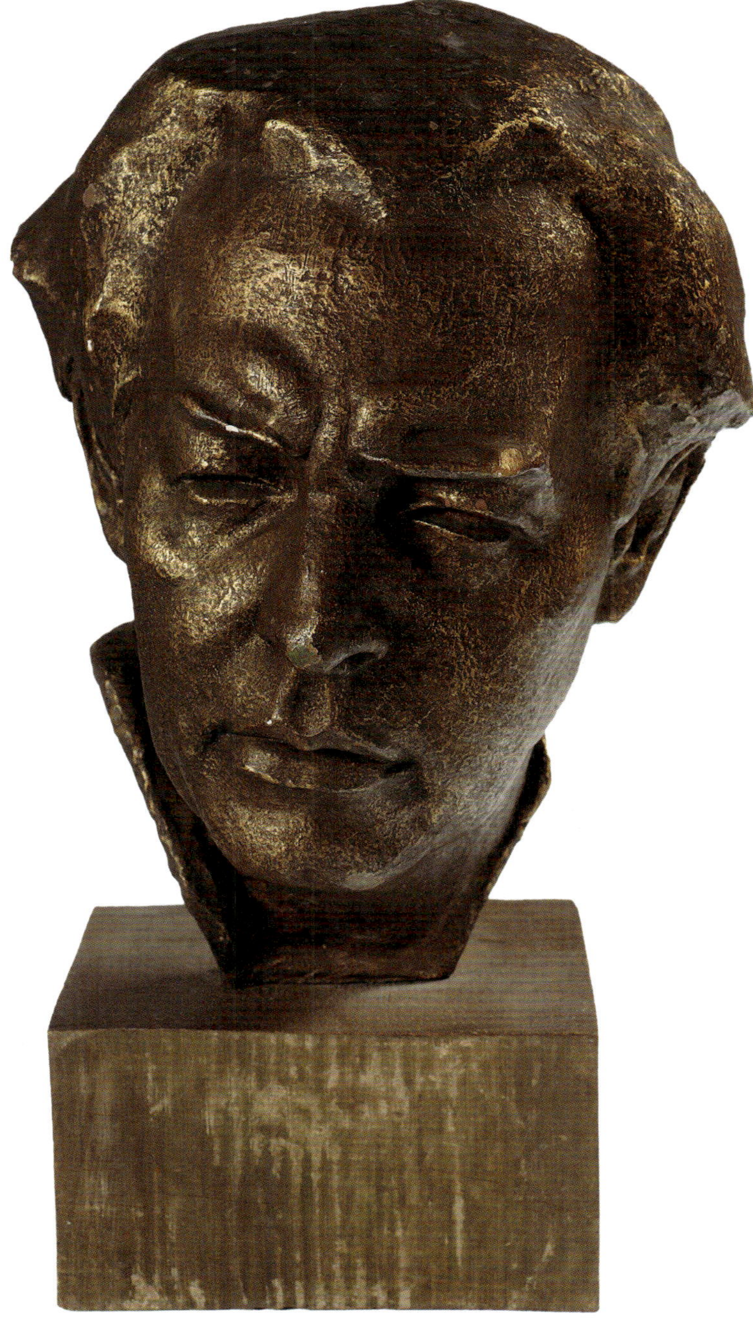

In 1914, just before the tragic intervention of the
First World War, Bomberg took these Vapour Baths
as the starting point for his masterpiece *The Mud Bath*
(1914, fig. 6), a large and prodigious painting where
figures purged of all excrescences are reborn in a
stripped-down, streamlined amalgam of humanity
and the machine. It was the climax of Bomberg's
precocious early career, which led him towards
studying at the Slade between 1911 and 1913. He had
been born in Birmingham, the son of a Polish leather-
craftsman who was driven from his native Poland by
fear of the pogroms. Abraham Bomberg and his wife
Rebecca already had four children, and they lived in
a desperately cramped and unhealthy working-class
neighbourhood. That is why they soon moved on
to Cardiff and then Whitechapel, where the ever-
expanding Bomberg family settled in a top-floor flat
with no bathroom or lavatory of its own. But Rebecca
made sure that young David's burgeoning talent as an
artist was encouraged, and she eventually obtained a
room in the flatlet next door where he could focus on
painting and drawing.

He made rapid progress, with the help of first-
hand contact with Sargent and Sickert, before visiting
the landmark London exhibition *Manet and the
Post-Impressionists*. Curated by Roger Fry, it opened at
the Grafton Galleries in November 1910 and enraged
many conservative visitors. Young rebels of Bomberg's
generation were, however, immensely stimulated by
the opportunity to encounter so many paintings by
Cézanne, Van Gogh and Gauguin. The achievements
of these artists strengthened Bomberg's resolve, and
Leftwich recalled that he seemed to be 'supremely
confident, full of himself and completely different
from Rosenberg who was taciturn'.[4] In April 1911
the Slade registered him as a student, and the

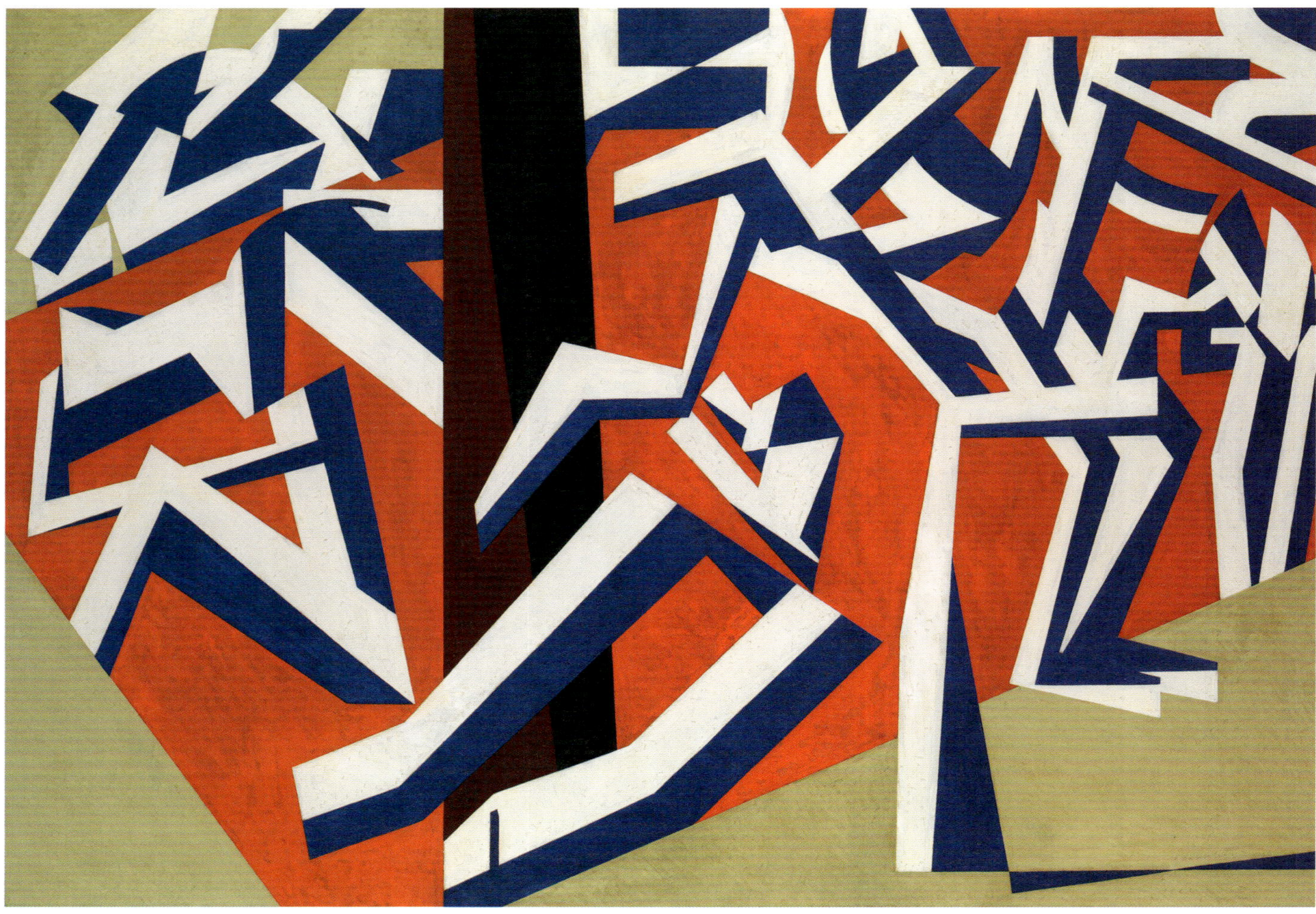

impoverished Bomberg was delighted when the Jewish Education Aid Society provided him with the funds to attend this outstanding school. He was even more fortunate to attend the Slade at the same time as many other top-flight students. Apart from Gertler (cats. 10 and 12) and Rosenberg (cat. 13), these included Jacob Kramer (cat. 14) and Bernard Meninsky (fig. 7), both of whose families had emigrated from Ukraine to the north of England, Paul Nash, C. R .W. Nevinson, Ben Nicholson, William Roberts, Stanley Spencer, Edward Wadsworth and Clare Winsten (cat. 15). So Bomberg was able to share his fascination with the avant-garde, and to realise just how dramatically British art in the fast-changing new century was being transformed by Cubism, Expressionism, Futurism and all the other modernist movements vying with each other to gain international attention.

In a series of paintings, ranging from *Vision of Ezekiel* and *Ju-Jitsu* to the extraordinary schematic virtuosity of *In the Hold* (*c.*1913–14, fig. 1), Bomberg proved himself an audacious young pioneer before the First World War. But he never stopped drawing as well, and a large chalk and wash study entitled

Racehorses (1913, cat. 9) shows just how experimental he had become. The subject could hardly have been more traditional, and yet Bomberg strips it of all conventional descriptive detail. The animals are reduced to their essential form, as 'primitive' as many of the works he admired on his visits to the British Museum. He must also have agreed with the witty observation, in the catalogue of Roger Fry's *Manet and the Post-Impressionists* exhibition, that 'a good rocking-horse is more like a horse than the snapshot of a Derby winner'.[5] The animals rushing through space in the distance, at the upper right area of this drawing, are as speedy as anything in a Futurist picture. Even so, the daring and reductive style deployed in *Racehorses* was bound to provoke hostile comments as well. The *Jewish Chronicle* declared that Bomberg's watercolour version of *Racehorses*, displayed in a ground-breaking show of *Twentieth-Century Art* at the Whitechapel Art Gallery in May 1914, depicted 'horses that could never possibly win races'.[6]

Bomberg had an immensely stimulating time when he was invited, with his friend Jacob Epstein (cat. 19), to select painters and sculptors for this Whitechapel Art Gallery exhibition. Its subtitle was *A Review of Modern Movements*, and the gallery's director asked Bomberg to curate a 'Jewish section' for the show. In his capacity as curator, he met Modigliani and Soutine on a trip to Paris with Epstein, who had studied there earlier in the century and knew Modigliani well. Bomberg was also able to contact artists as fascinating as Derain and Picasso, thereby ensuring that the Whitechapel exhibition was filled with experimental vitality. In May 1914, just before the show opened, Bomberg was interviewed by The *Jewish Chronicle* and insisted with characteristic conviction that:

[T]he new life should find its expression in a new art, which has been stimulated by new perceptions. I want to translate the life of a great city, its motion, its machinery, into an art that shall not be photographic, but expressive.[7]

London was, of course, a metropolis transformed by machine-age dynamism, and the Futurists' leader Marinetti was especially excited by travelling on the Underground. Bomberg refused to join any of the avant-garde movements, even though his *Jewish*

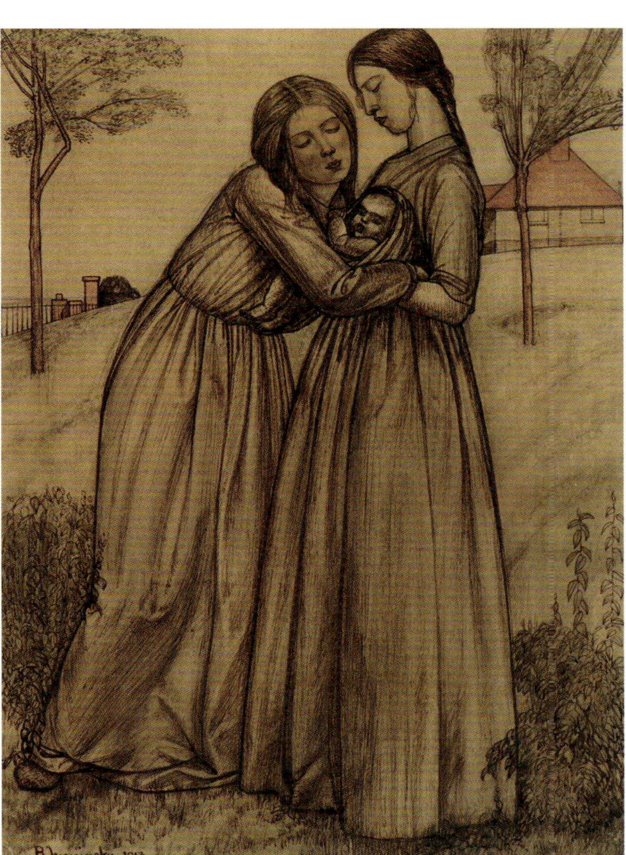

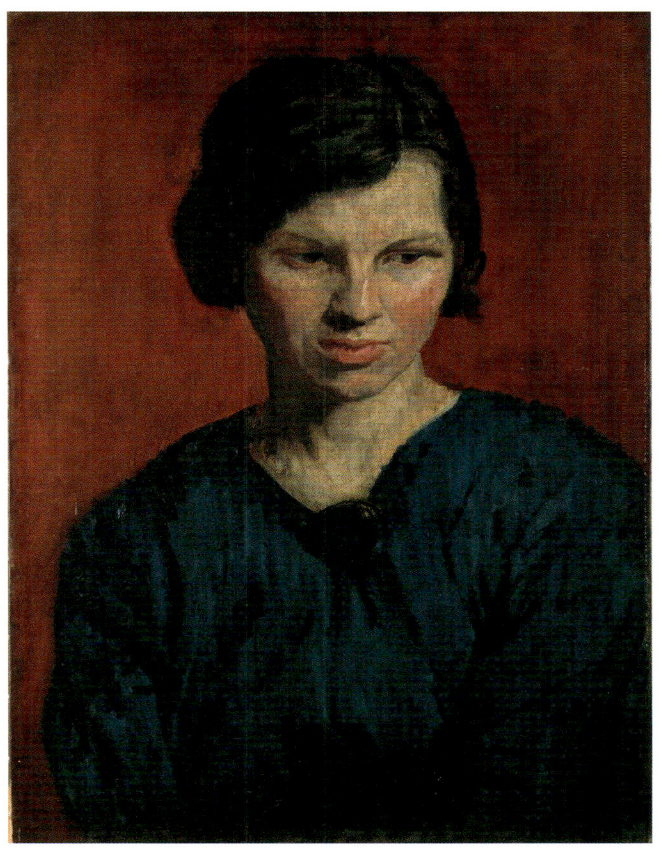

Chronicle interview was headlined 'A Jewish Futurist'. But he was laughingly prepared to tell his interlocutor that 'Futurism is in accordance with Jewish law, for its art resembles nothing in heaven above, the earth beneath, nor the waters under the earth.'[8]

Although Mark Gertler was one year younger than Bomberg, he had gained a place at the Slade before his East End friend. Mark's immigrant father could never have afforded the fees, so once again the indispensable Jewish Education Aid Society provided crucial financial assistance. The Gertler family was large, and his parents had suffered great privation after they left Galicia in the latter years of the previous century. Their gifted son Mark was fortunate indeed to enter the Slade, where his poised draughtsmanship and

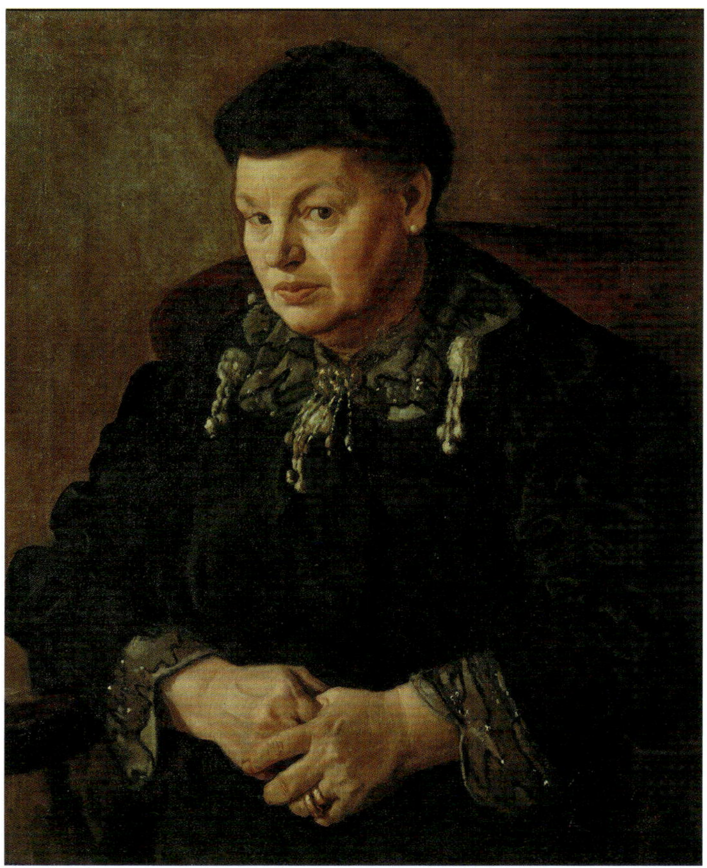

grasp of portraiture soon won him several awards. But while most of his lively student contemporaries were galvanised by the challenging new art exhibitions, he preferred to haunt the National Gallery. No hint of the heretical Cézanne ruffles his 1909 self-portrait (fig. 10), and a painting of his parents completed in 1910 is equally reluctant to ally itself with the avant-garde.

A year later, his mother Golda became the sole subject of another painting (1911, fig. 9), and the full force of her personality is made oppressively clear. Arrayed in a majestic dress, she stares out at her son with unsmiling wariness. Although her fiercely clenched hands indicate the strength of her will, they also convey an intense anxiety which might well have centred on her son's future. Talented and admired he might have been, but how could young Mark earn a living from his art? And how soon would his new middle-class friends at the Slade tempt him away from the family circle in Whitechapel for ever? Gertler was certainly asking himself the same questions. They would continue to plague him for many years, and the economic problem dogged his life to the very end. By 1914, after he had left the Slade and confronted the hazards of a career outside the art-school womb, they began to surface in his painting.

The East End was now becoming a remote place in his eyes, inhabited by people like the figures in one of his most powerful drawings of the period, *Rabbi and Rabbitzin* (1914, cat. 10). While at the Slade, Gertler had often tried to resist the influence of avant-garde movements. But this remarkable drawing suggests how important Cézanne, Gauguin and Van Gogh had now become to the rapidly developing young artist. Deploying watercolour and pencil with immense certitude, Gertler defines the essential structure of the man and woman as they lean on a table and link

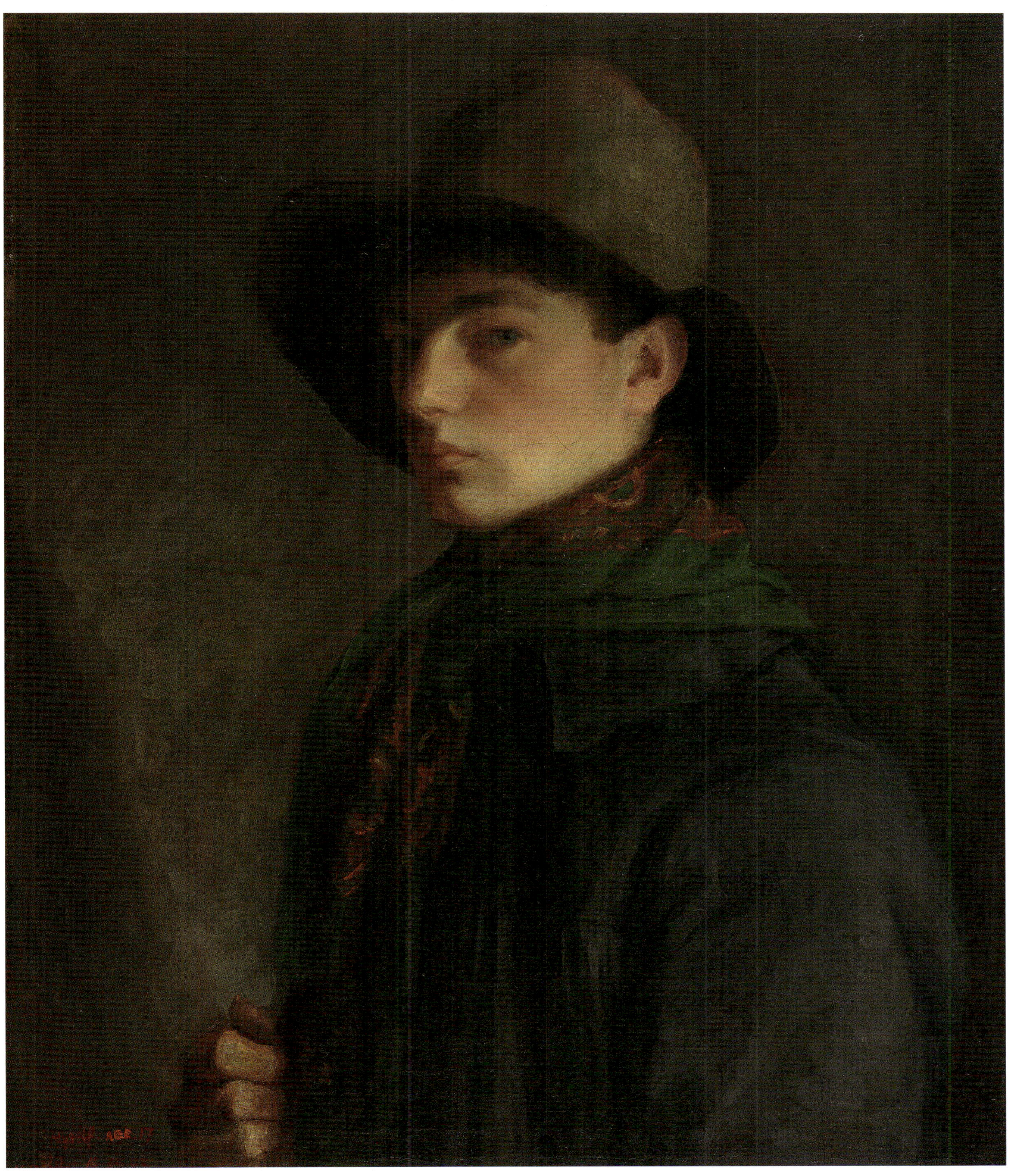

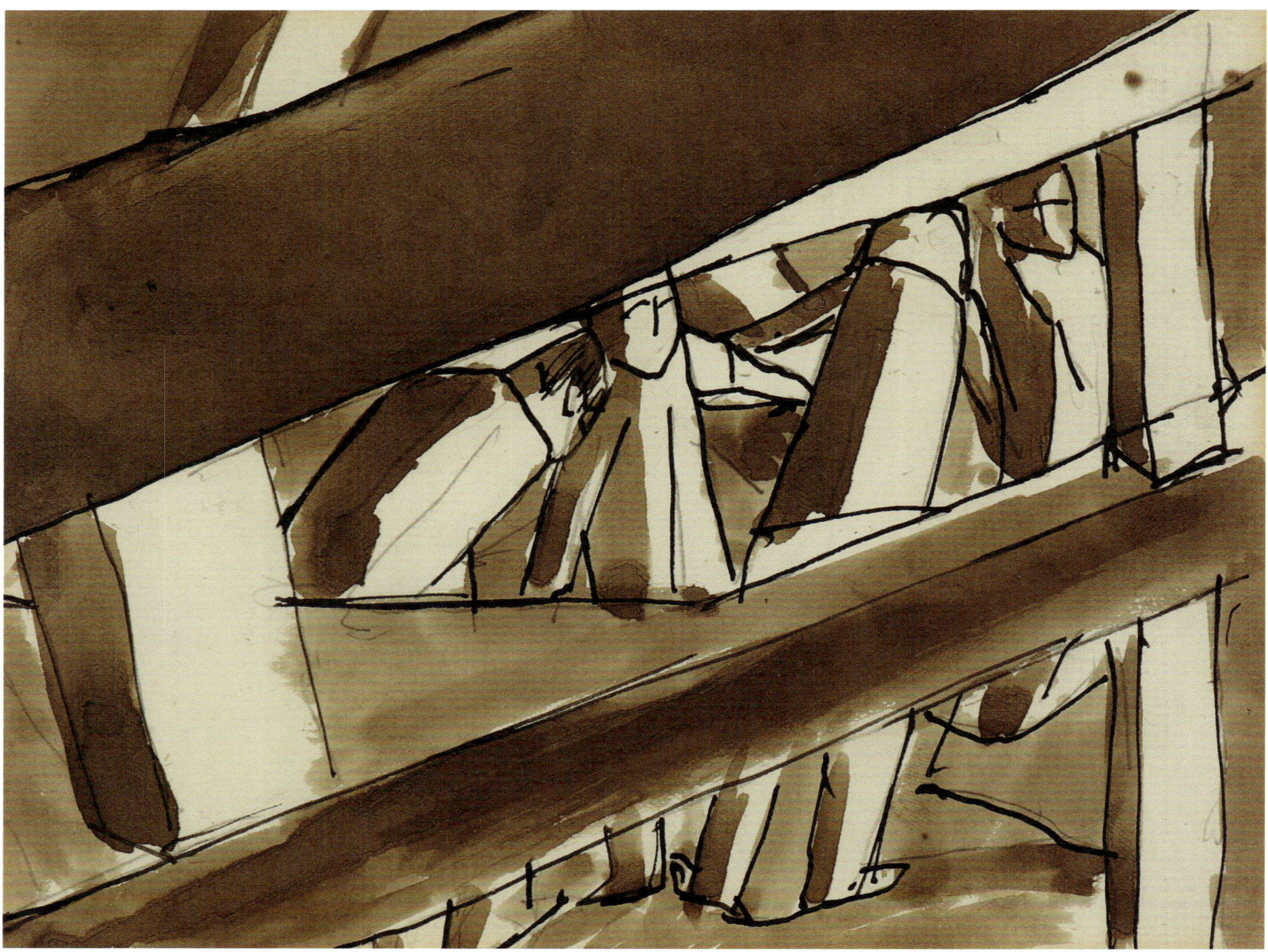

arms. The elongated Rabbi's haggard face is lined with misgivings, and he looks haunted by melancholy. But the Rabbitzin is younger, more comfortably built. Her hands are placed together in a more placid pose than that of the Rabbi, who crosses his fingers and makes his thumbs curve upwards in a manifestation of inner tension. They both appear admirably brave and determined, in spite of all the difficulties which must have beset their lives.

By this time, Gertler felt his loyalties torn between his love of family and a commitment to new friends such as the collector Eddie Marsh, or to the writers he had met while spending summer breaks at Lady Ottoline Morrell's house near Oxford. The conflict within him was immense, and by 1915 Gertler had left the East End to settle in Hampstead. On one level, he felt enormously relieved to break free from family constraints at last. The sense of liberation must have given him the energy to tackle *Merry-Go-Round* (1916,

cat. 12), the largest and most unforgettable painting he ever produced. In 1914 Gertler had reacted to the onset of the First World War by becoming a conscientious objector. He abhorred the conflict, and by 1916 nobody could ignore the appalling loss of human life generated by this alarmingly mechanised catastrophe. 'Lately the whole horror of war has come freshly upon me,'[9] he confessed to Dora Carrington, his fellow-student and former lover. Yet he also told William Rothenstein in April that 'I feel this last year or so much surer with my work. I have never felt quite like it before.' He went on to reveal how:

I live in a constant state of over-excitement, so much do my work and conception thrill me. It is almost too much for me and I am always feeling rather ill. Sometimes after a day's work I can hardly walk![10]

Merry-Go-Round, which uses a funfair carousel on Hampstead Heath as a metaphor for the unstoppable

Fig. 11   David Bomberg, *Sappers Under Hill 60*, 1919.
Ben Uri Collection

Fig. 12   David Bomberg, *Study for Ghetto Theatre I*, c. 1919–20.
Ben Uri Collection

insanity of war, is a macabre tour de force. I will never forget seeing it for the first time at the Ben Uri Art Gallery in Dean Street, where this masterpiece was for many years a prized painting in the collection. All Gertler's most despairing emotions about the supremacy of aggression, and humanity's helplessness in the face of cold, machine-age barbarism, were channelled into the pictorial equivalent of a yell. The most horrifying aspect of this engulfing picture lies in the glee with which each rider remains ensnared by the whirligig's dizzying rhythms. War is regarded as an insidiously addictive drug capable of giving the riders the elation they all crave. Worse still, it reduces them to the level of automata. Soldiers and civilians alike have been robbed of the ability to experience any real feeling, and Gertler feared that a similar malaise had blighted his own relationship with the unresponsive Dora Carrington.

Even his friends experienced overwhelming fear when they first saw *Merry-Go-Round*. D. H. Lawrence, who was away from home and asked Gertler to send him a photograph of the painting, wrote a letter filled with emotion:

Your terrible and dreadful picture has just come. This is the first picture you have ever painted: it is the best *modern* picture I have seen: I think it is great, and true. But it is horrible and terrifying. I'm not sure that I wouldn't be too frightened to come and look at the original.

Clearly very moved by *Merry-Go-Round*, Lawrence went on to reveal that 'in this combination of blaze, and violent mechanized rotation [...] and ghastly, utterly mindless human intensity of sensational extremity, you have made a real and ultimate revelation'.[11]

Neither Bomberg nor Rosenberg shared Gertler's commitment to becoming a conscientious objector. Rosenberg, a very talented poet as well as a painter, lost his life during the war, and Bomberg was driven to such an extreme state of despair by his gruelling experiences in the trenches that he shot himself in the foot. After hospital treatment, the wound healed and his adjutant gave him 'the post of Runner for his Unit, which meant going through the hottest part of the firing'.[12] But at least he survived, whereas Rosenberg was undermined, both physically and mentally, by the anguish of a scarcely endurable spell in the trenches during the winter of 1917. A year earlier, Rosenberg

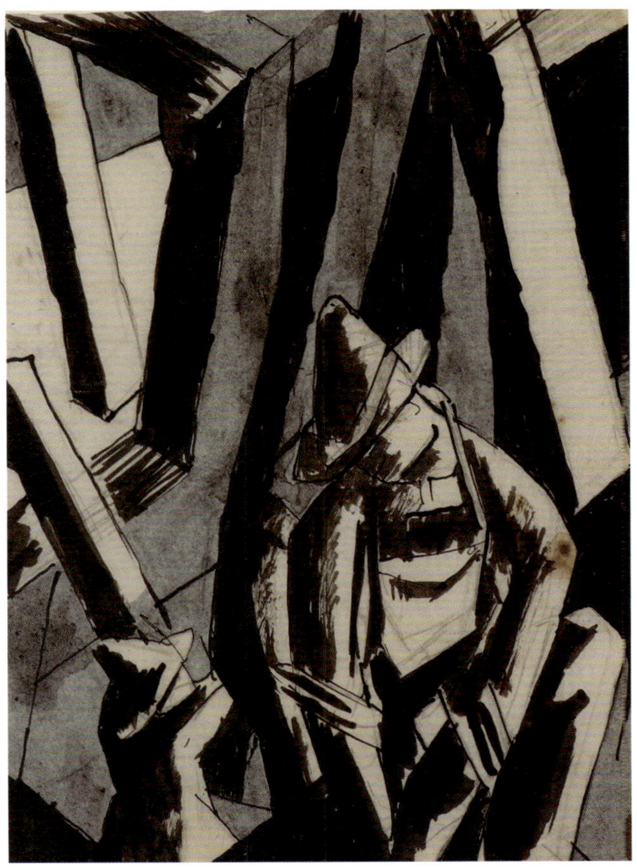

had prophesied his fate in a chalk, wash and gouache drawing called *Self-Portrait in a Steel Helmet* (1916). Executed on crumpled brown wrapping paper, this haunted image mixes fear with foreboding. It exudes a sense of weariness, even though Rosenberg is trying to maintain his composure. He gazes apprehensively to one side, as if expecting an assault at any instant. And in January 1918 Rosenberg became so desperate that he wrote to Eddie Marsh, in a letter cancelled by the censor: 'What is happening to me now is more tragic than the "passion play". Christ never endured what I endure. It is breaking me completely.'[13] A few months later, he was killed on night patrol, thereby confirming all Gertler's fears about the insanity of war.

Although *Merry-Go-Round* is an extraordinary achievement, it exposed so much of Gertler's private and social despair that he was weakened by the effort involved in its execution. His health, never robust, worsened with the discovery of tuberculosis. And his depressions became acute, forcing him for a while to abandon work altogether in 1919. Bomberg fared better, and succeeded in executing an impressive painting called *Sappers at Work: A Canadian Tunnelling Company Hill 60, St Eloi* (fig. 11). But its radical style was rejected by the Canadian War Memorials Fund, and in 1920 a disconsolate Bomberg returned to the East End subjects which had inspired so much of his pre-war art. An eloquent painting entitled *Ghetto Theatre* (1920, cat. 16). shows part of the audience watching a play at the Pavilion Theatre in Whitechapel. Bomberg had enjoyed the stylised acting favoured there, and his impressive 1913 chalk drawing *Jewish Theatre* was energised by the dramatic gestures of several feverish spectators. By the time he painted *Ghetto Theatre*, however, all this bodily dynamism was replaced by a strong feeling of confinement. Far from reacting with vitality to the performance on stage, the audience here seems oppressed. Bomberg uses the theatre's architecture, as well as the railing, to emphasise a sense of caged-in helplessness. These hunched people all look trapped, and their air of beleaguered gloom helps to explain why Bomberg himself decided that he could never live in the East End again.

Recovering from the trauma of prolonged military conflict was difficult for everyone who had survived the ordeal. No wonder, then, that Joseph Leftwich appears apprehensive in the portrait Clare Winsten (cat. 15) painted of him around 1920. Here, Leftwich clenches his hands as if steeling himself to muster enough determination for the life ahead. Winsten's brushwork catches her sitter's vivacity as well as his misgivings. She succeeds in conveying the complexity of Leftwich's mind, where justifiable pride in the achievements of The Whitechapel Boys mingles with a stoical awareness that, in the post-war world, nothing could ever be the same again.

Fig 13   Clare Winsten (Clara Birnberg), *Attack*, c.1910.
Ben Uri Collection

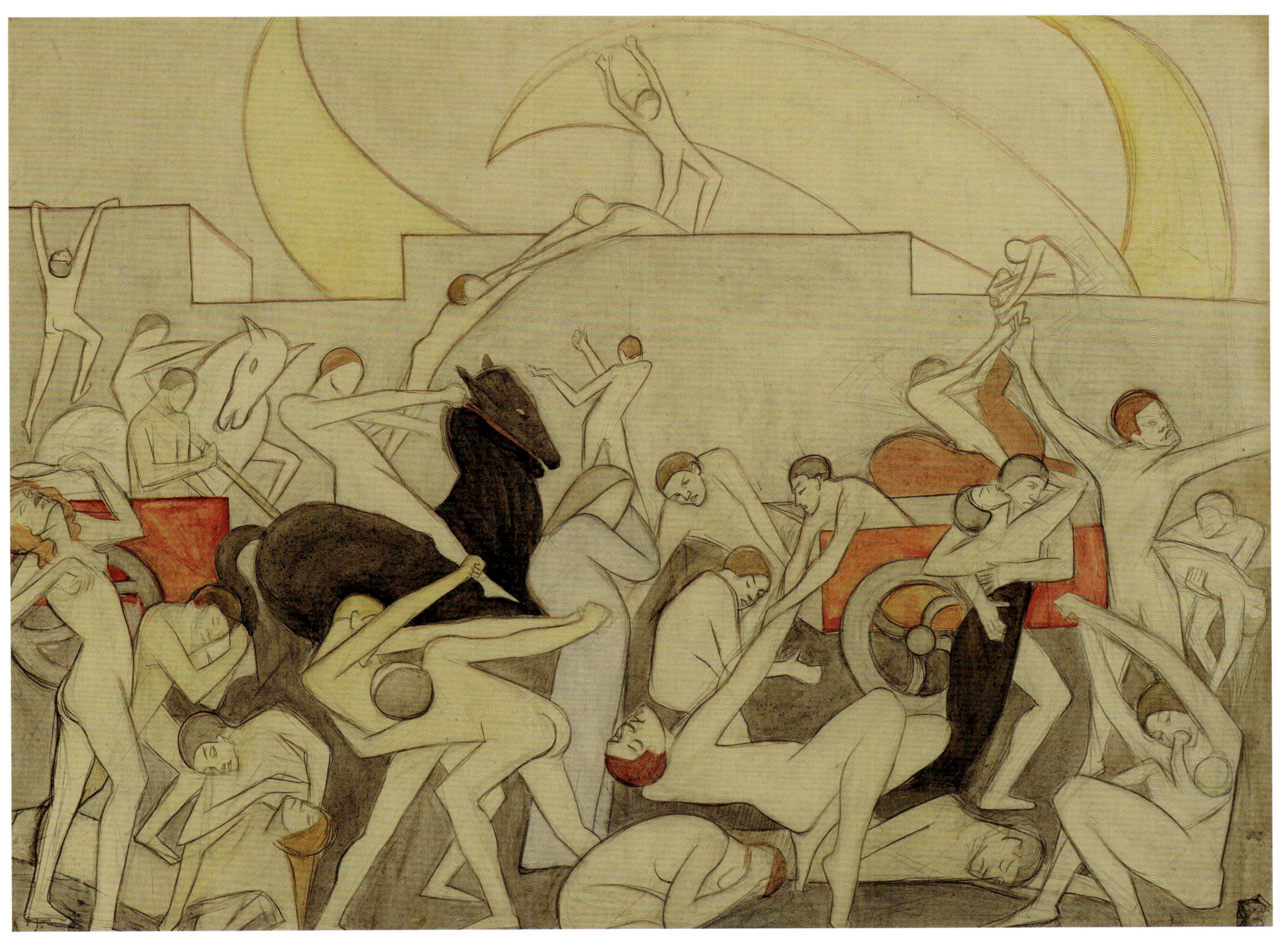

Soutine, Chagall
and the School
of Paris

Sarah MacDougall

2

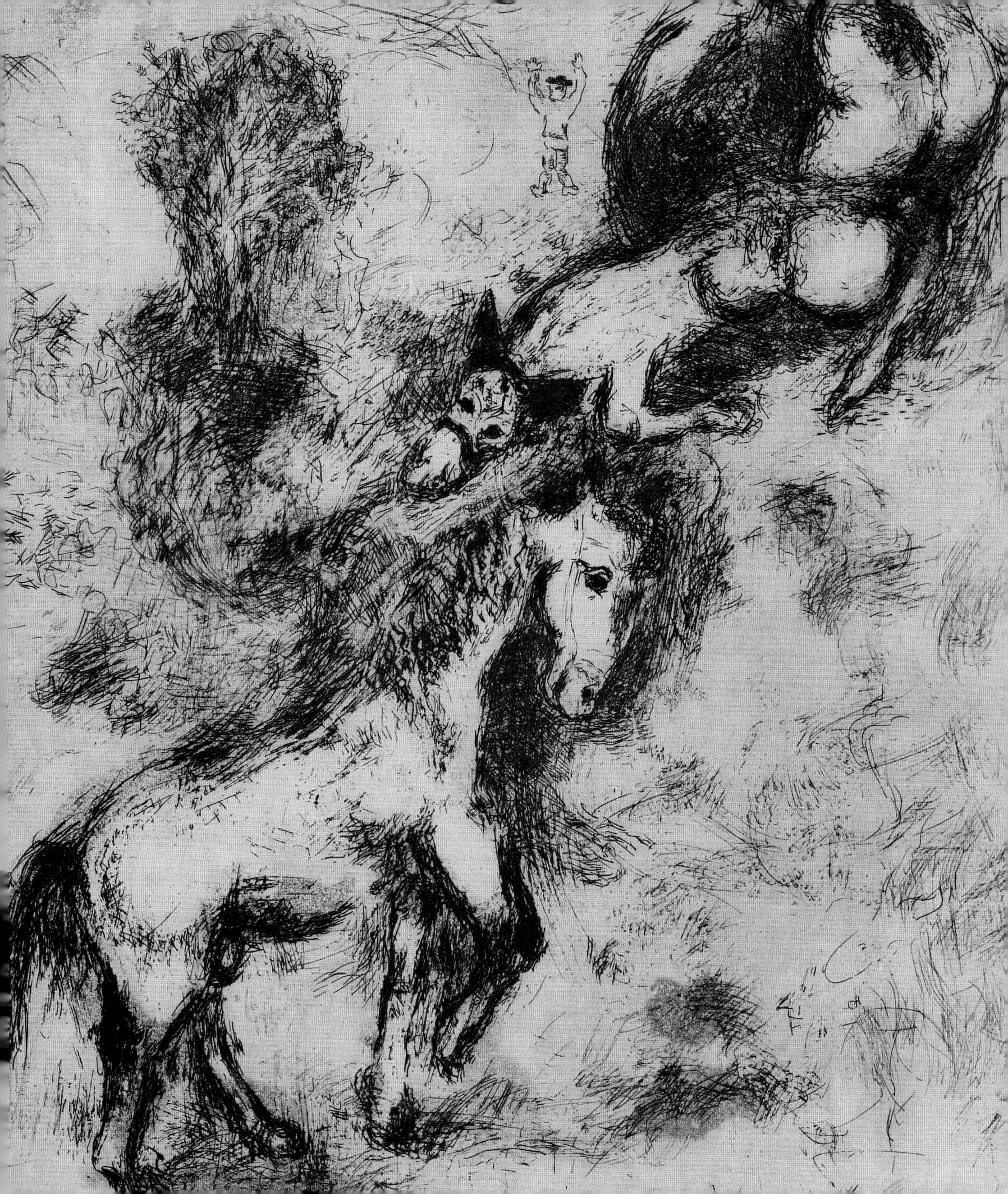

The contribution to twentieth-century visual culture by Jewish artists from an eastern-European background is considerable. During this century of widespread conflict and mass migration, the significant displacement of Jewish artists originating in eastern Europe led to a wide dissemination of artistic influences and ideas. In London, this gave rise to the Whitechapel Boys, who though mostly from eastern-European backgrounds were either born, raised or worked in London's East End in the first two decades of the twentieth century and made a significant contribution to British modernism.[1] In Paris, a still wider influx gave rise to the loose, informal association of artists who came to be known as the École de Paris, comprising a number of non-French émigrés, mostly of eastern-European Jewish origin. Among the best-known are: Marc Chagall (1887–1985), Moïse Kisling (1891–1953), Amedeo Modigliani (1884–1920),[2] Jules Pascin (Julius Pincas, 1885–1930) and Chaïm Soutine (1893–1943), who shared a figurative style loosely known as poetic Expressionism, which formed 'the most distinctive strand in French painting between Cubism and Surrealism'[3], and became leading members of the avant-garde. To this first group should be added the sculptor Jacques Lipchitz (1891–1973), who became one of the first sculptors to embrace Cubism around 1914.

As Sophie Krebs has established, the term École de Paris first arose from a row at the Salon des Indépendants in 1923[4] following the decision to hang works by nationality. The largest section was naturally the French School (*École Française*) and all foreigners were excluded no matter how long they had been in France. In his defence of this group the critic Waldemar George 'invented a subset of the School of Paris, the "Jewish School"'. It was this group who, in flight from the poverty, persecution and restrictions of their native lands had converged on Paris, the 'City of Light', in search of personal and artistic freedom, mostly (though not exclusively) in the first two decades of the twentieth-century.

Beyond the salons the term soon expanded to include all foreign artists who had settled in Paris at the turn of the century – Picasso was the most prominent among them – and then further still to include all manner of progressive artists in this period for whom Paris was undoubtedly the artistic centre. For the purposes of this essay, however, the term is applied exclusively to those eastern-European Jewish émigrés, *Les Peintres Juifs de l'École de Paris*, represented in the Ben Uri Collection.

The majority spoke Yiddish.[5] Chagall and Soutine, who lived and worked together in the collection of studios known as La Ruche ('the Beehive') (fig. 15) near the old Vaugirard slaughterhouses of Montparnasse, were joined there by Lazar Berson (1882–1954), Isaac Dobrinsky (1891–1973), Henri Epstein (1891–1944), Michel Kikoïne (1892–1968) and Isaac Lichtenstein (1888–1981), among others. Many of them also studied under Professor Cormon at the École des Beaux-Arts and exhibited at the progressive Salon d'Automne.

As Avram Kampf has observed:

Jewish artists, because of their common language and common background, tended to meet frequently. Some historians speak about an enclave of Jewish artists, others about a Jewish School of Paris. The gathering of a relatively large number of Jewish artists in Paris is a fact of twentieth-century art and of Jewish social and cultural history'.[6]

Many stayed on after the First World War,[7] often applying for French citizenship.[8] Although the artistic

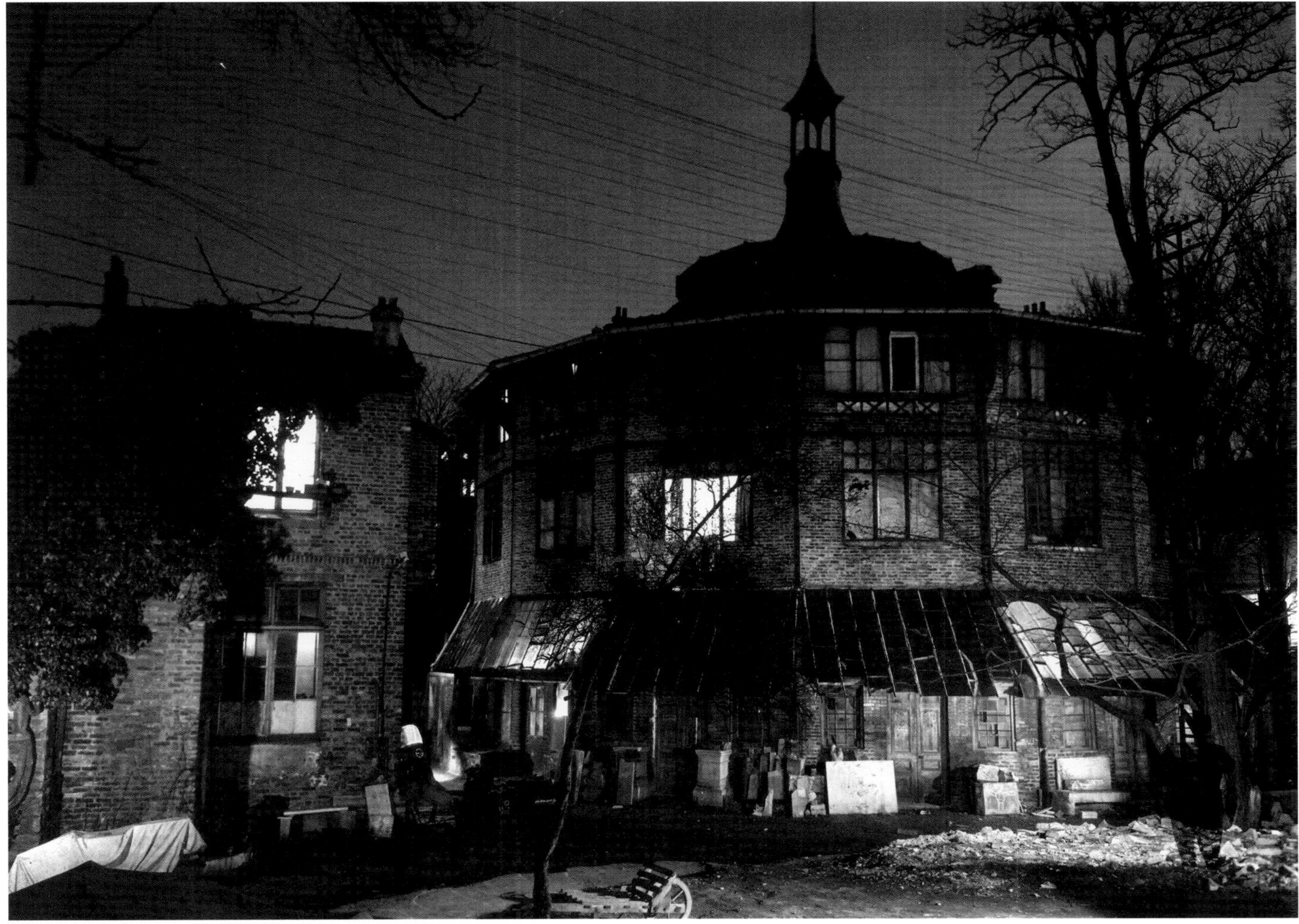

centre shifted from Montparnasse to the Left Bank, they remained in Paris until the events leading up to and during the Second World War forced them to flee or to hide; a much smaller number remained after the Liberation.

In 1910, Chagall's former teacher Léon Bakst (1866–1924) arrived in Paris (having been exiled from St. Petersberg as a Jew without a residence permit). His collaboration with artistic director Serge Diaghilev resulted in the founding of the revolutionary Ballets Russes, whose fame his celebrated designs – colourful, decorative and uninhibited – helped to promote. Despite Bakst's commission to produce his exotic and rhythmic designs for *La Péri* (fig. 16) in 1911, Diaghilev cancelled the production after the composer Paul Dukas tried to insist that his mistress Natasha Trouhanova (whose name appears in the top right corner of the work) perform the main role.

The majority of artists, though figurative, were only loosely connected, and a huge range of styles and subject matter prevailed, but there were also a number of other ties.

Several illustrated books: Berson's three fine, intricate designs (see cat. 11) for the Ben Uri, which he founded in London in 1915 following his time in Paris, were probably influenced by the *Machmadim* ('Precious Ones'), a textless, Jewish art journal produced in Paris in 1912 by a number of artists including Isaac Lichtenstein. Born in Plonsk, Poland, in 1888 and raised in Warsaw and Lodz, Lichtenstein was widely travelled, studying painting in Krakow, Rome, Florence and Munich before joining the Bezalel School of Art in Jerusalem in 1908. In 1911 he moved to Paris living alongside Henri Epstein at La Ruche.

This tiny and little-known group created important links with other Jewish artists connected by personal ties to a Yiddish avant-garde network that extended to a number of European cities including Berlin and London. This later gave rise to a series of specifically Yiddish artistic and literary magazines including *Renesans* (Renaissance) produced in London for six issues in 1920, which had close links to both Ben Uri and the Whitechapel Boys (Lichtenstein was

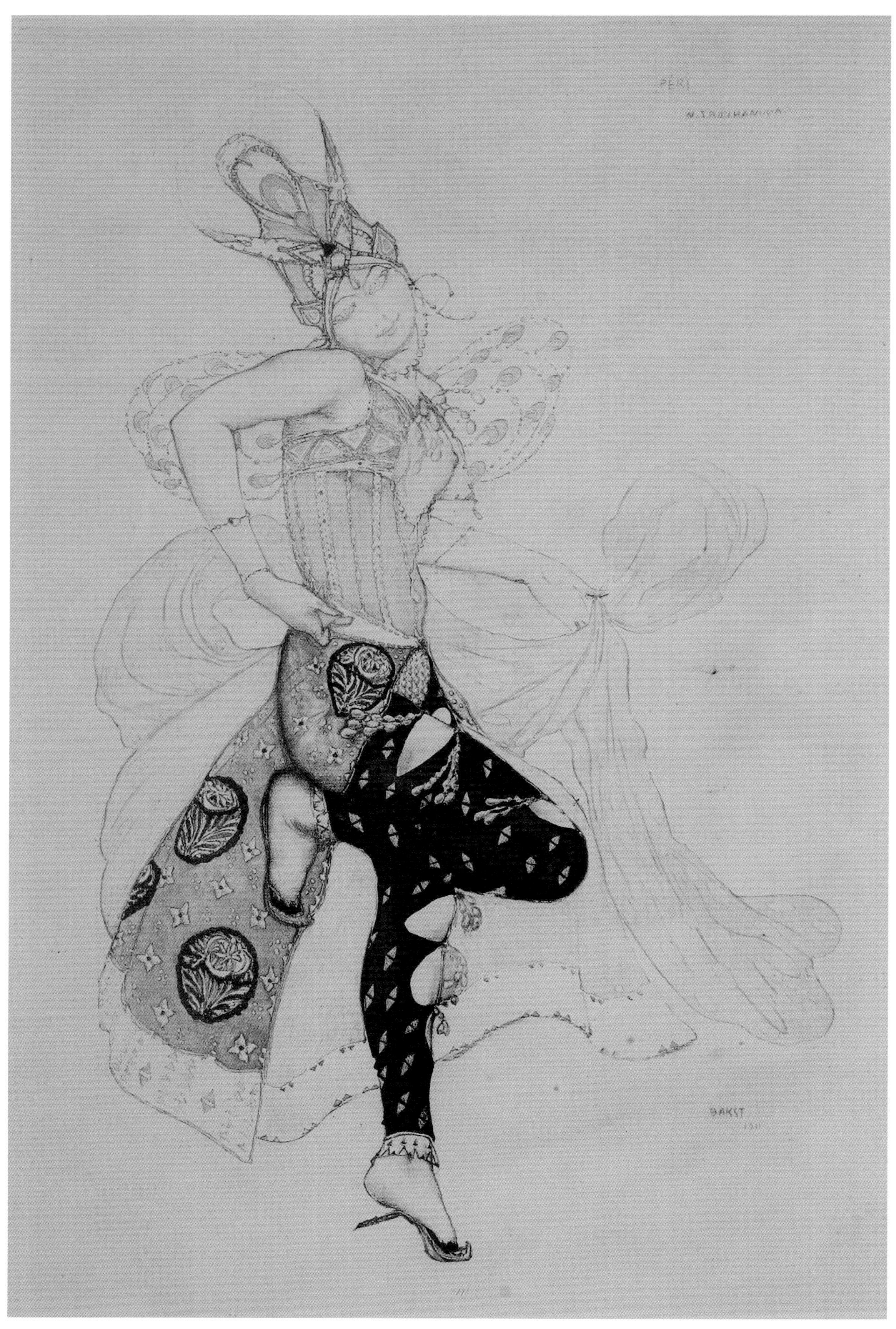

PERI
N. TROUHANOVA
BAKST
1911

published in volume 2). During the First World War, Lichtenstein travelled to London with Berson, then on to the United States before volunteering to join the Jewish Legion in 1918 and serving in Palestine. After the war, he moved between London, Poland, Paris, and the United States, where he spent most of his life, reviving the Machmadim Publishing House devoted to the production of artistic Yiddish books. Lichtenstein's painting *The Blind Fiddler* (1924, fig. 17) combines traditional folk iconography, in the manner of Chagall, with Cubist forms. The urban cityscape particularly evokes the strong colours and geometric shapes of the Orphic Cubists, Robert and Sonia Delaunay.

In 1927 the dealer Ambroise Vollard invited Chagall to produce a series of etchings to illustrate the seventeenth-century French poet La Fontaine's famous *Fables*. *Le Cheval et l'âne (The Horse and the Donkey)* (fig. 14) belongs to this series. The commission caused much controversy, as commentators asked why a Russian Jew, a foreigner to French culture, should be selected to illustrate a classic of French literature. Vollard responded that Chagall's aesthetic had something akin to La Fontaine's: it was 'at once sound and delicate, realistic and fantastic'. Chagall frequently used animals for symbolic purposes bringing together aspects of French tradition and Russian folklore in dream-like settings. Here, a horse and a donkey are shown with a despairing farmer behind them: the horse after refusing to share the donkey's heavy load must now carry his dead companion.

Born into a family of blacksmiths in Belarus, Ossip Lubitch (1896–1990) spent his teenage years at the Odessa Fine Art Academy. He moved to Berlin in 1919, then to Paris in 1923 to take up a contract to decorate a Montmartre Cabaret and was encouraged

to train as a painter by Antoine Bourdelle. In 1934 he published the album *Cirque*, comprising ten etchings and aquatints of circus scene with a poem preface by Georges Rouault.

Among the artists who produced specifically Jewish subject matter in Paris was Jankel Adler (cat. 22), whose *Ein Jude* was probably executed in 1926 on his second visit. During this period Adler deliberated the question of a 'new Jewish art', concluding 'there are still regrettably few Jewish artists' (though he numbered Chagall among these few).[9] The twenties heralded a second wave of Jewish émigrés to Paris including painter, printmaker, designer and co-

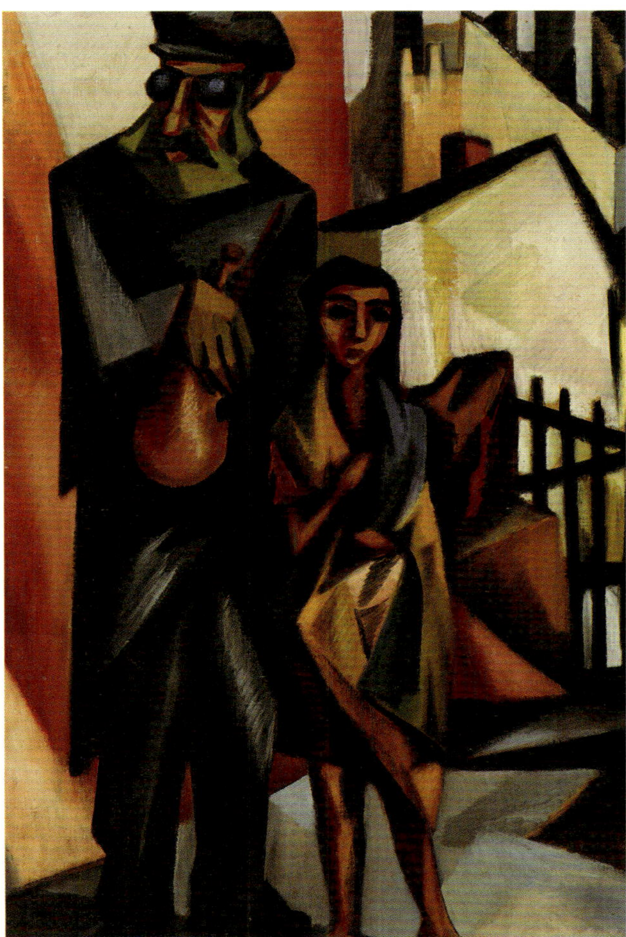

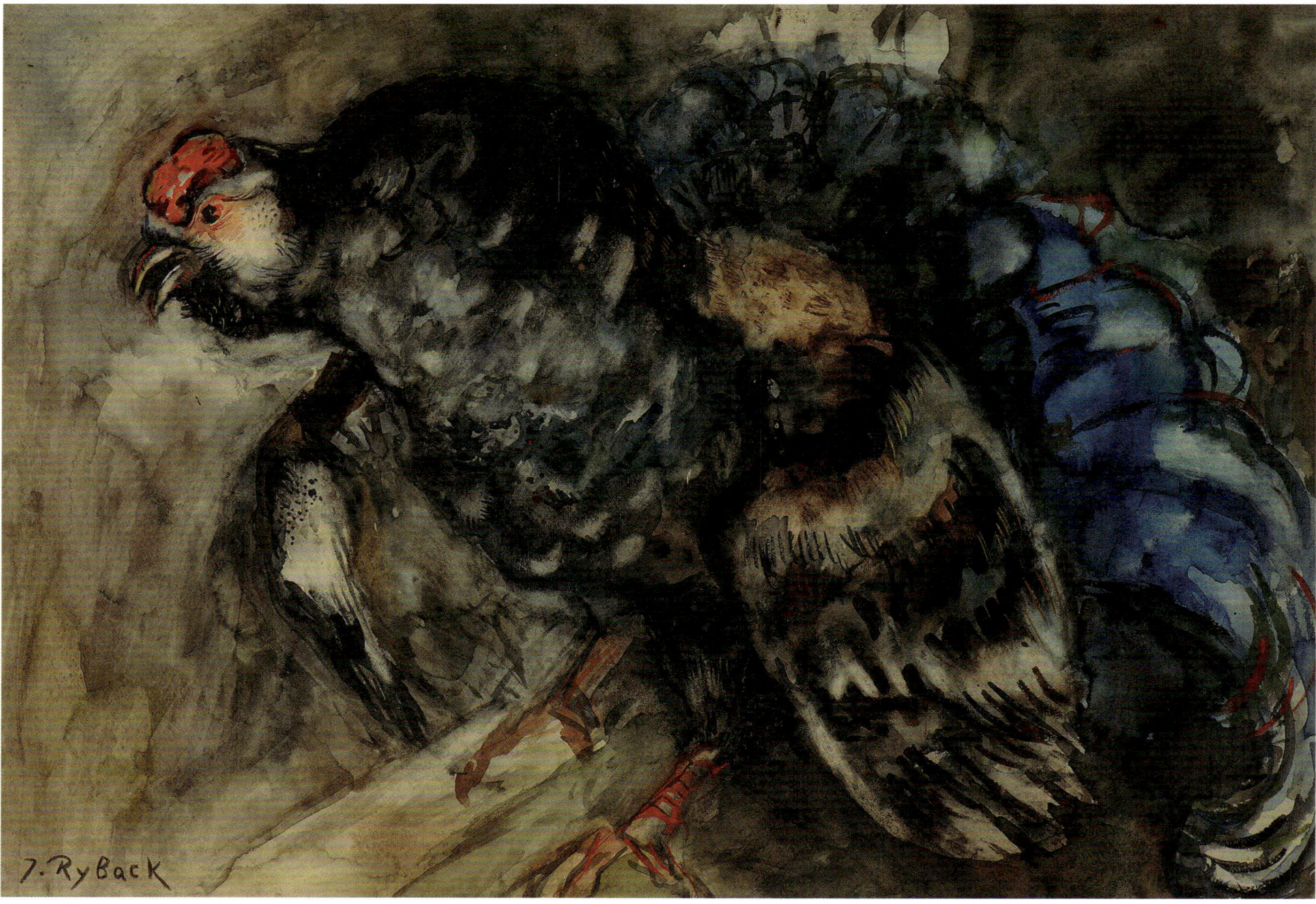

founder of the Kultur-Lige, Issachar Ber Ryback (1897–1935). In 1916, Ryback and his fellow Russian artist (Lazar) El Lissitzky (1890–1941) were commissioned by the Jewish Historical and Ethnographic Society to travel around the small towns of present day Ukraine and Belarus, copying paintings in wooden synagogues and carved gravestones in Jewish cemeteries. This trip was the beginning of Ryback's sustained interest in Jewish folk art, whose iconography he continued to collect and appropriate in his work. After the 1917 Russian Revolution, together with Chagall, Ryback was part of a significant national Jewish art movement based on ghetto folk-art, Jewish popular traditions and humour. His still life *Cock* (fig. 18) bears comparison both with Chagall's folkloric imagery combined with the expressionistic realism of Soutine's closely-observed still-life studies. A staple of the French tradition, the cockerel may also refer to the Jewish tradition of *kapparot*, in which the sins of a person are symbolically transferred to a fowl on the eve of Yom Kippur.

In the 1920s Ryback, like Chagall, spent time in Berlin, participating in the 'Der Sturm' group and completed an important series of lithographs depicting imaginary scenes of Jewish shtetl life. He later returned to Russia to design for the Moscow Theatre before settling in Paris, where his style became more Romantic and nostalgic. As well as Jewish subjects, he also painted flower pieces, portraits and animal studies including a sensitively-observed study of a horse at rest, animated by a vivid palette and the beautifully rendered landscape.

Yitzhak Frenkel-Frenel also arrived in the twenties having previously studied under the revolutionary designer Alexandra Exter in Odessa. In Paris he continued his studies at the École des Beaux-Arts, as well as working in the studios of Matisse and the sculptor Bourdelle. In these three fine works (rare both from this period and in terms of his style), *Shabbat Blessing* (cat. 17) and the two studies *Man with Torah* (Ben Uri Collection), he reinterprets traditional Jewish subject matter in a Cubist manner.

Ukraine-born Mané-Katz (who had originally intended to be a Rabbi) had arrived in Paris for the first time in 1913–14, where he enrolled alongside Soutine at the École des Beaux-Arts. Influenced by

Rembrandt, the Fauves and, briefly, the Cubists, he returned to the Ukraine during the First World War and was appointed professor at the Khar'kov (now Kharkiv) Academy after the 1917 revolution. He re-settled in Paris in 1921, focusing on studies of Jewish life, particularly the eastern-European ghetto peopled by Rabbis, students of the Talmud, comedians, beggars and musicians, and where it is possible that he observed his sensitive head study *Algerian Jew* (1934, Ben Uri Collection).[10]

Abraham Mintchine, initially apprenticed to a goldsmith, left his native Russia for Berlin in 1923. There he made a number of Cubist works (which he exhibited in 1925) and made set designs for the Jewish theatre in Palestine. He arrived in Paris in 1926, when he met Soutine; however all the work he produced before his arrival has since disappeared and his surviving work, including this landscape (fig. 19), therefore dates from his last six years (1926–31).

Zygmunt Menkes, a Pole trained at the Institute of Decorative Arts and at the Art Academy in Krakow, moved to Paris only briefly in the 1920s. In 1922 he settled in Berlin, studying under Archipenko before returning to Paris the following year and mixing with Chagall and others. He later returned briefly to Berlin and also visited Spain and, frequently, Poland. In 1939 he immigrated to the United States and settled in Riverdale, New York. His work frequently depicted Jewish subject matter including *The Scroll of the Law* executed in his typically expressive painterly style.

The rise of National Socialism in Germany in 1933 also impacted the School of Paris. Following earlier visits, Jankel Adler arrived in Paris in 1933, where he worked alongside the printmaker Stanley Hayter at *Atelier 17*, having already met Chagall in Berlin in 1922. He was forced to flee at the height of his success after his work was declared 'degenerate' and included in the infamous *Entarte Kunst* exhibition in 1937. Adler can be seen as part of a 'second wave' of artists from Russia who were drawn west to Germany, then France.

Although Soutine did not respond directly to politics or issues of his own ethnicity and never painted specifically Jewish subject matter, it is interesting to note that *La Soubrette* was painted around 1933, the year in which Hitler rose to power in Germany leading to the 'forced journeys' of many European artists, including Adler, as a result of cultural, religious or political persecution in their native lands. Moreover, Soutine's highly individual but anguished Expressionistic style has also been recognized as creating:

a new vision, toward which many other Jewish artists in Paris gravitated. Soutine, who had torn himself from his surroundings and his past, created an art which was filled with nervousness, anxiety and fear – the life experience of others who were less articulate in the medium. His work was believed to mirror the situation in which they and all European Jewry found themselves in the period between the two World Wars. It was later seen to prefigure the Holocaust.[11]

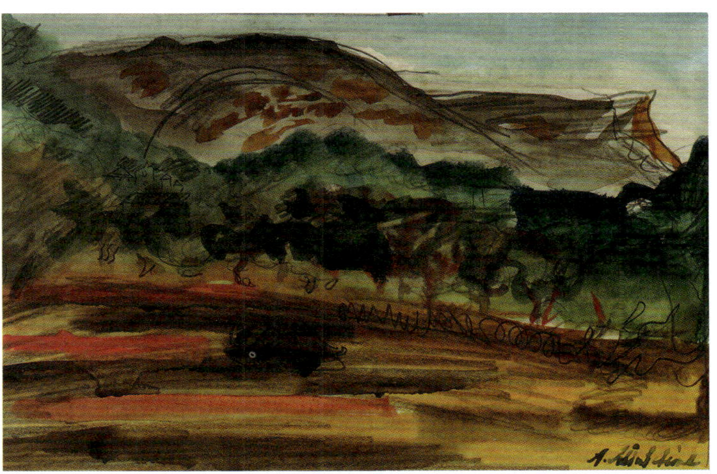

The German Occupation of Paris in 1940 had a major effect on the School of Paris. From 1941 Soutine sought refuge in the village of Champigny-sur-Veuldre in Touraine, using a false identity card. He returned to Paris two years later, suffering from perforated stomach ulcers, but died on the operating table on 9 August 1943. Chana Kowalska (1907–1941), whose deceptively naïve paintings evoke the fast-disappearing shtetl (cat. 27), from which many of the École de Paris *juifs* originated, was among the earliest to perish. It is a tragic irony that not only the shtetl way of life, but the artist herself and her husband were shortly afterwards extinguished by the Holocaust. Henri Epstein (1891–1944) was also arrested by the Gestapo, deported and killed in Auschwitz in 1944. His enclosed, northern *Forest of Rambouillet* (*c*.1931, fig. 20) contrasts with the open, light-filled, southern French landscapes of Zygmund Landau (who fled to

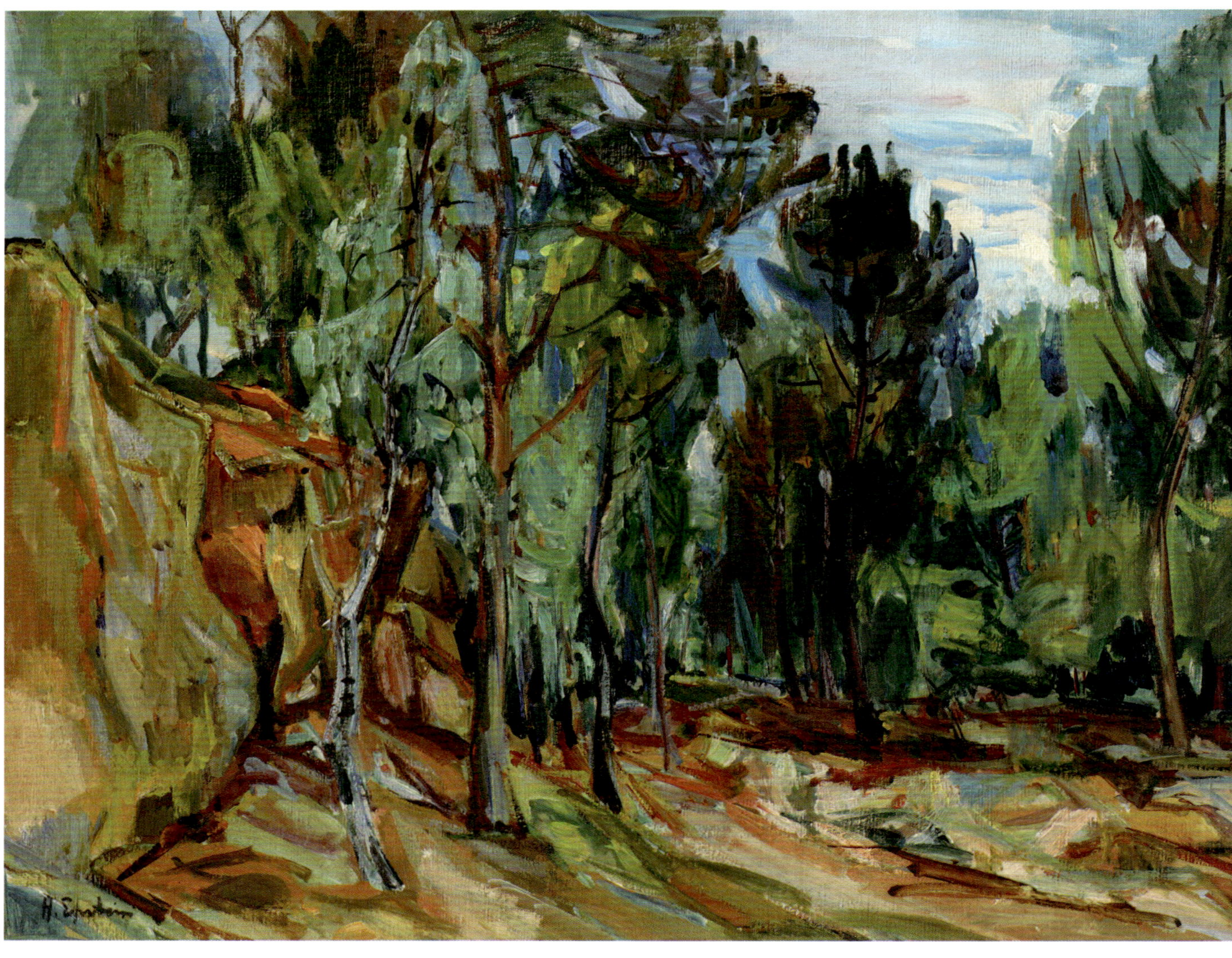

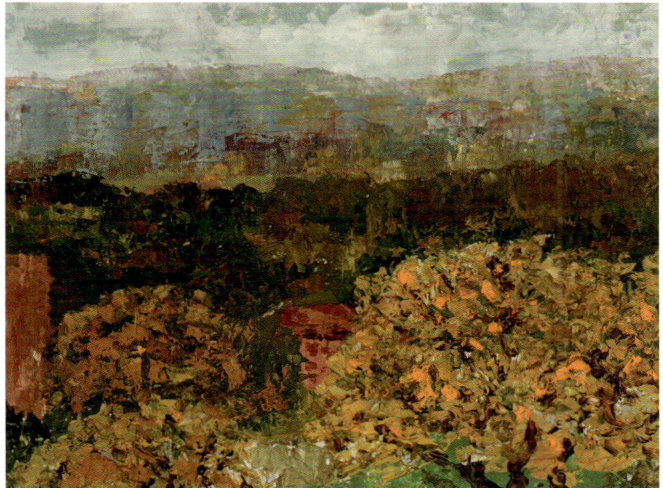

Saint-Tropez) and Zygmund Shreter (fig. 21), who fleeing Berlin in 1934, settled first in Cannes then in Paris. Remarkably, he remained in his Paris studio, protected by his neighbours throughout the Occupation. Ossip Lubitch, who failed to register as a Jew, continued painting at his Montmartre studio until he was denounced and arrested by the Gestapo in 1944. Although sent to Drancy concentration camp, he managed to avoid the last convoy to Auschwitz and resettled in Paris after the war, bequeathing a portfolio of Drancy drawings to Yad Vashem in memory of the victims of the Holocaust.

A number of artists served either in the French army or with the French Resistance. Kikoïne was mobilized to serve the Réserve near Soissons, where he painted gouaches of garrison life, until in 1942 he and his family found refuge in Toulouse, returning to Paris after the war. Henri Hayden (1883–1970) had arrived in Paris to study for one year in 1907 but never left. He associated with Picasso and Lipchitz among others, exhibiting regularly until he turned against his earlier Cubist style in 1922, returning to the study of nature. He took refuge in the South of France during the occupation, meeting Robert and Sonia Delaunay then moving to Roussillon d'Apt, where he was involved with the Resistance and became friendly with the writer Samuel Beckett. Maurice Blond (Maurice Blumenkrantz, 1899–1974), who had arrived in Paris in 1924 and volunteered for the French army in 1939, was soon demobilized and sent to the Avignon region, where he found refuge working in the home of a local peasant. His Parisian street scene of 1945 records the resumption of everyday life after the Liberation of the city.

Chagall spent the war in exile in New York. His important Jewish crucifixion *Apocalypse en Lilas,*

Capriccio (cat. 40) was probably the first work he created after emerging from mourning for his late wife, Bella (who had died suddenly in September 1944). Probably painted in April 1945 in direct response to the Holocaust, as the shocking news unfolded through press reports and newsreels, its complex imagery includes a clock, its hour hand apparently missing, indicating the onset of apocalypse.

Although the first wave of the École de Paris was broken up by the Second World War, among those

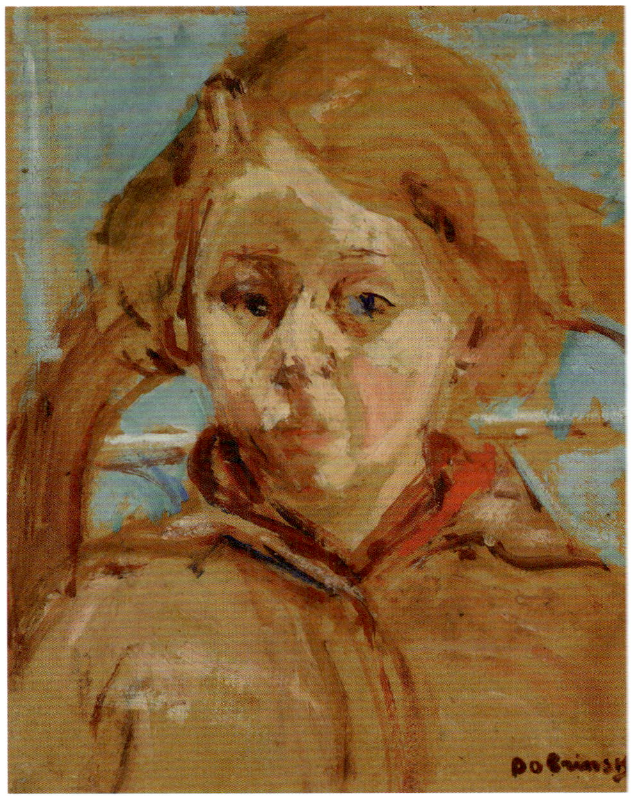

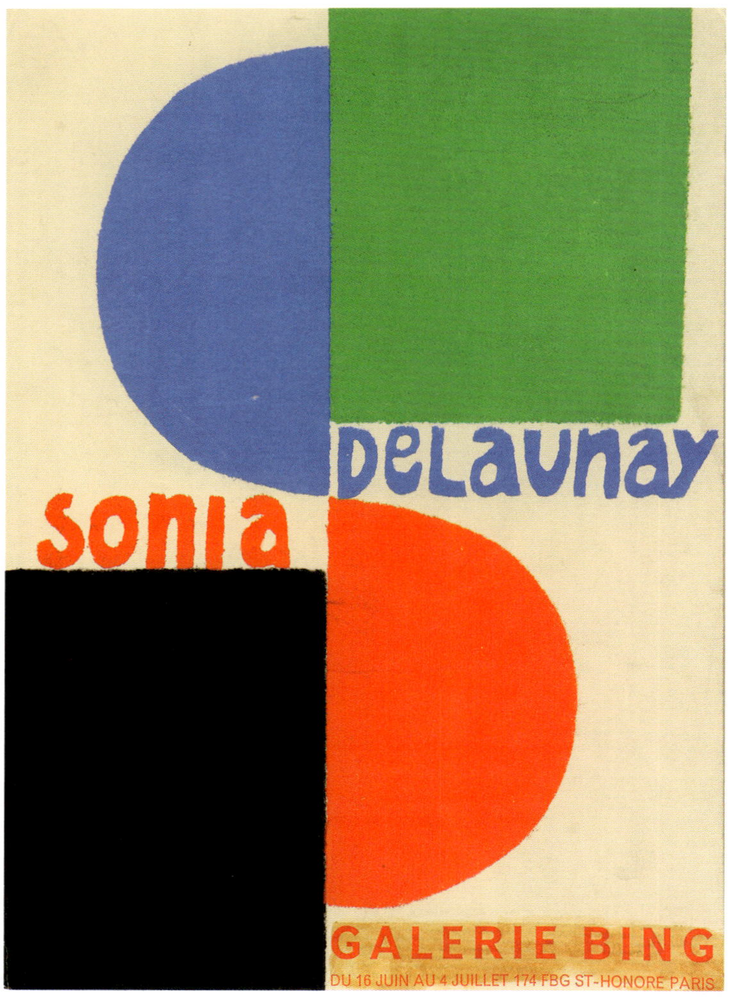

Fig. 23   Sonia Delaunay, *Poster for Galerie Bing*, 1964.
Ben Uri Collection

Fig. 24   Jacques Lipchitz, *Study for between Heaven and Earth*, 1971–2.
Ben Uri Collection

commissions in both the USA and Israel from the sixties onwards. *Study for between Heaven and Earth* (1971–72, fig. 24) is a later reworking of a motif he explored in earlier variations for the Nelson-Atkins Museum in Kansas City and the Los Angeles County Music Center between 1967 and 1969.

Soutine's influence on artists as various as De Kooning, Pollock, Dubuffet and Bacon has been much discussed in recent decades.[12] Most recently, Maurice Tuchman and Elli Dunnow in *Soutine/Bacon* (Helly Nahmad Gallery, New York, 2011) demonstrated Soutine's substantial influence in Britain on the later 'School of London' group, particularly Francis Bacon, as well as Lucian Freud, Frank Auerbach and Leon Kossoff, a subject further explored by Martin Hammer in 'Soutine Mania in Post-war British Art'. Chagall has also been the subject of two major exhibitions at Tate Liverpool (2013) and, most recently, in Milan and Brussels, in which *Apocalypse en Lilas, Capriccio* is included. While these major figures deservedly continue to be highly influential and much revisited, by contrast the many less celebrated artists whose contribution was nonetheless valuable have also been included in a number of exhibitions on the School of Paris,[13] and are part of the legacy which the Ben Uri is proud to preserve through its permanent collection and continuing exhibition remit.

who stayed on were pioneering painter, graphic artist and designer Sonia Delaunay, who had first arrived in the city in 1905. Her colourful, original graphics (cat. 47 and fig. 24) relate to her 1964 exhibition at the Galerie Bing (where Soutine had exhibited before her) and indicate a new postwar optimism. Kikoïne also remained in Paris, but made frequent visits to the new state of Israel. In the 1950s Dobrinksy (fig. 22), who had found refuge in Bergerac during the war worked at the Chateau de Chabannes, which cared for around 200 children orphaned by the nazis, painting numerous studies of both staff and children.

Others left Paris for good. Lipchitz fled the Occupation for Toulouse in 1940, later departing for the USA and settling in New York. His work was shown widely throughout the States, and he took part in Documenta in Germany in 1959 and 1964. Lipchitz's second wife Yulla inspired his later interest in the political fate of Israel and the conventions of Jewish orthodoxy and he received important

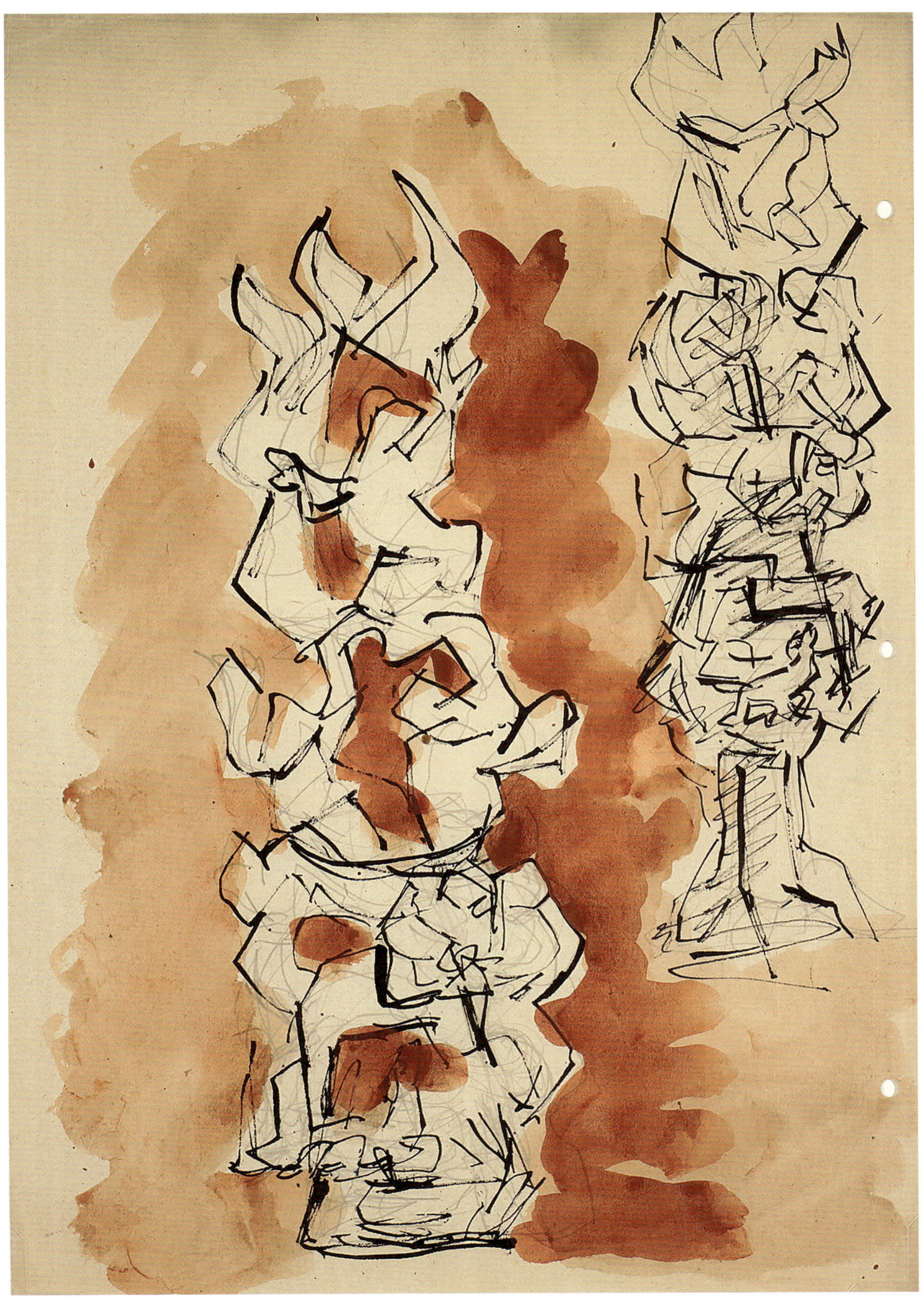

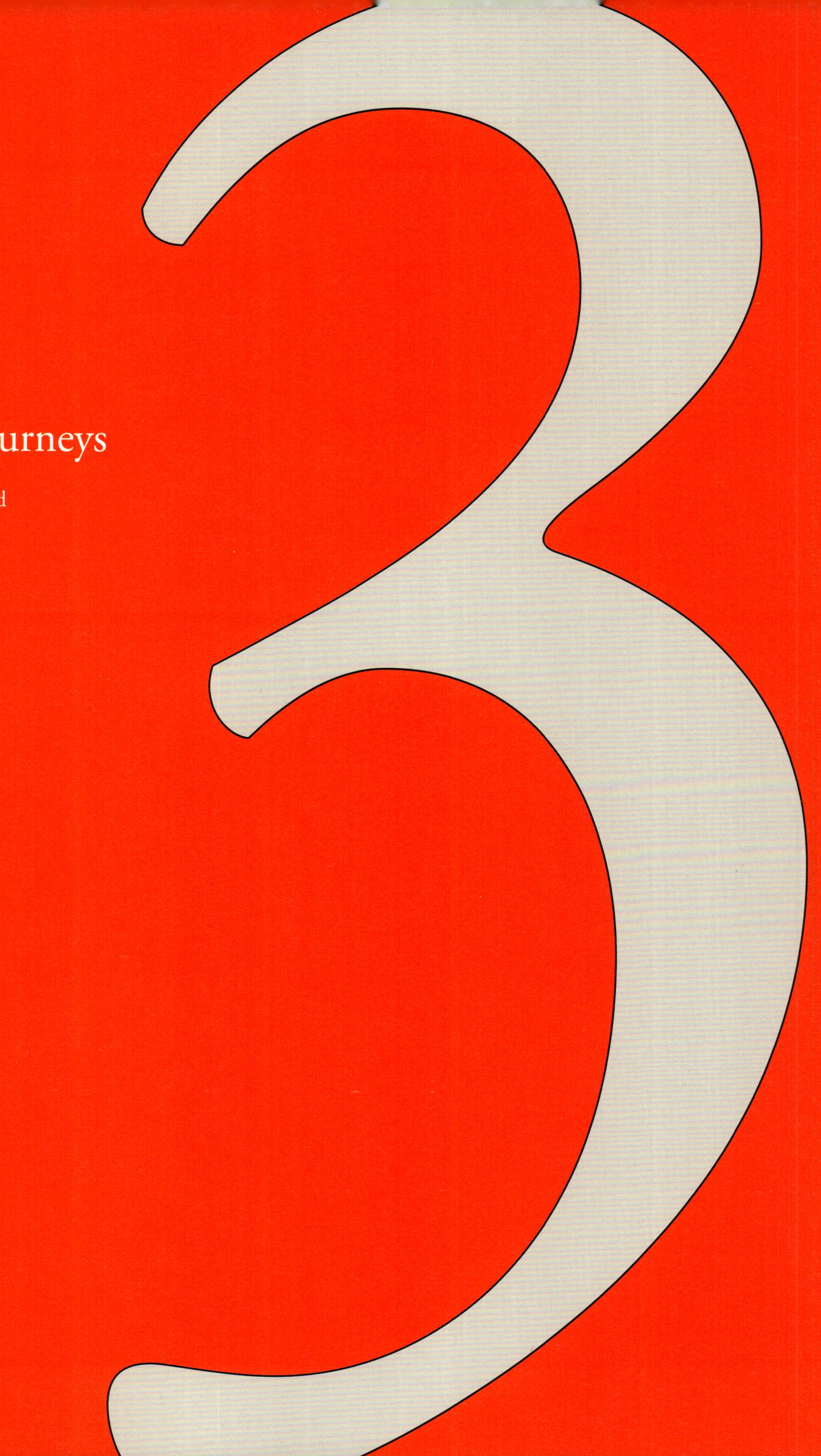

Forced Journeys

Rachel Dickson and
Sarah MacDougall

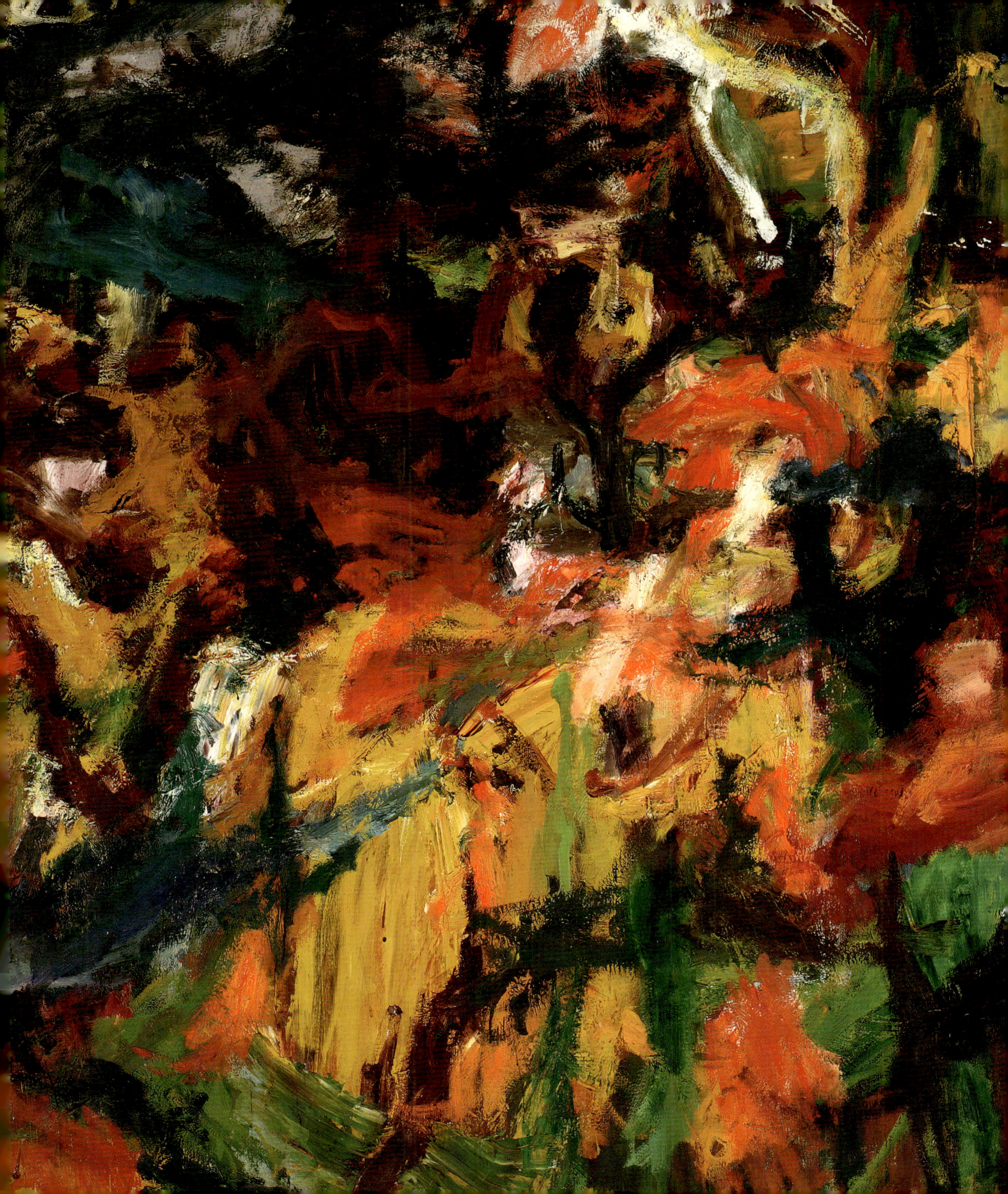

The iconography of exile cast its shadow over the work of many refugee artists of German and Austrian descent. As Sabine Eckmann has pointed out in *Exiles and Emigrés: the Flight of European Artists from Hitler*:

Neither the term exile nor the term emigration is entirely straightforward in its meaning. Emigration is generally distinguished from exile by the active and voluntary nature of the decision to leave one's country for political, economic, or religious reasons. In the case of exile the same motivations apply, except that here the state is the active party, compelling the individual to relocate by 'deprivation of citizenship, banishment, persecution.' [1]

Jutta Vinzent has documented in *Art and Migration* (2005) that between 1933 and 1945, whether for religious, political or artistic reasons, over 300 painters, sculptors and graphic artists immigrated to Britain.[2] Among them, mostly German or Austrian-born, but fleeing for a variety of reasons, were the following: Walter Nessler, who was firmly opposed to National Socialism; Fred Uhlman, an active Socialist; Hans Feibusch (fig. 26), Ludwig Meidner (cat. 21), Oskar Kokoschka, Kurt Schwitters and Jankel Adler (Polish, cat. 22), who were all included in the 1937 *Entartete Kunst* (Degenerate Art)[3] exhibition in Munich; and Palestinian-born but German-based Jussuf Abbo (fig. 27) who left to sustain patronage of his work.[4] For the majority of artists, simply being Jewish, or having a Jewish spouse, was reason enough to leave. Some came directly to Britain; others via Czechoslovakia (assisted by the Artists' Refugee Committee, co-founded in the summer of 1938 by Uhlman); and still others via more circuitous routes through various European countries. A number hoped to settle finally in the USA; but most of the artists in

this essay intended to stay in Britain for at least the duration of the war, with the majority remaining permanently and going on to make a substantial contribution to the British post-war art scene.

Freedom, however, was by no means guaranteed, particularly since after their arrival in Britain, many refugees, often to their considerable personal distress, were rounded up and interned as 'enemy aliens', initially in transit camps,[5] then in a series of internment camps.

As Jessica Feather has pointed out in *Art Behind Barbed Wire* (2004), however, internment gave the exiled artists 'a degree of freedom to practise what had been banned in Germany.'[6] Yet the indiscriminate nature of internment was, nevertheless, bewildering to the internees. The Berlin-born anti-Fascist and self-taught artist Jack Bilbo (originally Hans Baruch) had only narrowly escaped Nazi arrest before immigrating to England, via France and Spain, arriving in 1936. He recalled his deep shame at his subsequent arrest for internment in his country of exile:

I, who had suffered so much from the nazis, whose father was forced by them to commit suicide, whose mother was most probably in their hands and for all I knew murdered [...] I, who had sacrificed everything in my fight against them, was now a nazi suspect myself. I didn't know where to look.[7]

Some of the internees had already been in German concentration camps – Ernst Eisenmayer (cat. 34), Dachau and Erich Kahn (fig. 25), Welzheim, near Stuttgart – and were haunted by their memories. Many found that the families left behind were subsequently deported and murdered.[8] The internees were also uneasy at their ambiguous status, wondering whether, in the event of invasion, they would be handed over to the Germans from whose influence

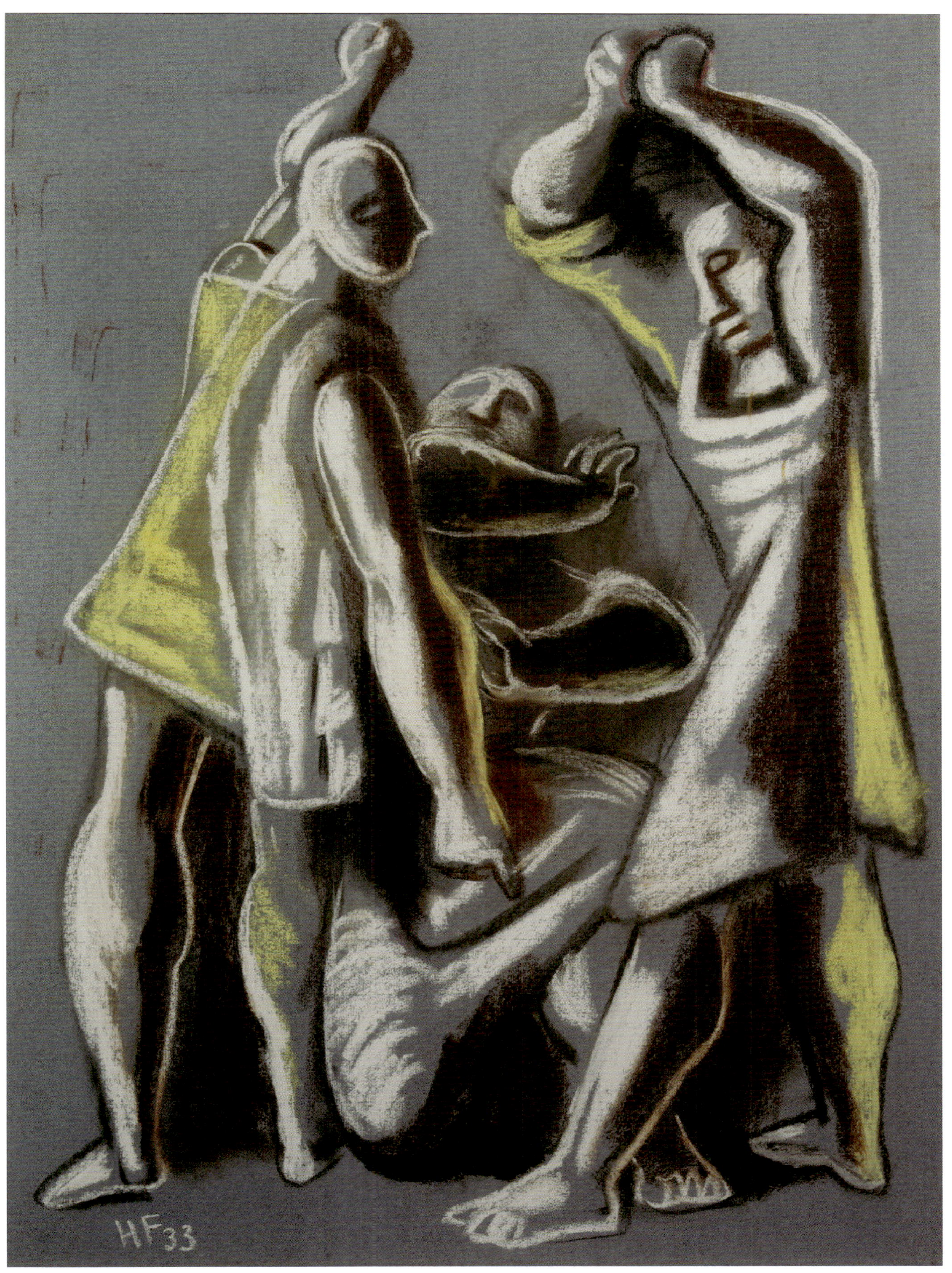

HF33

they had already fled. Some, like Weissenborn, for whom: 'Loss of freedom […] was an intolerable thought', felt further that:

the fact of being interned would have been bearable if one could have known the length of such imprisonment. For myself at this moment it meant for life, or in the last resort delivery to those dark forces from which I believed I had escaped.[9]

Erich Wolfsfeld was interned only briefly on the Isle of Wight, while Bilbo was interned for six months at Onchan Camp on the Isle of Man; there, with exemplary vigour, he organised art exhibitions shown to 1500 internees.[10] Eisenmayer, interned from October 1940 until September 1941, was also at Onchan, as well as Central and Ramsey camps in Douglas, where he recalled producing many character drawings. However, the main camp for the artists was Hutchinson, where Hermann Fechenbach, Erich Kahn, Fred Uhlman, Paul Hamman and Helmuth Weissenborn were joined by Klaus Hinrichsen, who acted as Secretary and then Head of the Cultural Department until his release in 1941,[11] as well as Dada-artist Kurt Schwitters and German Expressionist Ludwig Meidner.[12] Weissenborn noted that of the 2,000 men in Hutchinson: 'Germans, Austrians and a few Italians, people of all social circles, ninety percent [were] Jews.'[13]

Meidner, initially in transit at Huyton Camp, Liverpool, filled large sketch books with studies. Encountering some of his former students from Cologne,[14] he was a particular beneficiary of the rich cultural life provided by the close confinement of such an educated émigré intelligentsia – one of the unexpected advantages of internment. Weissenborn later declared, 'It was a miracle of the human will to live and to work, changing a miserable prison camp into a kind of university.' In spite of which, 'the time of imprisonment' was for him 'a continuous torment.'[15] By contrast, Meidner found camp life so positive that he even applied to have his stay at Hutchinson extended beyond his official release date, refusing to sign a letter from the other camp artists campaigning for release.[16] Meidner's output during this period was prolific, particularly portraiture and landscape. Ironically, as Vinzent notes, internment was his happiest experience in exile.[17] On release, Meidner, who had converted to Orthodox Judaism, barely scraped a living as a caretaker in a morgue, sketching corpses during air raids for identification purposes.

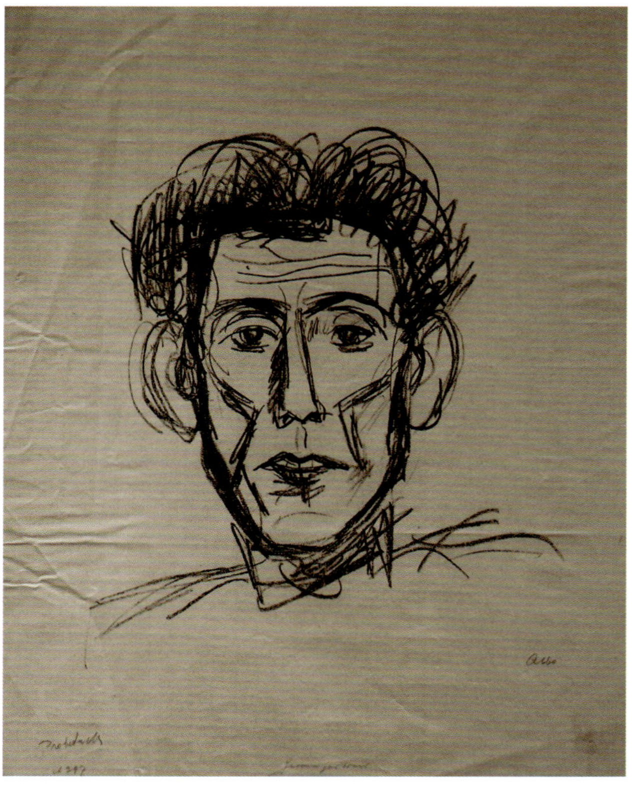

Meanwhile, his wife and former protégée, the talented painter Else Meidner, was forced to work as a domestic during the war, an experience common to many female refugees. Postwar, the Meidners received no artistic recognition, beyond their joint exhibition at Ben Uri in 1949,[18] existing in poverty; eventually their marriage disintegrated and they separated with Ludwig returning to Frankfurt in 1952 and later moving to Darmstadt (where his reputation was re-established), while Else remained in London, drifting into obscurity.

Kahn, though he suffered considerable postwar *angst* and was the subject of psycho-analysis, also enjoyed perhaps his happiest period under the enforced but stimulating and co-operative atmosphere of his nine-month confinement. Pre-exile he had studied at Stuttgart Arts and Crafts School under Professor Schneider and with Fernand Léger in Paris in 1926, before establishing his reputation exhibiting in Stuttgart and Berlin.[19] In Hutchinson, Kahn collaborated with 'house captain' Hinrichsen on the camp almanac, for which he provided engravings, and, through Fechenbach, joined a wider artistic circle, which included the sculptor Hamann, Weissenborn, Meidner and Schwitters, as well as the art dealer who would later represent him, Siegfried Oppenheimer.

Others, such as Walter Nessler and Hugo Dachinger were both interned initially in transit at Huyton Camp, Liverpool (which also housed Martin Bloch (cat. 28) before his transfer to Sefton Camp, Isle of Man). Born to Jewish middle-class parents, Dachinger had studied art in Liepzig (1929–32), afterwards working as a graphic designer and developing his own lettering system. He immigrated to England in early 1939, via Denmark, and pre-internment, established a successful London advertising business. In Huyton, he produced an astonishing output of work covering a huge diversity of subject-matter.

During internment in Huyton, Nessler also drew fellow internees, including Kurt Jooss (1901–79), the ballet choreographer; Bloch; and the German art dealer Erich Cassierer, as well as topographical landscapes dominated by barbed wire. However, these monochrome images are not typical of his varied output, to which an exploration of colour and new materials (including, later, sand and polyester) was central. Nessler – not Jewish – was violently opposed to Hitler's National Socialism, and was summarily dismissed from his job as a window dresser after replacing the star on the Christmas tree with a Star of David for a joke.[20] His savage lampoon of Hitler, *Das Hitler ABC* was smuggled out of Germany by his future wife, Prudence Ashbee, (one of the daughters of the Arts and Crafts designer and architect C. R. Ashbee) in 1937, and Nessler soon followed to escape Nazi Party membership and military service.

Martin Bloch, who later remarked that he had 'never seriously considered himself a Jew until the Rise of Hitler', had been forced to leave Berlin in 1934, after his work was removed from from the *Reichskammer der Bildenden Künste* (RBKD) exhibition. Bloch convened a protest meeting and, as a result, was expelled and felt his life threatened. He travelled to Britain with his family after taking temporary refuge in Denmark and, despite the initial alienation of his new London surroundings, produced a number of vivid cityscapes during the 1930s, reflecting his energetic response to this new challenge. 'In contrast,' noted his grandson Peter Rossiter, 'the wartime and immediate post-internment work demonstrates the serious struggle to survive and express personal suffering'.[21] Fellow internee Nessler noted how during internment Bloch for a time 'could not draw at all […] [he] was very sad and negative'.[22]

The experience of internment also spawned highly ephemeral forms of art: after immigrating to England in 1939, the Berlin-born sculptor Pamina Liebert-Mahrenholz spent a month in Holloway Prison, where she sculpted with bread. Similarly, during internment Kurt Schwitters assembled *Merz* from junk, porridge, linoleum and paint. Born in Hanover, Schwitters became involved with the 'Sturm' group and the Dadaists in 1918, writing poetry, building collages from scraps and constructing his famous *Merzbau* first in Hanover (later destroyed by bombing), and then after 1937, in Norway. His work was included in the *Entartete Kunst* exhibition and following the Nazi invasion of Norway in April 1940, Schwitters left for Edinburgh on a Norwegian icebreaker, reputedly 'in the entourage of the Norwegian King',[23] with his son Ernst and daughter-in-law.[24] Immediately after their arrival on 19 June 1940 Schwitters (and Ernst) were arrested and interned on the Isle of Man for 18 months. Despite his inclusion in two high-profile London exhibitions: *International Surrealist Exhibition* (1936) and the *Exhibition of Twentieth Century German Art* (1938), letters written to the authorities on his behalf by British admirers, and his and Ernst's own letter of protest to the *New Statesman*, Schwitters' small circle of friends in England, lack of political connections and lack of identity as an established antifascist, as well as his 'odd artistic preoccupations, scant English, […] general intractability […] and concerns about both his politics and his ability to support himself on the outside',[25] may all have contributed to his 'unusually long' internment.

In Hutchinson, however, Schwitters readily joined in the many cultural activities, as well as continuing to write and paint, entertaining fellow inmates with his 'witty Dada-poems and Dada-symphonies',[26] and producing some 200–300 works of mainly realistic portraiture for a small fee. 'You could have your portrait painted [by Schwitters] for five pounds', recalled a fellow internee. 'You could buy a collage of Mr. Schwitters for three or four pounds.'[27] Schwitters was finally released in December 1941 and joined his son in London, where he created a number of collages referencing his experience of war and exile.[28]

Sculptor Pamina Liebert had married the Prussian-born photographer Rolf Mahrenholz[29] in 1929, and studied as a 'master pupil' under Professor Klimsch at the Berlin Academy, winning the *Prix de Rome* in 1932 (which she was unable to receive) and gaining admittance to the Berlin State Museum as an exhibitor two years later.[30] Mahrenholz immigrated to London in 1938, in the knowledge that he would be unable to return, and worked as a freelance photographer for magazines including *Harper's*. Liebert-Mahrenholz followed in 1939, bringing only the £10 allowance and leaving nearly all her belongings behind.[31] Both were interned separately on the Isle of Man, c.1940–42, allowed to meet for only two hours once a month at a camp café.[32] Little is known of her internment but Liebert-Mahrenholz's post-war experience is typical of the wider experience of many exiles, in that her best work was done pre-exile, and that the trauma of exile contributed to a diminution of her output. After internment, unable to sculpt, she first worked in a lampshade factory then in a derelict barn batching kindling; afterwards she earned her living as a china restorer, eventually returning to sculpture, painting and drawing.

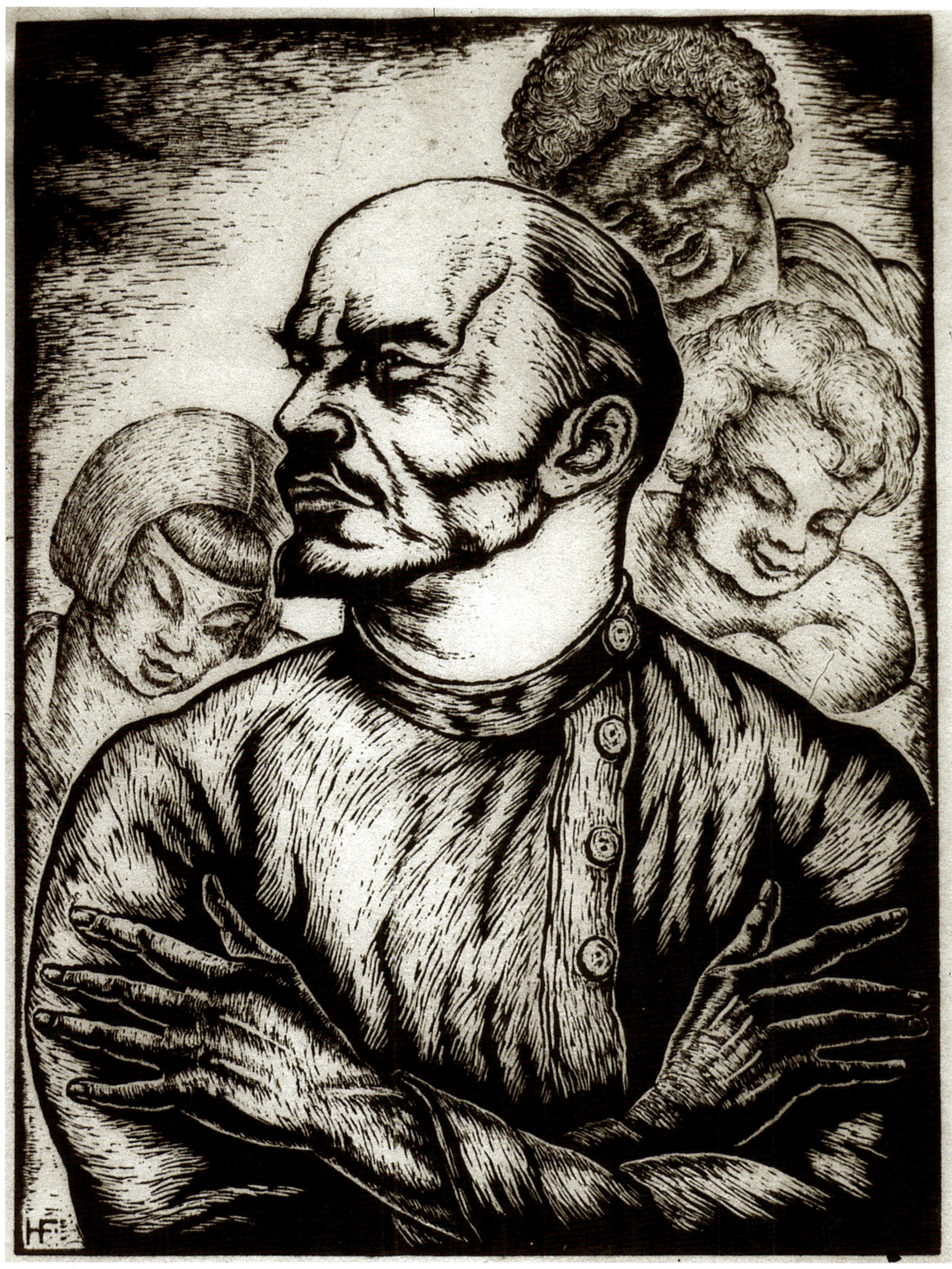

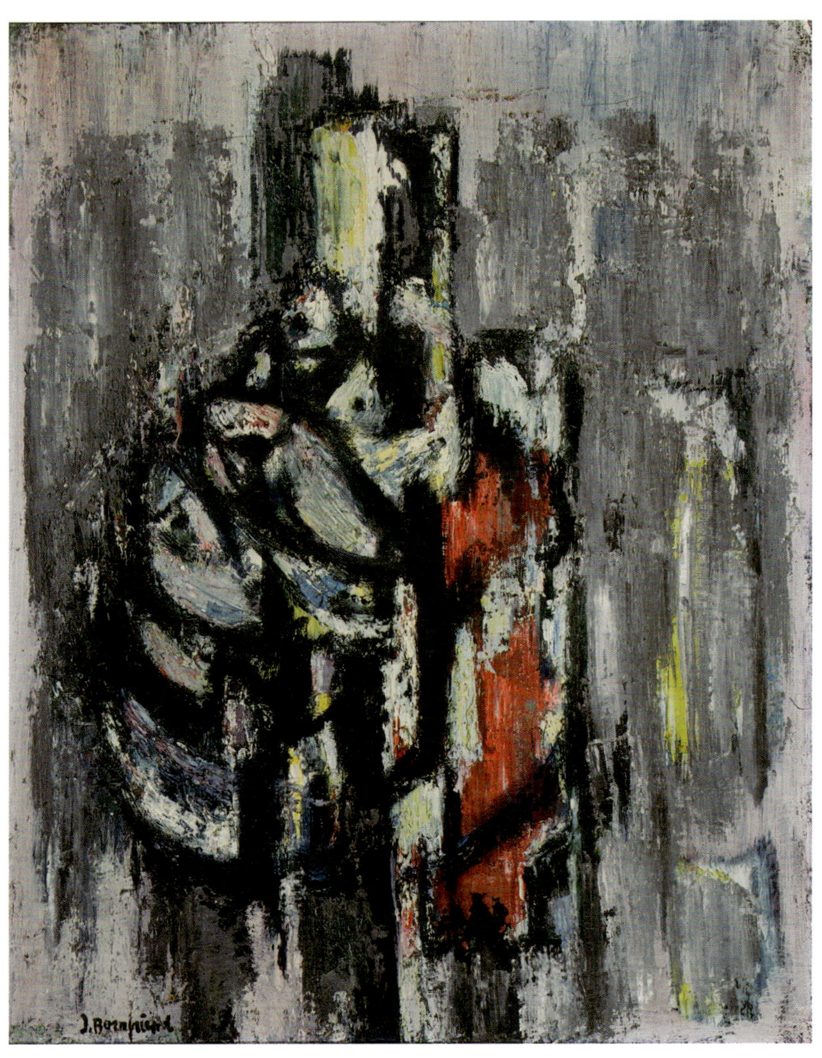

Fig 29   Jacob Bornfriend, *Blue Grey Fishes.*
Ben Uri Collection

As Vinzent has noted,[33] although many of the artists, such as Liebert-Mahrenholz, Wolfsfeld, Schwitters and Meidner had established significant reputations or teaching careers at renowned academies in Europe pre-war, they arrived in Britain as unknowns. Hampered by their lack of English (English lessons were among the most popular classes for internees), those who failed to secure teaching jobs or engage gallery support, often had to utilise their creative talents in more modest directions to survive. Jacob Bornfriend (fig. 29), who fled from Czechoslovakia in 1939, having trained at the Academy of Fine Art in Prague, found employment as a diamond cutter; his obituary recorded simply that he 'spent the war working in factories unable to paint.'[34]

In this spirit, a number of self-help organisations affiliated to the country of origin, such as the Austrian Centre with its different sections for theatre, musical, literary and fine arts, the Free German League of Culture (FGLC), first based at Uhlman's Hampstead home,[35] the Anglo-Sudeten Group and the Czech Institute, were established to provide not only a network of contacts and social activities, but also facilities ranging from a publishing house, library and café, to intensive language tuition. The Jewish Polish Centre for Cultural and Social Activities also formed the Ohel Club between 1943–44, with its active lecture programme, under the guidance of the brothers Alexander and Benjamin Margulies, the former closely involved with Ben Uri from 1948.

Images of 'the Other' were a particular interest (though not the exclusive preserve) of female artists, including Margaret (Grete) Marks (fig. 30) and Eva Frankfurther. Frankfurther, who had immigrated to Britain with her family aged nine, made pioneering studies of London's postwar multi-cultural communities, particularly the Black British post-colonials, whom she worked alongside at the famous Lyons Corner House. Her acute ability to capture feeling and pathos (without sentiment), and her particular sympathy for women, is exemplified in portraits such as *West Indian Waitresses* (cat. 44).

The Postwar Legacy

The range of contributions made by artists in exile in postwar Britain, not only as painters, printmakers, designers or sculptors, but as individuals who helped to shape the increasingly complex and changing art world in mid-century Britain, is considerable. They established key commercial galleries, became leading members of the graphic design and advertising industries, gained notable reputations within the applied arts, and enriched the teaching of art at a number of prominent institutions, both in London and in the provinces. Increasingly, they were absorbed into and effected significant changes within the broader landscape of the British art world.

A further affirmation of the degree of assimilation into the British art scene was the inclusion of a number of artists in exile within the exhibitions held, and the decorative and architectural schemes and public sculptures commissioned, as part of the Festival of Britain in 1951.[36] 'It has long been England's policy to give asylum to refugees, and its hospitality has enabled them to make their contribution to the stream of British culture' the *Jewish Chronicle* noted in reviewing the opening of the Festival. 'A glance through the list of architects and designers shows how many refugees have been employed at the South Bank. Each has doubtless added something of his own to a trend of design that is having a great influence on future work in England.'[37]

Josef Herman (cat. 36) was commissioned to make a painting of miners for the Pavilion of Minerals and Feibusch's mural panel *The Return of the Prodigal Son* was included in the main visual arts exhibition *60 Paintings for '51* curated by the Arts Council; he was also commissioned to design a crucifixion mural for the newly restored Festival Church of Saint John in nearby Waterloo Road. Feibusch – painter, designer and muralist – had been one of the Jewish artists included in the original list of 'degenerate' artists in 1937. Despite being awarded the German Grand State Prize for Painters by the Prussian Academy of Arts in Berlin in 1930, he was no longer able to work in Germany and left for in Britain in May 1933. By the autumn of the same year, with the foundation of the Nazi *Reichskulturkammer* to which all artists and designers had to belong in order to practice their profession, all Jews, Communists, Social Democrats or 'avant-garde' artists were effectively banned form working in Germany. Like Nessler, his work of the early 1930s is dark and prescient.

The Hungarian-born Jewish émigré Georg Mayer-Marton, who arrived in England in 1938, leaving his parents behind, also contributed significantly to English church decoration. On receiving the terrible news of their death in summer 1945, following the liquidation of the Jewish population of Gyor, he painted the powerful and haunting *Woman with Boulders*.[38] As with Feibusch, Mayer-Marton retained no obvious trace of his Jewish identity once he had settled in England. With a distinguished prewar artistic career in Europe, as designer, illustrator, poet, painter and curator, having trained in Munich and Vienna academies from 1919–24, and as a member of the Hagenbund,[39] he first obtained a modest teaching post at the private St Johns Wood School of Art, followed by a peripatetic role as a Guide Lecturer for CEMA, the precursor to the Arts Council. After a catastrophic fire destroyed his studio home and all its contents, Mayer-Marton relocated to the north of England, becoming Principal Lecturer at Liverpool School of Art.

Now less well-known than her celebrated fellow Viennese émigré Lucie Rie (1902–95), ceramicist Margaret (Grete) Marks had received solid, practical training at the internationally-renowned Bauhaus School of Arts in Weimar, which specialised in architecture, design and crafts and where she had studied from November 1920, receiving instruction from both artists and craftsmen in each subject.

In 1923 Grete and her husband, Gustav Loebenstein, established the Hael-Werkstätten for Artistic Ceramics Co Ltd at Marwitz, outside Berlin. The company was a member of the *Deutscher Werkbund*, an organisation committed to progressive design, and employed 120 workers at its height, producing simple geometric forms for tableware, decorated with coloured glazes, which were sold internationally. On the death of her husband, Grete continued to run the factory until 1932, but increasing anti-Semitism eventually forced her to sell the business at a much reduced price in 1935.

Helmuth Weissenborn, together with his second wife Lesley (whom he married in 1946 and who worked for the Baynard Press), made a remarkable contribution to British postwar printmaking (Weissenborn's first Jewish wife and son having left for the USA prior to his internment). In establishing the Acorn Press,[40] one of the most interesting private imprints to flourish after the war, the Weissenborns aspired to continue the Arts & Crafts tradition of hand press printing and, with their publications, to

match the quality of book production of smaller firms such as the Curwen Press.

In contrast to the experiences of Wolfsfeld and Ludwig Meidner, Bloch was able to resume his teaching career in Britain after the end of the war, despite the tremendous dislocation between life before and after the conflict. An influential teacher, Bloch had established a school of painting in Berlin in 1926 with the artist Anton Kerschbaumer, until his status as a 'degenerate' artist forced him to leave Germany. Arriving in England in 1934 via a safe haven in Denmark, Bloch opened the School of Contemporary Painting with Roy de Maistre.

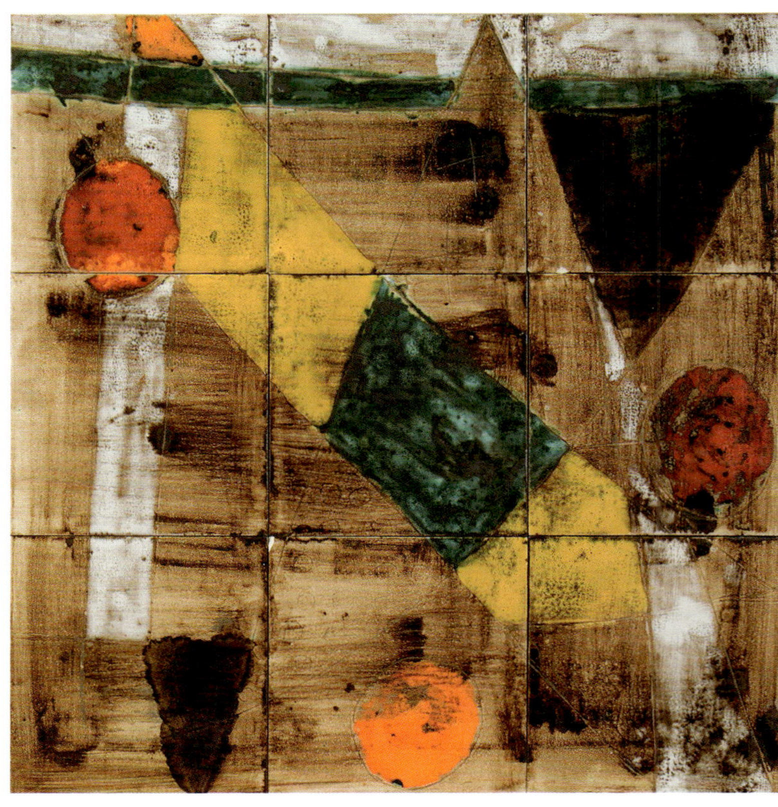

Although Bloch had applied for British citizenship, the outbreak of war delayed this process and he was interned. Post-war, he resumed his teaching as a guest lecturer at Camberwell School of Art, standing out in the post-war period as an exponent of rather unfashionable and little understood German expressionist painting whilst also inspired by Matisse and the Fauves. Bloch's daring approach found favour with a number of his students, notably Gillian Ayres and Bernard Evans. Ayres commented on how Bloch 'swept the life room,'[41] offering aesthetic liberation in contrast to the restrictive orthodox methods of Professor William Coldstream and his followers.

Weissenborn also taught part-time, 'enough to remain in touch with young people interested in the arts',[42] first during the war at Beckenham School of Art and later Ravensbourne College of Art, where he remained for 30 years. The Romanian-born émigré, Arthur Segal (cat. 24), opened his eponymous Painting School for Professionals and Non-Professionals in London in 1937 (moving it to Oxford in September 1939, before relocating back to London in 1943). It remaining open until 1977, committed to teaching artists and amateurs alike and acknowledging the importance of art as therapy.[43] Julius Rosenbaum and his wife Adele Reifenberg[44] also opened a small London school, which they too relocated to Oxford during the Blitz.

Some of the most important galleries of the period (a number of which are extant), such as Crane Kalman and Marlborough Fine Art, were established by émigrés and retained an empathy towards showing works of émigré artists. Often their very English names belied their continental roots: Marlborough Gallery, established in 1948 by Frank Lloyd and Harry Fischer, introduced Britain to the major Expressionists of *Die Brücke, Blaue Reiter*, and to Kokoschka. Molton Gallery, Annely Juda's first premises and precursor to Annely Juda Fine Art, showed a complementary range of Modernism, mostly Russian, or the geometrical abstract art of Holland and Central Europe; Crane Kalman Gallery established by the Hungarian, Andras Kalman, showed the work of émigrés including Mayer-Marton alongside British artists including L. S. Lowry and held a retrospective of Martin Bloch in 1974. Roland, Browse & Delbanco in Cork Street, founded by Henry Roland and Gustav Delbanco, 1930s refugees from Germany, showed a number of refugee artists including Herman and Bornfriend.

Hence, this highly talented and diverse group of émigrés not only 'broadened the scope of our galleries and museums and dented the belief, established by Roger Fry, that no art of any quality had ever come from beyond the Rhine',[45] but also implicitly understood that 'culture' was an essential part of daily living. It is this characteristic, known in German as *Bildung*,[46] and perhaps most easily translated as 'self-cultivation', compounded with a desire to share this enrichment with the greater community, that marks the extraordinary contribution made by these artists in exile.

Postwar: Jews, Art
and Refugees
1944–75

David Herman

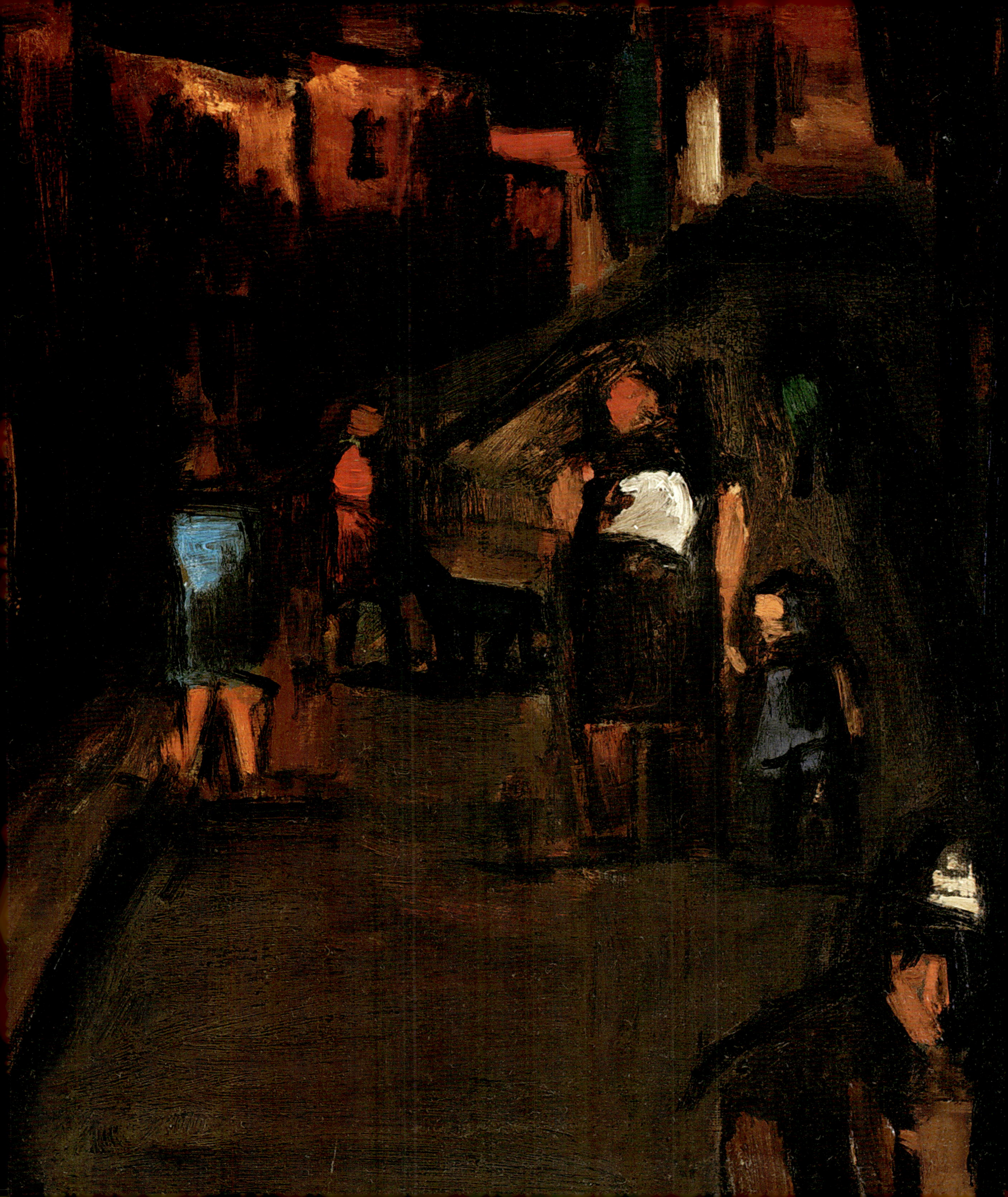

In January 1944 the Ben Uri re-opened after wartime closure. Its opening exhibition included an impressive range of Jewish artists, both British and European: from Jacob Epstein (cat. 19) and Mark Gertler (cats. 10 and 12) to Max Liebermann (cat. 23) and Camille Pissarro (fig. 32). The cosmopolitanism is all the more striking when you consider how the war had cut off British art from the European mainstream.[1]

It is tempting to see the Second World War as a crucial dividing point in the history of the Ben Uri, as it was for twentieth-century Britain. Before the war there were two generations of Anglo-Jewish artists: leading painters of the nineteenth and early twentieth centuries, such as Solomon Hart (cat. 1), Solomon J Solomon (cat. 18) and Alfred Wolmark (cats. 6 and 7);

then the Whitechapel Boys: Gertler, David Bomberg (cats. 9, 16 and 30), Isaac Rosenberg (cat. 13) and Jacob Kramer (cat. 14), among them. On the other side of the great divide come the postwar artists: the late work of Bomberg and Epstein in the 1950s, refugees such as Martin Bloch (cat. 28), Josef Herman (cat. 36) and Ludwig Meidner (cat. 21) and Else Meidner (fig. 33), and then younger artists such as Leon Kossoff (cat. 45), Frank Auerbach (cats. 43 and 57) [2] and Lucian Freud, later acclaimed as among the best British artists of their time.[3]

However, it is not just a question of individual names. The Second World War seems to divide two different worlds. Many of the Whitechapel Boys (and one Whitechapel girl, Clare Winsten née Clara Birnberg, cat. 15) were drawn to Jewish tradition in

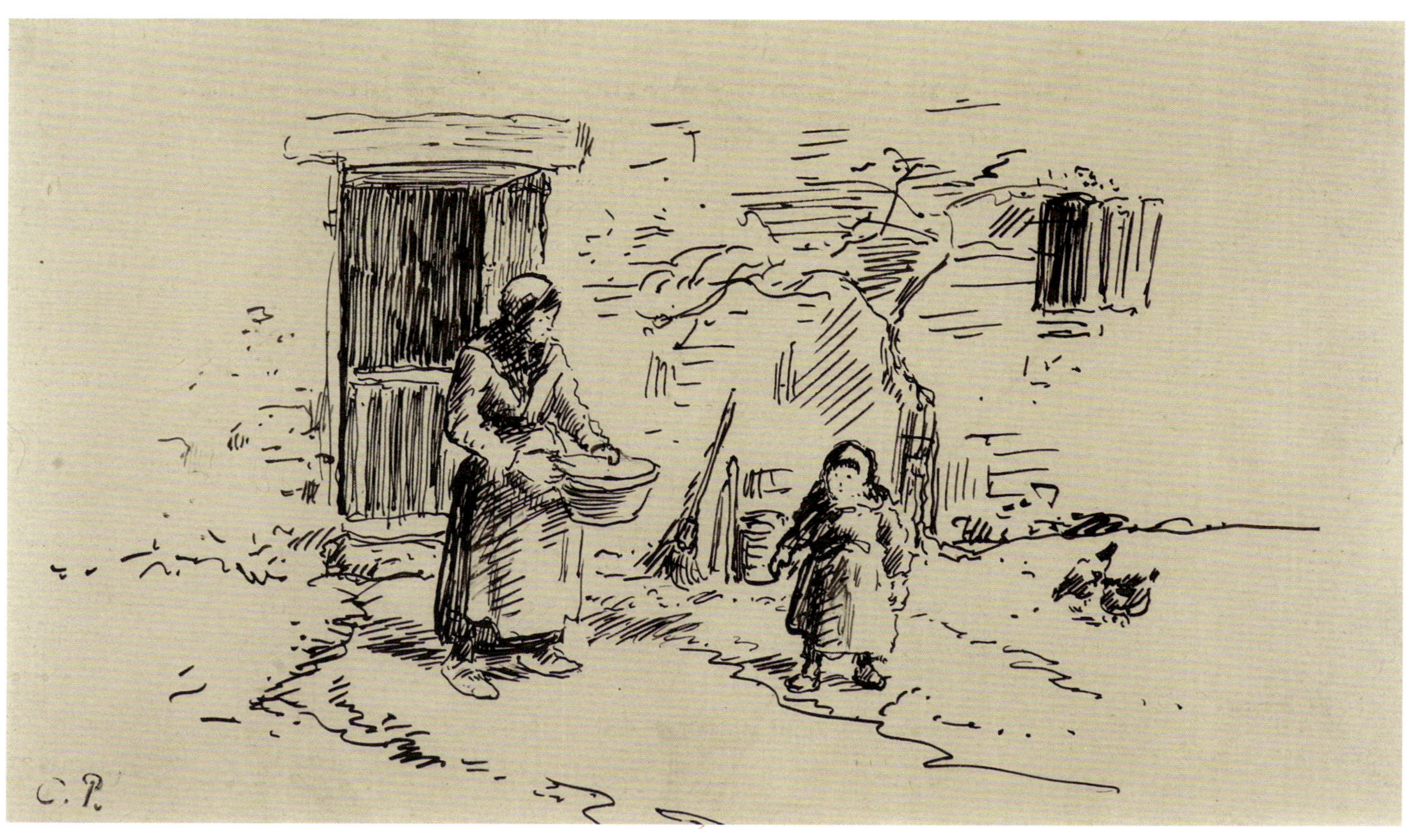

their work, an elegiac evocation of rabbis and ritual. Think of Gertler's *Rabbi and Rabbitzin* (1914, cat. 10) or Kramer's *Day of Atonement* (1919). But it was Jewish tradition with a Modernist twist. These artists worked at the heyday of Modernism. The Ben Uri opened in 1915, soon after Roger Fry's famous Post-Impressionist exhibitions of 1910 – the beginning of the modern period in British art according to Herbert Read[4] – and 1912, and two years after the 1913 Armory Show in New York, which brought Modernism to America. It was the year after the first exhibition of The London Group and the only Vorticist exhibition. This was the highpoint of the École de Paris and Bloomsbury. D. H. Lawrence wrote to Gertler that his painting, *Merry-Go-Round* (1916, cat. 12) was 'the best modern picture I have seen.'[5] The Ben Uri and the Whitechapel Boys are a crucial chapter in the history of Modernism in Britain.

The Whitechapel Boys also came of age during the First World War, in which many of them served. Rosenberg was killed on the Western Front, while Bomberg shot himself in the foot to be invalided out, only to be returned as a runner for his unit; Gertler, Bomberg and Rosenberg produced some of the great masterpieces of the war, both visual and literary.

They were a remarkably homogenous group: all born in the 1890s, Yiddish-speaking, from eastern-European-Jewish immigrant homes, brought up in the East End and educated at the Slade on the eve of the First World War.

The 1930s refugees who started to make a real impact in Britain after the war could hardly have been more different. The Whitechapel Boys engaged with the great formative experiences of their time. In the work of the refugees from the 1930s, the emphasis was on absence rather than engagement. Judaism and the

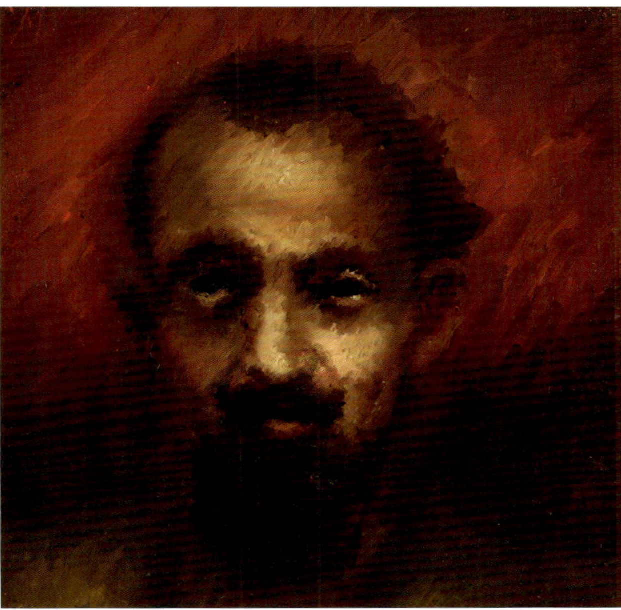

Jewish world of eastern Europe and the Russian Pale barely appear in their work. With a few notable exceptions, the Holocaust is a striking absence. Instead, we have a very different human and social landscape: Herman's Welsh coal miners, the great nudes of Lucian Freud (fig. 38), the powerful cityscapes of Auerbach, Bloch and Kossoff. Unlike the generation of 1910–20, the refugees created an artistic world virtually without Jewish imagery. And unlike Rosenberg, Bomberg and Meninsky, few of these post-war artists served in the war.

There was also nothing in their experience comparable to the moment of high Modernism on the eve of the First World War. Although there was still the continuing and intimidating challenge of Picasso, otherwise there was little more than a succession of trends and fashions, from Abstract Expressionism to Pop Art, which they largely ignored. For them, the

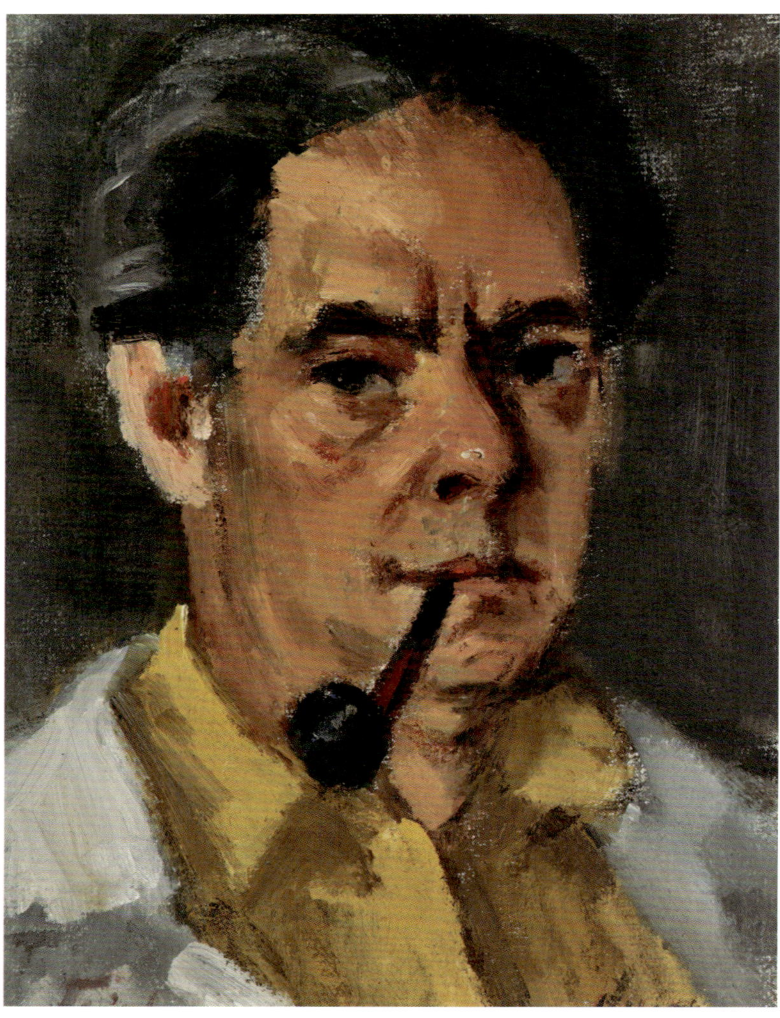

more important artistic context was German Expressionism. Both Ludwig Meidner and Else Meidner were out-and-out Expressionists, while for many central European refugees Expressionism was part of the culture that had formed them. Unfortunately, this made them seem all the more alien to British tastes. '[T]he characteristic style of the Northern latitudes,' Herbert Read called Expressionism, rather sniffily. 'It is also', he added, 'the characteristic style of the Jews [...]'[6]

The prewar artists had remarkably similar backgrounds. The postwar artists were diverse, impossible to categorise. They made up three generations, born half a century apart. Artists such as Arthur Segal (cat. 24), Bloch and Meidner, were born in the 1870s and 1880s. Herman, Walter Nessler and Dodo Bürgner, were born just before the First World War. Freud, Frankfurther (cat. 44) and Auerbach came to Britain in the 1930s as young children.

Perhaps just as importantly, the postwar artists were geographically diverse too. Else Meidner, Frankfurther, Auerbach and Freud were *Westjuden* from Berlin. Jacob Bornfriend (fig. 29) and Fred Feigl (fig. 34) were Czechs, Jankel Adler (cat. 22) and Herman were *Ostjuden* from Poland. When Herman met Adler and the Estonian sculptor Benno Schotz in wartime Glasgow, they spoke together in Yiddish, the common language for eastern European Jews.

The more than 300 creative figures who came to Britain as refugees from central Europe were not only painters but also included designers and typographers, sculptors and photographers, illustrators and cartoonists, publishers, architects and art historians. Elizabeth Friedlander was a designer and typographer who was responsible for many of the post-war designs

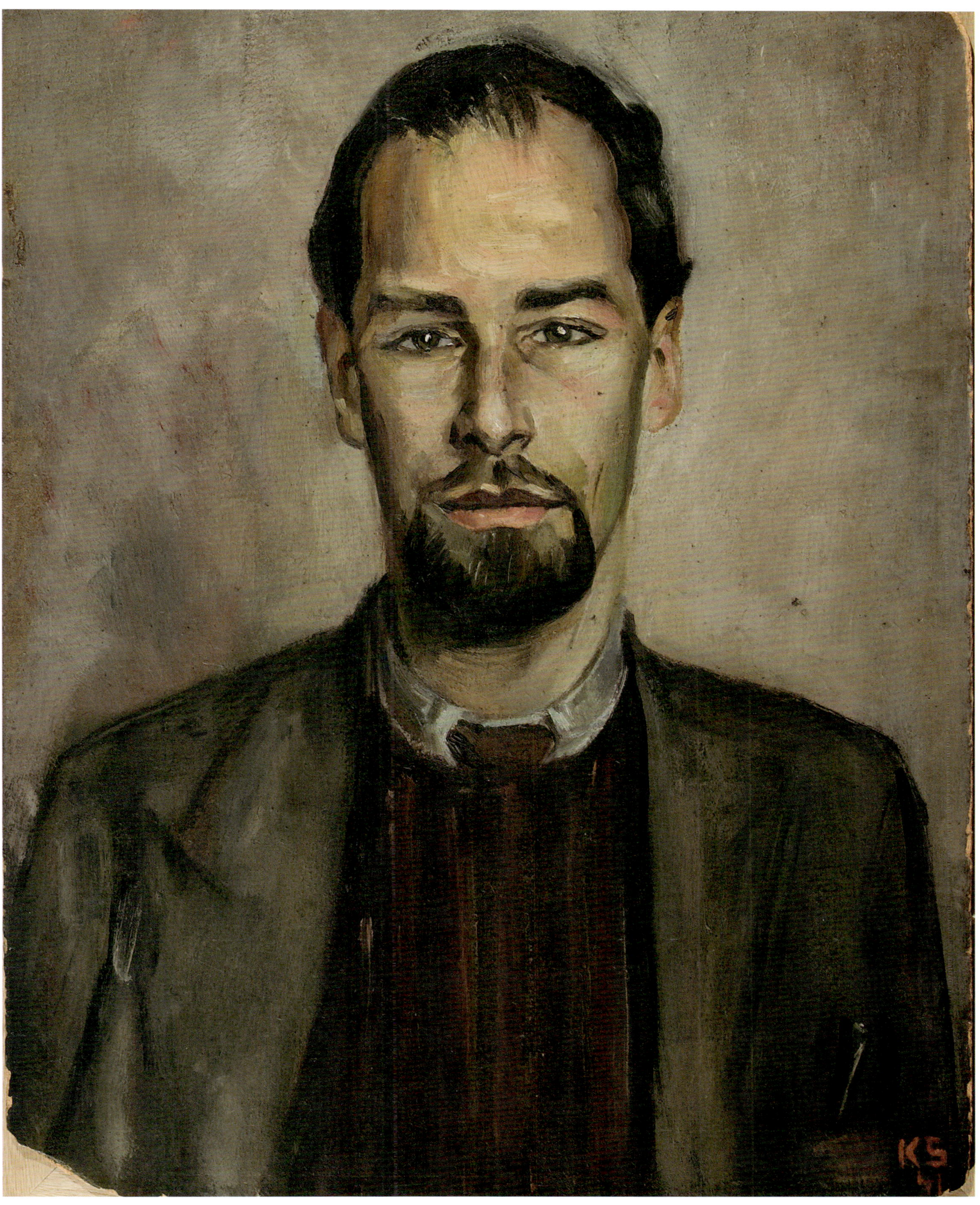

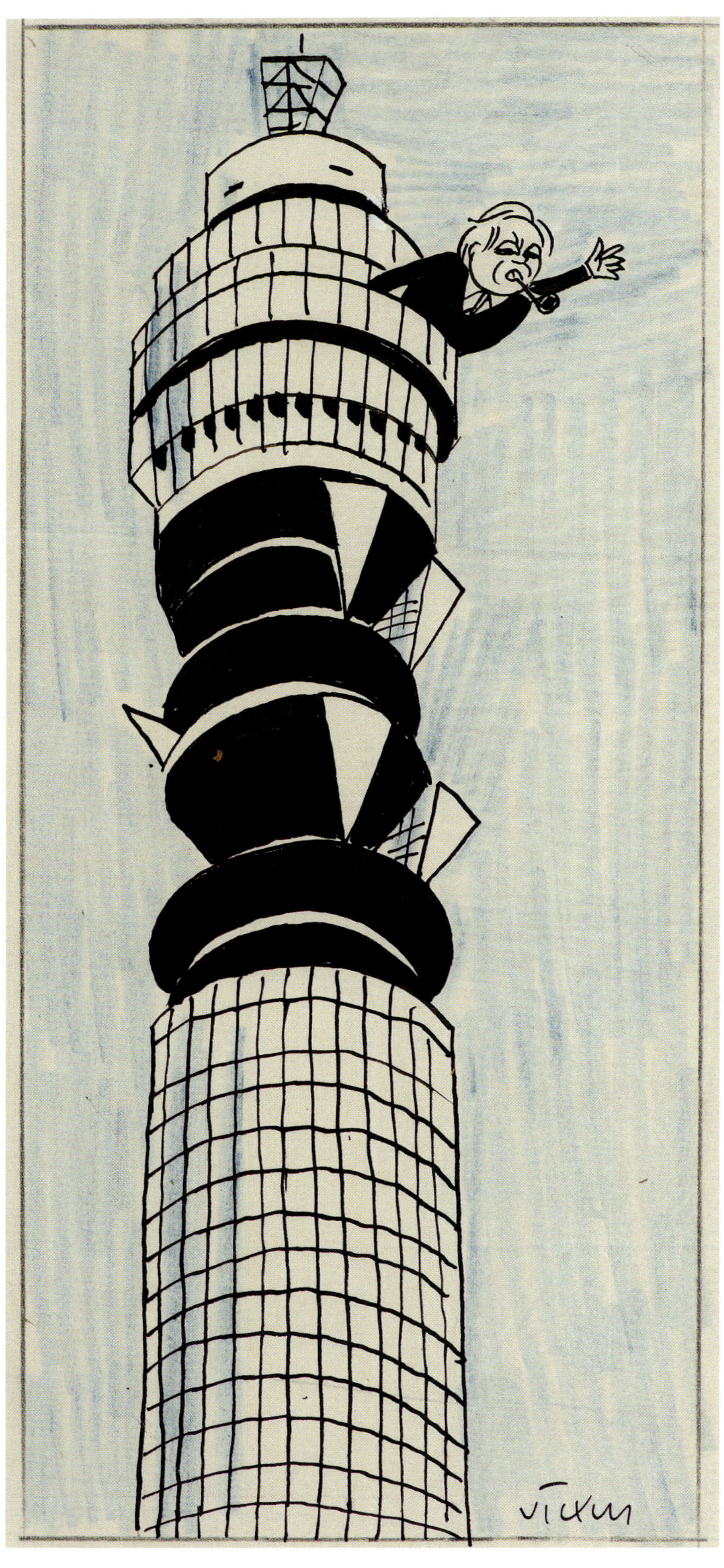

Fig. 36   Victor Weisz ('Vicky') *East of Suez.*
Ben Uri Collection

of Penguin Books, Hans Feibusch designed posters for Shell and Susan Einzig was a well-known illustrator of children's books. Ken Adam was the set designer for the first seven James Bond films, Hein Heckroth won an Academy Award for the costumes and sets for *The Red Shoes*, Hans Schleger designed the logo for John Lewis and made posters for London Transport. Refugees enriched every part of British visual culture. The Ben Uri recognised this range of achievement with acclaimed exhibitions of posters by Abram Games and cartoons by 'Vicky' (Victor Weisz, fig. 36).

There were very different reactions to the Holocaust in the work of these postwar artists. Few engaged directly with the Holocaust in their work, most did not and then there were those who both did *and* did not over the course of their careers. Jankel Adler painted his astonishing work, *The Orphans* (fig. 37) in 1942, one of the first works of art produced in response to the news of mass murder in Poland. Morris Kestelman's *The Persecution* was shown in the Ben Uri's *Summer Exhibition* in 1944, a year after his painting, *Why hast Thou Forsaken Me?* In an exhibition at the Ben Uri in the winter of 1946–47, Felix Topolski exhibited *After Liberation, In a Concentration Camp* and *Belsen, April 1945*.[7] Several artists, including Emmanuel Levy and especially Chagall, used the image of the crucifixion as a way of representing the destruction of European Jewry. See, for example, Levy's *Crucifixion*, 1942 (cat. 37), and Chagall's *Apocalypse en Lilas, Capriccio*, 1945/7 (cat. 40). Freud, Bloch and Bomberg, however, were among the many artists who chose not to take on the Holocaust as a subject.

Perhaps the most curious example is Josef Herman, who produced searing images of pogroms and refugees in the early 1940s, but then abandoned Jewish subjects for more universal themes. Then there is an equally complex group, containing those like Auerbach and Freud who did not explicitly engage with the traumatic history of the mid-century but whose work in the 1950s, with its imagery of isolation and darkness, could be described as 'Art of an Aftermath'.[8]

Finally, there is the extraordinary stylistic diversity of these refugee artists. Their work ranges from the bright yellows and reds of Bloch to the dark palette of early Auerbach and Kossoff, from the linocuts of London by Helmuth Weissenborn and Ernst Eisenmayer to more than 30 church murals by Hans Feibusch from the ceramics of Lucie Rie and Margaret Marks to the 200 delicate drawings by Fred Uhlman, produced when in internment on the Isle of Man, and the West Indian subjects painted by Eva Frankfurther in the late 1950s. Even within the work of a single artist there could be tremendous diversity. Schwitters' beautiful and traditional portraits of fellow-refugees Fred Uhlman and Klaus Hinrichsen (fig. 35), made in internment, are completely different from his mixed-media work, created in Germany and in Britain just a few years later. Herman's traditional Jewish subjects produced in Glasgow between 1940 and 1943 could not be more different from his monumental miners from South Wales painted in the 1950s.

At first, then, it might be tempting to see the Second World War as marking a great historical and cultural divide between two completely different groups of Anglo-Jewish artists, utterly different in their approach to Jewishness, Judaism, war and Modernism. However, it would be tempting but misleading.

The Second World War is not the straightforward watershed it seems. First, there are crucial similarities between those who came before the conflict and the postwar artists. Then there are continuities as well as discontinuities. These tell us a great deal about the history of Ben Uri and about postwar art by Jewish artists in Britain, but, perhaps above all about the larger history of British culture in the mid-twentieth century. Although these three histories, taken together, may seem to be about discontinuity, they are in fact more about continuities: about insiders and outsiders, and the place of Jews and immigrants in British culture.

Whether they originated from the Russian Pale or from Nazi-occupied central Europe, both groups of artists were outsiders. They were on the margins, as both Jews and immigrants, and as artists, too, they were outside the dominant English artistic traditions. When the English artist Paul Nash died in July 1946, Herbert Read wrote of his 'fidelity to a certain nativeness, a quality representing the historic English tradition in English art.' Read continued,

'[I]t is a quality which we find in the delicate stone tracery of an English cathedral, in the linear lightness and fantasy of English illuminated manuscripts, in the silver radiance of stained glass. It returns, after an eclipse, in our interpretation of classicism – in our domestic architecture, in our furniture and silver, in Chippendale and Wedgwood. The same quality is expressed, distinctly, in our poetry and music. It is a conscious tradition, as inevitable and as everlastingly vernal as an English meadow.'[9]

It is telling that the word 'English' is used four times. For Read it means a culture which is Christian, historic, medieval even, socially privileged ('in our furniture and silver, in Chippendale and Wedgwood') and pastoral ('as everlastingly vernal as an English meadow'). Note, too, the word 'our' ('our domestic architecture', 'our furniture and silver', 'our poetry and music'). Who is this 'we'? More importantly, who does the use of 'our' exclude? Whether you were a Jewish immigrant, or the son or daughter of immigrants from the Russian Pale such as Bomberg or Epstein, or a central European refugee, how included would you have felt reading this in 1946?

A few years later, in 1951, Herbert Read wrote an introductory book, *Contemporary British Art* in which he focuses on seventy British artists. Only three of them are Jews and there are passing references to no more than four Jewish artists in the entire book.

Another major figure in British mid-twentieth century art was Kenneth Clark, later Lord Clark, Surveyor of the King's Pictures, Director of the National Gallery and, like Read, a great admirer of Paul Nash and Englishness in English art. In his two-part autobiography, the only Jews Clark mentions are, in volume one, Berenson, Warburg and a few art collectors, and, in volume two, passing references to a dozen or so Jewish art historians and publishers, and TV and film producers. Not a single reference to the great Anglo-Jewish artists of his time: Bomberg, Epstein, Auerbach or Freud; plenty of references to Piper and Pasmore, Paul Nash and Henry Moore, all of whom Clark passionately collected, but not one modern Jewish artist.[10]

Between 1944 and 1959, Clark was editor of the *Penguin Modern Painters* series. Over 15 years this produced 19 volumes on artists as diverse as Moore, Graham Sutherland, Duncan Grant, Matthew Smith, Stanley Spencer and Ben Nicholson. There is, however, only one Jewish artist in the whole series: the American Ben Shahn.[11]

Read and Clark were two of the leading figures in British culture in the mid-twentieth century. Their sense of 'we' and of Englishness contrasts with the neglect felt by so many Jewish immigrant and refugee artists of the time. For almost a quarter of a century, from 1929 to 1953, Epstein received no large commissions. David Sylvester, along with John Berger and Clark one of the great English art critics of the 1950s, dismissed Freud, writing that he did not seem 'radical enough in style to be relevant to the future of painting.'[12] Bomberg lived from hand to mouth for years. In his essay on Bomberg for the *Dictionary of National Biography*, Richard Cork writes, 'Bomberg suffered continual rejection during the Second World War. The last one-man show he ever held in London was staged at the Leger Gallery (1943), and the only art school to accept him as a teacher was the Borough Polytechnic, London'.[13] In a passionate plea to the Ben Uri in 1938, Bomberg wrote,'The Jewish artists are starving, none of us can work, most of us receive one form of charity or another – we can make a market for ourselves if we organise.'[14]

These artists came from a world far removed from Read's vernal meadows and English cathedrals. In his memoir, *Related Twilights*, the artist Josef Herman, recalled his friend Jankel Adler, a fellow refugee from Poland and an Orthodox Jew: 'His conversation ranged wide: art linked with philosophy, philosophy linked with folklore; a Chassidic tale or a quotation from the Jewish book of mysticism, the Zohar [...]'[15]

A few pages later, Herman recalls another wartime encounter, this time with 'that phenomenal draughtsman of expressionistic portraits and painter of explosive landscapes and cityscapes,' the German refugee artist, Ludwig Meidner, also an Orthodox Jew. Meidner, he wrote, 'would wave his little red fists: "Our century is the century of the big city! ... We need to paint the truth! The city's savagery, its chaos, and the dark passions pent up in man!"'[16]

What could be further from Read's 'historic English tradition in English art' than Adler's Chassidic tales or Meidner's talk of 'the city's savagery'? In 1949 Meidner and his wife, Else, had a joint exhibition at the Ben Uri, the only British gallery to exhibit his work. The exhibition, however, was not a success. Meidner likened it to 'a second-class funeral' and in 1953 he returned to Germany, after twenty years of neglect in Britain, while Else remained behind. By then Adler was already dead. On his death, he had left Herman a Jewish prayer shawl which Herman kept in his studio for the rest of his life. This eastern-European Jewish world of prayer shawls and Adler's Chassidic tales are far removed from the England of Clark and Read.

If Clark and Read neglected these Jewish artists, the Ben Uri exhibited nearly all of them. One of the first whose work it bought was David Bomberg. In 1920, for example, Ben Uri acquired four of his works, including his masterpiece, *Ghetto Theatre* (1920, cat. 16), fresh from The London Group exhibition. In 1944 when the Ben Uri re-opened, its first exhibition included nine works by Epstein. In 1949 it exhibited both Meidner and Herman (in a joint exhibition with Bloch). In 1951, its contribution to the Festival of Britain celebrations, the *Anglo-Jewish Exhibition, 1851-1951* included work by Adler, Bomberg, Epstein and Herman, among many other refugee artists also shown, including Bloch, Hermann Fechenbach and Feibusch. Five years later, in the *Tercentenary Exhibition of Contemporary Anglo-Jewish Artists*, celebrating three hundred years of Jews returning to England, the Ben Uri featured works by more than twenty refugee artists and sculptors. During these years, then, the Ben Uri was the nearest these outsiders had to an artistic home.

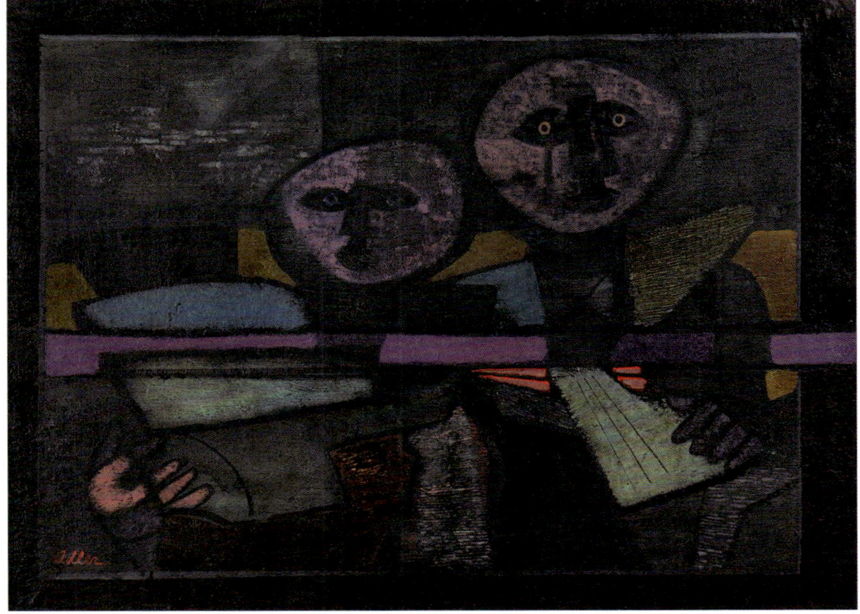

Although most of the refugee artists arrived in Britain before the Second World War, they only became established and found their artistic voices during, and more often after, the war – if at all. There were several important group shows during the 1930s and Bloch had his first British one-man show at the Lefevre Gallery on Bond Street in February 1939, but this was an exception; he was already in his mid-fifties with a distinguished reputation from Germany.

There are many reasons for their emergence in the late 1940s and 1950s but a few stand out. Several key artists caught the mood of postwar Britain, or, rather, two very different prevailing moods. Herman's images of Welsh coal miners (fig. 31, Ystradgynlais) and working people spoke to the atmosphere of social democratic Britain, the Britain that voted in their millions for Labour in the 1945 and 1951 elections.[17] In contrast, the pictures by the young Freud (fig. 38) expressed a deep sense of loneliness and isolation and seemed part of what some referred to as 'the age of anxiety'[18]. Like the work of his contemporaries, Francis Bacon and Auerbach, Freud's paintings

'[C]oncentrated on the human figure found, often alone, in a bare interior, neither diminished nor enhanced by the kind of data which, suggesting social or professional rank, would distract from the raw facts of existence. The approach is merciless, extreme [...]' [19]

Alongside this, however, were other more material factors. Artists were not the only refugees. A number of leading gallery owners also fled to Britain, among the best-known of whom were Erica Brausen at the Hanover Gallery, the Viennese **émigrés** Frank Lloyd (who changed his name from Kurt Levai) and Harry Fischer, who co-founded Marlborough Fine Art together in 1946, Annely Juda who later founded Annely Juda Fine Art, and Henry Roland (birth name Heinz Rosenbaum), who with fellow-refugee Gustav Delbanco, co-founded Roland, Browse and Delbanco on Cork Street in 1945. The Hanover Gallery gave the young Freud one-man shows in 1950 and 1952. Herman had his first solo show with Roland, Browse and Delbanco and exhibited with them for almost 30 years, while Bornfriend exhibited from 1948–1961. Auerbach and Kossoff had their first one-man shows in the mid-1950s with the Beaux Arts which was run by Helen Lessore who, while not herself a refugee, was the daughter of central European immigrants. New refugee gallery-owners and new refugee artists created important networks together in the years after the war. This was a very different artistic world from that of the Whitechapel Boys.

Another reason for the rise of so many artists in the 1940s and 1950s was money. The postwar state funded art schools which in turn employed many leading refugee artists as teachers. For example, Bloch and Karel Vogel taught at Camberwell, Bomberg taught at Borough Polytechnic from 1945 to 1953, Freud taught at the Slade for a decade, Klaus Meyer taught at Hornsey College of Art and then Kilburn Polytechnic during the 1960s and 1970s and Heinz Koppel taught at Camberwell, Hornsey College of Art and Liverpool College of Art.

Just as importantly, a new generation of students emerged from the art schools immediately after the war. To give just a small selection of the number of Jewish artists who benefited from the new opportunities: Frankfurther, Auerbach and Kossoff studied at St. Martin's, while Auerbach and Kossoff, along with Gustav Metzger, also studied with Bomberg at the Borough Polytechnic.

The economic boom of the 1950s and 1960s led to a new affluence after the decades of austerity both before and immediately after the war. 'Austerity and anxiety are words often applied to the decade immediately following the Second World War,' writes Frances Spalding in *British Art Since 1900*.[20] The 1950s were very different, however, and in Britain as in America, a generation of newly affluent buyers wanted to buy works by new artists.[21]

The rise of so many galleries and the emergence of an affluent middle class keen to buy art had serious implications for the Ben Uri. Each group represented a fresh kind of competition: galleries interested in new Jewish artists and buyers who could outbid the Ben Uri for their work. Just as it had not been lack of talent that led to important artists being marginalised in the 1940s, so it was not only talent that led to the success of a new generation of artists after the war. Economic circumstances favoured their emergence.

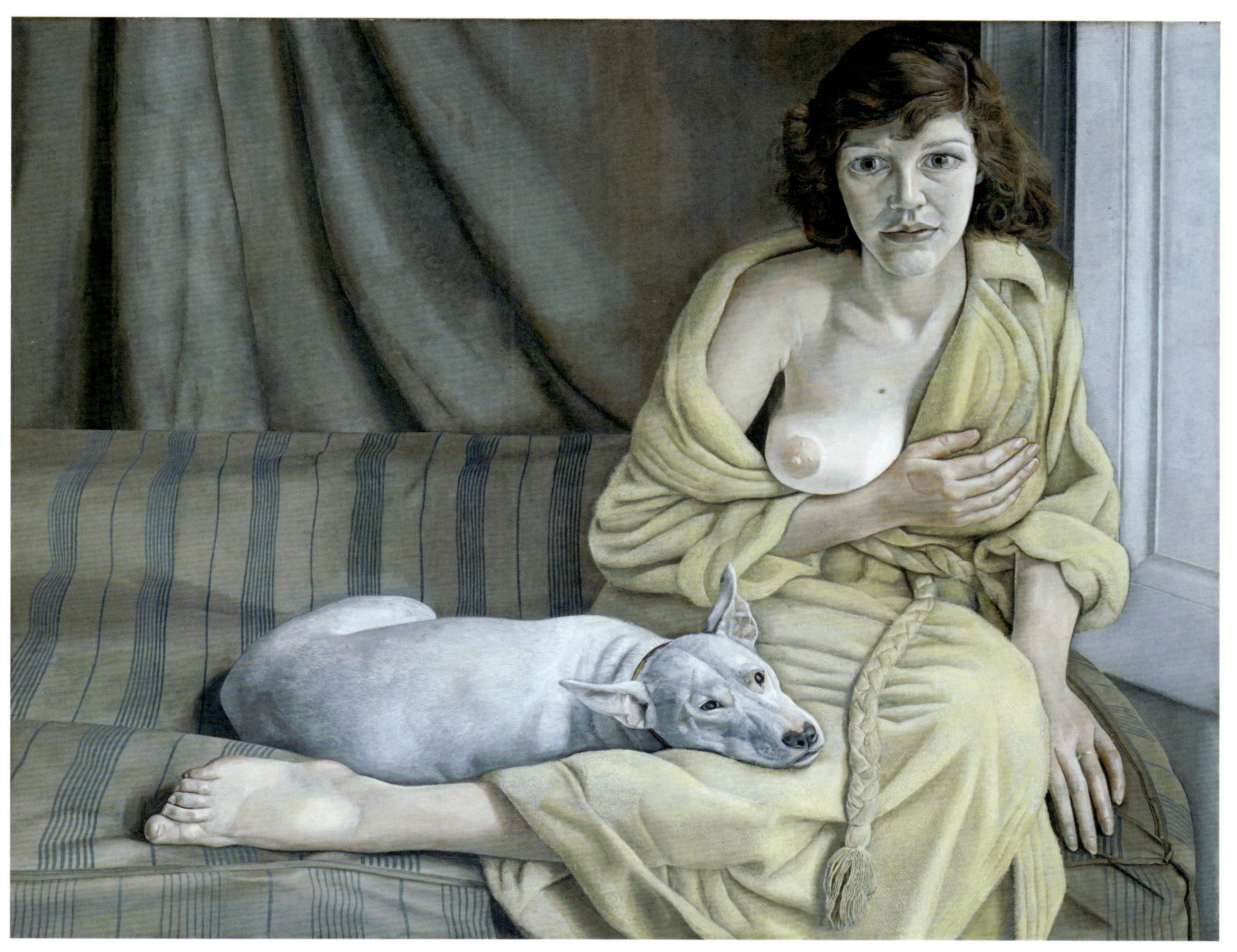

Fig. 38 Lucian Freud, *Girl with a White Dog*, 1950–51.
Tate

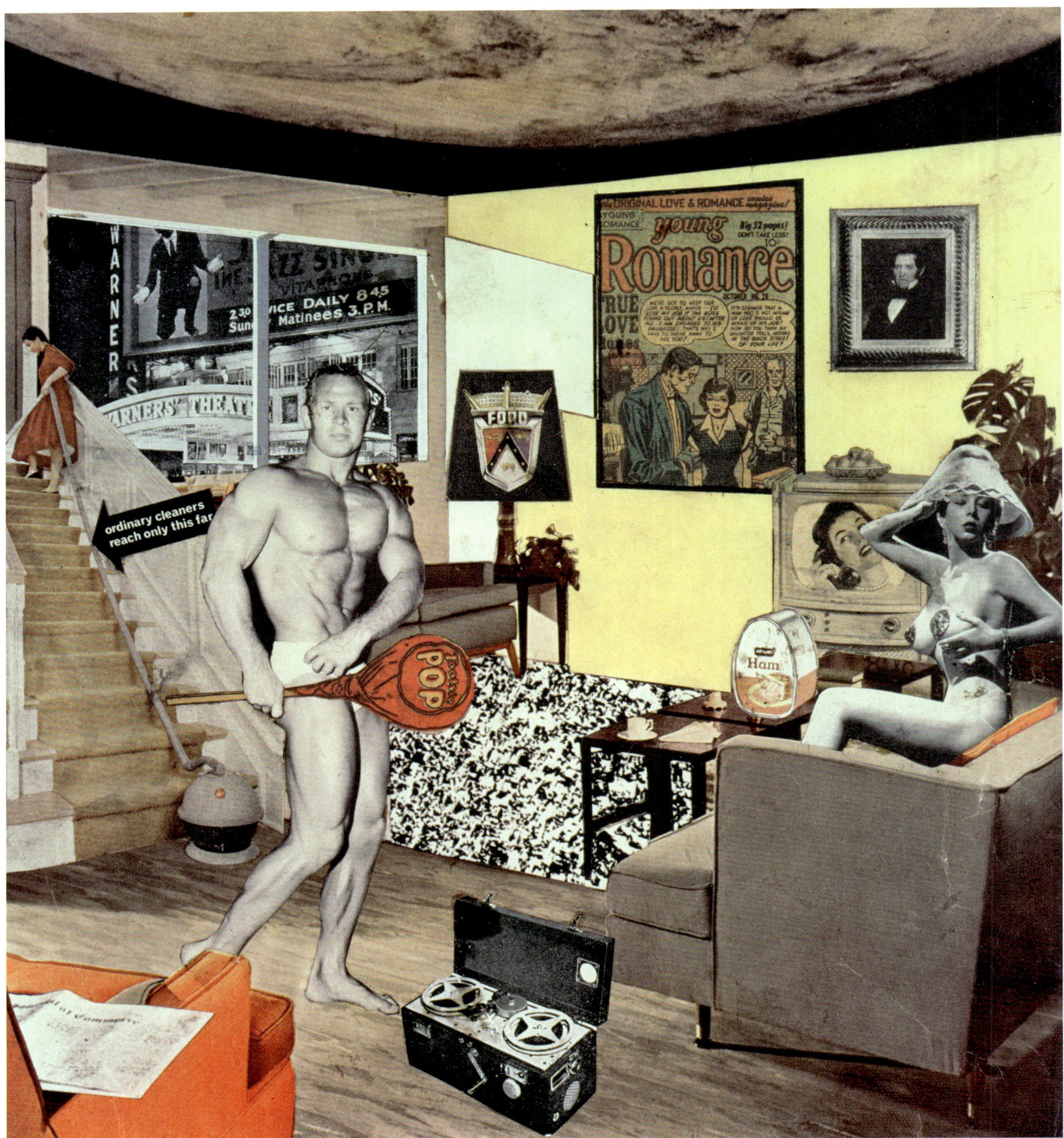

WARNER'S
THE JAZZ SINGER
VITAPHONE
2.30 ICE DAILY 8.45
Sunday Matinees 3 P.M.
WARNERS' THEATRE
ordinary cleaners reach only this far
FORD
POP
THE ORIGINAL LOVE & ROMANCE comics magazine!
YOUNG ROMANCE
young
Romance
Big 52 pages!
DON'T TAKE LESS!
10¢
OCTOBER NO. 26
TRUE LOVE Romance
Ham

The new affluence of the 1950s had other consequences for postwar Jewish artists. In 1957 Prime Minister Harold MacMillan said, 'most of our people have never had it so good'; in 1958 JK Galbraith wrote *The Affluent Society*; in 1959 a cartoon in *The Spectator* showed Harold MacMillan at Number 10: around the table are a car, a washing machine, a fridge and a television which MacMillan thanks for helping the Conservative Party achieve victory in the 1959 election – a victory generally attributed to the economic boom of the late Fifties.[22] It is worth noting that in the Ben Uri's recent exhibition, *Refiguring the 50s*, there were no images of washing machines, fridges or televisions. By contrast, in Richard Hamilton's famous collage, *Just What Is It That Makes Today's Homes So Different, So Appealing?* (1956, fig. 39), the first famous work of British Pop Art, a television and a hoover can be clearly seen in a modern living room. The rise of Pop Art, the bright cheery colours of Hockney and Hamilton, owed a great deal to the new affluence of the late 1950s and 1960s. The darker work of Jewish refugee realists and Expressionists, however, suddenly seemed out of touch and old-fashioned, something from the long nineteenth century. The real dividing point in Britain and in British art in the twentieth century came not with the Second World War then, but later, in the late 1950s and early 1960s, with the economic boom, the new consumerism and popular culture (television, pop music, new fashion, youth culture). The years of austerity, on either side of the Second World War, seemed far away. On 26 January 1964 the *Sunday Times Colour Magazine*, only recently founded, published an article by the art critic, David Sylvester, 'Art of the Coke Culture'. The new language he uses is revealing: 'consume', 'advertising', 'popular entertainment', 'supermarket', 'the billboard'. This is a long way from Meidner's 'century of the city' or the lonely figures of Auerbach and Freud. The refugee artists who seemed so at home in the social democratic moment after 1945 and in the 'age of anxiety' never seemed to connect with the new 'Coke Culture', either in form, colour or content.

In 1975 the Ben Uri celebrated its 60th anniversary. It was a very different world from 1944, one transformed by the social and cultural revolution of the 1950s and 1960s. Margaret Thatcher had just been elected as leader of the Conservative Party. The golden years of the economic boom came abruptly to an end. The post-war era of Anglo-Jewish art was giving way to something new and very different. Except for a few 'grand old men', the age of the refugees who had dominated Jewish art in Britain for almost forty years was over.

Je Suis Juif:
A Personal Response to British Figurative Painting since the Second World War

James Hyman

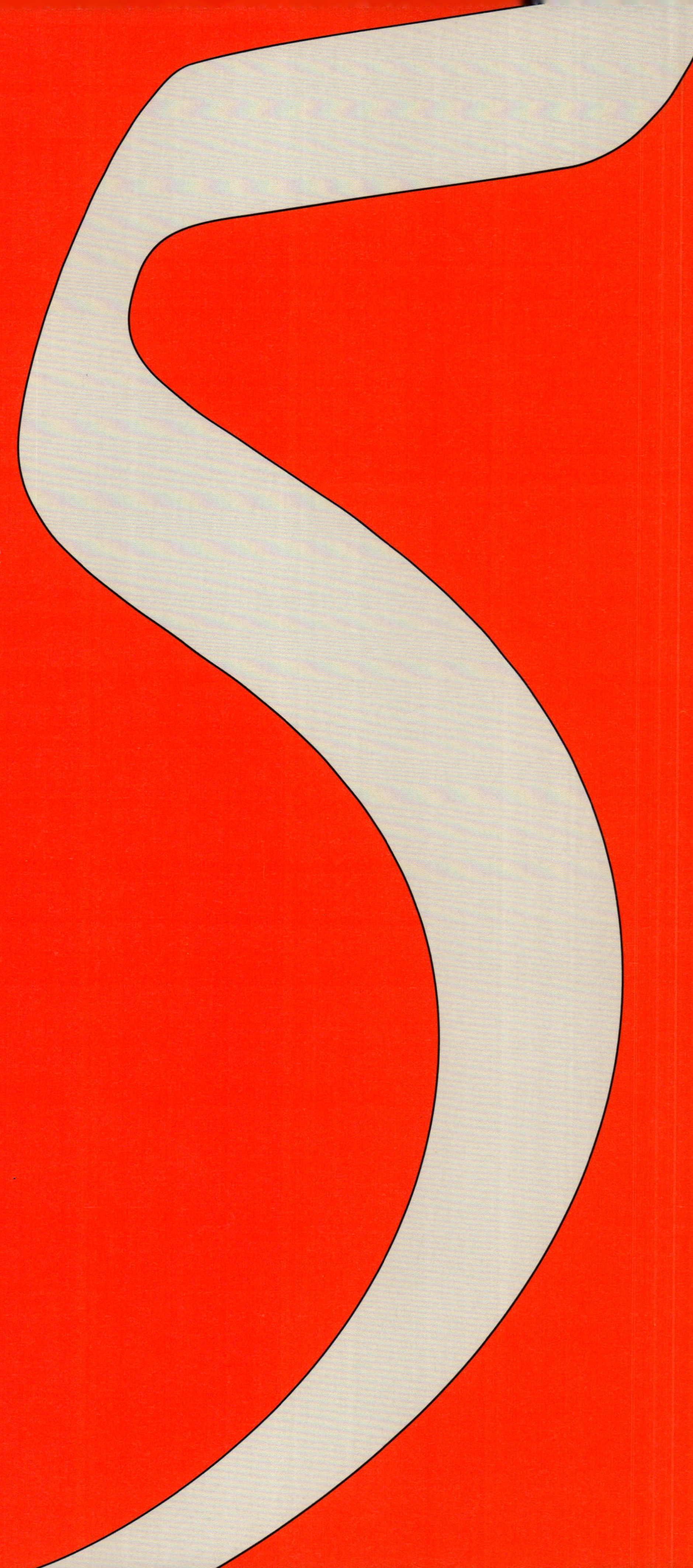

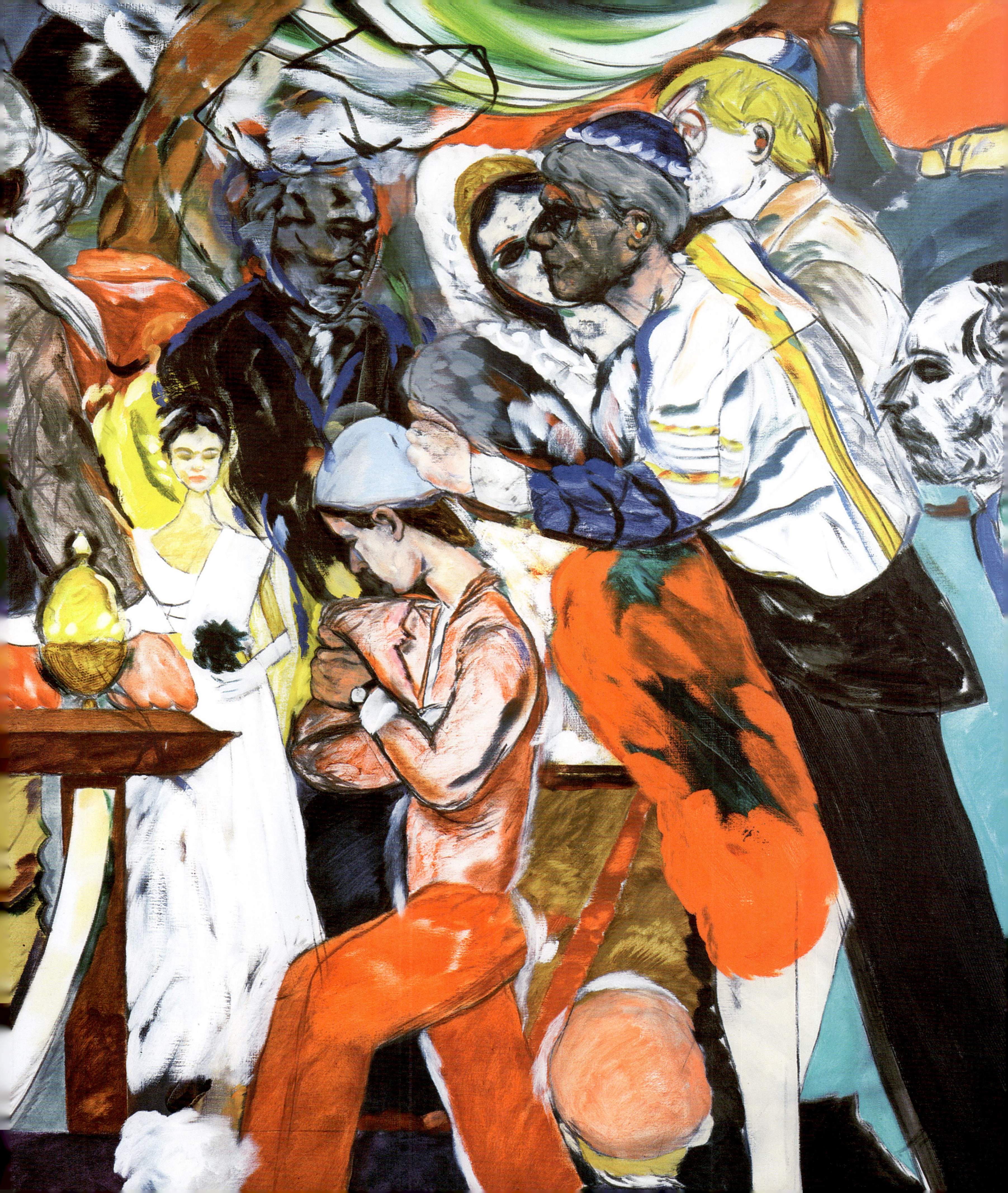

Fig. 40 *(previous page)*   R. B. Kitaj, *The Wedding* (detai), 1989–93.   Tate

At lunchtime on 11 September 2001 art critics, collectors and friends assembled at a gallery in Mayfair in London for the launch of my first book, *The Battle for Realism: Figurative Art in Britain during the Cold War (1945–60)*.[1] It was an enormously exciting moment that marked the culmination of ten years of work, first for my PhD at the Courtauld Institute of Art and then as an author for Yale University Press. In the book I traced the development of figurative art in Britain in the period after the Second World War and argued that the battle for realism was a key moment in the history of British art. This was the moment, in the late 1940s and 1950s, when a School of London was proposed for the first time as a challenge to the hegemony of the École de Paris and the New York School.[2] As with Paris and New York, the roll call of immigrants is long – Jankel Adler, Frank Auerbach, Lucian Freud, Naum Gabo, Josef Herman, and many, many more – and appropriately this is one of the strengths of Ben Uri's permanent collection. This was also a moment when British art was elevated to a heightened status through the international reputations gained by artists such as Francis Bacon, Graham Sutherland, Freud and Henry Moore. While in New York Clement Greenberg's 'abstract expressionists' and Harold Rosenberg's 'action painters' were prioritising the painted surface and the properties of the paint to create a radical new abstraction, in London Bacon, Freud, Auerbach and Leon Kossoff defiantly pushed figurative painting to its limits to create a radical modernist realism that gave a central place to the artist's own actions on the surface of the picture.

Their work was at the centre of a battle fought between two competing visions of realism: social or socialist realism, and modernist realism. Leading the two sides were two of the twentieth century's greatest art critics: David Sylvester, the insider *par excellence*, and John Berger, a combative outsider. Berger advocated a social realism that was an accessible art that would communicate with an audience, whilst Sylvester's existentialist realism addressed the human condition and presented the artist as a loner, a solitary genius revealing important truths.

That lunchtime in London, as we sipped wine, nibbled canapés and enjoyed the paintings around us by Auerbach, Freud, Kossoff, Moore, William Scott and Graham Sutherland, the first news came through of planes crashing into the twin towers of the World Trade Centre in New York. At that moment none of us appreciated the enormity of the event or the way that it would change the world so fundamentally.

In an essay for the *Guardian* newspaper entitled 'Fifty Years of Hurt', that I wrote later that day, I attempted to convey the continuing potency of this earlier battle for realism in the light of contemporary events.[3] I concluded:

Today, when so much art has become entertainment, serving a public hungry for sensation, and when the notion of high culture is attacked so routinely, it may seem misplaced to recall the high seriousness of that battle. Yet […] the indebtedness of today's leading artists to these post-war pioneers seems clear […]. As modern artists continue to grapple with humanity's vulnerability in a violent world, they are creating a new realism that places them as heirs to the legacy of this earlier battle. Fifty years ago it was the chimneys of Auschwitz and the atom bomb plume at Hiroshima that prescribed the artistic struggle. Now, in the aftermath of the terrorist atrocities in America, the battle for realism has assumed a chilling new resonance.[4]

An event of the magnitude of 9/11 can be embodied, encapsulated, evoked by a memorable line, a significant personal narrative, a defining image. The photograph of an aeroplane about to crash into the towers is etched into our collective memory and gives poignancy to the precarious twin towers of Anselm Kiefer's *Jericho* (fig. 41) which were memorably installed in the courtyard of the Royal Academy in 2007.

Herbert Mason's famous photograph of *St Paul's Cathedral in the Blitz* (1941, fig. 42) has a similar potency. Both these photographs embody a defining moment and each encapsulates a shift in consciousness of such profundity that those who experienced the event first-hand or through an image in the media would be changed forever.

Mason's iconic, widely reproduced photograph was declared to be 'war's most famous picture' and embodies resilience and an inviolate, unbroken spirit. Jeremy Paxman's characterisation of its resonance helps explain its potency and provides an insight into why three of the greatest paintings of St Paul's should be by Jews: '[T]he best-known picture of the Blitz, the picture that told the British people they would never be beaten [...] this sense of being uniquely persecuted and uniquely guarded'.[5]

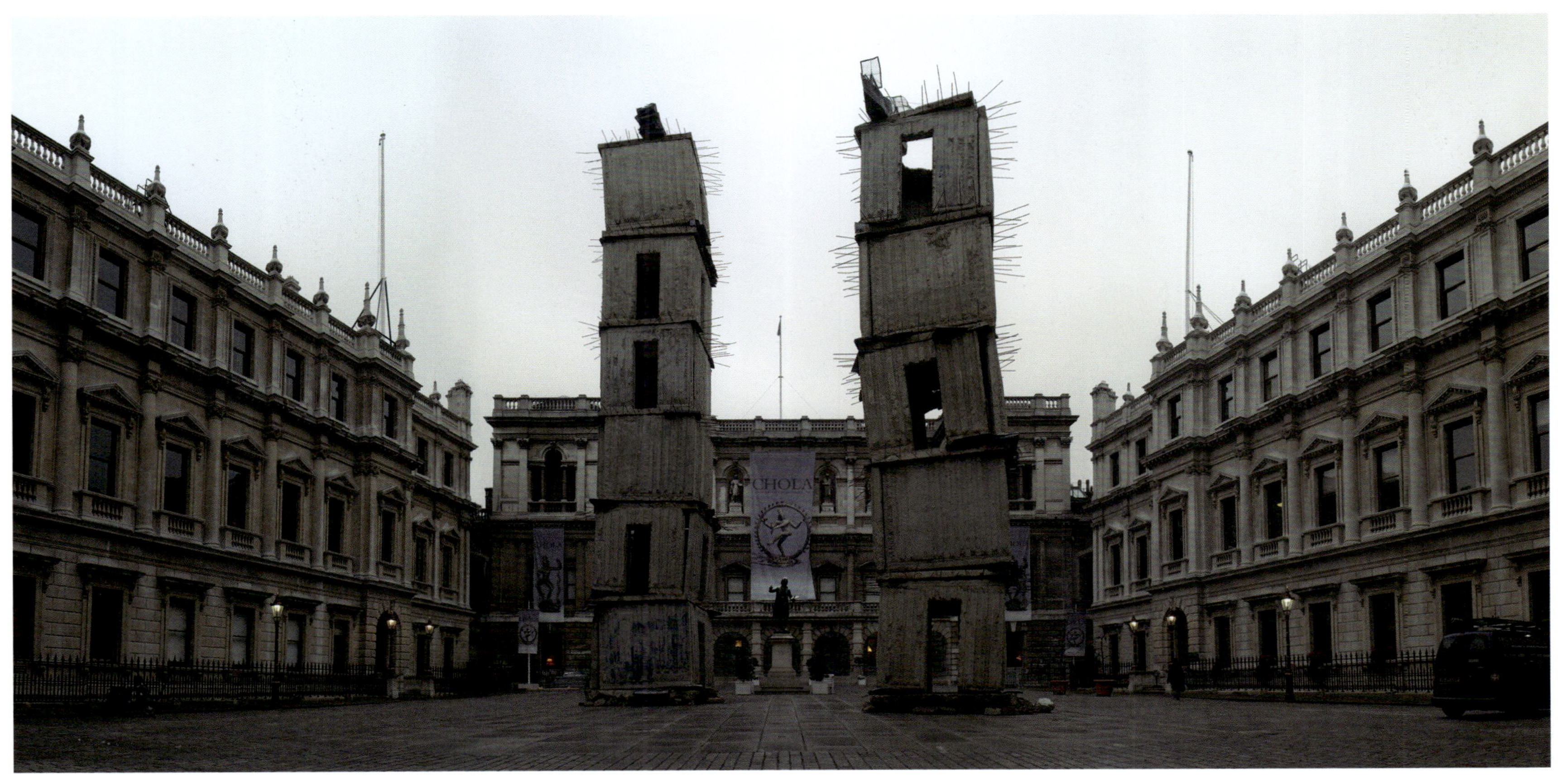

Fig. 42 *(right)*   St Paul's Cathedral in the Blitz, 1941.
Herbert Mason / Associated Press

Fig.43 *(below)*   David Bomberg, *Evening in the City of London*, 1944.
Museum of London

Fig. 44 *(far right)*   Leon Kossoff, *St Paul's*, 1954.
Annely Juda FineArt

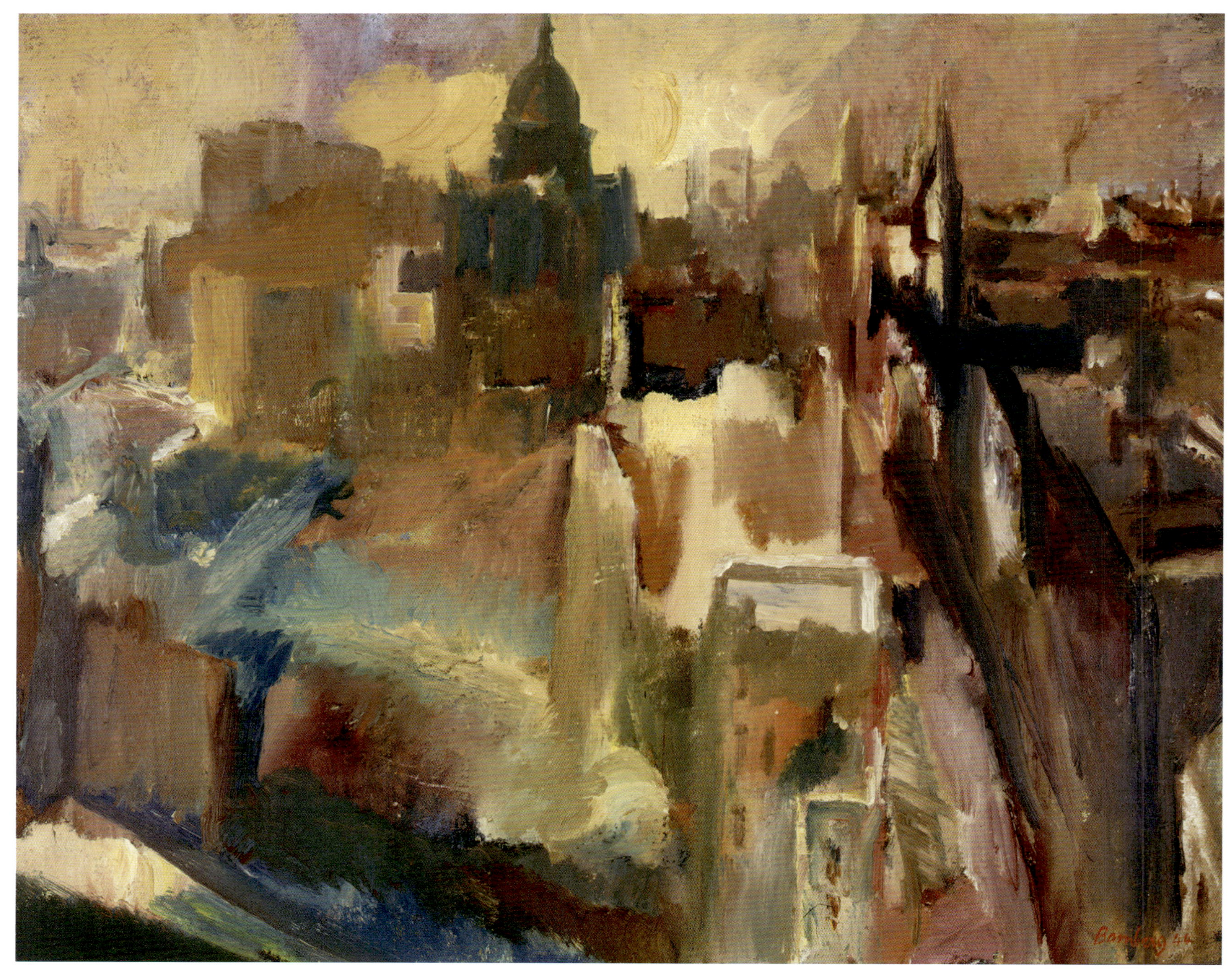

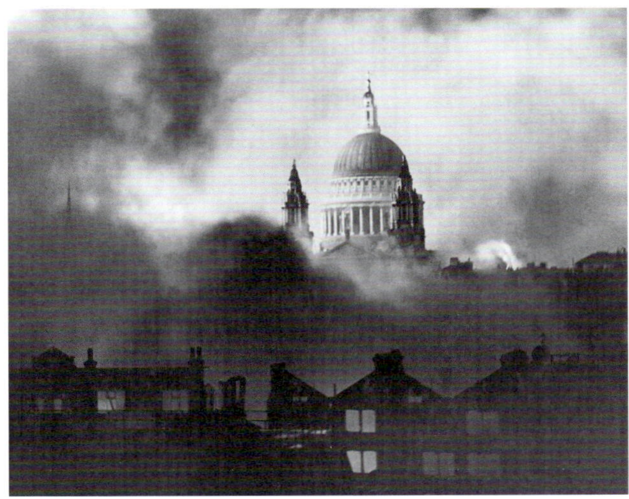

In David Bomberg's *Evening in the City of London* (1944, fig. 43) the city is tinged with glorious pinks and oranges and St Paul's dome rises proudly above it. In Kossoff's breakthrough painting, *St Paul's* (1954, fig. 44), the cathedral ascends vertiginously heavenwards and in Auerbach's complex *St Paul's Building Site* (1955) the builders construct a New Jerusalem.[6] Each artist's vision elevates one from the immediate to the transcendent.

In 1962 Michael Andrews produced what has become one of his most famous paintings, *The Colony Room* (fig. 45). This group portrait has assumed canonical status in its presentation of members of the so-called School of London in the infamous Soho drinking club that was frequented by Michael Andrews, Auerbach, Bacon and Freud amongst many other distinguished cultural and political figures. The iconic status of this painting is matched by that of a celebrated group photograph taken by John Deakin, *Wheelers Lunch* (1963) that shows Andrews, Auerbach, Bacon and Freud sitting around a dining table at the celebrated restaurant. Again the image encapsulates the friendship of a circle of painters and celebrates ideas of bohemia.

If, however, one looks beyond these over-familiar pictures, there is another group portrait that tells a different story, one that celebrates a different context: R. B. Kitaj's painting *The Wedding* (1989–93, fig 40). Here we are given another construction, one that takes us from a drinking club and a seafood restaurant and places us instead inside a synagogue. Our familiarity with the earlier pictures of Andrews and Deakin makes Kitaj's intervention all the more audacious.

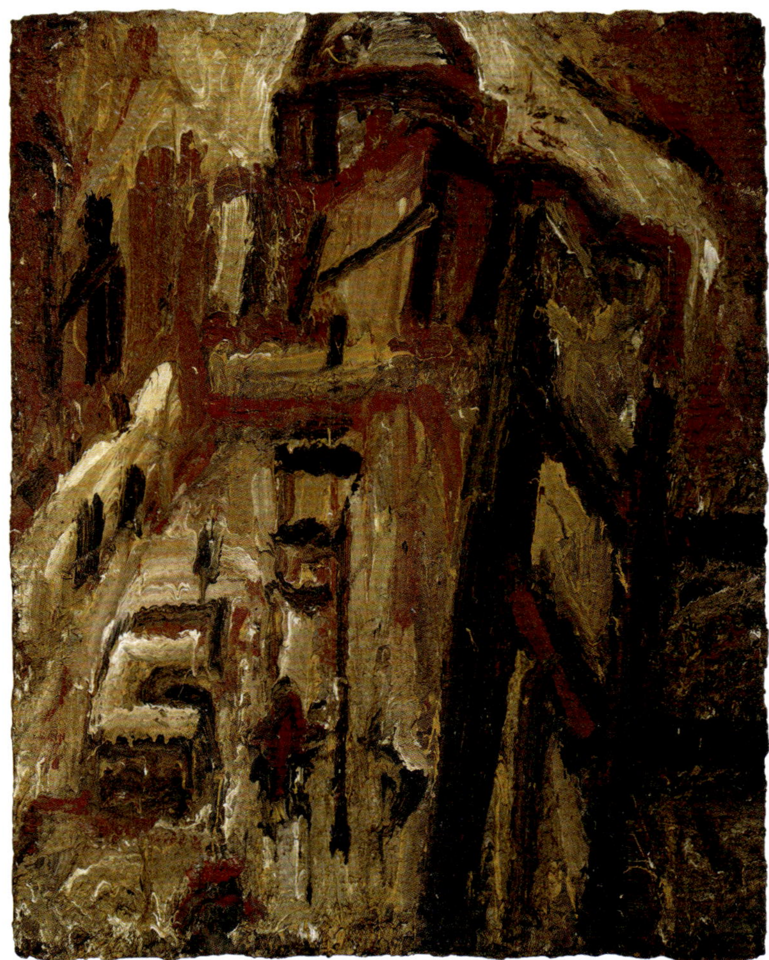

When I first saw this painting, which is now in the collection of the Tate, on a visit to Kitaj's studio in Chelsea in 1992, I was shocked by it.[7] It seemed to be a provocative reclaiming of Jews who had spent their lives seeking to create a place for themselves in the mainstream.

In contrast to the verdant landscape of lush greens in Andrews' *Colony Room*, Kitaj's declamatory painting is a brash commemoration of the artist's marriage ceremony. The setting is the oldest Spanish and Portuguese synagogue in London, Bevis Marks. In the centre of the picture, under the *chuppah*, stand Kitaj and his bride, fellow painter Sandra Fisher. Surrounding them is a roll call of some of England's most famous painters: Lucian Freud, the grandson of Sigmund Freud and an immigrant from Berlin; Frank Auerbach, an orphaned Jewish refugee from Berlin; and Leon Kossoff, the son of Russian Jewish immigrants. Obscured, to one side, is Kitaj's best man, his close friend since student days in the early 1960s, David Hockney.

At first sight the painting is a joyful celebration of the worlds of painting and Judaism. However, it also includes signs of the complexity that remains a key to diaspora experience. Freud appears to turn his back on marriage and Judaism, whilst Kitaj's adopted daughter is dressed in a sari having chosen this as the moment to assert her own ethnicity.

Kitaj had begun work on this painting at a time when he was also exploring the ideas that he would publish in 1989 in what he called his *First Diasporist Manifesto*.[8] More personal credo than rallying cry, it was a touching attempt to address his own identity and sense of place as a Jew in the diaspora. As Kitaj explained in his manifesto:

Diaspora is most often associated with Jews and their two-thousand-year-old scattering among the nations (longer by other accounts). Exile [...], has become a way of life and death – consonant with Jewishness itself [...]. I think that memories, events and beliefs are sacred dreams for paintings and so the mode of my life is translated into pictures […]. After 1945, the world changed for the Jews. If your world changes, your paintings change. Your hand, charged by heart and mind, goes at its task in new ways [...]. After 1945 [...], Jewish painting has new things to face, events never faced before, a profoundly different world view, an art to remodel.[9]

In making such statements, Kitaj was both an insider and an outsider: a figure at the heart of the contemporary British art establishment, who nevertheless was an American and a Jew. This duality is evident in the way that Kitaj championed the British art in which he believed. In the years prior to this painting, Kitaj had been tireless at promoting British figurative painting, most famously in the exhibition he curated entitled *The Human Clay* (Arts Council, 1976).[10] This mainly comprised drawings and was accompanied by a highly personalised catalogue essay, inspired in large part by Kitaj's recent return to life drawing and by his belief in the importance of this practice for both figuration and abstraction.[11] In the catalogue Kitaj briefly wrote of a 'School of London', using the term loosely, as he later explained to me:

I meant that a School had arisen, like School of Paris and School of NY, where a number of world-class painters and a larger number of good painters had appeared in London maybe for the first time [...]. Like NY and Paris, the London School will continue until its best painters die […]10 years after *The Human Clay*, the School of London has no peer abroad [...] the artists are just plain gifted beyond the resources of other schools. For the moment, NY seems played out and Paris doesn't count.[12]

Fig. 45   Michael Andrews, *The Colony Room*, 1962.
Pallant House Gallery

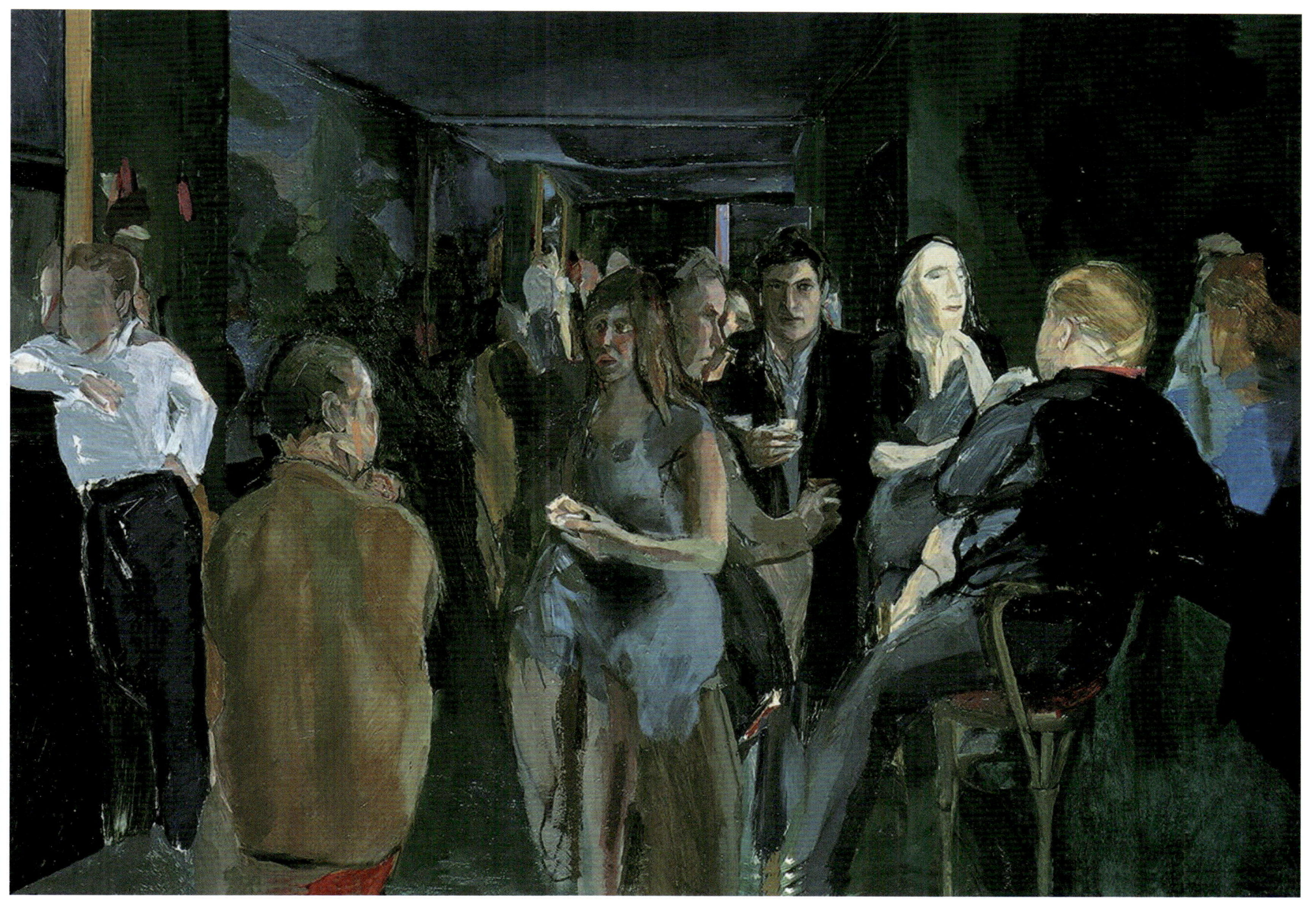

As a testament to the continuing relevance of
Kitaj's ideas, in 2011 on the 35th anniversary of Kitaj's
exhibition, I curated *Beyond the Human Clay* to
address its legacy and to propose a new generation of
artists.[13] In a catalogue designed in homage to the
original graphic design, and an essay that adopted
Kitaj's polemical tone, I wrote:

Over the last half-century the chimneys of Auschwitz and
the atom bomb cloud at Hiroshima, the atrocities of
Vietnam and the terror of the Cold War have moulded
the psyches of artists. Now with wars in Iraq and Afghanistan,
civil conflict across the Middle East, nuclear meltdown
in Japan, global financial crisis and street protest, it is
appropriate that the most powerful art of today should seek
to address the human predicament and to do so with
a new seriousness.[14]

Today Kitaj's paintings and writing about
immigration, identity and persecution have taken
on a fresh urgency and possess an acute universal
relevance, recognised not least in the way that Ben
Uri has reformulated its mission since 2001 to reach
beyond its Jewish constituency.[15]

In 1983 Kossoff painted one of his greatest group
portraits, *Family Party*. A massive, monumental
masterpiece, this painting provides us with another
context to contemplate: the subject for such grandeur
was not an important event, or a gathering of eminent
figures to be memorialised forever. Or perhaps it was.
Kossoff draws from the figure paintings of Rubens and
echoes the composition of a great Gothic tympanum
frieze to aggrandise the humble subject of the family.
This, for him, is what is most worthy of attention.

Kossoff brings us into the home and into an inner
world.

It is this very humanity that makes the work so
moving, for what is more important than those
around us? It is precisely this particularity and
intimacy that makes a great painting speak to us:
Auerbach returns to the same streets of his
neighbourhood, Freud paints the same models.
Each response to the personal creates an art that
is touchingly universal. At times of crisis, what we
cling to is the familiar.

Indeed it is striking that the growing international
stature of artists such as Bacon, Freud, Auerbach and
Kossoff has come post 9/11 as a reassessment of art-
world priorities has encouraged a new seriousness.
Furthermore, whilst much of the art of the last 20
years already has a passé *fin-de-siècle* decadence, serious
artists have gained new heights and younger artists
have turned increasingly to them for inspiration.[16]
Damien Hirst has shown paintings that imitate Bacon.
Jenny Saville draws from Freud. Kitaj's legacy can be
seen in works by artists as diverse as Marlene Dumas,
Luc Tuymans and Neo Rauch.

This embrace by the establishment and by the art
market obscures the fact that previously, for much of
their careers, the artists of the School of London had
occupied the position of marginalised outsiders.
Moreover, as the artists of the battle for realism have
grown in international stature, so the status,
appreciation and perception of their work has shifted.
These shifts, from private to public, outsider to
establishment, obscurity to celebrity, radical to
conservative, parallel what can be read, too, as a case
study in assimilation.[17] From being outsiders, whether
due to ethnicity, religion, sexuality, even artistic
practise, they have travelled to the mainstream and

then the establishment: Freud and Hockney, for example, both accepted the Order of Merit from the Queen.

Downplaying the ethnicity and origins of the School of London artists, and avoiding historical assessment, also obscures the fact that for much of their careers these artists had a deeply uneasy relationship with British art. It was only in the 1980s and 1990s that they became assimilated. However, I would like to propose that from today's perspective it is precisely their status as outsiders clinging to what is most personal and familiar that make the example of these artists so potent.[18]

A century ago, in May 1914, the Whitechapel Art Gallery staged a massive exhibition entitled *Twentieth Century Art: A Review of Modern Movements*, in which a group of works were labelled 'The Jewish Section'.[19] Today, such ghettoisation would be unthinkable. Moreover, it is because of, rather than despite, their fidelity to their roots half a century ago, and precisely because of their high seriousness, that pictures that could be dismissed as anachronistic remain urgent, even essential, in today's dangerous world. This, too, is where the idea of transcendence comes in, for to suggest that these are miserable pictures is to misunderstand their redemptive function. As I argued in an essay entitled 'From Tragedy to Joie de Vivre: Some Thoughts on the Work of Bacon, Freud, Kossoff and Auerbach', however black the roots, these paintings are increasingly uplifting. This is a matter of content as well as form: a lightening of mood, an increased joyfulness in colour and a compelling celebration of the properties of paint.[20] Bacon's

ejaculatory paint and smeared bodies show his urgent commitment to the human subject and the role he gave to chance in the creation of his paintings. Freud's worried surfaces reflect his alchemical desire that paint should become flesh. Auerbach's flowing paint conveys an ecstatic moment in which a heightened awareness of paint suddenly coexists with the springing to life of the subject. Kossoff's expressive response captures the intensity of a specific encounter and its personal resonance.

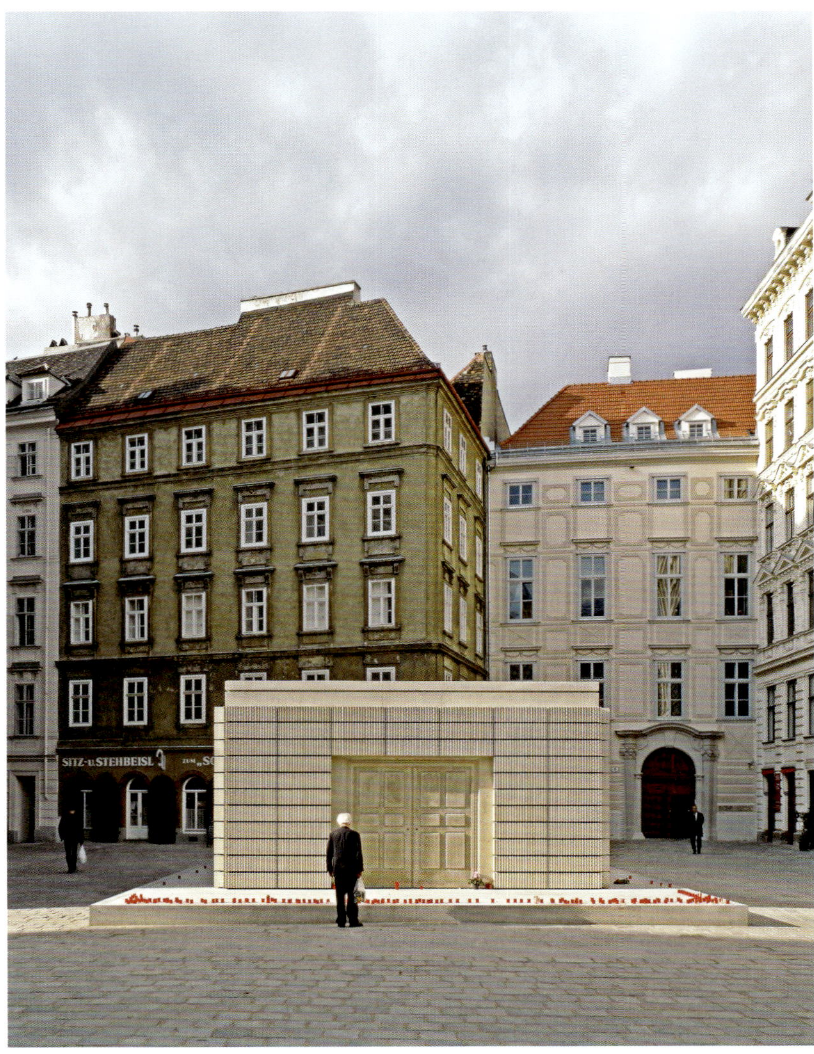

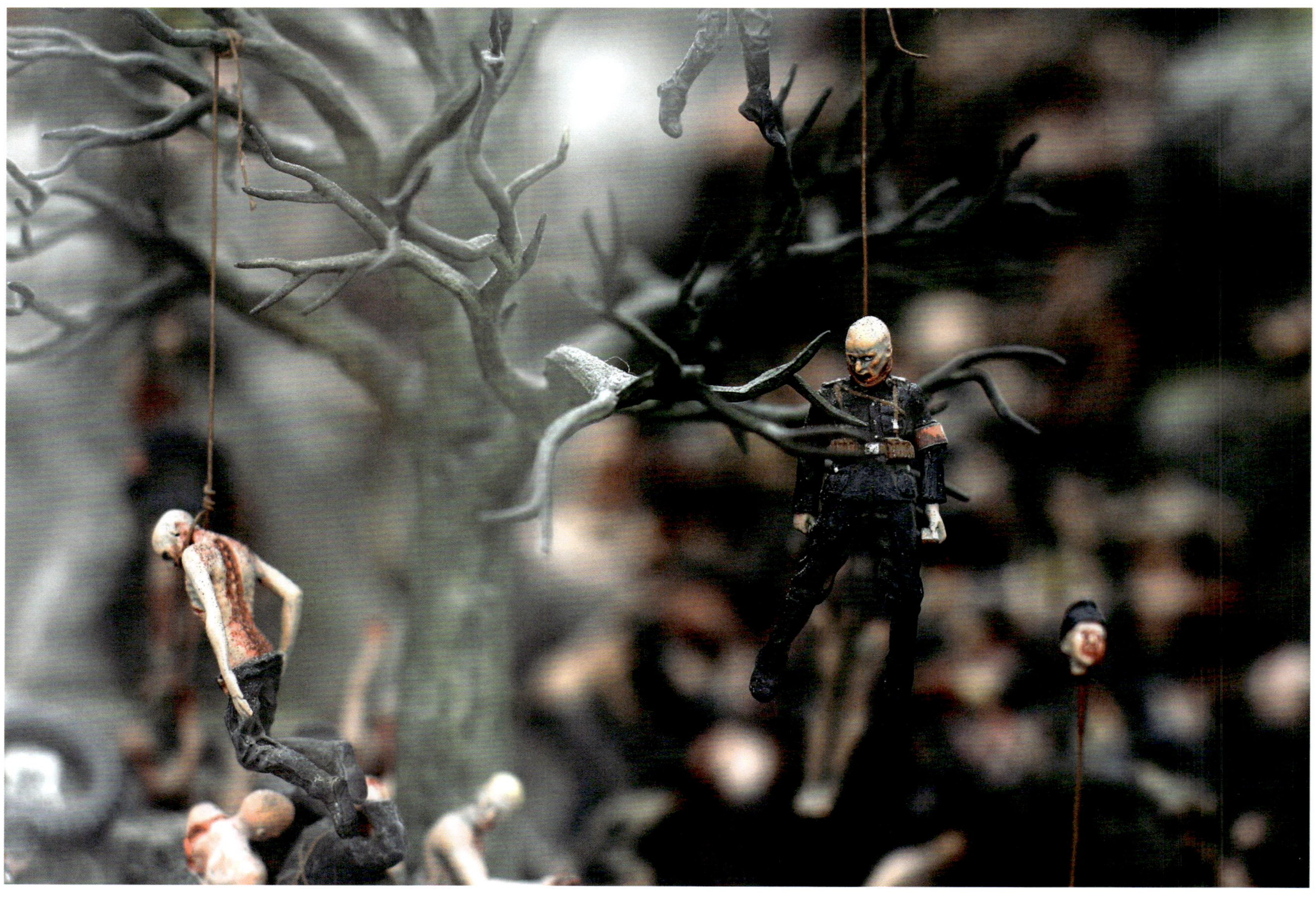

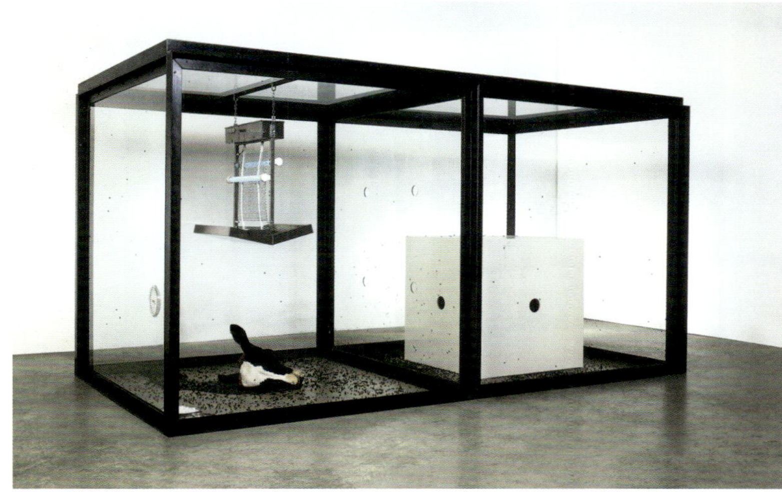

However, whilst these painters remain meaningful, little has been able to grow in their shadow and one of the striking features of the last 30 years is how little legacy they have left in terms of radical painting in Britain. Instead, if one is to locate their legacy, one must turn to other media. Originally, when the so-called *Young British Artists* (YBAs) emerged from Goldsmiths and other art colleges at the end of the 1980s, their values seemed antithetical. Yet 25 years on, I would propose that several of the best of these artists can be read as the heirs to the School of London. It's the language that has changed, not the preoccupation with our common humanity, vulnerability and mortality.

One of Rachel Whiteread's most powerful commissions is her eerie *Holocaust Memorial* (2000, fig. 46) for the Judenplatz in Vienna. The Chapman brothers' most profound tableau, *Hell* (2000, fig. 47), depicts the Holocaust. Anya Gallaccio's moving installation, a floor of 10,000 dying roses entitled *Red on Green* (1992, fig. 48) poetically traces death on a mass scale. For all the differences in medium, Damien Hirst's boxed and butchered animals (fig. 49) are the descendants of Bacon's paintings of man as meat, and Whiteread's impassive monuments the equivalents of Giacometti's stoical figures.

I began with the Schools of London, Paris and New York, so let's end with another journey through time and place. Let's travel from the Blitz in London and past the twin towers in New York and on to the streets of Paris and the recent murderous attacks on the satirical magazine *Charlie Hebdo* and a Jewish supermarket. In Paris and across the world people declared *Je suis Charlie*, and at mass demonstrations the placards, held by people of all faiths and none, also declared *Je suis Juif*. From the particular to the universal, from the personal to the public, it is this message of our shared humanity that is embodied by the great art of our age. This surely is the message, too, of Ben Uri as it continues to reformulate its mission for its second century.

Timeline

WORLD HISTORY TIMELINE

1905
Aliens Act, Britain.

1914
Outbreak of World War I

300,000 Jews in Britain. 100,000 in Whitechapel / Aldgate area.

1915
Passports made compulsory in Britain.

1917
Russian Revolution: The Tsar is overthrown and Lenin takes power.

1924
Jewish immigration to USA limited by Johnson Act.

1927
The Jazz Singer heralds the era of Talkies.

1928
First 5-Year Plan in USSR.

1929
Wall Street Crash.

ART TIMELINE

1905
*c.*Beginnings of *Ecole de Paris* group of artists.

1906
Exhibition of Jewish Art and Antiquities, Whitechapel Art Gallery.

1910
Roger Fry organizes controversial *Manet and the Post-Impressionists* exhibition in London.

1912
Roger Fry's *Second Post-Impressionist Exhibition* held at the Grafton Galleries, London.

1913
Armory Show in New York introduces Modernism to USA.

1913–14
Epstein's *Rock Drill*.

1914
First exhibition of the London Group.

1916
Isaac Rosenberg's, *Self-Portrait in a Steel Helmet*. Mark Gertler's *Merry-Go-Round*.

1918
Isaac Rosenberg killed on the Western Front.

1919
Jacob Kramer, *Day of Atonement*.

1920
David Bomberg, *Ghetto Theatre*.

1926
Decision of the Tate to exhibit contemporary European art.

1929
MOMA opens in New York.

BEN URI TIMELINE

1905

1915
July, Ben Uri Society founded in Whitechapel by Lazar Berson, over 100 members.

1916
Release of fundraising album, first Yiddish art publication in Britain. Berson leaves under mysterious circumstances.

1919
First acquisitions: nine works by outcast Pre-Raphaelite, Simeon Solomon.

1920
Acquisition of four works by David Bomberg, including *Ghetto Theatre*.

1925–26
Opens in Great Russell Street, WC1, with first collection display and catalogue.

1928
Bomberg lectures on 'Palestine Through the Eyes of an Artist'.

1931

Empire State Building in New York is completed.

1932

Oswald Mosley founds the British Union of Fascists. At its peak it has 36,000 members.

1933

Hitler comes to power. *c.* 565,000 Jews in Germany.

1933–39

70,000 Jewish refugees come to Britain.

1935

Anti-Semitic Nuremberg Laws restrict Jews in their everyday lives.

1936

Battle of Cable Street: Jews in the East End fight Mosley's Blackshirts.

1937

Spanish Civil War.

1938

Austrian Anschluss: *c.*120,000 Jews leave Austria.

1939

Germany and USSR invade Poland. Outbreak of Second World War.

130,000 Jews in Germany.

1940

Fall of France.

Churchill succeeds Chamberlain as Prime Minister. Battle of Britain

1940–41

'Collar the Lot!' Internment of refugees in Britain.

1941

German army invades USSR.

1941–45

The Holocaust.

1943

Warsaw Ghetto Uprising

1944

D-Day Landings in Normandy.

1945

Labour wins the Genreal Election by a landslide.

The end of the Second World War in Europe and in the Pacific.

1933

Beginning of exodus of Jewish refugee artists from Germany and later from Nazi-occupied Europe, including Jankel Adler, Martin Bloch, Ludwig and Else Meidner, Lucien Freud and Frank Auerbach.

1935

First entirely abstract exhibition in Britain.

1937

Entartete Kunst (Degenerate Art) exhibition in Germany.

Picasso's *Guernica*.

1938

Exhibition of Twentieth-Century German Art, New Burlington Galleries.

1940–41

Refugee artists interned, including Martin Bloch, Ludwig Meidner and Kurt Schwitters.

1944

Lucien Freud's first one-man show at Alex Reid and Lefevre Gallery, London.

1945–53

Bomberg teaches at the Borough Polytechnic. Pupils include Auerbach and Kossoff.

1930–2

Ben Uri Jewish Art & Literary Society moves to Jews Temporary Shelter, 63 Mansell Street, E1.

1932

Gift of pictures by Ben Uri to new Tel Aviv Museum in Palestine.

1933

Becomes Ben Uri Jewish Art Gallery. Sends representative to Boycott Conference in Paris. Sholem Asch and Cecil Roth lecture.

1933–36

Moves to Jewish Communal Centre, Woburn House, Upper Woburn Place, WC1.

1934

Opening exhibition features Marc Chagall, Amadeo Modigliani, Moïse Kisling, Chaïm Soutine, Jules Pascin, Camille and Lucien Pissarro. Vilna Troupe hosted.

1935

Alfred Döblin lecture: 'The Tragedy of the German Jews and its Consequences'. First annual open exhibition. Israel Zangwill Exhibition: George Bernard Shaw and H. G. Wells invited.

1936

Moves to Anglo-Palestinian Club, 43-44 Great Windmill Street, W1. Exhibits Martin Bloch work before any other UK Museum

1937

16 artists now in the Collection included in Nazi *Degenerate Art* exhibition. Jankel Adler *Still-Life* acquired and Reuben Ruvin exhibited before any UK museum.

1938

'Artists' revolt' led by David Bomberg: 'The Jewish artists are starving'.

1939

Closure at the Anglo-Palestinian Club. Collection in store.

1943–60

Moves to 14 Portman Street, W1. Opening exhibition highlights Max Liebermann, Camille Pissarro and Josef Israels.

1945

Leicester Gallery donates Gertler's *Merry-Go-Round.*

1946

Winston Churchill's 'Iron Curtain' speech in Fulton, Missouri.

1947

Indian Independence and Partition.

1948

Establishment of the State of Israel

HMS Windrush brings 493 Caribbean people to Britain.

1951

Festival of Britain

1953

Coronation of Queen Elizabeth II

1957

Harold MacMillan: 'Most of our people have never had it so good.'

1960

Harold MacMillan's 'Winds of Change' speech acknowledges independence in Africa.

1961

Eichmann Trial in Jerusalem. Berlin Wall built.

Percentage of British population born abroad passes 5% for the first time.

1948

David Sylvester writes of "the School of London".

1949

Francis Bacon's first one-man show at the Hanover Gallery.

1950

Lucian Freud's first one-man show at the Hanover Gallery

1951

Festival of Britain

1951–60

John Berger, art critic, *New Statesman*.

1952–68

Bryan Robertson, Director of the Whitechapel Gallery.

1953

Graham Sutherland, one-man show at Tate Gallery.

1953–56

The Beaux Arts Quartet and Kitchen Sink Realism.

1954

Francis Bacon at the Venice Biennale, catalogue introduction by David Sylvester.

1956

Modern Art in the USA at the Tate Gallery introduces Abstract Expressionism to Britain.

Frank Auerbach's first one-man show (Beaux Arts Gallery)

Richard Hamilton, *Just What Is It That Makes Today's Homes So Different, So Appealing?* The first famous work of Pop Art in Britain.

1957

Leon Kossoff's first one-man show at Beaux Arts Gallery.

1958

R. B. Kitaj arrives in Britain.

Lawrence Alloway coins the term 'Pop Art'.

1959

The New American Painting at Tate Gallery.

1961

First Rothko exhibition in Britain at the Whitechapel Art Gallery.

1946

Donation of a Soutine by Mrs Robert Solomon and Epstein bronzes by Moshe Oved.

1948

Josef Herman works exhibited before any other UK museum. Recital by renowned émigré violinist Norbert Branin of the Amadeus Quartet.

1948–55

More than a dozen exhibitions with an Israeli theme following Israel's independence.

1949

Ludwig and Else Meidner's retrospective at Ben Uri; his only exhibition in exile.

1950–76

Barry Fealdman, Secretary of the Ben Uri

1951

Festival of Britain Anglo-Jewish Exhibition, 1851–1951, Art Section at Ben Uri.

1953

Coronation Exhibition of Paintings and Sculpture.

1956

Ben Uri's 40th Anniversary Exhibition and *Tercentenary Exhibition of Contemporary Anglo-Jewish Artists*. Leon Kossoff works exhibited before any other UK Museum.

1959

Jacob Epstein Bronzes and *Recent Drawings* by 'outsider' artist, Scottie Wilson.

1960

Moves to Endsleigh Street, WC1.

1961–64

Moves to Berners Street, London W1.

1964

Civil Rights Act in USA.

1965

Race Relations Act makes some discrimination unlawful.

1967

Israel: Six-Day War.

1968

Asian immigrants start to arrive from Kenya.

Enoch Powell makes his controversial 'Rivers of Blood' speech on immigration. The Race Relations Act is passed.

1972

27,000 Asians come to Britain after being expelled from Uganda under Idi Amin.

1973

Israel: Yom Kippur War.

1976

New Race Relations Act. Commission for Racial Equality established.

1978

Winter of Discontent, UK.

1979

Margaret Thatcher elected, beginning almost twenty years of Conservative rule.

1982

Unemployment passes 3,000,000 for the first time since 1930s.

1989

Fatwā calling for Salman Rushdie's assassination issued by Ayatollah Khomeini.

Fall of the Berlin Wall symbolises end of Communism in Central & Eastern Europe.

1990

Nelson Mandela released from prison. German reunification.

1991

Fall of Soviet Communism.

1992

Six minority ethnic MPs elected. First Asian judge appointed

1993

Schindler's List released and opening of Holocaust Museum in Washington D.C.

1962

Andy Warhol's first New York solo pop art exhibition.

1967

David Hockney, *A Bigger Splash*.

1969

Kenneth Clark presents *Civilisation* on BBC2.

1972

John Berger presents *Ways of Seeing* on BBC2.

1975-6 Freud's portraits of his friend Frank Auerbach.

1977

Pompidou Centre opens in Paris

1981

A New Spirit of Painting, The Royal Academy includes Auerbach, Freud and Bacon.

1982–84

Zeitgeist exhibition includes Georg Baselitz, Julian Schabel and Howard Hodgkin, Berlin and MOMA, New York.

1983

British Jewish Artists 1900-1945–The Migrant Generation, Jewish Museum, New York.

1985

Saatchi Galley opens in St. John's Wood, London.

1988

Freeze exhibition organised by Damien Hirst.

1990–91

Chagall to Kitaj: Jewish Experience in 20th Century Art , Barbican Art Gallery.

1991

Damien Hirst's shark in formaldehyde

1992

Saatchi Gallery stages the Young British Artists exhibition, featuring Damien Hirst's "shark"

1993

Lucian Freud awarded OM.

Tate Gallery, St Ives opens.

White Cube gallery opens. Tracey Emin's first solo show at White Cube.

1962

Douglas Fairbanks Jr presents a prize at *Housewives Art Exhibition* .

1964–96

Moves to 21 Dean Street, Soho, W1. Lawrence Olivier sends congratulations.

1966

Ben Uri 50th Anniversary *Special Exhibition*.

1967

Sells Modigliani.

1968

Ben Uri orchestra performs with Yehudi and Hephzibah Menuhin.

1976

'Vicky' caricature exhibition, visited by Michael Foot.

1980

Epstein Centenary exhibition.

1983

Roman Vishniac exhibition.

1984

Ben Uri sells Gertler's *Merry-Go-Round* to the Tate.

1987

First *Catalogue of Permanent Collection* published by Lund Humphries.

1990

Ben Uri Highlights Key Works and Figures 1915-1990 75th Anniversary exhibition.

1992

Jewish Artists at the Slade: Exhibition of Works from the Ben Uri Collection.

Rachel Whiteread's installation *House* in East London.

1994

End of *apartheid* in South Africa .Nelson Mandela elected first black President.

Genocide in Rwanda.

1997

Tony Blair elected Prime Minister in Labour landslide victory. Ends 20 years of Conservative hegemony.

2000

Holocaust exhibition opens at the Imperial War Museum

2001

Twin Towers in Manhattan attacked by Al-Qaeda terrorists.

2004

Eight East European countries join the European Union.

2008

Global financial crisis.

1995–96

Brilliant! Group exhibition including Chapman Brothers, Tracey Emin and Damien Hirst.

1996

Leon Kossoff retrospective at Tate Gallery

Term YBAs (Young British Artists) coined.

1997

Charles Saatchi's *Sensation* at the Royal Academy: Hirst's shark, Emin's tent, Quinn's blood head exhibited.

1999

Tracey Emin, *My Bed*.

2000

Tate Modern opens.

Chapman Brothers, *Hell*.

Rachel Whiteread, *Holocaust Monument*, Judenplatz, Vienna.

2002

Freud: full retrospective at Tate Britain to mark his 80th birthday.

2008

Lucian Freud solo show at MOMA, New York.

1994

Second edition of *Catalogue of Permanent Collection* published by Lund Humphries.

1995

80th Anniversary of Ben Uri.

1997–99

Moves to 126 Albert Street, NW1.

2000

Moves to The Manor House, 80 East End Road, Finchley, N3, shared with other liberal Jewish organisations. David Glasser appointed Chairman. Moves from Finchley to reinforce new policy without religious alignment and positioning in the centre of UK mainstream museum sector. Ambitious programme of exhibitions, acquisitions, education, outreach and wellbeing – a platform for a future central London building.

2001

The Ben Uri Story exhibition at Phillips Auctioneers, Bond Street, W1 and publication of '*The Ben Uri Story from Art Society to Museum*'.

2002

Ben Uri acquires Gertler's *Rabbi and Rabbitzin*. Moves to 108a Boundary Road, NW8.

2004

Ben Uri acquires Emmanuel Levy's *Crucifixion*.

2005

Fundraising Reception at 10 Downing Street.

2006

Awarded the opportunity to curate and tour worldwide exhibition *Auktion 392: Reclaiming the Galerie Stern, Dusseldorf*, highlighting Nazi Looted Art and restitution.

2007

Jewish Artists in Britain. Exhibition celebrating the 350th Anniversary of the Return under Cromwell, The Arts Depot, London N2. Receives Sandford Award in recognition of its contribution to heritage education and learning within the historic environment.

2008

Launches its pilot 'Wellbeing' project at Hammerson House Residential Home, London N2.

2009

Barack Obama becomes first black American President.

2009

Frank Auerbach, *The London Building Sites, 1952–1962*, Courtauld Gallery.

2009–10

Forced Journeys: Artists in Exile in Britain, c.1933-45 marks the 70th anniversary of internment, touring to Sayle Gallery, Isle of Man, and Williamson Gallery, Birkenhead. Acquires Frank Auerbach, *Mornington Crescent, Summer Morning II* and Marc Chagall, *Apocalypse en Lilas, Capriccio* (1945).

2010

Cross Purposes: Shock and Contemplation in Images of the Crucifixion curated by Nathanial Hepburn creates media controversy. Acquires George Grosz *Interrogation.*

2011

Census shows that the percentage of UK population born abroad is 13.4%.

2011

Lucian Freud dies

2011

Acquires *Portrait of John Rodker* by David Bomberg and *Portrait of Sonia* by Isaac Rosenberg. *Selected Masterworks from our Israeli Modern and Contemporary Collection* at Bonhams, London W1. School Learning Programmes shared with London Grid for Learning, automatically accessible to over 2,500 schools across London.

2011–12

Josef Herman Warsaw Brussels, Glasgow, London 1938-44 touring to Royal West of England Academy, Bristol.

2012

David Hockney awarded OM.
Hockney: *A Bigger Picture* at the Royal Academy

2012

Acquires Chaim Soutine's *La Soubrette, Waiting Maid* (*c.*1933). Hosts 'a conversation with American artist, Judy Chicago,' at the Whitechapel Gallery. Second Sandford Award. Expands its Learning programmes with the National Education Network; now accessible to 16,000 schools nationwide.

2013

Features in international media after the discovery of Cornelius Gurlitt's hoard of Nazi looted artworks. Underbidder to Zaha Hadid for the 35,000 sq. ft. Design Museum on the South Bank.

2014

ISIS in Syria and Iraq. Conflict in Ukraine.

2014

Ben Uri awarded HLF grant towards its centenary exhibition.

2015

Conservatives win the election with an outright majority

2015

Frank Auerbach retrospective at Tate Britain.

2015

May: Loses out to a commercial theatre and retail project to occupy 60,000 sq. ft. at Tower Bridge.

July-December: *Out Of Chaos Ben Uri: 100 Years in London* at the Inigo Rooms, Somerset House East Wing, King's College London, Strand, London WC2R 2LS. Presented in association with the Cultural Institute at King's College London.

Selected Exhibition History

1925

Official opening of the Ben-Uri Gallery and Club, 68 Great Russell Street, WC1

1927

Exhibition arranged by Mrs. L. Pilichowski, 7 Hill Road, NW8

1931

Exhibition of Paintings in Oil and Water Colours by Nathan Spiegel, Mansell Street, E1

1934

Opening of the Ben Uri Jewish Art Gallery and an Exhibition of Works by Jewish Artists, Woburn House, WC1

1935

Exhibition of Water Colours, Drawings and Sketches of Old Synagogues in Poland and Eastern Europe, XIV-XVIIIth Centuries, by George Lukomski

Annual Exhibition of Works by Jewish Artists

1936

Israel Zangwill Memorial Exhibition

1944

Opening Exhibition, Portman Street, W1

Exhibition of Paintings and Drawings by Mark Gertler (1892–1939)

Memorial Exhibition of Original Lithographs and Etchings by Herman Struck

1945

Exhibition of Paintings by A.A. Wolmark (Konstam Collection) Dobrinsky – Paris and Selected Works from the Ben Uri Art Collection

1946 Recent Additions to the Permanent Collection and Works by Pissarro, Liebermann, Epstein, Modigliani, Chagall

1946

Solomon J Solomon and Lily Delissa Joseph

1947

Exhibition of Paintings by Walter Trier and Sculpture by Else Fraenkel and Erna Nonnenmacher

1948

Exhibition of Children's Art

Ink and Wash Drawings Done in Terezin Concentration Camp by Bedřich Fritta (1907–1944)

1949

Famous Jewish Artists of the Past: Israels, Liebermann, Modigliani, The Pissarros, Soutine

Martin Bloch, Josef Herman: Paintings and Drawings

Drawings of Ludwig Meidner (1920–1922 and 1935–1949), Paintings and Drawings of Else Meidner (1935–1949)

1950

Exhibition of Recent Acquisitions, Friends of Tel Aviv Museum of Israel

Cartoons and Caricatures

1951

Festival of Britain: Anglo-Jewish Exhibition, 1851–1951, Art Section

Michael Kikoine (Paintings and Water Colours), Zechariahu Erlichman (Water Colours), Bruno Simon (Sculpture)

1952

80 Posters and Other Work by A. Games,

Memorial Exhibition of Works by Amy J. Drucker (1873-1951)

1953

Paintings by Emmanuel Levy

Coronation Exhibition of Paintings and Sculpture (from the private collections of Friends of the Ben Uri Art Society)

1955

Type Design, Lettering and Bookwork by Elizabeth Friedlander

Sculpture by Freida Brilliant, Georg Ehrlich, Jacob Epstein, Lippy Lipshitz, Abraham Lozoff, Karel Vogel, Ben Uri Art Gallery

1956

Fortieth Anniversary Exhibition Paintings Drawings Sculpture

The Tercentenary Exhibition of Contemporary Jewish Artists

1957

Drawings, Lithographs and Etchings by the Israeli Artist Yehuda Bacon

Jankel Adler (1895–1949), Mark Gertler (1891—1939), Bernard Meninsky (1891–1950)

Contemporary Jewish Artists of France

1958

First London Exhibition of Painting, Drawings and Lithographs by Alfred Cohen (USA)

Twelve Contemporary Artists: Archibald Ziegler,

Alfred Harris, Claude Rogers, Jacob Bornfriend, Morris Kestelman, Frank Auerbach, John Coplans, Kalman Kemeny, Josef Herman, Alfred Daniels, Henry Inlander, Fred Feigl

1959

Sir Jacob Epstein Exhibition of Bronzes

'Scottie' Wilson: Recent Drawings

1962

Ruth Abrahams and Ernest Eisenmayer

Housewives' Art – 6th National Exhibition presented by the people

1963

Eva Frankfurther Retrospective Exhibition

Abstract Art

Mane-Katz

Martin Bloch - Memorial Exhibition of Paintings and Drawings

1964

Paintings from Terezin: Bedrich Fritta, Karel Fleischmann, Otto Ungar, Peter Kein

1965 Josef Herman

1965

Horace Brodzky: Retrospective Exhibition

1966

Ben Uri 50th Anniversary Exhibition accompanied by *1915–1965 fifty years achievements in the arts,* edited by Jacob Sonntag

1968

Max Liebermann (1847–1935), Isidor Kaufmann (1853–1921), Lesser Ury (1862–1931), E.M. Lilien (1874–1925), Hermann Struck (1876–1944), Jacob Steinhardt (1889–1968)

Sandra Blow, Henry Inlander, Leon Kossoff, Helena Markson, Archibald Zielger

1970

Hans Feibusch Paintings, gouaches, drawings

Paintings from the Ben Uri Art Gallery, Russell-Coates Art Gallery & Museum, Bournemouth

1971

Some of my Best Jokes are Jewish - a new collection of cartoons by Nero

1973

Exhibition of Woodcuts by Arthur Segal

1975

Shmuel Dresner Paintings

1976

Original 'Vicky' Cartoons and Drawings together with items from the permanent collection

Roman Halter

1977

Hans Feibusch: Sculptures and Gouaches

1978

Graphic Work by George Him

New Works by Emmanuel Levy

1980

Selected Works from the Permanent Collection

David Bomberg and Family: David Bomberg, Lilian Holt, Leslie Marr, Dinora Mendelson: An Exhibition of Paintings and Drawings

1982

Mark Gertler – the early and the late years

Jerusalem – Then and Now: Lithographs by David Roberts, Paintings by David Thomas

1983

Roman Vishniac's 'A Vanished World'

David Bomberg in The Holy Land 1923–1927

Jacob Kramer reassessed

1985

Four Naïve Painters at the Ben Uri: Perle Hessing; Moshe Maurer; Dora Holzhandler; Scottie Wilson

1986

Marcel Ronay - Drawings and Watercolours: Vienna 1929–36

1987

Jewish Artists: The Ben Uri Collection, held to celebrate the publishing of the Collection catalogue

1988

Manchester Jewish Artists

1989

Emmanuel Levy: A Memorial Exhibition

1990

Solomon J Solomon RA

'Innocence and Persecution': The Art of Jewish Children, Germany 1936-1941

1991

Abram Games: Designs for Jewry

1992

Jewish Artists at the Slade: Exhibition of Works from the Ben Uri Collection to be shown with recent acquisitions

Drawings by Arnold Daghani

1993

Paintings, Drawings and Prints by the Negev Group of Artists: Anna Andersch Marcus, Rina Sthelman, Joseph Rac, Sally Levin Bar, Moty Assiag, Sadeh, Dorti Dinur, Rachel Kroupp

1994

Bernard Cohen

Visages du Ghetto: Paintings, Drawings and Etchings of Pre-War Jewish Europe by Paul Jeffoy (1898–1957)

Jewish Artists: The Ben Uri Collection (2nd Edition)

1995

Hans Feibusch: The Heart of Vision

1996

Paintings Drawings and Sculpture by Austrian Artists Whose Lives Were Disrupted by the Holocaust (Hans Schwarz), loan exhibition from private collections and the Ben Uri Art Society

1996-7

Jewish Artists: The Ben Uri Collection, touring to: University of Leeds, Grundy Art Gallery, Blackpool; University of Essex

1999

Jewish Stage and Costume Designers

2001

A Singular Vision: Drawings and Paintings of Bernard Meninsky

The Ben Uri Story from Art Society to Museum, held at Philips, London W1

2002

Mark Gertler: A New Perspective

Ludwig and Else Meidner

2003

William Roberts & Jacob Kramer: The Tortoise and the Hare, touring to Leeds University

A Storm in Europe: Béla Kádár, Hugó Scheiber and Der Sturm Gallery in Berlin

2004

Jenny Stolzenberg: Forgive and Do Not Forget

International Jewish Artists of the Year Awards

Rediscovering Wolmark: a pioneer of British modernism

2005

Maximum Meaning, Minimum Means: Abram Games

Children of Jerusalem: Painting Pain, Dreaming Peace

Joash Woodrow Retrospective

Chagall and his Circle

2006

Love Revealed: Simeon Solomon and the Pre-Raphaelites, touring from Birmingham Museum and Art Gallery and Museum Villa Stuck, Munich

Embracing the Exotic: Jacob Epstein and Dora Gordine

Auktion 392: Reclaiming the Gallerie Stern, Dusseldorf

2007

Bomberg's Relevance: David Bomberg, Responses by Michael Ajerman, Simon Keenleyside, Sarah Lightman, Jane Millican, Gideon Rubin, Joe Schneider, Adriana Swierszczeck, Polly Townsend

David Breuer Weil: Project 3

Regard & Ritual: Julie Held and Shanti Panchal

International Jewish Artists of the Year Awards

2008

Ambiguous Realities: Colour Photographs by Dorothy Bohm

Schmatte Couture, held at Rivington Gallery, London EC2

Homeless and Hidden: Highlights of the Ben Uri Collection 1938–1988

Robert Lenkiewicz: Self Portraits

Israel & Art: 60 Years Through the Eyes of Teddy Kollek

Whitechapel at War: Isaac Rosenberg and his circle, touring to Stanley and Audrey Burton Gallery, University of Leeds

2009

Jacques Lipchitz: Master Drawings, Anatomy of a Sculptor

2009–10

Forced Journeys: Artists in Exile in Britain c.1933-45, touring to Sayle Gallery, Douglas, Isle of Man and Williamson Art Gallery, Birkenhead

2010

Cross Purposes: Shock and Contemplation in Images of the Crucifixion

Apocalypse: Unveiling a Lost Masterpiece by Marc Chagall, held at Osborne Samuel, London W1

The Land of Light and Promise: 50 Years Painting Jerusalem and Beyond Ludwig Blum 1891–1974, touring to MOBIA, New York

Josef Herman – Warsaw Brussels, Glasgow, London 1938–44, touring to the Royal West of England Academy, Bristol

2012

The Inspiration of Decadence: Dodo rediscovered, Berlin 1920–30s, touring from the Sammlung Modebild, Lipperheidesche Kostümbibliothek, Staatliche Museen zu Berlin

From Russia to Paris: Chaim Soutine and his contemporaries

Judy Chicago and Louise Bourgeois, Helen Chadwick, Tracey Emin: A Transatlantic Dialogue

2013

Looking In: Photographic Portraits by Maud Sulter and Chan-Hyo Bae

Boris Aronson and Avant-garde Yiddish Theatre in conjunction with La Galerie Minotaure, Paris and Tel Aviv

Uproar: The first 50 years of The London Group 1913–1963

2014

Max Weber: An American Cubist in Paris and London 1905–1915 in conjunction with the University of Reading

Roman Halter: Life and Art through Stained Glass

Suzanne Perlman: Painting London

Still Fighting Ignorance & Intellectual Perfidy: Video Art from Africa

Refiguring the 50s: Joan Eardley, Sheila Fell, Eva Frankfurther, Josef Herman, L S Lowry

2015

Notting Hill Carnival: The A-Z of Elimu Carnival Band, 1980–2014

Out of Chaos: Ben Uri – 100 Years in London, Inigo Rooms, Somerset House, in association with the Cultural Institute at King's College London

Endnotes

1   The Whitechapel Boys

1   Joseph Leftwich, interview with Richard Cork, 15 September 1980. Quoted in Richard Cork, *David Bomberg* (New Haven and London: Yale, 1987), p.20.

2   Ibid., p.19.

3   A.B. Levy, *East End Story* (London: Constellation Books, n.d.; *c.*1951), p.26.

4   Leftwich, quoted in Cork, *David Bomberg*, p.22.

5   Desmond MacCarthy (with notes from Roger Fry), introduction to the catalogue of *Manet and the Post-Impressionists* exhibition, Grafton Galleries, London, November 1910–January 1911.

6   'Jewish art at Whitechapel', *Jewish Chronicle* (15 May 1914), p.10.

7   David Bomberg, interview with *Jewish Chronicle* (8 May 1914), p.13.

8   Ibid., p.13.

9   Mark Gertler to Dora Carrington, quoted in John Woodeson, *Mark Gertler: Biography of a Painter 1891–1939* (London: Sidgwick & Jackson, 1972), pp.225-6.

10   Mark Gertler to William Rothenstein, 4 April 1916, quoted in Noel Carrington ed., *Mark Gertler Selected Letters*, (London: Rupert Hart-Davis, 1965), p.110.

11   D.H. Lawrence to Mark Gertler, 9 October 1916, quoted in Woodeson, *Mark Gertler*, p.226.

12   Alice Mayes, *The Young Bomberg 1914–1925*, memoir dated 1972, p.22. Collection of the Tate Archives, TGA 7312.

13   Isaac Rosenberg to Edward Marsh, 26 January 1918, quoted in Joseph Cohen, *Journey to the Trenches: The Life of Isaac Rosenberg 1890–1918* (London: Robson Books Ltd, 1975), p.3.

2   Soutine, Chagall and The School of Paris

1   For a fuller account of their origins see Richard Cork in this volume; Rachel Dickson and Sarah MacDougall in Whitechapel at War; and Sarah MacDougall '"Something is Happening There": early British modernism, the Great War and the Whitechapel Boys' in ed., Michael Walsh, *London, Modernism, and 1914* (Cambridge UK: Cambridge University Press, 2010), pp.122-147. There was clearly a crossover between the two groups with David Bomberg and Jacob Epstein visiting Paris to select works for the 'Jewish Section' at the exhibition, *Twentieth-Century Art: A Review of Modern Movements* at the Whitechapel Art Gallery in 1914.

2   No longer represented in the Ben Uri Collection. His work was published in *Renesans*.

3   This group also included Tsugouharu Foujita (1886–1968), who is beyond the scope of this essay.

4   Sophie Krebs, 'L'École de Paris, une invention de la critique d'art des années vingt' (unpublished PhD Thesis, Institut d'Études Politiques, 2009), pp.31-32, translated by and cited in Andrew W Symons, 'A Phenomenological Approach to Chaïm Soutine's Portraits' (unpublished MA Dissertation, Courtauld Institute of Art, 2014), unpublished, p.15, n. 26.

5   Mark Gertler in Paris in 1920 was introduced to a group of artists, whom he described as 'mostly foreigners' and mainly Jewish. They included Ortiz de Zarate, a particular friend of Modigliani's, with whom he conversed in Yiddish.

6   A. Kampf *From Chagall to Kitaj: Jewish Experience in Twentieth-Century Art* (London: Lund Humphries/Barbican, 1990).

7   During the First World War Soutine enlisted in the work brigades but was soon dismissed with health problems, having developed the stomach problems which later killed him.

8   Among those who left was Elie (Eliasz) Nadelman (1882–1946), who departed at the onset of war for New York. His first solo show

at Stieglitz's gallery was a tremendous success and he became a naturalised citizen in 1927. Ruined by the 1929 stock market crash, much of his work was accidentally destroyed in 1935. He became a virtual recluse, developing a heart condition in 1945 and committing suicide in 1946.

9   Ulrich Krempel and Karin Thomas, *Jankel Adler 1895–1949* (Köln: DuMont Verlag, 1985), pp. 24–5.

10   He also painted landscapes and flower studies in an expressionist and baroque manner. After the fall of France in 1940, he fled to New York, later returning yet again to Paris. He visited Israel annually from 1948 and died in Tel Aviv before being buried in Haifa where he had bequeathed his collection and today a museum stands in his name.

11   A. Kampf, op. cit., pp. 75–81.

12   Maurice Tuchman, *The Impact of Chaïm Soutine (1893–1943): De Kooning, Pollock, Dubuffet, Bacon* (Ostfildern: Hatje Cantz 2001).

13   These include *Dobrinsky, Paris and Selected Works from the Ben Uri Art Collection* at Portman Street in 1945; *Shtetl Scenes: A Selection from the Society's Permanent Collection together with new Acquisitions* at Dean Street in 1990; *From Russia to Paris: Chaïm Soutine and his Contemporaries* at Boundary Road in 2012; and *Chagall, Soutine and the School of Paris* at Manchester Jewish Museum in 2013.

3   Forced Journeys

1   Eckmann, Sabine 'Considering (and Reconsidering) Art and Exile' in ed., Barron, S *Exiles and Emigrés: the Flight of European Artists from Hitler* (California: Los Angeles County Museum of Art, 1997), pp. 30–42.

2   Powell, Jennifer and Vinzent, Jutta *Art and Migration Art Works by Refugee Artists from Nazi Germany in Britain*, (Birmingham: George Bell Institute, 2005), p.7.

3   In 1937 the Nazis held an exhibition of modern art in Munich entitled *Entartete Kunst*, or 'Degenerate Art'. Its purpose was to signal

to the German people that certain modern artists and artworks were not acceptable under various criteria, including being un-German, Jewish or 'Bolshevik'. During the *Entartete Kunst* campaign over 20,000 works by more than 200 artists were confiscated. The exhibition traveled within Germany and to Austria.

4   See Powell and Vinzent, op. cit., p.65; although in 'Jussuf Abbo' in eds., Krug, H and Nungesser, M *Kunst im Exil in Großbritannien 1933–45* (Berlin: Orangerie, Charlottenburg Castle, 1986), p.133, his reason is given as escaping Jewish persecution. (We are grateful to Ulrike Smalley for translation of this piece.)

5   Jack Bilbo was in Kemptor Park, then Warth Mill (near Bury, Manchester) together with Hermann Fechenbach and Hellmuth Weissenborn. Fred Uhlman was in a transit camp at Ascot; Dachinger and Nessler at Huyton Camp, Liverpool. Ernst Eisenmayer was in transit at Prees Heath in Shropshire; Erich Wolfsfeld on the Isle of Wight. See Powell and Vinzent, op. cit., pp. 34–40.

6   Feather, Jessica *Art Behind Barbed Wire* (Liverpool: Walker Art Gallery, 2004), p.11.

7   Cited Powell and Vinzent, op. cit., p.35.

8   Among the victims were Bilbo's disabled mother; the mother of Austrian-born Eisenmayer and Marie-Louise von Motesiczky's brother, Karl, who were both deported to Auschwitz; graphic artist Hans Schleger's mother, Bianca, who died in the Minsk ghetto and Georg Mayer-Marton's parents, who were deported from the Gyor ghetto. His mother was killed immediately, and his father transported with 5,000 others before being killed.

9   Weissenborn, Hellmuth in *Hellmuth Weissenborn, engraver: with an autobiographical introduction by the artist* (Andoversford: Whittington Press, 1983), p.13.

10   Powell and Vinzent, op. cit., p.66.

11   Behr, Shulamith 'Klaus E. Hinrichsen: The Art Historian behind 'Visual Art behind the Wire', in Behr and Malet, *Arts in Exile in Britain 1933-45 Politics and Cultural Identity*, The Yearbook of the Research Centre for

German and Austrian Exile Studies, Volume 6 (Amsterdam and New York: Rodopi, 2004), p.18.

12   See Smalley, Ulrike 'Lecture on the Lawn', in *Forced Journeys, Artists in Exile in Britain c. 1933-45*, eds Dickson, Rachel and MacDougall, Sarah, (London: Ben Uri, 2008), pp. 50-63.

13   Weissenborn, Hellmuth *Hellmuth Weissenborn, engraver,* op. cit., pp. xiii-xiv.

14   Including Ernst Levy, Arno Kahn, Erwin Weinberg, Ernst Meyer and a former pupil named Bier, whose first name has not been traced. See Powell and Vinzent, op. cit., p.37.

15   Weissenborn, Helmuth, op. cit., p.xiv.

16   Powell and Vinzent, op. cit., p.82.

17   Vinzent, Jutta DNB: 'Despite the paucity of artistic acceptance he produced numerous works, including charcoal, chalk, and watercolour series, ranging from political themes, such as *Massacres in Poland* (1942–5, Stadtarchiv Darmstadt, Germany), to burlesque prints, for example, *Cafés, Theater, Variété (und Comics)* (1951; priv. coll.). These series reflect the influence of William Blake, who, as Meidner felt, was a kindred spirit in visionary painting and writing.' See also Powell and Vinzent, op. cit., pp. 82–3.

18   Else Meidner was supported by the Czech émigré art historian and writer, J. P. Hodin, following Ludwig's departure. He became the recipient of hundreds of handwritten notes, letters and poems, blurring the boundary between professional art critical interest and personal and emotional prop. At the end of Else's life, Hodin became official guardian of her works, organising their bequest to the city of Darmstadt. He facilitated two exhibitions at Ben Uri for Else: *A Retrospective* (22 October -13 November, 1964) which he opened, and her 70th birthday exhibition, delayed, which ran from 19 June to 14 July, 1972.

19   Bateson, Matthew 'Erich Kahn: The Forgotten Expressionist', unpublished typescript, dated 04/08/03.

20   Buckman, David 'Walter Nessler, Obituary', the *Independent*, 12 January 2002.

21   Podro, Michael, Rossiter, Peter and Johnson, Nichola *Martin Bloch: A Painter's Painter'* (Norwich: Sainsbury Centre for Visual Arts, University of East Anglia, 2007), p.55.

22   Cited Feather op. cit., p.11.

23   Weissenborn, Hellmuth, op. cit., p.xiv.

24   Behr, Shulamith, 'Klaus E Hinrichsen: The Art Historian behind "Visual Art Behind the Wire"', in Behr and Malet, op. cit., p 35, n. 10. It is tempting to see a retrospective reference to this exile in his 1946 relief, *C64 Ship in the Sea* (fig. 33). However. Dr, Karin Orchard comments that 'Schwitters used these "C" numbers in 1946/67 for a series of works, probably preparing them for an exhibition. Throughout his life he always had some kind of personal numbering systems. The title 'Ship on the sea' might refer to the dark/yellow form in the right upper corner over the blue part which reminds one of the shape of a boat turned upside down. But it would be very unusual if the title refers to an event long ago in Norway or even the Isle of Man. If Schwitters refers to an actual event or scene it's more likely something around the actual production time of the work, for example, […] [in] Lake Windermere. (Dr. Karin Orchard, Kurt Schwitters Archiv, Sprengel Museum, Hannover), November 2008.

25   Copeland Buenger, Barbara in ed., Barron, S *Exiles and* Emigrés, op. cit., p.81.

26   Weissenborn, Hellmuth, op. cit., p.xiv.

27   Hallgarten, Fritz cited *Living With the Wire*, op. cit., p.53.

28   Copeland Buenger, Barbara op. cit., p.81.

29   b. 1902, Konisgberg, East Prussia. After release he worked initially as a portrait photographer then later as a photographer of objects and landscape.

30   Katz, Agi 'Two Berliners: Margaret Marks and Pamina Liebert-Mahrenholz', private view card, (London: Boundary Gallery, September 2008).

31   Liebert-Mahrenholz, Pamina 'A brief autobiographical profile of Pamina Liebert-Mahrenholz: sculpture, painting and drawing', July 1994, courtesy of Agi Katz.

32   Ibid.

33   Helmuth Weissenborn taught at the Leipzig Academy.

34   *Jewish Chronicle*, 19 November 1976, p.24.

35   Uhlman and Hamman were already friends pre-internment and were both former Chairmen of the FGLC (artists' section). Both were the main reps of this section from 1938 until they were interned in June 1940. Afterwards they continued to remain active members and both were present at a meeting in 1942. Müller-Härlin, Anna 'It all happened in this street, Downshire Hill', in Behr and Malet, op. cit., p.253.

36   'The South Bank Exhibition alone included around 100 murals executed by as many different artists.' See Pearson, Lynn *Roughcast Textures with cosmic overtones: a survey of British murals, 1945–80* (London: Decorative Arts Society Journal, Volume 31, 2007). Émigré sculptors included Siegfried Charoux, Peter Peri, Georg Ehrlich, Heinz Henghes.

37   *Jewish Chronicle*, 4 May 1951, p.13.

38   In the collection of the Imperial War Museum, London.

39   Mayer-Marton designed a poster for Max Rheinhardt's production of Georg Büchner's *Dantons Tod* in 1929.

40   In 1949, Weissenborn illustrated Richard Friedenthal's *Goethe Chronicle* with 15 wood engravings. He was to work as an illustrator for 30 London publishers, in addition to Acorn Press. One of his most ambitious undertakings was his joint translation (with Lesley) of Hans Jacob Christoffel von Grimmelshausen's *Simplicius Simplicissimus*, the first English version of the 1669 German baroque novel; it took seven years and Lesley became fluent in German (London: John Calder, 1964, illustrated with 45 wood engravings). In the early 1970s Acorn Press began an association with John Randle, then production manager at Heinemann Educational, who was keen to print using some of Weissenborn's original boxwood blocks through the independent Whittington Press. Afterwards, a string of books was published jointly under the Acorn and Whittington Press banner, including *Ruins* (1977), *Roads Rails Bridges* (1979) and *Proverbs* (1979).' By the time of Hellmuth's death, in 1982, his work was being shown fairly frequently again in Germany, with a large exhibition at Guteberg Museum, Mainz, in 1980. See 'Obituary of Lesley Weissenborn', the *Independent*, 14 June 2001.

41   British Library Archival Sound Recordings: Gillian Ayres, National Life Story Collection: Artists' Lives, shelf reference C466/91, 1999–2000.

42   *Hellmuth Weissenborn,* engraver, op. cit., p.XV.

43   In 1933 Segal fled Berlin where he had settled with his family and opened an art school, and moved to Palma de Mallorca, remaining until October 1936 and the outbreak of the Spanish Civil War. On moving to London Segal opened his painting school, which transferred to Oxford in 1939, to escape the Blitz. During 1940 Segal was interned on the Isle of Man. He returned to London with his family in 1943, reopening his art school at 1 Englands Lane, Hampstead, in north London. Arthur Segal's work is represented in the Ben Uri Collection.

44   Rosenbaum and Reifenberg's work is represented in the Ben Uri Collection.

45   Sewell, Brian 'A Debt to Pay, A Monument to Make', in ed., Rathbone, Gillian *The Ben Uri Story from Art Society to Museum* (London: Ben Uri Gallery / The London Jewish Museum of Art, 2001), p.21

46   'Bildung macht frei' – culture brings freedom – was the motto of Cotta, the 19th-century Jewish bookseller and publisher of German classics, a phrase which contrasts ironically with the chilling 'arbeit macht frei' above the gates of a number of the Nazi concentration camps. See Mucznik, Esther in Berardo, José Manuel et al *Forgotten Generation: Erich Kahn – Jewish Survivor, German Expressionist* (Sintra: Berado Collection, 2005), p.19.

4   Postwar

I am most grateful to Rachel Dickson, Claire Jackson, Sarah MacDougall and Harriet Powney for all their time and advice.

1   See Shulamith Behr's essay, "Exhibitions and Beyond: Ben Uri, Politics and Émigré Identities in the Critical Years, 1944–1949", *Ben Uri History* companion volume, 2015, for a more detailed discussion.

2   Auerbach and Kossoff first exhibited at the Ben Uri in the *Tercentenary Exhibition of Contemporary Anglo-Jewish Artists*, November 15th December 23rd 1956.

3   See James Hyman's essay in this volume for a more detailed account of the School of London.

4   'The modern period in British art may be said to date from the year 1910, when the first Post-Impressionist Exhibition was held in London.' Herbert Read, *Contemporary British Art* (London: Pelican Books, 1951), p.14.

5   D. H. Lawrence to Mark Gertler, 1916: see Richard Cork's essay in this volume.

6   Read, *Contemporary British Art*, p.20.

7   See Behr, "Exhibitions and Beyond: Ben Uri, Politics and Émigré Identities in the Critical Years, 1944–1949", *Ben Uri History* companion volume, 2015, for a more detailed discussion of the 1946–47 Ben Uri exhibition.

8   The phrase "Art of an Aftermath" is David Sylvester's. See *About Modern Art: Critical Essays, 1948–96* (London: Chatto & Windus, p.71–74. He uses it to describe the aftermath following the great period of High Modernism, but it could also apply to the traces of the Holocaust in postwar art.

9   Herbert Read, *The Philosophy of Modern Art* (London: Faber & Faber, 1952), p.194.

10   Kenneth Clark, *Another Part of the Wood: A Self-Portrait* (London: John Murray, 1974) and *The Other Half: A Self-Portrait* (London: John Murray, 1977).

11   For a more positive view of Clark's relationship with émigré artists, with evidence of his support for the sculptor, Georg Ehrlich, see Sarah MacDougall, "'Separate Spheres of Endeavour?' Experiencing the Émigré Network in Britain, *c.*1933-45" in Burcu Dogramaci und Karin Wimmer, eds, Netzwerke des Exils (Berlin: Mann Verlag, 2011).

12   Sylvester, *About Modern Art: Critical essays, 1948-96*, p.19.

13   Richard Cork, 'Bomberg, David Garshen (1890–1957)', rev. *Oxford Dictionary of National Biography*, Oxford University Press, 2004; online edn, Jan 2012

14   David Bomberg, *cit.* Rachel Dickson, "'Neither Gospel Nor Creed': The London Group 1928–49" in *Uproar! The First 50 Years of the London Group 1913–63*, ed. by Sarah MacDougall and Rachel Dickson, London: Ben Uri in association with Lund Humphries, 2014, p.46.

15   Josef Herman, *Related Twilights: Notes from an Artist's Diary* (London: Robson Books, 1975), p.70.

16   Herman, *Related Twilights: Notes from an Artist's Diary*, p.80.

17   It is often forgetten that though Churchill won the 1951 election, Labour received 13,948,385 votes.

18   W.H. Auden, *The Age of Anxiety: A Baroque Eclogue* (1947; first UK edition, 1948).

19   Frances Spalding, *British Art Since 1900* (London: Thames & Hudson, 1986), p.143.

20   Ibid., p.143.

21   See James E. B. Breslin's account of the new post-war art market in New York in *Mark Rothko: A Biography* (Chicago: University of Chicago Press, 1993, especially pp 251, 299, 340, 420-2, 607n42, 608 n44, 609n49.

22   Dominic Sandbrook, *Never Had it So Good: A History of Britain From Suez to the Beatles* (London: Little, Brown, 2005), pp.80, 102.

5   *Je suis juif*

1   James Hyman, *The Battle for Realism: Figurative Art in Britain during the Cold War (1945–60)* (London and New Haven: Yale University Press, 2001).

2   A School of London was first proposed by the great art critic and curator, David Sylvester, in a three-part series of essays on British Art that was one of his most substantial early pieces of writing, and was aimed at boosting the international standing of British art. See Hyman, *Battle for Realism*, introduction.

3   James Hyman, 'Fifty Years of Hurt', *Guardian* (22 September 2001).

4   Hyman, 'Fifty Years', ibid

5   Jeremy Paxman, *The English: A Portrait of a People* (London: Penguin, 1998).

6   On Kossoff's paintings of London, and their relationship to those of Bomberg and Auerbach, see James Hyman, 'Golden Builders and the Crowd: Leon Kossoff and London' (MA thesis, Courtauld Institute, London, 1990). I also explored these ideas in James Hyman, 'Kossoff's London', *Tate* magazine (Summer 1996). Writing of St Paul's I argued: 'For Kossoff hope lies in reconnecting with the past and identifying its legacy in the present. A lost innocence may be recaptured, a childhood memory recollected. Remnants of the past may survive, renewed. Paintings of London are an exhortation for a new world created not from promises of progress or modernity but through redemption and the renewal of a mythologised past. St Paul's Cathedral, for example, serves as a general emblem of faith (Kossoff himself is a Jew), represents the City and provides a signifier for the artist's own childhood. It suggests the possibility of redemption, a glimpse of an elusive spirit of place and a return to a lost innocence'.

7   On Kitaj's *The Wedding* see James Hyman, 'The Chimney that Chills', BBC World Service, 1992. This was part of a series of six broadcasts that I wrote and presented on Jewish artists. A version of this text was subsequently published by the Jewish cultural affairs journal, *Manna*, Winter, 1993.

8   R. B. Kitaj, *The First Diasporist Manifesto* (London: Thames & Hudson Ltd, 1989).

9   Ibid.

10   In the catalogue Kitaj championed a School of London but it was an exhibition characterised by its diversity and scope in which drawing was presented as central to all painters, whether figurative or abstract. Such promotion gave especial prominence to art school teaching and to the fundamental importance of life drawing. Frequently the suggestion of continuity, through the presentation of such 'traditions' as an essential characteristic of the best British art, was used as a riposte to the supposed decadence to be found elsewhere, particularly in America.

11   In *The Human Clay* Kitaj did include those artists now considered to constitute the core of the 'School of London' – namely Michael Andrews, Francis Bacon, Lucian Freud, Frank Auerbach and Leon Kossoff – but he also deliberately blurred distinctions between abstract and figurative artists and to this end selected over 40 other artists. Arts Council records show that the exhibition attracted over 10,000 visitors, but it appears to have had little immediate impact. Critical priorities were elsewhere and Kitaj's reference to a 'School of London' passed unnoticed. Indeed when in 1981 it was proposed once again, this time by the painter, teacher and art historian Lawrence Gowing, he had apparently forgotten Kitaj's earlier reference and claimed authorship of the idea.

12   In the years after Kitaj and Gowing's references to a 'School of London', their broad conception of a 'School' became honed down to an almost fixed core of six or seven painters. This 'School of London', including Andrews, Auerbach, Bacon, Freud and Kossoff as well as Kitaj, swiftly gained powerful promotion. The label 'School of London', despite the often-used prefix 'so-called', soon became the dominant framework for the presentation of post-war British figurative painting, despite the reservations of the artists themselves. Nonetheless the idea has been greeted with little enthusiasm either by the chief beneficiaries or by those to whom it might be extended.

The presentation of a small core of artists owes most to Michael Peppiatt, and much to the British Council exhibition which he curated *A School of London: Six Figurative Painters* (British Council, touring exhibition, 1987). Presenting Andrews, Auerbach, Bacon, Freud, Kitaj and Kossoff, this powerful exhibition provided a template for future presentations of a 'School of London' such as *From London: Bacon, Freud, Kossoff, Andrews, Auerbach, Kitaj* (London: British Council, 1995). Despite differences, both exhibitions sought to characterise these very different artists in a way that suggested a commonality of interests. Above all, this was a group of artists for whom the Second World War and its aftermath provided a formative milieu and who, with the radicalism of Giacometti in Paris and de Kooning in New York, created a radical contemporary vision of urban man attuned to a new existentialist sensibility. The same line was also pursued in other exhibitions that stressed the distinctive qualities of the immediate post-war period and its resonance for the painters of the 'School'. Prominent among these were *The Hard Won Image: Traditional method and subject in recent British art* (Tate, 1984), *The Forgotten Fifties* (Sheffield City Art Galleries, Sheffield, 1984) and *The Transformation of Appearance – Auerbach, Andrews, Bacon, Freud,* Kossoff (Tate Gallery Collection exhibition, Sainsbury Centre, (Norwich, 1991). An apotheosis was reached in 1987, when the core artists of the 'School of London' held centre stage in the main gallery of the Royal Academy's controversial survey *British Art of the Twentieth Century: The Modern Movement.* This gave Andrews, Auerbach, Bacon, Freud and Kossoff the main gallery of the exhibition. It thereby placed figurative painters of diverse ethnic backgrounds, physically and symbolically at the heart of a national tradition. The same formula was true of an exhibition entitled *British Figurative Art of the Twentieth Century* which I curated for the British Council for the Israel Museum in Jerusalem in 1992. The initial proposal was that I should curate an exhibition of British artists of Jewish heritage, namely Auerbach, Bomberg, Freud, Kitaj and Kossoff, inspired by the idea of a core group of 'School of London' artists, but this was soon replaced by extending the scope of the exhibition to painters of all backgrounds, by moving back and forwards in time and widening this middle generation. The effect of such exhibitions was

to stress national continuity and specifically to secure the perception that contemporary figurative practice was embedded within a national 'tradition' of art school teaching. The creation of international contexts for British figurative painting would add an entirely new dimension, reasserting the radicalism and contemporary resonance of these artists. Examples of such international contextualisation for British figurative art are rare but include Jean Clair's Venice Biennale exhibition, *Identity and Alterity: Figures of the Body 1895–1995* in 1995, and, more recently *Paint Made Flesh*, Phillips Collection, Washington, DC, USA, in 2009.

13 James Hyman, 'Introduction' in *Beyond the Human Clay* (London: James Hyman Gallery, 2011). See also the coincidental essay, James Hyman, 'The Human Clay', in *Art of England*, (Summer 2011, pp. 64-7).

14 Ibid.

15 Kitaj was, for example, inexplicably omitted from the otherwise impressive *The Mystery of Appearance: Conversations between Ten British Post-War Painters* at the Haunch of Venison, London, 2011. This omission was despite the fact that no artist was more central to the 'conversation' it presented between the 'School of London' and British Pop Art painters.

16 I most recently addressed this contemporary resonance in: James Hyman, 'The Battle for Realism: British Figurative Painting in the Age of Celebrity' (lecture given in Munster, Germany, 5 February 2015). This lecture took place at the time of the LWL-Museum für Kunst und Kultur's exhibition, *Bare Life: From Bacon to Hockney – London Artists Painting from Life, 1950–80* (Munster, 2014–15).

17 I first addressed the mechanisms behind these shifting approaches to British art in two essays for *Art Monthly* as long ago as November 1991. There I wrote about the idea of a 'School of London', declaring that 'the nationalism of the idea and of a proposed tradition of English empiricism adds further problems. Is it valid to trace a lineage back through Coldstream and the Slade and through Euston Road and Camden Town? Is there really such a figurative tradition within British art? If there is, then

does it provide a useful conceptual framework for discussion of post-war figuration? What of Francis Bacon, for instance? Within the context of the School of London, Bacon's relationship to French art is almost ignored and his indebtedness to Surrealism altogether hidden. Furthermore, if one wishes to find examples of fidelity to the subject and the rigours of life drawing one might equally well look abroad. Given the familiarity of his work and his personal links with British artists, one is unlikely to find a more relevant artist than Alberto Giacometti. When it comes to the post-war years we still seem to be in the grip of a persistent, even pernicious "Little Englandism", an insularity that presents figurative artists of whatever background as part of a national tradition and marginalises their place as part of a band of international painters whose bloody-minded pursuit of "appearance" was intensified by the hegemony of abstraction.'

18 In the 1980s it became apparent that in the promotion of British figurative painting, it was not the new heights reached by these artists, nor their radical pursuit of the real, that was at the forefront of the claims made for them. Instead, all too often, their work was appropriated and presented as an antidote to the excesses perceived in international vanguard culture. In Britain, the critic Peter Fuller had an undeniable importance through his pioneering essays of the 1970s and 1980s, championing critically neglected artists such as Bomberg, Auerbach and Kossoff, but all too frequently his acute insights into these artists were blunted by the role he assigned to them as a riposte to all that he deplored in contemporary, especially American, culture. Similarly, in America, Robert Hughes used the pages of *Time* to deride the art he saw around him in New York and to praise the supposedly antithetical values represented by Freud and Auerbach.

19 Including fifty-four works, the Jewish section was guided by the choices of David Bomberg and the display included not just familiar Anglo-Jewish artists such as Mark Gertler, Horace Brodsky, Isaac Rosenberg, Bernard Meninsky and Alfred Wolmark but also, following a visit by Bomberg and Jacob Epstein to Paris, works by Amedeo Modigliani, Jules Pascin and Moïse Kisling. I addressed the issue of ghettoisation in response to this

exhibition in an essay for the catalogue of the Ben Uri Gallery exhibition, *Making Waves*, in 2003. The exhibition included mainly non-Jewish artists and had a particular emphasis on landscape, which could be used as a foil to much of the work in the Ben Uri's own collection and encourage the identification of difference: 'Whilst many Jewish artists might be said to inhabit a realm of earth and fire, these British artists inhabit a lighter world of air and water [...]. Whilst twentieth-century art by Jewish artists has often been characterised as expressionist and figurative – an urban art of domestic interiors and mundane neighbourhoods – the British artists in the present exhibition are more emotionally detached as they explore the countryside from land, sea and sky or pursue innovative new Modernist paths.' Nevertheless, I concluded, 'Almost ninety years since the Whitechapel's survey of Modern Art, today's Jewish artists fight against any such separation, their social and cultural assimilation a riposte to any such ghettoisation. Furthermore, the most significant British artists of today – ranging from painters such as Freud, Auerbach and Kossoff to the sculptors Anthony Caro and Anish Kapoor – long ago assumed their rightful place alongside the major figures of post-war art not as "Jewish" artists but as powerful and distinct individuals. It is fitting, then, that this exhibition should be shown at the Ben Uri, where the story of Jewish art really is the story of art.'

20 James Hyman, 'From Tragedy to Joie de Vivre: Some Thoughts on the Work of Bacon, Freud, Kossoff and Auerbach', in *Bacon, Freud, Kossoff, Auerbach* (Berlin: Galerie Sander, 2003; London: Blains/James Hyman Fine Art, 2003), unpaginated.

Bibliography

Books

Bryan Appleyard, *The Pleasures of Peace: Art and Imagination in Post-war Britain* (London: Faber & Faber, 1989)

Stephanie Barron, *Exiles and Emigrés: the Flight of European Artists from Hitler* (California: Los Angeles County Museum of Art, 1997)

Shulamith Behr and Marian Malet eds., *Arts in Exile in Britain 1933–1945: Politics and Cultural Identity* (Amsterdam and New York: Rodopi, 2005)

Jonathan Boyarin, *Storm from Paradise: The Politics of Jewish Memory* (Minneapolis: University of Minnesota Press, 1992)

David Cesarani and Tony Kushner eds., *The Internment of Aliens in Twentieth-Century Britain* (Abingdon and New York: Frank Cass, 1993)

Joseph Cohen, *Journey to the Trenches: The Life of Isaac Rosenberg 1890-1918* (London: Robson Books Ltd, 1975)

Richard Cork, *David Bomberg* (New Haven and London: Yale, 1987)

David Feldman, *Englishmen and Jews* (New Haven: Yale University Press, 1994)

William Fishman, *East End Jewish Radicals 1875–1914* (London: Duckworth, 1975)

Sigmund Freud, *Moses and Monotheism*, trans. Katherine Jones (London: Hogarth Press and Institute of Psycho-Analysis, 1939)

Lloyd Gartner, *The Jewish Immigrant in England: 1870–1914* (London: George Allen & Unwin, 1960)

Paul Gilroy, *The Black Atlantic: Modernity and Double Consciousness* (London: Verso, 1993)

Josef Herman, *Related Twilights: Notes from an Artist's Diary* (London: Robson Books, 1975)

Robert Hewison, *Under Siege: Literary Life in London, 1939–45* (London: Weidenfeld & Nicolson, 1977).

Robert Hewison, *In Anger: Culture in the Cold War, 1945–60* (London: Weidenfeld & Nicolson, 1981).

John Higham, *Strangers in the Land* (New York: Atheneum, 1978)

James Hyman, *The Battle for Realism: Figurative Art in Britain during the Cold War (1945–60)* (London and New Haven: Yale University Press, 2001)

Dominique Jarrassé, *Existe-t-il un art juif?* (Paris: Biro, 2006)

Avram Kampf, *From Chagall to Kitaj: Jewish Experience in Twentieth-Century Art* (London: Greenwood Press, 1991)

R.B Kitaj, *The First Diasporist Manifesto* (London: Thames & Hudson Ltd, 1989)

Ulrich Krempel and Karin Thomas, *Jankel Adler 1895-1949* (Köln: DuMont Verlag, 1985)

Tony Kushner ed., *The Jewish Heritage in British History: Englishness and Jewishness* (Abingdon: Frank Cass, 1992)

Tony Kushner, *Anglo-Jewry since 1066* (Manchester: Manchester University Press, 2009)

Cecile Esther Kuznitz, *YIVO and the Making of Modern Jewish Culture: Scholarship for the Yiddish Nation* (Cambridge: Cambridge University Press, 2014)

Leksikon fun der Nayer Yidisher Literatur (Biographical Dictionary of Modern Yiddish Literature) 1–8 (New York: 1956–1981)

A.B. Levy, *East End Story*, (London: Constellation Books, *c.* 1951)

Louise London, *Whitehall and the Jews 1933–1948: British Immigration Policy and the Holocaust* (Cambridge: Cambridge University Press, 2000)

Sarah MacDougall, '"Something is Happening There": Early British Modernism, the Great War and the Whitechapel Boys' in ed., Michael Walsh, *London, Modernism, and 1914* (Cambridge UK: Cambridge University Press, 2010)

David Mazower, *Yiddish Theatre in London* (London: Museum of the Jewish East End, 1987)

Mosheh Oved, *Visions and Jewels* (London: Faber and Faber, 1952)

Griselda Pollock and Michael Silverman eds., *Concentrationary Memories: Totalitarian Terror and Cultural Resistance* (London and New York: I. B. Tauris, 2014)

Jennifer Powell and Jutta Vinzent, *Art and Migration Art Works by Refugee Artists from Nazi Germany in Britain* (Birmingham: George Bell Institute, 2005)

Leonard Prager, *Yiddish Culture in Britain: A Guide* (Frankfurt: Peter Lang, 1990)

Herbert Read, *Contemporary British Art* (London: Pelican Books, 1951)

Herbert Read, *The Philosophy of Modern Art* (London: Faber & Faber, 1952)

Helen Rosenau, *Women in Art: From Type to Personality* (London: Isomorph, 1944)

Michael Rothberg, *Traumatic Realism: the Demands of Holocaust Representation* (Minneapolis and London: University of Minnesota Press, 2000)

Raphael Samuel and Paul Thompson eds., *The Myths We Live By* (London: Routledge, 1990)

Dominic Sandbrook, *Never Had it So Good: A History of Britain From Suez to the Beatles* (London: Little, Brown, 2005)

Dominic Sandbrook, *White Heat: A History of Britain in the Swinging Sixties* (London: Little, Brown, 2006)

Moshe Sanders, *Jewish Books in Whitechapel* (London: Duckworth, 1991)

Frances Spalding, *British Art Since 1900* (London: Thames & Hudson, 1986)

David Sylvester, *About Modern Art: Critical Essays, 1948-96* (London: Chatto & Windus)

Feliks Topolski, *Three Continents 1944–45* (London: Methuen, 1946)

Maurice Tuchman, *The Impact of Chaim Soutine (1893-1943): De Kooning, Pollock, Dubuffet, Bacon* (Hatje Cantz, 2002)

Robert Weinberg, *Stalin's Forgotten Zion: Birobidzhan and the Making of a Soviet Jewish Homeland* (Berkeley: University of California Press, 1998)

E. Thomas Wood and Stanisław M. Jankowski, *Karski: How One Man Tried to Stop the Holocaust* (New Jersey: John Wiley, 1994)

John Woodeson, *Mark Gertler: Biography of a Painter 1891-1939* (London: Sidgwick & Jackson, 1972)

Exhibition Catalogues

Manet and the Post-Impressionists (London: Ballantyne & Company Ltd., 1911)

Opening Exhibition (London: Ben Uri Art Gallery, 1944)

Subjects of Jewish Interest (London: Ben Uri Art Gallery, 1946)

Richard Calvocoressi and Philip Long eds., *From London: Bacon, Freud, Kossoff, Andrews, Auerbach, Kitaj* (London: British Council in association with the Scottish National Gallery of Modern Art, 1995)

Colin Cruise, *Love Revealed: Simeon Solomon and the Pre-Raphaelites* (London: Merrell, 2006)

David Glasser ed., *Chagall and his Circle* (London: Ben Uri, 2005)

David Glasser and Sarah Lightman eds., *Bomberg's Relevance* (London: Ben Uri, 2007)

James Hyman, *Beyond the Human Clay* (London: James Hyman Gallery, 2011)

James Hyman ed., *Making Waves: Modern British Masterpieces from a European Trust* (Ben Uri, 2003)

Leo Kenig, 'Jews and Plastic Art', in *Catalogue and Survey of Activities, Ben Uri Art and Literary Society* (London: Ben Uri, 1930)

R.B. Kitaj, *The Human Clay* (London: Arts Council of Great Britain, 1976)

Sarah MacDougall ed., *Mark Gertler: A New Perspective* (London: Ben Uri, 2002)

Sarah MacDougall ed., *Refiguring the 50s: Joan Eardley, Sheila Fell, Eva Frankfurther, Josef Herman and L. S. Lowry* (London: Ben Uri, 2014)

Sarah MacDougall and Rachel Dickson eds., *Whitechapel at War: Isaac Rosenberg and his Circle* (London: Ben Uri in association with Lund Humphries, 2009)

Sarah MacDougall ed., *Josef Herman: Warsaw, Brussels, Glasgow, London 1938-44* (London: Ben Uri, 2011)

Sarah MacDougall and Lauren Barnes eds., *From Russia to Paris: Chaïm Soutine and his Contemporaries* (London: Ben Uri, 2012)

Sarah MacDougall and Rachel Dickson eds., *Rediscovering Wolmark: A Pioneer of British Modernism* (London: Ben Uri, 2004)

Sarah MacDougall and Rachel Dickson eds., *Uproar! The First 50 Years of the London Group 1913-1963* (London: Ben Uri in association with Lund Humphries, 2014)

Sarah MacDougall and Rachel Dickson eds., *Forced Journeys: Artists in Exile in Britain c. 1933-1945* (London: Ben Uri, 2009)

Paul Moorhouse, *The Transformation of Appearance – Auerbach, Andrews, Bacon, Freud, Kossoff* (London: Tate, 1991)

Michael Peppiatt, *The School of London: Six Figurative Painters* (London: The British Council Visual Arts Publications, 1987)

Gillian Rathbone ed., *The Ben Uri Story: From Art Society to Museum* (London: Ben Uri Art Society, 2001)

Walter Schwab and Julia Wiener eds., *Jewish Artists: The Ben Uri Collection* (London: Ben Uri Art Society in association with Lund Humphries, 1994)

Jacob Sonntag ed., *Ben Uri 1915–1965: Fifty Years Achievement in the Arts* (London: Ben Uri Art Society, 1966)

Articles

'Bergen-Belsen: Photos from the Liberation of the Notorious Camp', *Life* (30 April 1945)

'A Russo-Jewish Artist: Interview for the Jewish Chronicle with Mr Eliezer Berson', *Jewish Chronicle* (10 September 1915)

'Ben Uri / Proud Possession of Anglo-Jewry', *Jewish Vanguard* (7 December 1962)

'Jewish art at Whitechapel', *Jewish Chronicle* (15 May 1914)

Sadie Buchler, 'Jewry in Art', *Manchester Guardian* (17 October 1946)

Rachel Dickson, '"Jewish Artists will be lost to Jewry without Jewish Support": Ben Uri Art Society and Émigré Artists 1933–1959', in *Netzwerke des Exils: Künstlerische Verflechtungen, Austausch und Patronage nach 1933*, eds., Burcu Dogramaci and Karin Wimmer (Berlin: Gebrüder Mann, 2011)

Lloyd Gartner, 'Notes on the Statistics of Jewish Immigration to England, 1870–1914', *Jewish Social Studies* 22, no. 2 (1960)

James Hyman, 'Fifty Years of Hurt', *Guardian* (22 September 2001)

James Hyman, 'Kossoff's London', *Tate Magazine* (Summer 1996)

David Mazower, 'Lazar Berson and the Origins of the Ben Uri Art Society' in *The Ben Uri Story: From Art Society to Museum*, ed., Gillian Rathbone (London: Ben Uri Art Society, 2001), pp. 37–58

Julie Miller and Richard I. Cohen, 'A Collision of Cultures: The Jewish Museum and the Jewish Theological Seminary, 1904-1971', in, *Tradition Renewed: A History of the Jewish Theological Seminary, Vol II: Beyond the Academy*, ed., Jack Wertheimer (New York: The Jewish Theological Seminar of America, 1997)

Robin Ostow, 'From Wandering Jew to Immigrant Ethnic: Musealizing Jewish Immigration', in Visualizing and Exhibiting Jewish Space and History, ed., Richard I. Cohen, *Studies in Contemporary Jewry*, Vol XXVI (Oxford: Oxford University Press, 2012)

Sarah MacDougall, '"Separate Spheres of Endeavour": Experiencing the Émigré Network in Britain c.1933–1945' in *Netzwerke des Exils: Künstlerische Verflechtungen, Austausch und Patronage nach 1933*, eds., Burcu Dogramaci and Karin Wimmer (Berlin: Gebrüder Mann, 2015)

Kathrin Pieren, 'Negotiating Jewish Identity through the Display of Art', in *Whatever Happened to British Jewish Studies?*, eds., Hannah Ewence and Tony Kushner (London: Vallentine Mitchell, 2012)

Jankel Sountag, 'The Yiddish Theatre: Seventy Years Development', *Our Time* (December 1946)

Isabel Wollaston, '"Negotiating the Marketplace: The Role(s) of Holocaust Museums Today," *Journal of Modern Jewish Studies*, 4.1 (2005)

Artists as teachers: a legacy

Frank Auerbach (b.1931) taught first in secondary schools (1955-) and then until 1968 for one day a week at various art colleges including Ravensbourne; Camberwell College of Arts (1958–1965); Ealing School of Art, Design and Media; Sidcup Art College and the Slade School of Fine Art. Pupils include Ray Atkins (b.1937), Christopher Couch (b. 1946), Mike Knowles (b.1941), Peter Prendergast (1946–2007) and John Virtue (b.1947)

Martin Bloch (1883–1954) ran an art school in Berlin, the Bloch–Kerschbaumer School of Painting (1923–33), first with Anton Kerschbaumer (1885–1931), then from 1926 with Schmidt-Rottluff (1884–1976); he subsequently ran The School of Contemporary Painting in London from 1936–39 with Australian artist, Roy de Maistre (1894–1968); taught briefly at the Walker Arts Centre in Minneapolis and at Princeton University when travelling in America (1948); and at Camberwell School of Arts and Crafts, London (1949–1954). Pupils included Harry Weinberger (1924–2009) and Heinz Koppel (1919–1980)

David Bomberg (1890–1957) taught painting at Borough Polytechnic (1945–1953). His pupils included Frank Auerbach (b. 1931), Leon Kossoff (b. 1926), Gustav Metzger (b. 1926) and Dennis Creffield (b.1931).

Hermann (1892–1988) and Erna Nonnenmacher (1889–1980) taught modelling and pottery at Morley College (1949–1970); Hermann also taught private pupils in his studio. Pupils included Inge King (b. 1915).

Paul Hamann (1891–1973) organised life drawing classes with Hugo Dachinger (1908–1995) in North London.

George Him (1900–1982) was Senior Lecturer in Graphic Design at Leicester Polytechnic, elected RDI in 1977.

Henry Inlander (b. 1925) was art adviser to the British School in Rome (1955–56) and again in 1971; he taught painting at Camberwell School of Arts and Crafts, London (1957–79).

Kalman Kemeny (1896–1994) taught at Hammersmith College of Art (1947–79) and Chelsea School of Art.

Heinz Koppel (1919–1980) taught art to both children and adults, running an art centre in Dowlais, Wales under the Merthyr Settlement, later for the Education Authority; he subsequently lectured at Camberwell School of Art, Hornsey College of Art and at Liverpool College of Art from 1956.

George Mayer-Marton (1897–1960) taught at St Johns Wood School of Art, followed by a peripatetic role as a Guide Lecturer for CEMA, the precursor to the Arts Council. After a catastrophic fire destroyed his studio home and all its contents, Mayer-Marton relocated to the north of England, becoming Principal Lecturer at Liverpool School of Art.

Bernard Meninsky (1891–1950) taught painting and drawing at the Central School of Arts and Crafts, London (1913–40); appointed as a tutor of life drawing at Westminster School of Art (continuing to teach part time at the Central School), (1920–39); taught at Oxford City School of Art (1940–45), returning to Central School in 1945. Pupils included George Weissbort (1928–2013), Susan Einzig (1922–2009), Grahame King (1915–2008), Marion Milner (1900–1998), Nancy Durrell (1912–83) and Edward Ardizzone RA (1900–1979).

Klaus Meyer (1918–2002) taught at Hornsey College of Art, then at Kilburn Polytechnic in the 1960s and 70s, where he became Head of the Art Department.

Julius Rosenbaum (1897–1956) and Adele Reifenberg (1893–1986) From 1942 Julius gave private tuition and in 1948 he and his wife Adele established a private art school in Belsize Park, London.

Arthur Segal (1875–1944) ran the Arthur Segal Painting School for Professionals and Non Professionals in London and Oxford from 1937–44 with his wife and daughter, Ernestine and Marianne Segal. Pupils included pioneering art therapist Elsie Davies as well as fellow émigrés Joseph Horovitz, George Weissbort (1928–2013) and Nikolaus Braun (1900–1950). The School remained open until 1977, committed to teaching artists and amateurs alike, acknowledging the importance of art as therapy.

Willi Soukop (1907–1995) taught part-time at Dartington Art School and at Blundell's School (1935–40, apart from nine months when he was interned in Canada. He established the sculpture department at Blundell's, setting up other sculpture departments at Bryanston School in Dorset and at the Downs School in Worcestershire. He moved to London and taught at Bromley College of Art (1945–46), Guildford College of Art (1945–47) and subsequently at Chelsea Art College (1947–72); he was also a Master of Sculpture at the Royal Academy Schools (1969–82) and a member of the Faculty of the British School in Rome; visiting teacher at the Glasgow School of Art. His pupils included Elisabeth Frink (1930–1993).

Willy Tirr (1915–1991) began teaching at Leeds Polytechnic in the 1950s becoming Head of Fine Arts in 1968, a position he held until his retirement in 1981.

Harry Weinberger (1924–2009) took a teacher training diploma in Brighton and taught art at a school in London and then at Reading School before joining Didsbury teacher training college in Manchester; in 1964 he was appointed Lecturer at Lanchester Polytechnic (now Coventry University) eventually becoming Head of Department, a position he held until early retirement in 1983.

The Queen Mother and pottery tutors
Hermann and Erna Nonnenmacher, 1958

Ben Uri People

The list below highlights those who have occupied significant positions – often more than one - within Ben Uri's governanace and management and have made a lasting contribution to the organisation, beginning with its Yiddish Founders in Whitechapel.

VC = Vice Chairman, VP= Vice President

Lazar Berson   1915–16   *Founder / Director*
Edward Good   1915–56   *Founder member, Council, VC, VP*
D Simkovitz   *c.*1915–17   *Founder member*
A Bezalel   1915–16   *Secretary*
W Victor   1916–26   *Council, Finance Committee, Honorary Treasurer*
L Good   1916–37, 1944   *Council, brother of Edward Good*
Judah Beach   1916–49   *Founder member, Finance, Exhibitions Committee, Yiddish Circle*
Max Rose   1916   *Council*
Y Brindberg   1916–22   *Council, Chairman*
H Brindberg   1916–21   *Council*
Bernard   1916   *Council*
Halpern   1916   *Council*
Rowley   1916   *Council*
Sofer   1916   *Council*
Shapiro   1916   *Council*
Gasson   1916   *Council*
Jacob Slivko   1916–25   *Council*
Polyikov   1917   *Council*
Susman   1922   *Council*
A M Kaiser   1921–37   *Council, Secretary*
J Lash   1922–25   *Council*
L Hersh   1922–38   *Council*
Adolph Michaelson   1922–55   *Council, Chairman, VP*
A Mundy   1922–37   *Council, Chairman*
Miss Margolin   1922–24   *Council*
Israel Zangwill   1922–23   *President*
Pilichowski, L   1923–24, 1930–33   *VP, Council, Hon President*
W J Simons   1923–33   *Council, Secretary*
Alfred Wolmark   1923–59   *Art Committee, Council, VP*
Solomon J Solomon   1924   *Hon President*
Schlowsky   1924–25   *Council*
Dr Mme Zarchi   1924   *Council*
Wolfson   1924   *Council*
Dr Fraenkel   1924–25   *Council*
Newton   1924–25   *Council*
David Checkanover   1924–34   *Council, Chairman*
S White   1924–37   *Council*
Jack Seres   1924–60   *Council*
Ethel Solomon   1931–66, 1975, *Art Committee, Council, Exhibition Committee, Chairman, Trustee (Mrs Robert B Solomon)*
Samuel Moses   1928–30   *Hon Secretary*
Marcus Lipton   1933–38   *Council, Secretary*
B Mlavsky   1933–39   *Council*
J Dorf   1933–34   *Council*
Israel Sieff   1934–37, 1948–68   *VP, President*
H Snowman   1936   *Council*
Otto Schiff   1936   *Patron*
Jacob Epstein   1936–37   *Patron*
Cecil Roth   1936–37   *Art Committee*
Gilbert Solomon   1936–52   *Art Committee, Chaired in absence of Ethel Solomon*
Cyril J Ross   1938–73   *Press and Publications Committee, Treasurer*
Fritz Solomonski   1943–45   *Administrator / Secretary / Curator – salaried*

Carica Davidson   1944–61   *VP*
Hans Feibusch   1944–51   *Council, Art Committee*
Siegfried Oppenheimer   1944–71   *Exhibition Committee, Art Committee, Council*
Phillip Kaufmann   1944   *Press & Publications Committee*
Mitzman   1944   *Press and Publications Committee*
Sadie Buchler   1945–50   *Secretary/Curator*
Kenneth Snowman   1946–56   *Chairman Studio Group, Council*
Franz Reizenstein   1946–47   *Music Committee*
Archibald Ziegler   1947–48, 1951, 1964–71   *VP, Hanging Committee, Art Committee*
Ruth Gollancz   1947–48   *Council*
J Yahuda   1947–48   *Council*
Kalman Kemeny   1948–76   *Council, Art Committee*
B Stross MP   1949–52   *Council*
Max Sokol   1949–68   *Art Committee*
Henry Sanders   1949–51   *Studio Group committee*
W Scharf   1949–51   *Studio Group committee*
Mrs A Lerner   1949–52, 1965–68   *Council*
Fred Feigl   1949–63   *Art Committee*
Maurice Sochachewsky   1949–68   *Art Committee*
Barry Fealdman   1950–76, 1993   *Curator / Secretary, Permanent Collection Committee*
Ian Stoutzker   1950–51, 1965–68   *Music Committee Chair, Council*
Joseph Leftwich   1951   *Art Committee*
Max Sokol   1951   *Autumn Exhibition Hanging Committee*
Alexander Margulies   1951, 1958–1962, 1965–90   *Art Committee, VC, Chairman, President*
A N Stencl   1951–1954   *Friends Of Yiddish*
Selig Brodetsky   1952–1954   *President*
Benno Elkan   1951   *VC*
Paul Brandenburger   1951–52   *Orchestra, Secretary*
J E Posnansky   1952–68   *Council*
Israel Feldman   1953–80   *VP*
Charles Aukin   1953–68, 1975   *Council, Trustee*
Charles Spencer   1956   *Exhibition Committee*
Mrs J Steinberg   1956   *Exhibition Committee*
Alfred Harris   1956–68; 1972–73   *Art Committee.*
Alex Lerner   1956–68   *President*
Sydney Fixman   1958, 1962–92   *Conductor of Ben Uri Orchestra, Council*
Jacob Bornfriend   1962–68; 1972   *Art Committee*
Raymond Davoud   1965–69   *Council*
Hazel Rose   1965–68   *Council*
Mrs Basil Samuel   1965–68   *Council*
F Worms   1965–68   *Art Committee, Council*
Mrs I Stoutzker   1966–68   *Art Committee*
Fritz Kormis   1967–68   *Art Committee*
Ethel Solomon   1968–1985   *President*
Joyce Lipman   1968–91   *Council, Hon Secretary*
Mrs Neville Blond   1969–70   *Council*
G Baron-Cohen   1972   *Council*
Henry Lewis   1972   *Music Committee*
Ernst Eisenmayer   1972   *Art Committee*
Henry Inlander   1972   *Art Committee*
Martin Paisner   1972, 1975, 1985–86   *Literary Committee, Trustee, Council*

Lawrence Lowenthal   1974, 1976–85   *Hon Secretary, VC*
Henry Rudolf   1974–77   *Council, Treasurer*
Phineas May   1974–93   *Council*
William Margulies   1975   *Trustee*
Barnett Shine   1975   *Trustee*
Cyril Stein   1975–76   *Trustee, VP*
Trevor Chinn   1975   *Patron*
Alan Nabarro   1975   *Patron*
H Rothenberg   1975   *Patron*
Samuel Sebba   1965–69   *Council*
Concita Abrahams-Curiel   1968–88   *Council*
Naomi Blake   1975–93   *Art Committee, Council*
Alice Schwab   1975–99   *Council, Hon Secretary, Hon Curator*
Chaim Bermant   1975–77   *Council*
Agi Katz   1979–85   *Curator*
Richard Fisher   1980–90   *Hon Treasurer, VC*
Harvey Chesterman   1980–81   *VC*
Walter Schwab   1985–95   *Hon Secretary, Council, VP*
Mrs C Sebag-Montefiore   1986–89   *Council*
Leslie Michaels   1987–2000   *VC, Permanent Collection Committee, Council, Hon Treasurer, Chairman*
Sharon Lancer   1988   *Curator*
Maggie Pope   1989–90   *Curator/Administrator*
Edward Toledano   1990–92   *Council*
Julia Weiner   1990–96   *Curator*
Robert Lewin   1990–98   *Permanent Collection Committee, Council*
Lewis Goodman   1990–2001   *Council, VC*
Jack Lass   1990–93   *Council*
Estelle Lovatt   1991–93   *Art Committee*
Lois Peltz   1992–2000   *Art Committee, VC*
Sydney Levinson   1992–2001   *Council*
Joanne Shaw   1993   *Council*
Caro Conrich   1993   *Permanent Collection Committee*
Irene Scheinmann   1993   *Art Committee*
Jo Velleman   1997–2000   *Administration Director*
David Glasser   1997–99, 2000–   *Council, Chairman*
Irving Grose   1997, 2000–01   *Council, Hon Secretary*
Michael Posen   1988, 2001–   *Council, VC*
Gerald Rothman   1997–2000   *Hon Secretary*
Myra Waiman   2000–08   *Council*
David Stern   2001–2006   *VC*
Andrew Balcombe   1999–2000   *Council, VC*
Andrew Coleman   1999–2000   *Honorary Treasurer*
Peter Gross   2000–2004   *VC*
Simon Bentley   2005, 2007–09   *Co-chairman*
Peter Hoffman   2000, 2007–09   *Council*
Simon Wagman   2007–09   *Council, Hon Secretary*
Jonathan Horwich   2004, 2007–08   *Council*
Marilyn Rosenfelder   2000, 2007–08   *Council*
Keith Graham   2010–14   *Finance*

CURRENT BOARD
David Glasser   2000–   *Exec Chair*
Mike Posen   2001–   *Deputy Chair*
Hillary Bauer   2014–   *Deputy Chair*
Amanda Lewis   2014–   *Trustee*

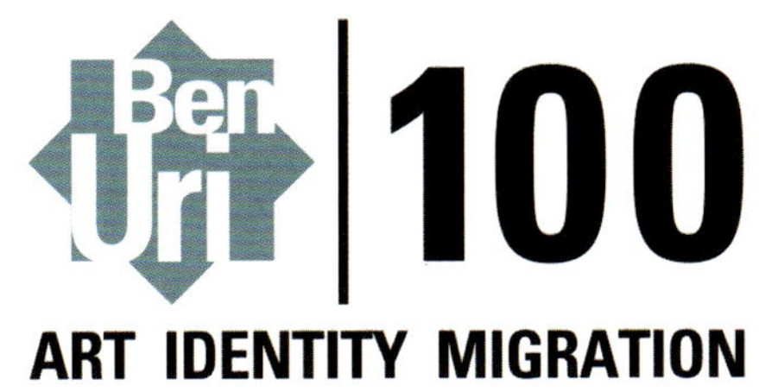

Short History and Mission Statement

Ben Uri, 'The Art Museum for Everyone,' focuses distinctively on Art, Identity and Migration across all migrant communities to London since the turn of the 20th century. It engages the broadest possible audience through its exhibitions and learning programmes. The museum was founded on 1 July 1915 by the Russian émigré artist Lazar Berson at Gradel's Restaurant, Whitechapel, in London's East End.

The name, 'The Jewish National Decorative Art Association (London), "Ben Ouri" ', echoed that of legendary biblical craftsman Bezalel Ben Uri, the creator of the tabernacle in the Temple of Jerusalem. It also reflects a kinship with the ideals of the famous Bezalel School of Arts and Crafts founded in Jerusalem nine years earlier in 1906.

Ben Uri's philosophy is based on our conviction that, by fostering easy access to art and creativity at every level, it can add weight to our two guiding principles: 'The Dignity of Difference' and 'The Equality of Citizenship'. Ben Uri connects with over 300,000 people a year via its various creative platforms.

The museum positively and imaginatively demonstrates its value as a robust and unique bridge between the cultural, religious, political differences and beliefs of fellow British citizens.

Our positioning of migrant artists from different communities in London within the artistic and historical, rather than religious or ethnic, context of the British national heritage is both key and distinctive. Through the generous support of our 'Preferred Partner' Manya Igel Fine Arts, we provide free entry to all our exhibitions, removing all barriers to entry and participation.

Ben Uri offers the widest access to all its extensive programming and physical and virtual resources including exhibitions, publications, website and outreach through:

- **THE PERMANENT COLLECTION:** comprising 1300 works, the collection is dominated by the work of first and second generation émigré artists and supported by a growing group of emerging contemporary artists, who will be a principal attraction in the generations to come. The largest collection of its kind in the world, it can be accessed physically via continued exhibition, research, conservation and acquisitions or virtually.

- **TEMPORARY EXHIBITIONS:** curating, touring and hosting important internationally-focused exhibitions of the widest artistic appeal which, without the museum's focus, would not be seen in the UK or abroad.

- **PUBLICATIONS:** commissioning new academic research on artists and their historical context to enhance the museum's exhibitions and visitor experience.

- **LIBRARY AND ARCHIVE:** a resource dating from the turn of the 20th century, documenting and tracing in parallel the artistic and social development of both Ben Uri and Jewish artists, who were working or exhibiting in Britain, as part of the evolving British historical landscape.

- **EDUCATION AND COMMUNITY LEARNING:** for adults and students through symposia, lectures, curatorial tours and publications.

- **SCHOOLS:** Ben Uri's nationally available 'Art in the Open' programme via the 'National Education Network' and The London Grid for Learning' is available on demand to 16,000 schools across the United Kingdom. Focus-related visits, after-school art clubs, family art days and competitions are also regular features.

- **ARTISTS:** regular artists' peer group programmes, international competitions, guidance and affliation benefits.

- **WELLBEING:** a pioneering set of initiatives addressing the young with special needs and the elderly who may be living in some isolation or with early stages of dementia. The programmes recognise the significant importance of the carer within the relationship and uses art practice as an effective bridge for positive engagement.

- **WEBSITE:** provides an online educational and access tool, to function as a virtual gallery and reference resource for students, scholars and collectors.

The strength of the museum's growing collection and our active engagement with our public – nationally and internationally – reinforces the need for Ben Uri to have a permanent museum and gallery in the heart of Central London alongside this country's great national institutions. Only then will the museum fulfil its potential and impact the largest audiences from the widest communities from home and abroad.

Picture Credits

All Ben Uri Collection and Ben Uri Archive photographs are courtesy Justin Piperger except for:

Michael Illas: cats, 6, 8, 25

Annely Juda Fine Art: fig. 44

AKG: fig. 15 (photo: Walter Limot)

Associated Press Images / Herbert Mason: fig. 42

DACS: figs. 47, 48, 49 (photo: Roger Wooldridge)

Gagosian Gallery: fig. 46 (photo © Werner Galigofsky)

James Hyman Gallery, London: fig. 48

Kunsthalle Tübingen / Bridgeman: fig. 39

Morley College, London: fig. 50

Museum of London: fig. 43

National Portrait Gallery, London: fig. 10

Pallant House Gallery: fig. 45

Private Collection, Birmingham: fig. 27

Private Collection, London: fig. 2

Private Collection, London: fig. 35 (photo: Roy Fox)

Private Collection: fig. 37

Tate, London 2015: cat. 12, figs. 1, 6, 9, 38, 39, 40

Werthwhile Foundation, London: fig. 26

White Cube Gallery, London: fig. 41 (photo: Todd White Art Photography)

Copyright

Jussuf Abbo © Jerome Abbo

Jankel Adler © DACS 2015, All Rights Reserved

Nirveda Alleck © The Artist

Michael Andrews © the Estate of Michael Andrews, courtesy of James Hyman Gallery, London

Oreet Ashery © The Artist

Frank Auerbach © The Artist

Yaki Assayag © The Artist

Zeev Ben-Zvi © The Estate of the Artist

Lazar Berson © The Estate of the Artist

Martin Bloch © Martin Bloch Trust

Dorothy Bohm © Dorothy Bohm Archive

David Bomberg © The Estate of David Bomberg. All Rights Reserved, DACS 2015

Jacob Bornfriend © The Estate of the Artist

David Breuer-Weil © The Artist

Marc Chagall © ADAGP, Paris and DACS, London 2015

Jake and Dinos Chapman © Jake and Dinos Chapman, All Rights Reserved, DACS 2015

Bernard Cohen © Bernard Cohen, courtesy Flowers, London & New York

Arnold Daghani © Arnold Daghani Trust

Sonia Delaunay © Pracusa, Spain

Isaac Dobrinsky © ADAGP Paris and DACS London 2015

Shmuel Dresner © The Artist

Amy J. Drucker © The Estate of the Artist

Natan Dvir Ernst Eisenmayer © Jan Daws

Jacob Epstein © The Estate of Sir Jacob Epstein

Hermann Fechenbach © Rosa-Maria Breinlich

Frederick Feigl© The Estate of the Artist

Eva Frankfurther © The estate of Eva Frankfurther

Yitzhak Frenkel-Frenel © The Artist's Estate

Lucian Freud © Lucian Freud Archive / Bridgeman Images

Anya Gallaccio © Anya Gallaccio. All rights reserved, DACS 2015

Rachel Garfield © The Artist

George Grosz © 2015 Estate of George Grosz

Leo Haas © DACS 2015

Richard Hamilton © The Estate of Richard Hamilton

Josef Herman © The Estate of Josef Herman

Damien Hirst © Damien Hirst and Science Ltd. All Rights Reserved, DACS 2015

Anselm Kiefer © Anselm Kiefer

Erich Kahn © The Estate of the Artist

R. B. Kitaj © Marlborough Fine Art

Leon Kossoff © The Artist / Annely Juda Fine Art, London

Jacob Kramer © William Roberts Society

Isaac Lichtenstein © The Estate of the Artist

Jacques Lipchitz © The Estate of Jacques Lipchitz

Margaret Marks © Frances Marks

Herbert Mason © Associated Press. All Rights Reserved

Else Meidner © Ludwig Meidner-Archiv, Jüdisches Museum der Stadt Frankfurt am Main

Ludwig Meidner © Ludwig Meidner-Archiv, Jüdisches Museum der Stadt Frankfurt am Main

Bernard Meninsky © The Estate of the Artist

Reuven Rubin © The Rubin Museum, Tel Aviv

Zygmund Schreter © The Estate of the Artist

Kurt Schwitters © VG Bild-Kunst, Bonn

Victor Weisz © The Estate of the Artist

Rachel Whiteread © The Artist

Clare Winsten © Jonathan Harrison

Alfred Wolmark © The Artist's Family

Ongoing efforts are being made to seek formal permission from the estates of the artists currently untraced. Ben Uri offers its appreciation to all those who have granted permission and apologises to those with whom we have been unable to make contact.